BABE'S PLACE:

The Lives of Yankee Stadium

Michael P. Wagner

BABE'S PLACE: The Lives of Yankee Stadium

Originally printed in USA by 48HrBooks (www.48HrBooks.com) in 2012

Dedication

This book is dedicated to my parents, Jack and Bernice Wagner, for their love, and for giving myself and my brothers, Alan and Mark, such a wonderful childhood. This dedication extends to my Aunts Elsie and Elaine, as well as Grandpa Meyer Director, and Grandmas Rose Director, and Sarah Wagner, for doing the same. I have such wonderful memories of growing up. Also, for my stepmother Cecele, who encouraged me to follow my dreams.

I further dedicate this book to my wife, Carolyn, who has stood by me through thick and thin in life, as well as the long process of getting this book published. To my stepson, Dustin Warncke, and his wife Meagan, who were always supportive in offering many suggestions in this endeavor. And, to our grandson, Jackson Vaughn Warncke. May this book make him proud of his grandfather. A special thank you to friends Ray and Phyllis Davis. Also, to the many special other family members and friends who frequently and excitedly looked forward to the publication of this book.

Lastly, I dedicate this book to my New York Yankees heroes. Since childhood, I have been and will ALWAYS be a New York Yankees fan. No team has a prouder history or greater legacy.

Table of Contents

Preface

When the New York Yankees played at Shea Stadium during the 1974 and 1975 seasons, I went to see Marty Appel, the head of the Yankees Public Relations Department. His office was in a trailer near Shea.

I don't remember if I had an appointment or not to see him, but he was kind enough to see this almost 20 year old person. I told Mr. Appel that I wanted to write a book about Yankee Stadium. We spoke for perhaps 15 minutes or so, and he generously gave me some materials to take back home. I never did write that book, but I did collect autographs of celebrities, and of course Yankees, in the mail and in person.

About 2003 I was looking through my four photo albums of photos I took of Yankee games, whether they were from the regular season, Old Timers' Day games (my favorite), the World Series, and the renovation of Yankee Stadium. Surely, I thought, someone must have written a book about the renovation of Yankee Stadium. A search of the internet proved me wrong. Yes, there was some bits and pieces of information on this subject, but not much at all. I was very shocked.

After all, this was a major event in the life of Yankee Stadium. It had to be in order to close the sacred ballpark for two and a half years. I had about 230 photos of this event, as I was going to New York City Community College in Brooklyn at the time. A five hour wait for a writing class afforded me the opportunity to take the train to the Bronx to visit my beloved stadium. My trusty Kodak Instamatic 100 camera allowed me to record the historical progress. I've always enjoyed American History and Journalism.

The photos I've looked at 30 years after this major alteration of The House That Ruth Built rekindled my desire to write a book. Not just a book about Yankee Stadium, but one that would fill a niche. Of course the usual information had to be included, such as *Babe's Place* being built in 284 days. But, I'm an oddball. As such, I enjoy unusual things in life.

Having never written a book before, I must say that ignorance may have been one of my best friends. I wanted to write a book my way. I wanted it to come from the point of view of a fan who loves Yankee Stadium and the proud history of the New York Yankees. As mentioned, I wanted to include unusual information. Why write about the same thing that everyone did? Also, with no true deadline, I wanted to collect as much data as I could until it felt as though the well ran dry. I didn't want a deadline to make me cut corners, thereby shortchanging the reader or myself.

The main foundation of my book is the history of the 1973 thru early 1976 renovation of baseball's most historical baseball park and photos. Nearly every book I've seen of the modernization mentions only a few sentences about it, and has maybe one or two photos depicting this great upheaval. History demanded much more than these little crumbs of information. Yankee Stadium has been in the soul of America since it opened in 1923. So many historical events have occurred there that it has earned the telling of this very overdue story. And, not just about baseball. Popes have held masses there, many non-sporting events have occurred there, and the moving tribute to the 9/11 victims was also held at America's most famous palace.

Even though I started writing at that point, the book took on a life of its own. I felt it would be convenient for the reader to have a strong history of the pre-renovated Yankee Stadium in one volume. I've learned a lot about the Yankees and the Stadium, and about researching and writing a book.

My two main goals have always been to aim for 100% accuracy, and easy readability. I also wanted to give *Babe's Place* a personal feel, as it really is a personal story on many levels. Not just from me, but also the kind people who generously helped to make this a more complete story that is entertaining while being educational.

My favorite chapter is "The Heroes Speak." My thought was that even though we, the fans, have a personal interest in the national pastime and our heroes, they had the unique honor of living the dream that many of us share. Although I never was good enough to play for the Yankees, this dream will never die. What a thrill it was to receive answers in the mail from these idols, or converse by e-mail or talk to them in person or on the phone!

Babe's Place has been a wonderful experience. I've made great friends of people that I've only met on the internet or telephone. But, that's the magic of baseball. This is especially true of those of us that root for the same team. You automatically become friends because baseball naturally binds us together. In my case, once a Yankee, ALWAYS a Yankee! Just like Billy Martin.

-Michael Wagner

THANK YOU AND ACKNOWLEDGEMENTS

This book originally primarily focused on the history of Yankee Stadium through 1976, especially the 1973-1976 renovation, since that's when the 1970s remodeling of Yankee Stadium finished. Since no books have previously devoted much effort on this important episode in the life of the famed ballpark, I chose to do so. I made every effort to be 100% accurate with respect to the facts. Most of my information was taken from newspaper accounts of the day. Different newspapers sometimes had the same accounts. I found cases where a specific event also differed. It came down to a case of trying to corroborate questionable facts with support from another source. This was not always possible. I then based disputed data on best evidence. This story took about ten years of research. I've been writing it since 2006 and constantly updated and added details as they became available. This book is written from the point of view of a fan of the New York Yankees. Therefore, I wanted it to have humanity and personality, as well as facts and photos.

This list is in no particular order. But to all the people who were kind enough to help me on this project, I am so grateful to you. You didn't have to help me, but you did. Thank you for your time, wisdom, and guidance. This book isn't just my effort, but **ours**. I would like to thank the following for making this book possible.

My father, Jack Wagner, was a Yankee fan. I remember Dad taking us to a Yankee game in 1964. I remember that because I can still see the cover of the 1964 Yankee yearbook in my mind. Another event I remember was us being in the right field concourse and a Yankee nearly bumping into us. He said, "Excuse me." I saw the number 9 on his back. It was one of my favorite Yankees – Roger Maris! I also recall being in the upper deck behind home plate when Whitey Ford was pitching. I'm not sure if it was 1967, but I can still see us making our way to our seats during the first inning.

I paid Dad back by purchasing seats for the 1977 World Series. We saw Reggie hit his three home runs in game six. This was the only World Series Dad went to, which was a shock to me, given the fact he was born in 1932 in Queens, New York, and stayed in the New York metropolitan area during so many glory years. I'm so proud and happy to have been able to pay Dad back for being such a wonderful father and person, and introducing me to the legendary Bronx Bombers. Baseball connects fathers and sons for life. Dad, this book is dedicated to you more than anyone else because of your love, wisdom, and great sense of humor. What a blessing to be your son! Every child should be so lucky!!!

My wife, Carolyn, for her love and support. So often, whether at social functions or other events, Carolyn would tell people, "Michael's writing a book about the history of Yankee Stadium!" Nice food for the ego. Thank you, Carolyn.

Of course, the New York Yankees, without whom there would be no book. Everyone knows the Yankees are the most successful organization in the history of sports. As a Yankee fan, it was a great joy to work on this labor of love. Entering the gates of Yankee Stadium was always a great thrill and honor!

While ALL of the people listed in this part of this book have contributed to the success of this undertaking, the following individuals have truly earned my deepest thanks and gratitude for going well out of their way to make this venture a more complete and accurate history of Yankee Stadium. I hope I have not forgotten anyone.

Further thanks go to the former Yankees and opponents who played at Yankee Stadium, as well as umpires, executives, and people in the media. Thank you for your opinions, gentleman. I know I thoroughly enjoyed your expertise and kindness in responding to my query about your feeling about the renovation. Going out to the mailbox was a pleasure since I was receiving mail other than bills! Your kindness in responding will never be forgotten!

I remember going to Yankee games in the early 1970s and getting autographs from Yankee president Michael Burke, who was sitting to the left of the Yankee dugout. He was always so kind and gracious. I also recall he wore a nice cologne. Michael Burke will forever have my deepest love and respect. He has a special place in my heart because of his benevolence. He loved New York and Yankee Stadium. He kept the Yankees in New York. God Bless Him for his caring, kindness, and thoughtfulness to the fans. We each leave a legacy in the lives we lead. I'll cherish his forever! He's one of many people that have helped me to become a better human being through example. Thank you, Mr. Burke.

I remember very fondly the interaction with Mr. Burke and our baseball heroes. I do wish baseball would borrow part of its recipe from the past and engage in that endearing behavior once again - even to a slight degree. Mingling with our baseball diamond gods gives us joy and memories that last a lifetime.

My friend, Harry Swanson, who wrote the book, *Ruthless Baseball: Yankees Purified by Fire Stadium Construction* was a great source of advice and guidance. Harry was also kind enough to let me use much of the information published in *Ruthless Baseball* regarding the building of Yankee Stadium. Thank you for your kindness and generosity, Harry. *Ruthless Baseball* was such a joy to read because I learned so much about the construction of Yankee Stadium. The names and facts and figures you listed answered so many questions I've wondered about for so many years.

Tim Reid, who is a true and honest friend. Thank you for your friendship, honesty, and great advice, Tim. Also for your many words of encouragement and support on this long journey. Your knowledge and passion for baseball history is contagious.

Chris and Cindy Jones for your encouragement, support, and honesty, as well. Chris, your sense of humor gave me many great laughs, and laughter is truly the greatest medicine. Your enthusiasm to fight for what's right is a great attribute, too.

John Guilfoyle, another friend. Thank you for sending me stories and photos of Yankee Stadium, and leads with regard to information I could use for this book. And, for *New York Daily News* and New York Yankees magazines covering Yankee Stadium and team history. Thank you, John.

Gary Dunaier is a friend who is well known in the New York City area for taking fantastic photos of Yankee Stadium, Shea Stadium, and CitiField. His baseball knowledge is also amazing. Thank you for filling in so many pieces of the puzzle, Gary.

Steve Alevas, another friend, has sent me many photos of Yankee Stadium for the past few years. Thank you for your generosity and magnificent photos, Steve. They are always a treat to receive. You are also a great keeper of photographic expertise and history. Steve doesn't have red blood in his veins - it's colored Yankee blue!

Matt Visco, who is a trusted, honest friend. Matt also directed me to people with knowledge for my book, as well as honest critiques of some chapters I've written. He was also kind enough to post photos for me on *baseball-fever.com*, as well as send me blueprints of the renovated Yankee Stadium. Matt also kindly edited my book for historical accuracy and proofreading. Thank you, Matt.

John Meeks, who built an outstandingly beautiful model of Yankee Stadium as it appeared in 1973. John also proofread my manuscript and checked for historical accuracy and proofreading errors. Thank you John, for your fine work on my book, and such a magnificent replica of Yankee Stadium. Your solid friendship, wise advice, and honesty cannot be underestimated in my completing this book. You have the patience of a saint!!!

Richard Muller worked as an ironworker for Karl Koch Erecting for 19 months on the project. Besides speaking so beautifully, his wonderful stories and knowledge kept me enthralled. He's also a great historian. What a joy Dick brought to my research. Thank you, Dick.

Jay Schwall, president of Louisiana Chem Dism/Invirex. Jay was in charge of the demolition phase of the renovation. This generous, kind friend sent me information regarding the demolition and spoke to me on the phone numerous times. Thank you for your kindness and generosity, Jay.

Gabriel Schechter, a dear friend who is also a wonderful person and superb copy editor. Gabriel's exceptional skills added so much to the quality of this finished product. This book would not have been published without Gabriel's superior talents. Thank you for your friendship, patience, advice, and wisdom, Gabriel. Your esteemed reputation as a fantastic baseball copy editor is indeed truly earned!!!

Sara Hendricks, a former officer with the American Copy Editors Society, and a 30-year career in newspapers as a reporter and editor, edited the first chapter of *Babe's Place*. Sara is a great lady with superb skills and a good heart. Thank you for being an important asset to *Babe's Place*, Sara.

Steve Koch, who served as Project Engineer, then Project Manager, for Walsh Construction during the Yankee Stadium renovation of the 1970s. Thank you for your patience, kindness, and friendship in telling your story, Steve. You've solved some more of the mysteries I've wondered about, and you've added so much to the fascinating history of sacred Yankee Stadium. Also, deepest thanks to your kind daughter, Suzanne Koch Fabrizio, who got us together.

Doug Walker, a master carpenter on the project, spoke to me on a few occasions. His Scottish accent and the joy in his voice kept me asking more questions. Not just to get the story, but just to hear his brogue. Thank you, Doug.

Anthony Adonetti, President/CEO of Structural Contours, Inc., Greenwich, CT. This wonderful man has impressed me no end! He wrote the section on "Falsework" in the 1976 section of this book. Anthony also responded to my requests quickly, personally, and professionally. He didn't know me, yet here's a president of a company going out of his way to help me with my project! Anthony, thank you for treating me as though I were as important as Stephen King!!!

Kurt Rim, Chairman of the Osborn Engineering Company, Cleveland Ohio. This fine gentleman was one of the first people kind enough to help out this unknown author. Kurt impressed me with his marvelous geniality.

Mariano Molina, a principal of MDM Consulting Engineers, New York, NY, and Jersey City, NJ, is cut from the same mold as Anthony Adonetti. Mariano also showed nothing but kindness to me in the same exact way. For presidents of such successful companies as these to go out of their way to assist me...it still boggles my mind. All businesses should be led by such magnificent leaders as these outstanding gentlemen!

Edwin H. Brunjes, who served as the Director of Design, and Assistant Commissioner for the Department of Public Works, City of New York, from 1970-1975. Ed is another fine example of a business leader who has shown extreme kindness to a stranger who asked questions from out of the blue.

Judith Lillard, of URS Corp., New York City, who was a tremendous help in helping me receive permission to use the 69 page 1972 Yankee Stadium Modernization Plan. It's a very important document which gives the reader a greater appreciation into what went into the renovation. Thank you, Judith, for your tireless effort and patience, and URS for your kindness.

Patricia D. Kelly, Photo Archivist, at the National Baseball Hall of Fame and Museum, was a pleasure to work with. Pat patiently helped me select photos in the Baseball Hall of Fame's collection for use in *Babe's Place*. In September of 2010, Carolyn and I had the pleasure to visit the beautiful village of Cooperstown. Besides meeting Pat, James L. Gates, Jr., the Library Director of this magnificent institution, took time from his busy schedule to visit with me. I cannot count the number of wonderful people I've met in this long, exciting journey.

Michael Margolis, Manager, Media Relations and Publicity, New York Yankees, is a true gentleman in every sense of the word. I first had the honor and pleasure of meeting Michael in September 2010 the new Yankee Stadium. Steve Alevas took me to meet Michael at a designated location during a game at the Stadium. It was my first time there, so I was totally unfamiliar as to where to go. Michael immediately struck me as a very nice, honest man. I was very much impressed with him. Michael, likewise, seemed impressed by my manuscript for *Babe's Place*. Michael gave each of us a 2010 New York Yankees Media Guide. Michael is a trusted friend. The New York Yankees have a gem of a person in Michael Margolis. Thank you for all of your help, Michael.

Brad Turnow. Brad has been kind enough to advertise *Babe's Place* on his wonderful New York Yankees website, *www.HistoryOfTheYankees.com.* Brad also made a cover for my manuscript while I was searching for a publisher. He then spent a lot of time and effort creating the cover used in the book you are now reading. He's a true computer genius with great artistic talent. Your true friendship, wisdom, honesty, and advice greatly helped make this book possible. Thank you for your help and support, Brad.

Chris and Cindy Jones, Tim Reid, and Brad Turnow, have been exceptionally notable in ongoing efforts to preserve the memory and treasures of Old Yankee Stadium, which they rightfully praise as "the greatest stadium since the Coliseum of Rome". As leaders of the Committee to Commemorate Babe Ruth, the Committee to Commemorate Old Yankee Stadium, and *HistoryOfTheYankees.com*, they have engaged the public through a long series of historic preservation and media campaigns. These include very well-received musical slide-show videos creatively documenting and paying tribute to the history of *"The House That Ruth Built"*. (These videos, including *"SaveTheGate"*, *"YankeeUnderground*", and *"TheKingOfSwing714*," can be seen on *youtube.com* accounts) One of their most significant joint successes include saving of three (Gate 2) balconies for the citizens of New York. They and others continue to work with the City, general public, baseball world, and media, to improve commemorations of Old Yankee Stadium on its legendary former site.

Dave Ciambrone, president of the San Gabriel Writers' League, Georgetown, TX. Thank you for your wisdom, and guidance. Your encouragement and suggestions made this book easier to work on.

Gary Mitchem, Senior Acquisitions Editor, McFarland & Company, Inc., Publishers, Jefferson, North Carolina. I've learned a lot from working with you, Gary. Thank you for giving me the self confidence to publish this book. The dream is now a reality thanks to you and many other people that have helped me along the way.

These other remarkable people who worked on the renovation added credence to my research. My deepest thanks to: Stephen Offerman of Amsterdam Color Works, Bronx, NY; Ralph Drewes, who worked for NAB. Ralph was kind enough to speak with me on the telephone and answer a couple of my letters requesting information about the 1970s remodeling of Yankee Stadium, as was Robert Young, an engineer on the renovation; Harvey Simpson of NAB; Victor Strauss, President of Ben Strauss Industries, NY; I'm still amazed that such important, busy people as yourselves took time to assist me. You didn't have to help me, but you did. I humbly thank you for your time and generosity. These kind gentlemen spoke to me on the phone and corrected my drafts to ensure the accuracy of the facts.

Other people who sent me items or gave me information I could use for my book are: Cecele Wagner; Arthur Tauber; Elsie Director; Elaine Friedman; Carl & Lila Vogel; Mark Costello; Richard Lillard; John Trush; Mike Hagan; Tom Noonan; Paul Doherty; Tony Summo; Jacqueline Thompson; Dustin and Meagan Warncke; Joe & Candy Vogel; Robert Bluthardt and Jacob Pomrenke of the Society For American Baseball Research (SABR); Kyle Johnson and Carol Clark; Joe Garagiola, Jr.; Chris Kozicki (Chris suggested "*The Lives of Yankee Stadium*," as part of the book's title); Pat Trigani; Marty Appel; K. Jacob Ruppert; Ross Lewis, www.ys-stadiumphotos.com; Roy Slezak, formerly of Passaic, NJ, currently of Chandler, AZ; Jerry Marshall of Marshall/KMK Acoustics, Ltd., Chappaqua, NY; Rosanne Miskow, Secretary to Michael Burke, 1972-1982; John Lenaz, Corbett Inc., Somerset, NJ; Tim and Mary Crowley, www.TheCrowleyGroup.net, 300 South Legacy Trail, St. Augustine, FL 32092; Cynthia Montello, The Montello Agency, Jacksonville, FL; Howard Berk, former Vice President of the New York Yankees; Megan Walsh of Major League Baseball Properties, Inc.; Jay Latimer, Manager, Media Relations and Publicity, New York Yankees; Jennifer Reilly, Senior Director, Client Relations, New York Yankees; Brian Richards, Curator of the New York Yankees Museum, Yankee Stadium; Bobbie Jackson and The Bell County Writers Guild; Pruitt Davis and the members of the Sammons Community Center Writers Group, Temple, TX; Barbara Wilson of the Sammons Community Center Art Group, Temple, TX; Larry King of Jaffe Holden Acoustics, Norwalk, CT; Jim Long of Electro-Voice; Susan Milburn; Richard McCroskey; Herman A. Lindau of Hermann Lindau & Son, Inc., Huntington, NY; Brad Wilson; Mike Griffin; Scott Seaborn; Rich Gagliano; Marshall Fogel; Hannah Arnold and David Leavitt of Interstate Bakeries Corp.; Brian Kelleher aka Mack Maloney; LBJ Museum, Austin, TX; Matthew King; Debra Charles; Karen Vrotsos; Members of the San Gabriel Writers' League,

Georgetown, TX; Jeff Ellinport; John E. Schlimm II; Michael Maggi; Joe Kusiak; Greg & Nicole Slivanik; William Barret; Abraham Brown; Louis DiLullo; Dave Kaplan, Director of the Yogi Berra Museum, Montclair, NJ; Greg Schwalenberg of the Babe Ruth Museum, Baltimore, MD; Don Boeri; Larry Wiederecht; Michael Grossbardt; Benning De La Mater; Harvey Levene; Peter Kasten of United States Bronze, New Hyde Park, NY; Neil Poloncarz; Ginger Seidel of the National Ticket Company, Shamokin, PA; David W. Smith of retrosheet.org.; Neil deMause of *The Village Voice*, NY; Ralph & Mark Terowsky; Marjie Rynearson; Patrick Vecchio, Town Supervisor, and Marlene Wolke, Smithtown, NY; Eric Peither, Sherwin Williams Paint Co., Temple, TX; Big Guy, Drums, PA; yankees74, Saddle River, NJ; Joe Thordsen; Bruce Genther; Steve Sears; Gil Debner; Burge Smith, author of the book, "The 1945 Detroit Tigers,"; Eric Okurowski of www.stadiumpage.com; Robert Weintraub, author of the book, "The House That Ruth Built,"; Dr. Cary Goodman, Executive Director, 161 Street Business Improvement District, Bronx, NY; Steven Koch and his daughter, Suzanne Koch Fabrizio; Frances M. Walker, my English teacher for two years at Sewanhaka High School, Floral Park, NY; Ray and Phyllis Davis; Selma & Jim Steidley; David Kramer; friends and co-workers at Hill Country Transit District (The HOP), Belton, TX; Frances Bourgeois; Richard and Karen Pruitt; James Woodward; Linda Mullen; Joel M. Lowry; PACK 'N' MAIL, Temple, TX; Rick Petricca of Unistress Corp, Pittsfield, MA; Jack Smalling and Harvey Meiselman for their marvelous baseball address lists; zamzar.com for photo conversions; Patricia Benoit, Staff Writer, *Temple Daily Telegram*, Temple, TX; Marlisa Brown and Russ Schiemente; Mark Ravitz, Jeff Boettcher; Colin Mason, Director, Division of Fine Arts, Temple College, and his associate, Radha Beeram,Temple, TX; Sports Collector's Digest; Tim Waits, sports columnist in the *Temple Daily Telegram*, Temple, TX; Josh Arnold, Staples Office Supply, Temple, TX.

Thank you to the following for use of their resources: SUNY Stony Brook – Frank Melville, Jr. Memorial Music Library, Stony Brook, NY; Laura Tosi, librarian at The Bronx County Historical Society; Color Express, New Braunfels, TX; Sundance Print and Copy, New Braunfels, TX; Landa Photo, New Braunfels, TX; The UPS Store, Georgetown, TX; Linda Fryar, Public Library, Wichita Falls, TX.

The internet has been so invaluable in my research, that there are no words I can say that could thank these sources properly: *newspaperarchive.com*; *The New York Times* Archives; *Newsday*; *The New York Daily News; The New York Post; ebay*; and many other internet sites that deal with baseball have been of great assistance. *Outrageous Good Fortune*, the autobiography of Michael Burke, published by Little, Brown and Company, 1984.

Baseball Fever (baseball-fever.com) has a wealth of knowledgeable baseball fans that also have given priceless facts and benevolence to this project. This site is addicting and tremendously educational. My deepest gratitude to these magnificent baseball research sleuths and friends. Their kindness and generosity cannot be underestimated in the success of this project. Many facts found in the pages of this book are thanks to these remarkable individuals. Some of these exceptional people are: spiderico; Kaplanski; RichardLillard1; jimmyjimjimz; The Monument; TJH1923; SparkyL; WEB; YankeesFan; enchano; Gary Dunaier; paynoaks; BSmile; alpineinc; brooklyndodger14; Mattingly85MVP; David Atkatz; Gehrig27; monkeypants; cgcoyne2; stlfan; tdinan; nymdan; donut726; kobathecat; Swoboda4; IPO; YankeeStadium1923; MarcianoNY; Yankees73; Urbanshocker13; Aviator_Frank; six4three; shaneslatts; Tino24; Astros; NYFan1stYankFan2nd; whoisonit; Paul W; Mario Mendoza...HOF Lock; locke40; tugger; DaBigMotor; Milwaukee Stadium; RichieA13; bleacherbum73; stadiumbuilder; david (digger) odell; frank72; Mackenzie; NYSubway18; thestadiumguy; voodoochile; CrazyMind 2017; Andrew Harts; bkhockey3. *Note:* thestadiumguy posted his nearly six minute Super 8 film footage, "Yankee Stadium Renovation 1974-75," *on www.youtube.com*; James Wickham.

So many people have been a constant source of friendship, encouragement, and inspiration. They have contributed greatly in many ways to *Babe's Place*, whether through corrections, sending me materials for the book, or proofreading. Their baseball and Yankee Stadium love and knowledge is astounding, as is that of many people mentioned in this section of the book. The funny thing is that I've met hardly anyone in person or have spoken with them on the phone. Most of us have met only on the internet, yet there is a strong bond thanks to the magic love of Yankee Stadium, the New York Yankees, and baseball.

My computer skills are good only up to a point. April, Kelly, and Brittany, at 48 Hour Books (*48hrbooks.com*) have the patience of saints. They helped me with the photos and other aspects of publishing *Babe's Place.* I cannot thank you enough, ladies. I would recommend 48 Hour books to the world!

As strange as this may sound, I would also like to thank my old nemesis/friend, insomnia. I cannot count how many nights I was able to focus on researching and writing *Babe's Place.* I did accomplish a lot in the wee hours of the night. When harnessed, insomnia can be your friend in reaching a goal. And, this goal was very long in coming!

I was a United States Air Force Historian for 21 years. I've always enjoyed history, especially American History and baseball. The Air Force was great to me. I'm thankful for the many nice people I've known in my 27 years in the Air Force, and for the things I've learned. My training certainly helped me organize and write this book.

Ever since I was a child, I wanted to grow up to play baseball for the New York Yankees. I was not good enough for such a proud honor, however. I am therefore very thankful that *Babe's Place* is now published. Although I did not achieve the lofty ambition of putting on the sacred New York Yankee pinstripes, I will at least be forever associated with the New York Yankees thanks to my authorship. Even though I'm currently in my fifties, some dreams in life will never die.

Although *Babe's Place* spotlights Yankee Stadium through 1976, a number of photos in this book are from later dates. I had hoped to include the demolition of Yankee Stadium and the construction of the new Yankee Stadium in this book. However, the amount of research and writing precluded that decision. I may yet still write that book. I wanted to ensure that some of these magnificent photographs would be published, as they did occur at the first Yankee Stadium.

I would like to note that some photos I wished to have published in this book are not included, as I tried to obtain permission to use them. Since such approval was not granted, I regretfully had to leave them out in order to avoid copyright infringement.

Chapter One

A TEAM AND HOME ARE BORN

From its early days of spitballs and screwballs and outright cheating, baseball has and always will be about homeruns, fast pitches and diehard fans. No team like the Yankees and no player like Babe Ruth have captured the imaginations of old and young alike during its long history.

Behind the scenes, though, building a home for the team is a story about big business, political graft and the ups and downs of athletes who bring hordes of fans to the Bronx for hot dogs, beer and cheer.

It's all play -- fair or foul, on and off the field.

In the beginning

The National League has been in existence since 1876. Throughout much of its early history, baseball leagues came and went. When the National League dropped its franchises in Baltimore, Cleveland, Louisville and Washington after the 1899 season because of poor attendance, the Western League was poised to act. The minor league baseball organization was founded in 1893 and its teams played predominantly in the Midwest. Byron "Ban" Johnson had been president of the Western League from 1893 to 1900 and he had greater ambitions than a minor league for himself and baseball.

At the same time, in June 1900, a group of National League players organized the Players Protective Association. They wanted to create a stable baseball league where rowdy behavior, profanity and drunkenness by baseball players was not tolerated, umpires would be supported in their decisions and gamblers would no longer influence the outcome of games. Also of great importance, the players were fed up with low salaries and the reserve clause, which, in effect, made the National League owners the masters and the baseball players the slaves.

With all the bickering going on, Johnson, at the end of the 1900 season, saw an opportunity to proclaim his organization in the major leagues and renamed it the American League. Johnson was aided by St. Paul owner Charles Comiskey, who moved his team to Chicago. Johnson could now make improvements in baseball that the National League prevented.

In December 1900, the great baseball war began between the National and American Leagues. Johnson stole 45 players away from the senior league that year, with another 37 in 1901. The National League tried to recoup its losses in the courts but lost most battles. Over half of the National League's players, including many stars, were lured to the American League by bigger salaries and the promise of better treatment by the junior circuit. The list included such luminaries as Clark Griffith, the first National League star to join the new organization, Napoleon Lajoie, John McGraw, Cy Young and Joe McGinnity.

Baseball fans evidently agreed with the infant league's aim to make baseball a respectable form of family entertainment. In 1902, the National League counted 1.9 million spectators, more than a quarter million more than its new counterpart. The next season the American League overtook them with 2.2 million fans to National's 1.7 million.

Johnson then turned his sights on New York where he hoped to form a team to rival the New York Giants baseball players. He knew this great metropolis would support a second team and he wanted it to be a thorn in the side of John McGraw, a former American League manager who now managed the Giants and was known for intimidating umpires and opponents alike.

Chance smiled on Johnson when the bankrupt American League Baltimore Orioles franchise, under President Calvin Chan, was sold in 1902 to Bill Devery and Frank Farrell of New York for $18,000.

Baltimore had ended its first season with a 68-65 record, attracting 141,952 fans that first year, then finished dead last in 1902. When the team moved to New York in 1903, Joseph W. Gordon, former New York state assemblyman and ex-president of the New York Metropolitans American Association baseball club (a 19th century ball club), served as team president. This new team was named the Highlanders. Frank Farrell would follow in Gordon's footsteps from 1907 until 1915.

On January 9, 1902, with the Highlanders now in New York, American Leaguers Ban Johnson, Vice President Charles Somers and J.F. Kilfoyle met with club owners at the Criterion Hotel in Manhattan. Their National League counterparts, led by John Brush, assembled at the Victoria Hotel. Johnson secured $370,000 for an American League ball park in Manhattan. He disclosed details about a week later when he also announced that right fielder Willie Keeler, who had played for the Orioles, would join the Highlanders. "I signed Keeler myself," Johnson said, "and I found him an easy man to do business with." [1]

On January 10, 1903, the baseball war between the leagues ended when each appointed Peace committees to negotiate a treaty that came to be known as the Cincinnati Agreement. In part, it established an American League ballclub in New York. Keeler of Brooklyn, and Clark Griffith of Chicago, among others, would leave their National League teams to move to their rival American League clubs in 1901. Besides New York, the cities of Boston, Philadelphia, Washington, Cleveland, Detroit, Chicago and St. Louis would now field teams in the revamped

American League. The plan called for the 1903 American League season to start April 23 or 24, with 140 games scheduled.

Before leaving on a business trip to Washington, Johnson said he had abandoned a proposed site for an American League ballpark at Lenox Avenue and 142nd Street in Manhattan. He had options on three more sites – one in Manhattan and two above the Harlem River. "As to the property sites above the Harlem, all I can say is that we can start immediately, but I prefer Manhattan to the Bronx, and will not think of crossing the Harlem until forced to, which does not seem likely." [2] One Bronx property owner met with Johnson for over an hour, hoping to persuade him to consider building a ball yard above the river, as the underground railroad to the Bronx would soon be completed, making transportation a non-issue.

Apparently, his words did not move Johnson. He hired Thomas McAvoy, a Tammany Hall district leader, as contractor. McAvoy, in turn, hired laborers to build a park on Broadway between 165th and 168th Streets in Manhattan. Workers began hauling rocks and boulders from the location on March 16. A number of these laborers refused to return to work on March 30, because they had received only $1.50 per day instead of the promised $2. Still, the work continued and the high fence around the ballpark was now almost complete, and the grandstand would be started a few days later. [3]

Property owners, too, got into the fray. Some wanted a baseball park in the Washington Heights neighborhood; scores were opposed because they felt property values would decline due to the large crowds associated with sporting events. On April 9, the Washington Heights Local Board of Improvements cleared the way for construction to continue when they voted 4-3 to deny cutting new roads through 166th and 167th streets, which would have impeded progress on the park. This was welcome news to the Blind Asylum authorities, who leased the land to the baseball club.

The park that was destined to be the best in baseball had humble beginnings. Built in just six weeks, Hilltop Park became home to the New York Highlanders, later to become the Yankees. It was constructed near the highest elevation in Manhattan, making Highlanders an appropriate name for the team. Conjecture also abounds it was named for the Scottish Gordon Highlanders regiment. Since Joseph Gordon was the team president, it was a way to honor him.

Sitting on 9.6 acres, Hilltop was almost twice the size of most ball parks of the era. Most of the $300,000 spent on it went to blasting and excavating about 12,000 cubic yards of rock. Workers replaced the bedrock with 30,000 cubic yards of dirt. This process began on March 25. Spectators helped workers by scavenging bits of rock for souvenirs. Groundskeeper Phil Schenck laid out the field. He would later be instrumental in performing the same task at Yankee Stadium. The actual cost of constructing the home of the Highlanders was $75,000. Another $6,000 would be spent on rent its first year.

The New York Times issue of April 30 proclaimed that the brand new park "from now on will be known as American League Park, on Washington Heights." Although the park was not yet completed, the paper noted "enough progress has been made to enable the games being played." [4]

When Hilltop opened, the dimensions of the field were 365 feet to left field, 546 to center and 400 feet to right field – considerably greater than today's distances. A covered grandstand stretched from first to third base, with uncovered bleachers down both lines. A simple scoreboard was located near the left field foul line. The outfield was still in rugged condition, and right field still needed to be filled in, but conditions improved when the team returned from their road trip on June 1 to a completed field and stands.

The Highlanders name didn't enjoy the same sense of completion. The team was variously called the New York Americans, New Yorks, Greater New Yorks, New York Porchclimbers, New York Burglars and New York Invaders, among others.

The team of many names played its first game April 22, 1903, against the Washington Senators at League Park in Washington, D.C. Al Orth pitched a 3-1 victory over New York's Jack Chesbro, before almost 12,000 spectators. Nearly every seat was sold, and fans crowded the outfield. District Commissioner H.L. West and Senator Arthur Gorman participated in formally opening the game that went on for one hour and 45 minutes. The next day the Highlanders reversed roles by beating Washington by a score of 7-2 with Harry Howell on the mound.

The Highlanders won their inaugural home game on April 30, 1903, against the Senators, with Jack Chesbro besting Jack Townsend by a score of 6-2, in front of 16,000 spectators. The gates opened at 1 o'clock on a beautiful day for baseball. American League President Ban Johnson attended the festive event, along with Joe Gordon and G. Hector Clemes, one of the directors of the Washington club.

The box score consisted of the following players and positions:

New York		Washington	
Alphonzo Davis	lf	William Robinson	ss
Willie Keeler	rf	Albert Selbach	rf
Herm McFarland	cf	Ed Delahanty	lf
Jimmy Williams	2b	Jimmy Ryan	cf

John Ganzel	1b		George Carey	1b
William Conroy	3b		Bill Coughlin	3b
Ernie Courtney	ss		Gene DeMontreville	2b
Jack O'Connor	c		Lew Drill	c
Jack Chesbro	p		Jack Townsend	p
			*James Holmes	

*batted for Townsend 9th inning

The other players who played for the 1903 New York Highlanders were:

Norman Elberfeld	ss		Jesse Tannehill	p
Monte Beville	c		Clark Griffith	p, manager
Dave Fultz	of		Harry Howell	p
Herman Long	ss		Barney Wolfe	p
Jack Zalusky	c		John Deering	p
Pat McCauley	c		Ambrose Puttmann	p
Patsy Greene	3b		Elmer Bliss	p
Tim Jordan	1b		Merle (Doc) Adkins	p
Fred Holmes	1b		Eddie Quick	p
			Lewis Wiltse	p

To open the new arena, George M. Cohan sang "You're A Grand Old Flag" and "Yankee Doodle Dandy," while the 69th Regiment Band, led by Bandmaster William Bayne, played such favorites as "The Star Spangled Banner," "The Washington Post March," and "Yankee Doodle."

The Highlanders wore new white uniforms and caps of white flannel with white facings. On top of their uniforms they wore natty maroon-colored coats. Washington sported white shirts and blue pants.

Players on both teams waved little American flags, as did paying customers, who were given the gifts upon entering the ball park. The park contained 16,000 yellow pine and spruce seats, and about the same number could stand. Perhaps one of the best features of the park was that the fans sitting behind home plate were treated to a view of the Hudson River and New Jersey Palisades.

Thomas Connolly and Robert Caruthers umpired the Highlanders' first home game. The New York team dominated the hour-and-a-half contest from beginning to end.

The 1903 season saw the Highlanders finish in fourth place, with the team compiling a 72-62 record, and an attendance of 211,808. The next season, attendance at the park jumped to 501,000 when the Highlanders came close to winning the pennant.

Clark Griffith served as the first manager of the Highlanders. He also continued to pitch until 1907. Under his leadership the team was championship bound, thanks in large part to Jack Chesbro's 41-12 pitching season and Wee Willie Keeler's hitting. Unfortunately, on the last day of the series at Hilltop Park, Chesbro's spitball sailed over the catcher's head, letting the Boston Pilgrims runner on third base score in a 3-2 triumph.

Griffith left the team in 1908 after constant disagreements with the owners. There was also a crosstown rivalry between Griffith and John McGraw, who was playing for the Giants. Both had a hard-scrabble existence in their formative years, and both made their way onto National League teams in the old days when players treated fans to a raucous afternoon at the ballpark.

A few years after leaving the Highlanders, Griffith became part owner of the Washington Senators. There he persuaded President William Howard Taft to throw out the first ball at the Senators' Opening Day game in 1912, starting a tradition that continues to this day. Griffith was merely trying to boost fan attendance.

The Highlanders first exhibited their new light gray road uniforms in April 1905. Along with that, they were given yet another nickname, the Yankees, perhaps first printed in the *Sandusky Evening Star* in Ohio, on April 26, 1904. *The Post Standard* of Syracuse, New York, used the new name a month later. The *Boston Herald* followed suit when Patsy Dougherty came to the team from the Boston Pilgrims in a trade for Bob Unglaub. The headline shouted, "Dougherty as a Yankee." [5]

The New York Times came around when it published an article, "15,000 SEE YANKEES TAKE FIRST GAME," on April 15, 1906. This was perhaps the first time the *Times* referred to the team as the "Yankees." [6] On the same date, the *New York Herald* proclaimed, "Yankees win opening game from Boston, 2-1." Cy Young pitched for Boston while Jack Chesbro hurled for the Yankees in the 12-inning game.

Before that lively game, the stands were filling up early. A band was playing to keep the fans enthused. As *The New York Times* related, "A knot of a dozen had its own song to suit the occasion, and yelled it from a corner in the bleachers to the tune of 'Yankee Doodle,' in honor of their own Yankees of the Heights: The throng sang, 'Yankee Griffith came to town, A ridin' on a bean can, Collins furnished all the pork-, O joy! 'twas a cinch, man.'" Yankees manager Griffith was amused and when he led the Yankees onto the field to practice, the band and fans joined together in singing, "I'm a Yankee Doodle Dandy." [7]

It takes little imagination to envision this was not the first time the fans sang this particular tune at a game. Whether it was the song or newspapers wanting a shorter name for their headlines, the name Yankees stuck, and when "Diamond Jim" Brady threw out the first ball to start the team's home opener in April 1907, the *New York Times* used the new moniker. [8] The Yankees lost, 9-6, before 10,000 fans on a day of threatening weather. Trainer "Mike" Martin was ready in the wings should any injuries occur, but he couldn't heal the damage cause by the team's four errors.

Two years later, Willie Keeler was the last of the original Highlanders to depart the team, when he was released by the club at the end of the 1909 season. Second baseman, Jimmy Williams, lived the longest of the group. He died in 1965 at the age of 88.

Road to the Polo Grounds

Shortly after midnight on April 14, 1911, the main wooden grandstand of the Polo Grounds, home of the National League New York Giants, was destroyed by fire. It took the wind-fanned flames less than an hour to damage all but the left field bleachers and clubhouse. Frank Farrell, an owner of the Orioles and later of the Highlanders when the team moved to New York, immediately extended an invitation to the Giants to play at Hilltop until the Polo Grounds could be repaired. Charles Ebbets, president of the Brooklyn Superbas (later the Dodgers), offered the use of Washington Park, although they could only do so through April 20, as Brooklyn would open the season against Boston the following day.

The Giants accepted the Yankees offer until June 28 when they moved back home. The legendary Christy Mathewson pitched a 3-0 shutout over the Boston Rustlers on a blazingly hot day. Farrell's generosity in letting his rival use his ballpark led the Giants to extend their offer to let the Yankees play in the Polo Grounds when it was their turn to move.

On January 8, 1913, Farrell hired Frank Chance, former manager of the Chicago Cubs, to manage the Yankees. He offered $75,000 and 5 percent interest, over the span of three years. The $120,000 was quite a tidy nest egg for the time. Chance had planned to turn down any offer by Farrell, but changed his mind, saying, "Mr. Farrell, however, offered inducements much better than I had dreamed of, and, excluding my love for the game as a factor, I could not decline them." He further added, "I am not at liberty to give out the terms, but I can say I am to get the largest sum anybody ever got for piloting a ball club, and I am going to come as near earning it as I can." [9] He assumed his position on February 11, when he attended baseball meetings in New York. Following that, the club conducted spring training on a cricket field in Bermuda leased by Farrell.

Chance didn't like the numerous names the team had earned. Highlanders, Hilltoppers, Kilties and Yankees were unbecoming, he believed, and had no meaning outside of New York. His personal favorite was the New Yorks, but fans thought they would be confused with the rival Giants. They further pointed out that the name Highlanders should be replaced in case the club moved to the Polo Grounds. [10]

One New Yorker relayed, "… a shorter and snappier name would not hurt the team, and there is no better time than the present to rechristen the club." Another suggested honoring Chance by naming the team Bears or Bruins, as it was noted he resembled a big bear, also, that "no visitor leaves Manhattan without visiting Bulls and Bears of Wall Street." [11]

The team officially changed its name to the Yankees on April 10, 1913, the first year they played at the Polo Grounds. Washington defeated the locals in their first game at that ballpark by a score of 9-3 on April 17. In this year the Yankees played in front of 1,273,075 paying customers. Of this number, 357,551 patrons went to home games. The team had introduced their famous pinstripe uniform a year earlier. On the left breast the letters "NY" were interlocked and players wore white caps with a blue monogram and blue stockings with maroon stripes. [12]

Chance, however, didn't last out his contract, leaving in 1914 after one of many temper outbursts against the owners.

As fans predicted, the Yankees moved out of Hilltop when their lease expired. Even with improvements at Hilltop to make way for more seating, the Yankees left for the Polo Grounds in time for the 1913 season. The final game at Hilltop Park was October 5, 1912, with the Hilltoppers defeating the Washington Senators, 8-6. Hilltop Park was demolished in 1914 to make room for a one-story tabernacle for Billy Sunday, the baseball player turned evangelist. His building suffered the same fate as the ball park in 1925, when groundbreaking ceremonies began for the Columbia-Presbyterian Medical Center.

The colonels take the reins

A change of venue wasn't the only shakeup. Yankees owners Farrell and Devery hadn't been getting along, and the team had run deeply into debt. They wanted to unload it. Into the picture stepped Jacob Ruppert and Tillinghast L'Hommedieu Huston.

Though not yet owners of the team, the two money barons were already talking about moving the team to the Bronx because the National League didn't want to extend the Yankees' playing at the Polo Grounds past 1915, despite the Yankees having signed a 10-year lease with the Giants. The rent there was also excessive, making it impossible for the team to make money.

Negotiations for the sale of the Yankees were ongoing for weeks, culminating in the sale of the club to the two colonels on January 11, 1915, for $460,000. Ruppert's significant amount of real estate in the Bronx and Huston's vast resources were set to remedy the team's financial woes.

They hired "Wild Bill" Donovan as manager that same month. Shortly after the purchase, Ruppert wanted to change the team's name yet again – this time to the Knickerbockers. He scrapped that idea after the fans' outcry ruled against the move. He was hoping to promote his brewery's flagship beer along with the team.

By May of 1915, a rumor circulated that a baseball stadium for the club would be built on property belonging to the Astor family at Westchester Avenue and Clason Point Road, in the Bronx. This was a 10-minute train ride from the Simpson Street subway station. In reality, there were about six Bronx locations thought to be the future home of the Yankees. Ruppert and Huston had kept in close contact with American League President Ban Johnson concerning the search. Most sites in Manhattan would start at $1 million, making the building of a stadium unaffordable. Three locations had been deemed possible in Queens.

The Yankees would play at the Polo Grounds until 1922, even though the Giants were pressuring their tenants to leave, angry that the Yankees' attendance far exceeded their own, thanks in great part to the slugging of Babe Ruth, acquired from the Boston Red Sox on December 26, 1919. The Babe hit 29 home runs in 1919 and followed that with a whopping 54 the next season, his first in New York.

Harry Frazee, the Red Sox owner, was paid $100,000 and given a $300,000 loan, with Fenway Park as collateral to let Ruth go. He had little choice since he kept running short of money and star players because his heart was in putting on Broadway plays, which did not always succeed. He'd also bought the Red Sox on credit and had to come up with cash to pay loans. Additionally, he had numerous legal run-ins with American League President Ban Johnson over his franchise. Along with Ruth, the Yankees acquired pitchers Waite Hoyt, Carl Mays, Herb Pennock, catcher Wally Schang, shortstop Everett Scott, and third baseman Joe Dugan from Boston in the early 1920s. In essence, Frazee sold the Yankees the pennant, infuriating the Red Sox brethren. Frazee left baseball for good in 1923.

The American League held a special meeting in Philadelphia on August 24, 1920, and decided the Yankees would be allowed to have their own ballpark in New York. The Yankees owners felt the American League should help cover the cost of the new park, as their stadium would surpass the size of any yet completed.

A *New York Times* article on January 30, 1921, reported the club would purchase land owned by the Hebrew Orphan Asylum in Manhattan, at Hamilton Place, off Broadway and Amsterdam

Avenue, bordered by 136th and 138th Streets. The land cost was $750,000 and the stadium about $2 million. [13] The design would resemble the Polo Grounds, with an upper and lower deck, in a horseshoe shape. This location was perfect for mass transit access.

On January 31 *The New York Times* ran a story contradicting the sale of this land to the baseball team. Judge Joseph E. Newburger, president of the Hebrew Orphan Asylum, denied the acreage had been sold, declaring, "Permit me to inform you that there is no option outstanding for the sale of the Hebrew Orphan Asylum, nor are there any negotiations pending. Nor has any sale been consummated."

On the other side of the coin, P.P. Evans, vice president of the Osborn Engineering Company of Cleveland, Ohio, declared the contract was already signed and several plans were ready for the building of the stadium. Osborn, of which Huston was an owner, had previously built contemporary concrete and steel baseball parks for the Boston Braves, Cleveland Indians, New York Giants and Detroit Tigers. Colonel Ruppert had only one request of Osborn: "I want the greatest ballpark in the world." [14]

The engineering company, which began in 1892 under owner Frank Osborn, was to start building the edifice in June, with a two-year completion date, in time for start of the 1923 season. The construction contract between the Yankees and Osborn had been signed and most of the drawings finished.

The next day the *Times* reported the new home of the Yankees would seat 80,000 people. This would be double the seating capacity of the Boston Braves' home, which was at this time the largest baseball park in the world. It cost $650,000 when it opened in 1915, and had seating for 35,000 fans. Only the Yale Bowl in New Haven, Connecticut, which Yankee Stadium would be patterned after, would be in the same league in seating.

Now Ruppert and Huston said that, although the Hebrew Orphan Asylum had been considered for some time, no final resolution had been reached. Other sites under consideration were 225th Street in Manhattan and the 161st Street area of the Bronx.

At last, on February 6, 1921, *The New York Times* reported, "Yankees To Build Stadium In Bronx." The four-block, 10-acre site would range from 157th to 161st Streets and Doughty Avenue to River Avenue. An illustration of the new home of the Yankees was published. It was to be fully enclosed by a mezzanine and an upper deck. Osborn began site work on February 7. Drainage was a very important issue, as the Harlem River was nearby, and the field had to remain dry. The market price of steel, concrete and lumber remained a source of worry for the colonels as well. Coincidentally, Babe Ruth was born on February 6, 1895.

The Yankees and Ruth were riding high during this period, with the team clinching its first American League pennant in 1921 before being defeated in the World Series by the Giants, five games to three.

City plot 2106, lot 100

The home of The House That Ruth Built was on land bought in 1639 by Jonas Bronck, a sea captain of Swedish descent who moved to the Netherlands before becoming the first European to settle in the Bronx. He bought 500 acres in the area of Lincoln Avenue and 132nd Street in Harlem. Known as Broncksland, the territory would eventually become known as the Bronx. Another part of the future site of the baseball temple was land granted to farmer John Lion Gardiner by the British.

One of the streets that would eventually feed into the stadium is Jerome Avenue. It got its name about 1900 when Kate Hall Jerome, wife of high society millionaire Leonard W. Jerome, became angry when a street was named for a New York City alderman instead of her husband. She made her own bronze "Jerome" signs and had them placed on poles on a thoroughfare that maps from 1888 refer to as Central Avenue.

Mr. Jerome was an influential financier, *New York Times* stockholder, and the founder of the Academy of Music. He also helped organize the American Jockey Club at the Jerome Racetrack, which existed from 1867 to 1890. This racetrack was the early home of the Belmont Stakes. His daughter, Jennie, was of greater historical importance, as she gave birth to future British Prime Minister Winston Churchill in 1874.

A postcard from 1908 paints a tranquil scene of the intersection of Jerome Avenue and 161st Street. A gardener mows the lawn near a park bench. Across the wide street is a restaurant and a passing horse-drawn trolley. The rural feel left the area when an elevated subway opened for service on June 2, 1917. This easy access to mass transit was a major reason that Colonels Ruppert and Huston purchased the parcel of land destined to become Yankee Stadium.[15]

After the announcement of the location of the new Yankees home, several hundred fans visited the location. The comments were favorable. The locals, of course, were delighted that Babe Ruth and his teammates would play in their backyard, and the Manhattanites were happy that transportation to Babe's new playground would make their journey an easy one. By happenstance, this was the first property the colonels looked at as a potential home for the Yankees when they acquired the franchise in 1915. They originally voted against this location, believing Manhattan to be better suited, as this area had not yet had subway access. But once railroad service opened on June 2, 1917, the die was cast. This Macombs Dam Bridge setting also yielded more property to the colonels than the Hebrew Orphan Asylum site would, as it was about the same size as the Polo Grounds.

The subway carried fans from 42nd Street in Manhattan in 16 minutes and the elevated train only took two minutes more than it took to get to the Polo Grounds, which was just across the Harlem River. Of course, league rivalries were still alive and kicking. The colonels infuriated Charles Stoneham and John McGraw by building their spectacular new stadium a mere five-minute walk from their former landlords. Automobile access would also be simple.

The *New York Times* said the land, site of a lumber yard belonging to the estate of William Waldorf Astor, cost $500,000. Later, it was learned, the outlay was $675,000. The price tag to build the ball yard would be another $1,500,000. [16] In March, Osborn's engineers were testing the soil to decide the makeup of the foundation. Attorneys were checking deeds to make sure the title to the land was free and clear. But signing all the agreements with the Astor family took over a year, thanks to the Giants' Tammany Hall, a political organization that influenced elections and political patronage, and New York City bureaucracy.

William Waldorf Astor was an American-British financier who was born in New York City and went to school in Germany, England, and New York's Columbia University Law School. He served as a state assemblyman and senator for New York. In 1893, he built the Waldorf Hotel in New York, later to become the famous Waldorf-Astoria. As a millionaire, he gave generously to numerous war funds. He died in England, where the Astor descendants had lived. They rarely sold property, but this land was non-producing, and by selling it the family avoided a sizable inheritance tax.

Bernard Green, the chief architect at Osborn since 1919, designed and supervised the construction of Yankee Stadium, for which he earned $223,000. Green collaborated with Major Thomas Birmingham and Huston on design issues, as well supervising construction. Birmingham, a friend of Huston's, served as Yankee Stadium house engineer. Green's resume included the designing of the Polo Grounds, Boston Braves Field, Dunn Field in Cleveland and Navin Field in Detroit. John White, the general superintendent at Osborn, also oversaw construction.

The project, which was to be built in two phases to limit debt and get the Yankees out of the Polo Grounds sooner, was on paper and the first phase approved by the fall of 1921. Plans called for 21,000 temporary wooden bleachers in the grandstand. In Phase II these would be replaced by concrete, and the grandstand would be extended to encircle the stadium. Cost reductions lowered seating expectations from 80,000 to 50,000. Ed Barrow, the team's business manager, had led a troop of trained sitters in choosing the seats to be used in the new home. They sat in

The Polo Grounds, home of the New York Giants. The ballpark also served as the home of the New York Yankees from 1913-1922, until Babe Ruth and the upstart Yankees outgrew their welcome. Photo courtesy of the NATIONAL BASEBALL HALL OF FAME LIBRARY, COOPERSTOWN, N.Y.

numerous armed and armless rows of chairs brought into the Yankees office, trying to determine which would offer the most comfort for the fans. Seats for the new stands would be 18 inches wide.

By mid-November Osborn Construction had given blueprints to American Bridge Company of Coraopolis, Pennsylvania, for price quotes on steel fabrication of the grandstand. American Bridge, which 10 years later supplied the steel to build the Empire State Building, earned the contract with a bid of $102,500. The Taylor-Fichter Steel Construction Company of New York won the bid to furnish and erect the fabricated steel frame by using derricks and hoists to guide the steel beams, girders and trusses into place. Taylor-Fichter offered to complete the job for $42,300. Those two companies erected the stadium's steel skeleton.

The rest of the concrete and steel structure would be fireproof, with bids for structural steel to be used for the project going out on December 4, 1921. Special thought was given to the number of exits so the fans could leave the ballpark in a short time. The scissor ramps, measuring 20 feet wide behind the stands, could handle 3,000 people per minute. Wider aisles, seats and more room between rows would make fans more comfortable. In fact, every major league baseball park had been studied and their best features had been incorporated into making the home of the Yankees the most fan-friendly park ever created. The exception would be the 118 large posts holding up the second deck that blocked the view of many fans. The grandstand, offices, and Yankees' dressing room would have an estimated cost of $750,000. The mezzanine would be novel to this baseball stadium.

A December 18 article in *The New York Times* stated the building would officially be called Yankee Stadium. The name, "Yankee Field," had previously been bandied about as well. [17] On January 3, 1922, the Yankee colonels announced to the media details of the project. They placed classified ads asking for bids on construction for the job. All proposals were due January 18, except for lighting, elevators and heating, which had to be submitted sooner. Osborn Engineering handled all blueprint requests and collected all bids. General or subcontractors paid $12 to be mailed complete or partial sets of blueprints. These proposals called for carpenters, painters and other skilled workers, and supplies that included sod and bathroom fixtures. Forty contractors, subcontractors and suppliers sent proposals.

On April 19, 1922, *The New York Times* reported the White Construction Company, of 95 Madison Avenue in New York City, would serve as general contractor for the building of Yankee Stadium. Their motto was, "Let White Build It of Concrete." White bested 40 companies with a bid of $1,136,304. White would handle $736,151., and the sub-contractors would control $400,153. This included a $69,413 profit for White. [18] They signed the contract at the Yankees office at 226 West 42nd Street in Times Square on May 5th, 1922. Besides Colonels

Ruppert and Huston, Byron Clark, the Yankees attorney from the law firm of Fitch and Grant, 67 Wall Street in Manhattan, attended the occasion.

The day after the contract was signed, *The Times* published a report that the building would take two or three years to complete. Bernard Green, however, said, "A little teamwork will be necessary to accomplish this happy result. If the Yankee colonels will only make sure that their team wins the American League pennant, the contractors will do their best to see that the park is ready for the big series. That's a fair enough proposition." [19]

The *Times* related that 2,000 tons of steel and 18,000 cubic yards of reinforced concrete would be essential to build the massive structure. Also, plans called for right and left field walls to be 257 feet from home plate. This would be the first baseball park to feature covered stands. One of the biggest considerations in building the grandstand was its proximity to the train station and traffic flow of patrons entering and exiting the park.

H.E. Tear acted as White's general site supervisor and Raymond Bourne as head accountant. They believed the job could be completed in four and a half months, but the contract included an eight-month completion date in case of unforeseen circumstances. White Construction had a solid reputation in industrial and commercial construction projects. The Yankee Stadium project had been assigned number 567. Contract delays forced the company to take on other jobs. In April they took on jobs 566 and 568, projects for Vacuum Oil, of 61 Broadway. Those projects lasted from May through September, and brought in $185,000 and $25,000, respectively. [20]

Colonels Ruppert and Huston took possession of the Yankee Stadium site on May 16, after paying $500,000 to the Farmers Loan and Trust Company in Manhattan. Two months before they had made an initial payment of $100,000. Farmers Loan and Trust represented Charles Peabody and Clarence Baldwin, trustees of the William Waldorf estate. The Yankees made payment in Liberty Bonds. They used Equitable Trust Company as their bank to supply cash and to approve financing before receiving approvals from American and National Sureties for bonding.

The colonels had earlier promised a construction start date of March 1, 1922, firmly believing their team would be playing in the World Series that year, so they were relieved when Mayor John Hylan finally signed off on the plans to build Yankee Stadium on March 31. Site grading was almost completed by this time, and Monday, April 17, was the next chosen date for construction to begin.

Limited construction didn't actually begin until May 6. Most of the activity consisted of materials being brought to the site, as the formal work order to start work had not yet appeared. By May 21, trucks were unloading equipment, surveyors were hammering stakes into the ground, and wooden boards were being placed near curbs at 161st Street to make it easier for trucks to reach the site. Work had been delayed by 13 months, mostly due to political wrangling.

Ruppert and Huston chose Frederick K. Gaston, of 30 East 42nd Street as their insurance broker. White Construction and the Yankees went through Edwards and Booth Insurance for $125,000 worth of fire insurance, for a total premium cost of $187.50. They also received telephone service at their construction shanty at Cromwell Avenue on June 23. Four work locations were given the phone number MEL-4365, and White would pay 2½ cents per call. [21]

In May, 40,000 cubic yards of fill earth for grading was delivered. An extra 25,000 cubic yards was taken from the site in early June for footings, concrete supports, and foundations for the grandstand and bleachers. Rosoff Sand and Gravel promised delivery of sand and gravel from their Marlboro, New York, sand and gravel bank. James Reilly and Sons contracted to deliver these materials to 161st Street in their three dump trucks. Elevator Supplies Co. of Hoboken, New Jersey, supplied elevator erection and repairs.

One site for mixing cement and another for cutting lumber had been created. River Mill Corp. and Van Ness managed the wood cutting mill. By the end of the venture the 30,000 yards of concrete used required 45,000 barrels of cement, 30,000 yards of gravel, and 15,000 yards of sand. Roughly 2,500 tons of structural steel would be used for the stadium, plus another 1,000 tons of reinforcing steel to secure the concrete to the 169,000 square feet of wire mesh. The iron used in the seats added another 500 tons to the monolith. More than four miles of piping was used for hand rails, framing box seats and fencing. The Pipe and Rail Construction Company supplied and installed the pipes.

The (Thomas) Edison Portland Cement Company in New Village, New Jersey, supplied 180,000 bags at 94 pounds per bag of light brown super-hard Portland Cement for the exterior of Yankee Stadium. The curbs for Babe's Place would be gray. The Hutton Company of Kingston, New York, made the 8-inch by 2½-inch bricks for the new monolith, as did the Goldrick Brick Company of Haverstraw, New York. Kinnear Manufacturing Company of Columbus, Ohio, built the exterior steel doors, which were painted dark green. The underside of the upper deck roof and steel supports would display the same color. Grandstand and bleacher seats were to receive light green paint, and field level box seats sported white paint. Wadsworth, Howland and Company of New York supplied the Bay State Paint and Varnish paints, enamels, and concrete coatings used on the giant creation.

The wooden bleachers and concrete work form boards surpassed 2 million board feet, with another 600,000 linear feet for grandstand seating. The Yankees expected to replace the newly painted bright green bleachers in two or three years, as they also planned on extending the three concrete and steel grandstand levels around the whole stadium, for a total of 85,000 seats. As it now stood, these benches consisted of 40,000 square feet of Pacific Coast fir planks, made from

950,000 board feet of wood shipped through the Panama Canal. Between 21,000 and 22,000 fans could sit in this section of Yankee Stadium during a game.

More than 500 workers used trucks, horses, wagons and other equipment to finish this massive job. The four-acre baseball diamond required four to six inches of topsoil, which amounted to 13,000 cubic yards, covered with 116,000 square feet of Long Island sod. Phil Schenck, the groundskeeper for the team since they were known as the Highlanders, aided the field construction.

About 25,000 feet of clay pipe below the playing surface drained water from the field. These two drainage systems consisted of 11 nine-inch pipes for the outfield, and 24 smaller conduits for the infield. A concrete channel in front of the grandstand emptied into municipal sewers. The field had been constructed with a turtle-top slope so water could run off. The warning track around the field measured 24 feet wide and was made from red cinders 10 inches deep. The distance surrounding the perimeter of Yankee Stadium was 2,591 feet, plus an additional 705 feet on River Avenue. [22]

The beautiful art deco 16-foot-deep copper frieze, often mistakenly called a façade, would become the trademark of Yankee Stadium. It was bolted to steel supports at the roof's edge. Fashioned in gothic style and proportion, much like a European cathedral, it enclosed the full upper deck and was the color of brown copper when the stadium opened in 1923. Kinnear Manufacturing of Columbus, Ohio, made the 15-ton frieze, and U.T. Hungerford Brass and Copper in Manhattan supplied the copper. The Yankees originally wanted it painted a soft green to blend in with the grass, but found the cost prohibitive.

Rather than using galvanized metal as planned for the frieze, blueprints noted the use of 22-gauge toncan copper, because it would naturally turn green over time. This copper and iron alloy resisted corrosion and weathering, and proved to be cost effective. Each of the fascia measured slightly over 26 feet long, and 42 feet in length for the longer sections. Thirty-two flag poles were bolted on top of the frieze. These same vendors created the four-foot-tall letters for the exterior YANKEE STADIUM sign above the main entrance of the park. The letters were nearly 38 feet long. The letter "S" weighed 11 pounds. The letter "U" measured 24 inches wide. The letter "M" weighed 16.25 pounds, was one inch thick, and measured 34.5 inches long. The top of the flag pole bore a copper baseball above a three-foot-long copper baseball bat, which also served as a weather vane.[23]

The blueprints called for the high roof portion of the stadium to rise to a height of 127.5 feet, with the low point at 122.5 feet. The elevations for the Main Deck were 41 feet, with 64 feet for the Mezzanine and 112.25 feet for the Upper Deck. The South Amboy Terra Cotta Company in New Jersey bestowed the three nine-foot circular polychrome terra cotta panels detailing a dark red painted eagle. The bird had outstretched wings and gripped baseball bats. Two panels had been placed over the main entrance. Pittsburgh Plate and Glass supplied glass for the stadium, while Crittall Casement Company of Detroit, Michigan, provided casements for the windows.

Some of the many other contractors used included:

Davis Brown – plastering
Durand Steel Locker Co. – lockers in dressing rooms, New York/Chicago
J.W. Fiske Iron Works, New York City – ticket turnstiles
Gould Construction Company – miscellaneous iron
M. Limanti & Sons – tile, stone, terrazzo, mosaic work
Metropolitan Electric Manufacturing Co. – electrical - switchboards
Otis Elevator – elevators – New York
Philadelphia Fire Retardant Company – fire proofing
T.J. Rooney – curb setting
B. Rybakof – refreshment stands
Schenck and Gibbons – sod, topsoil, and landscaping

Several vendors who supplied materials included:

Allied Window and House Cleaning Company
American Glue Company – Boston and New York
Chicago Pneumatic Tool Company – New York
Colonial Sand and Stone Company
Eggleston Brothers Company
George H. Storm and Company
Jenkins Valves – New York
Lenex Sand and Gravel Company
New York Edison
New York Telephone
Spadaro Construction Company
Wadsworth, Howland and Company – paint – New York and Boston

Some of the costs for the project were estimated to be:

$19,768 – brick, tile, insurance

$35,669 – excavation, shoring, grading
$30,000 – construction supervision, engineers, site plan preparation
$429,302-- concrete work and forms, on-site labor, mill work, insurance
$129,305–carpentry work
$24,268 – cleaning and removal
$39,165 -- iron
$43,421 – painting
$ 7,399 -- plastering
$39,983 – plumbing
$76,989 – seats
$146,500 – structural steel and erection [24]

Not all competition is on the field

In response to the hoopla surrounding the building of Yankee Stadium, on July 25, 1922, the New York Giants announced the Polo Grounds would undergo a renovation that would create a better baseball stadium than the future home of the Yankees. They would raze their 12,000-seat wooden bleachers and expand their double deck grandstand, dramatically increasing grandstand seating from 26,200 to 53,200. Bleacher seats would be reduced to 5,000. They also planned to enlarge the playing field to encourage more inside-the-park home runs. [25]

The Giants also increased their football seating to 65,000 and 92,000 for boxing. This was a clear attempt to lure workers away from the building of Yankee Stadium and to earn more money for the Polo Grounds.

But the Giants didn't have the greatest draw of all – Babe Ruth. The Yankees played their last game at the Polo Grounds on September 10 before a crowd of 40,000 faithful. Another 25,000 had to be turned away.

The Giants gained some satisfaction when they beat the Yankees in the 1922 World Series four games to none, and a tie. The Babe hit a paltry .118 and only had one RBI. Huston was so angry he wanted to fire manager Miller Huggins, but relented when Yankees General Manager Ed Barrow said he'd quit if Huston didn't stop meddling in the operations of the club. Huggins and Barrow stayed. Radio station WJZ, based in Newark, New Jersey, broadcast the games. Box seats sold for $6.60, reserved for $5.50, upper grandstand unreserved went for $3.30, and for $1.10 you could sit in the bleachers.

Back at Babe's Place

On September 1, 1922, Osborn Engineering figured Yankee Stadium construction costs to be $308,924 with the stadium 27 percent finished. The three-tier steel frame was nearly halfway finished by September 19. By the end of the month, most of the wood framing for the bleachers was done. Also at this time, concrete work began along the left field upper decks, and United Roofing installed the Johns-Manville asbestos roofing material on the left field portion of the roof. Eight other major league stadiums had previously used this substance for sound protection, durability, and fire protection.[26]

The cost of building Yankee Stadium rose to $682,354 by October 31. With 60 percent of the stadium completed, the steel construction was nearly done. At this point, 21 Change Orders to the original stadium plans made the cost rise another $82,946. The largest came on November 1 with revision to the bleachers. Originally slated to cost $116,697, costs would now run $253,266 for longer-lasting seating. Modifications also consisted of building concrete footings, girder footings, exterior walls matching the exterior grandstand, decking, ramps and sidewalks. [27] The bleachers would weigh 11 tons, with wedging plates installed under concrete columns to support the weight. In December, the firm of Moran, Maurice and Proctor performed an independent load-bearing test on these seats by putting gravel-filled bags on them for 10 days, as requested by the Yankee colonels. The test was carried out to ensure the bleachers would safely hold its 21,000 fans.

Phil Schenck, whose tasks encompassed anything from laying the drainage system under the field, to adding top soil, to placing the sod on top of baseball's newest diamond, had finished laying sod in the new temple on the afternoon of November 27. Shortly thereafter, snow began to fall on the holy grounds. [28]

The Daly Brothers Company, Contractors and Excavators of New York, worked as subcontractor to White Construction for water mains, cellars, and other similar projects. Perhaps the most intriguing thing about Daly Brothers is that on December 26, 1922, a crew member opened a previously closed and covered water main for city inspection on the corner of 161st Street and River Avenue after Change Order No. 7 had been completed. Before recovering the main, this gentleman buried an item in the pit to bring good luck to the team in their new arena. Bookkeeping notes of White Construction showed the item to be a bottle. Quite possibly it was a Ruppert Beer bottle. History has shown this unidentified object has served the New York Yankees immensely well. [29]

White Construction built the manually operated 30-foot tall by 66-foot long scoreboard on top of the bleacher fence in right center field. The hollow structure held two-foot-high letters to show the score. J.I. Haas painted it. Jack Lenz, speaking through a megaphone on the field, acted as the first public address announcer. This scoreboard far surpassed the small, inadequate ones of the Polo Grounds and other parks. Twelve innings of play by all teams in both leagues could now be displayed on this new masterpiece.

Each tier of the facility held phone booths and the mezzanine had a central location for a large storeroom and refreshments distribution. The Harry M. Stevens Company of New York held the contract for food service. Sixteen large bathrooms, eight each for men and women, had been built to avoid congestion. Smoking and lounge rooms adjoined the men's toilets while the ladies enjoyed wicker chairs, dressing tables, and grass mats. These restrooms and terra cotta cost $5,000. Eugene Duklauer handled the plumbing while Hart and Hutchinson supplied the toilet parts. The Indiana Flooring Company furnished floor tiles and J.M. Jackson and Company completed the floor and tile work.

In order to help with the stadium's upkeep and maintenance, as well as to bring in extra income from other sporting and non-sporting events, 200,000 square feet of available rental space was provided several feet below the lower grandstand. This would come in handy to help pay the stadium's $75,000 debt. White Construction installed a 15-foot brick-lined vault with electric, telephone, and telegraph cables under the second base area. Many boxing matches took advantage of this cellar. The J.P. Hall-Smith Electric Company completed the electrical work for this area.

The main entrance to Yankee Stadium was located behind home plate at 157th and Doughty Streets. Another grandstand exit would be located at 157th Street and River Avenue (right field) and the bleacher exit at 161st Street and River Avenue. Each of these three locations had six wooden ticket booths with a copper roof. White Construction built and painted them. The J.W. Fiske Iron Works of 78-89 Park Place, New York City, manufactured the 40, 38-inch tall turnstiles used to enter the ball park.

The Yankees dugout was planned for the first base side of the field. The visiting team had to enter the Yankees dugout to enter their own clubhouse. Each clubhouse had 25 lockers and five showers. The Yankees bullpen had originally been planned for right field between the grandstand and bleachers. The visiting team's bullpen was to be in left centerfield between the grandstand and bleachers. The Yankees changed this plan and took the third base dugout as their own, as well as the left centerfield bullpen.

Almost 53,000 grandstand seats in two decks and the mezzanine were assembled on site and another 5,000 finished chairs had been delivered. Wooden seat slats were milled on site for consistent measurements and screwed down for the completed seat bottom. U.T. Hungerford Brass and Copper of New York City supplied the seat hardware. George Cornell provided his carpentry skills and installed all the seats at 50 cents per seat. Most were 18 inches wide. Over 1 million brass screws had been used to install the seat lumber and 600,000 linear feet of lumber was used to construct the seats. The Expansion Bolt Company furnished expansion bolts for the 80,000 holes drilled to anchor the seating to the cement floor.

Chittan Lumber, Tisdale Lumber, and Cress, Austin and Ireland delivered 400,000 boards of maple lumber, while Troy Foundry and Machine Company provided 135,000 prefabricated metal seat castings, weighing a total of 500 tons. The three levels of seats combined to form 80 rows. The Lower Field Level, the largest of the three, measured 127 feet from front to rear. The mezzanine afforded extra room and featured four wooden free-standing high back chairs. The aisles had been designed to be wider than that of other stadiums. The outcome resulted in 25,000 seats in the lower deck, 10,000 in the mezzanine, and the upper deck accommodated 13,000 rooters.

By December 15, the structure was 76 percent finished. Osborn figured construction costs at $858,063.96. Change Orders to the building now numbered 24, and had added another $134,668.71 to the bill.

White Construction was having difficulty paying its subcontractors in February. The company told the Yankees brass they were broke and workers were threatening to walk off the job. After legal delays, the Yankees released $50,000 on March 26 to their construction partner to cover $49,735 in debts.

Because construction had been held up for so long, cold weather impeded progress of this mammoth enterprise by six weeks.

Higher costs, inclement weather and strikes all added to growing differences between the Yankees owners, White Construction and Osborn Engineering. The Yankees and Osborn agreed to arbitration to resolve their differences, but failed to include White Construction. Ultimately, this plan failed. [30]

All parties now had the added worry as to whether the stadium would be open in time for the April 1923 baseball season.

Far from the sounds of hammers and squabbling, the Yankees started the baseball year with spring training at Pelican Park in New Orleans, Louisiana, on March 7. The first Yankee on the field for the two-hour practice was catcher Fred Hofmann. Eight of the 35 players had not yet reported to the club. This included Babe Ruth and Franklin "Home Run" Baker, who planned to retire.

Three days later, on March 10, Major Thomas H. Birmingham announced that Yankee Stadium was now 95 percent completed. He said the final cost of the stadium and the land purchase would be $3 million. The wooden bleachers were nearly completed, as were over 90 percent of the grandstand seats. A 24 feet-wide by 400 yard-long cinder running track surrounded the field. An extra $232,425 had been incurred by 50 Change Orders through April 1. Change Orders now totaled 78. [31]

Many interested fans visited the stadium shortly before completion to inspect the biggest ballpark in the United States. In mid-March some weekends saw 10,000 people visiting the site on a daily basis. Many of these enthusiasts commented that the mezzanine seats, composed of 19 rows with seating for 10,000 followers, were the best in the house.

Yankee Stadium opened on Wednesday, April 18, 1923, after 284 days of construction – Sundays not included -- nearly a month ahead of the deadline. The national pastime's new showcase took only 185 actual workdays to complete. The ball park was now 97 percent finished and had a capacity of 58,000 fans. The brand new ballpark booked at $1,226,010, with a depreciation of $30,650.25. Land costs for the ten acres the temple stood on came in at $525,500, with land improvements at $47,693.94.

All told, the total cost to Ruppert and Huston amounted to $2,196,888.54, excluding office equipment. [32] Hamilton & Wade, Inc. Insurance, Liberty Street, New York, covered accidents at the stadium. The $190,000 policy was with Lloyds of London, and the premium cost $1,375. The Yankees offices moved from 42nd Street in Manhattan to between the main and mezzanine decks of their new home. An elevator connected the headquarters to the main entrance.

Yankee Stadium was the first ballpark built since 1915, and by far the largest. Comiskey Park, home of the Chicago White Sox, for example, held 35,000 fans, Fenway Park, housing the Boston Red Sox, sat 30,000 devotees, and Sportsman's Park in St. Louis sat only 18,000 supporters, by far the smallest venue in the American League.

The Yankees' new masterpiece was 20,000 square feet larger than their former home, with left field, left center and right center field accounting for most of this added space. Yankee Stadium incorporated 138,000 square feet in fair ball territory, whereas the Polo Grounds had 118,000. This did not hamper Babe Ruth. The Babe himself stated of Yankee Stadium, "I don't see any fences there that I can't hit over." That was great news, considering the Yankees would play 77 scheduled regular season home games to inaugurate their new residence. Babe had already tested his new home on February 15, when he knocked a few balls over the fence with his favorite bat.

Sportswriter Fred Lieb dubbed the place, "The House That Ruth Built." [33]

The spectacular dwelling appeared to be modeled after Greco-Roman architecture. The neoclassical colossus greatly reminded one of the Roman Coliseum.

The field dimensions were:
Left Field Line: 257.6 feet
Left Center Field: 460 feet
Center Field: 490 feet
Right Center Field: 429 feet
Right Field Line: 257.6 feet [34]

The American League club was relieved as they had outdrawn the Giants in attendance for the past three years. The bitter Giants wanted to make up for the financial loss of losing rental fees paid by the Yankees by scheduling more games on Sunday to fill the void. They felt this would recoup $100,000 in lost revenue. The Yankees opposed this idea, saying this was an "entirely mercenary" move by their former landlords to make the American League look feeble and that "Sunday baseball might be overdone in New York City." [35] Even with a population of 10 million in New York City alone, the Yankees, Giants and Dodgers had to contend with numerous semi-pro and amateur baseball clubs.

Bitter though they were, it was baseball genius and Giants manager John McGraw who had Giants owner Charles Stoneham evict the Yankees from the Polo Grounds to "build a park in Queens or some other out-of-the-way place. Let them go away and wither on the vine." [36]

ROSTER OF THE 1923 NEW YORK YANKEES

Player	Pos.
Benny Bengough	c
*Joe Dugan	3b
Mike Gazella	if
Lou Gehrig	1b
Hinkey Haines	of
Harvey Hendrick	of
Fred Hofmann	c
Ernie Johnson	if
Mike McNally	if
*Bob Meusel	lf
*Wally Pipp	1b
*Babe Ruth	rf
*Wally Schang	c
*Everett Scott	ss
Elmer Smith	of

<u>PITCHERS</u>

Joe Bush
Waite Hoyt
Sam Jones
Carl Mays
Herb Pennock
George Pipgras
Oscar Roettger
*Bob Shawkey

*Aaron Ward 2b
*Whitey Witt cf

*played in lineup of opening game of Yankee Stadium on April 18, 1923.

Boston Red Sox who played against Yankees in the first game:

Chick Fewster	ss
Shano Collins	rf
Camp Skinner	cf
Joe Harris	lf
George Burns	1b
Norm McMillan	2b
Howard Shanks	3b
Al DeVormer	c
Howard Ehmke	p
Mike Menosky	ph for Ehmke in 8th inning
Carl Fullerton	p

Play ball!

The New York Yankees relished the opening of the 1923 season now that they had a dazzling new gem of a home they could call their own.

Manager Frank Chance led his visiting Boston Red Sox onto the glistening diamond at noon as they took batting and fielding practice first. The former Yankees manager was making his debut with the Beantown club. When they finished, the Yankees took their turn and the mighty Babe gazed out at the right field stands, exclaiming, "Looks pretty far out to that right field fence." No doubt he felt better after lifting four balls into the stands. [37]

Business Manager Ed Barrow ensured the 36 ticket windows would all be open, as would all 40 turnstiles in the edifice. The Yankees' offices on 42nd Street, the Winchester store on East 42nd Street near Madison Avenue, and Spalding's downtown Manhattan store at 126 Nassau Street had also been selling tickets for the day's monumental event. Gates opened at noon and the game would begin at 3:31 – only one minute late. Fifteen year-old Malcolm Drummond, who lived near Yankee Stadium, became the first fan to enter the new palace. He skipped school that day to make history. In an odd twist of fate, he died in 1973 – the last year of existence of the "old" Yankee Stadium.

An official crowd of 74,217 fans attended that first game. This was by far the most people to ever attend a game for the national pastime, eclipsing the previous record of the fifth game of the 1916 World Series at Braves Field in Boston, where 40,000 fans passed through the turnstiles. Inspector Thomas Reilly, in charge of the police outside the stadium, estimated another 25,000 hopefuls were turned away. The lucky ones filled up the stands a half-hour before game time. Fans stood three and four rows deep behind the seats. Some also viewed the game from the ramps.

Two men, Abraham Cohen, age 28, from Brooklyn, and the other, Sebastian Calabrese, 35, of Manhattan, were arrested for scalping tickets. One tried to sell a $1.10 grandstand seat for $1.25, and the other attempted to charge $1.50 for his grandstand ticket. Each was held in the night court prison, as they could not come up with the $500 bail. This offense carried a fine of $500 or one year in jail, or both. [38]

New York Governor Alfred E. Smith threw out the first ball. Yankees owners Ruppert and Huston, baseball Commissioner Kenesaw Mountain Landis, Bronx Borough President Henry Bruckner, Red Sox owner Harry Frazee, Giants owner Charles Stoneham, Mrs. Alfred E. Smith and other distinguished guests took part in the dedication ceremonies, which occurred shortly before game time. Numerous other local politicians and military guests also made sure they did not miss this huge event. American League President Ban Johnson planned to attend, but had to bow out because of a bout with influenza. New York Mayor John Hylan also missed the festivities. The Bronx Board of Trade held 2,000 seats for the festive event, the Bronx Lodge of Elks had 1,000, and other local organizations reserved other portions of the grandstand.

Part of the dedication included the Yankees, Red Sox and dignitaries marching to the center field flagpole to unfurl Old Glory and the American League pennant. Renowned bandmaster John Philip Sousa and the Seventh Regiment Band began the musical program at 1 o'clock with the "Star Spangled Banner" and the "Stars and Stripes Forever." The parade then returned to home plate, where Governor Smith threw out the ceremonial first ball from his seat in the stands to Yankees catcher Wally Schang. Schang then returned the ball to the governor.

The Yankees received a floral horseshoe during the event and Babe Ruth was given a case containing a big baseball bat. The team issued a round pin to the press. This design featured a white baseball surrounded by a blue and red enamel background with gold lettering, and was made by Dieges & Clust. The badge was inscribed, "Yankee Stadium – Opening Day April 18, 1923. After the ceremonies, Bob Shawkey pitched "Ball One" to Red Sox shortstop Chick Fewster for the historic first pitch. Tommy Connolly performed the role of umpire-in-chief behind home plate. Billy Evans arbitrated at first base and Howard "Ducky" Holmes was at third.

The Yankees inaugurated Yankee Stadium with a 4-1 win over the Red Sox. Bob Shawkey gave up only three hits in his fine game, defeating Boston's Howard Ehmke, and the Bambino hit the new stadium's first homer into the right field bleachers in the third inning, with Whitey Witt on third base and Joe Dugan on first. The two-and-two pitch landed about ten rows into the stands. Babe answered the jubilant crowd by lifting his hat to them after he crossed home plate.

The Babe had gotten his wish when he earlier said, "I'd give a year of my life if I can hit a home run in the first game in this new park." The game lasted two hours and five minutes. Colonel Ruppert hosted a party at the Hotel Commodore to celebrate the opening of his dream home. He boasted, "This is a wonderful occasion. I now have baseball's greatest park, baseball's greatest players and baseball's greatest team." [39]

Another historic event was that Yankees shortstop Everett Scott played in his 987th consecutive baseball game. The team worried he would not be able to play ever since he suffered an ankle injury a week earlier in Springfield, Missouri, during an exhibition game. He expected to play in his 1,000th straight game on May 2. (That same year, Lou Gehrig made his major league debut with the Yankees and would later shatter Scott's streak of 1,307 games played in a row.)

Scores of bleacher fans rushed onto the field shortly before the game ended and surrounded their hero, Babe Ruth. Order had to be restored so the game could continue. Once it was, a throng of joyful worshippers encircled the Yankees dugout. Some of the hometown heroes had trouble making it to the clubhouse.

YANKEE STADIUM FIRSTS:

First pitch thrown by Shawkey was a ball.
Boston's first batter, Chick Fewster, grounded out to the shortstop.
Shano Collins caught the first outfield fly ball, off Babe Ruth.
The first hit was by Boston's George Burns, a 2nd-inning single.
The first Yankees batter was Whitey Witt.
The first Yankees hit was a 3rd inning single by Aaron Ward.
Bob Meusel of the Yankees hit the first double in the Stadium.
Norman McMillan of Boston hit the first triple in the park.
Bob Shawkey scored the first run in Yankee Stadium on Joe Dugan's 3rd-inning single.
Bob Shawkey recorded the first strikeout.
Babe Ruth hit the first home run in the 3rd inning, scoring three runs. (There's a surprise!)
Babe also made the first error, a dropped fly ball in the 5th inning.
Wally Pipp, the Yankees first baseman, recorded the first putout.
Wally Pipp of the Yankees and George Burns of the Red Sox both attempted to steal a base, but both were thrown out. [40]

A few days later, on April 24, President Warren G. Harding saw the Sultan of Swat belt a home run when the chief executive visited Yankee Stadium. The Babe walloped a pitch well into the right field bleachers. Harding gave the slugger a long applause for the feat, for which the Babe tipped his hat to the Chief Excutive when he neared the Yankees bench. [41] Ruth hit 1.000 in the 4-0 win over the Senators, with a home run, two singles, and a base on balls.

Across the Harlem River, the Giants played their first home game at the Polo Grounds on April 26 before a crowd of 25,000 fans. New York City Mayor Hylan showed up for the game and pre-game festivities, which included Commissioner Landis presenting World Championship diamond rings to the Giants for defeating the Yankees in the 1922 World Series. Legendary former Giants pitcher Christy Mathewson appeared during the ceremonies and received a huge ovation. Art Nehf pitched the Giants to a 7-3 win over the visiting Boston Braves.

Yankee Stadium, Opening Day, April 18, 1923. The Bronx Bombers welcomed their fans with a 4-1 win over the Boston Red Sox. Photo courtesy of the NATIONAL BASEBALL HALL OF FAME LIBRARY, COOPERSTOWN, N.Y.

Babe Ruth (L), Manager Miller Huggins (C), and Lou Gehrig (R). These men began the Yankee tradition of winning. Photo courtesy of the NATIONAL BASEBALL HALL OF FAME LIBRARY, COOPERSTOWN, N.Y.

One owner down; two park World Series

Ruppert bought out Huston's half of the team on May 21 for $1,250,000. They had argued about personnel and policies, with Huston becoming especially riled that Ruppert refused to fire manager Miller Huggins. This stemmed back to October 26, 1917, when Ruppert hired Huggins as manager while Huston was in Europe with the American Army. Huston wanted his friend, Wilbert Robinson, to manage the club, but the interview with Ruppert did not go well, so Ruppert hired Huggins on the recommendation of American League President Ban Johnson. Huston did stay on as a team director, although he stayed in the background. [42]

The Yankees clinched their third straight league pennant on September 20 at the Stadium by defeating the St. Louis Browns, 4-3, behind the pitching of Sam Jones. The Babe capped off the year with 41 home runs, 205 hits, and a .393 batting average. The Giants coincidentally also won their third successive banner eight days later across the river, earning "Little Napoleon" John McGraw his ninth pennant. Art Nehf tossed a 3-0 shutout against the Brooklyn Robins (Dodgers) as his gift to McGraw.

This led to another World Series contest between the bitter rivals. This time, however, two ballparks would be used to stage the heady event. On September 30 both clubs announced applications could be made by mail to purchase one reserved seat for three World Series games for $16.50. Both parks would reserve lower grandstand seats. Polo Grounds upper stand and Yankee Stadium upper stand and mezzanine seats would be available for purchasers of general admission tickets. At 10 a.m. on the day of the game, fans could buy general admission unreserved seats for $3.30 and bleacher seats for $1.10. Scalpers along Broadway sold the $16.50 seats for an average of $27.50 and $10 for the $3.30 seats.

The third consecutive World Series between these two foes set new records in numerous ways. Yankee Stadium, with its capacity to seat 63,000 fans, and the Polo Grounds' seating capacity of 52,000 set the stage for breaking all baseball box office receipt records. Two days before the day of the first game at Yankee Stadium on October 10, the Bronx Bombers had already sold all 25,000 reserved seats. When the gates opened at 10 a.m., there was no doubt the remaining 18,000 unreserved grandstand seats and the same number of bleacher seats would be sold. The Yankees expected total receipts to reach $200,000. The Giants still had seats for sale.

During the regular baseball season the glistening "House That Ruth Built" sat 1,007,066 devotees in its first year. Most teams drew less than half the number. Not bad for a team that spent $300,000 on player salaries. Of that, $52,000 went to the Babe.

This, the first million dollar series, saw 301,430 fans shell out $1,063,815 to cheer the six games. Each player on the winning team earned a share of $6,160.46, and those on the losing team took home $4,112.88. These figures set new records for World Series play. The Yankees voted a share of $750 for groundskeeper Schenck. When the game started at 2 o'clock, the winner of the series was said to be a "toss up," with the Giants said to have better batting and the Yankees possessing superior pitching. [43]

It should be mentioned that across the nation, interest in this event was not at fever pitch. The usual routine of the Yankees vs. Giants had made people take this show for granted. Also, many people out of the New York area did not show much interest as in years past since it was again a New York affair. The name that seemed to bring the most passion was "McGraw." He was known as being shrewd, a great strategist and superior baseball psychologist. While Babe Ruth had a great year, people still remembered he had a terrible World Series the year before, batting only .118.

The first game at Yankee Stadium was the first to be broadcast on radio, with announcer Graham McNamee behind the mike. Baseball clowns Nick Altrock and Al Schacht set the tone for the day by entertaining fans before the start of the game. Commissioner Landis, Christy Mathewson, Connie Mack, Ban Johnson, John Heydler and Branch Rickey were there.

The most famous play of the game was an inside-the-park home run by 34-year-old Casey Stengel, who hit a screaming line drive between Yankees outfielders Whitey Witt and Bob Meusel, which rolled to deepest left center field.

The last game of the series was played on October 15, when the Yankees finally won the World Series at the Polo Grounds by a score of 6-4, in front of 34,172 souls. Although Giants starter Art Nehf gave up a first-inning home run to the Bambino, he was masterful, keeping the boys from the Bronx hitless from the third through the seventh innings. After a couple of hits and walks in the eighth, the final blow that sunk the Giants came thanks to a rally. Bob Meusel singled in three men with the bases loaded off Rosy Ryan, who came in to relieve southpaw Nehf. Two hits and three walks preceded Meusel's hit. He drove in two runs with his single, and the third scored on an error made on the play by center fielder Bill Cunningham.

The Giants' McGraw was denied his hankering to win three World Series in a row. It was a bad ending to a year that had already dealt him a blow. McGraw had a quick temper and a penchant for blocking runners when the lone umpire's eyes were on the ball, but he developed a close friendship with teammate Willie Keeler. Wee Willie was only 50 when he succumbed to heart trouble on the first day of 1923. Accounts say McGraw, whose brawls even included a time or two with Keeler, wept at his old friend's funeral.

Babe Ruth had a great Series, hitting three homers and batting .368. Frankie Frisch, the second baseman for the Giants, had an outstanding World Series. He hit .400 in the Series and made many sparkling plays on the field. The unflappable Casey Stengel led the Giants by batting .417. He also hit two four-baggers to win two games for McGraw's men. The Giants thanked him a few weeks later by trading him to the Braves, along with Dave Bancroft.

The Yankees truly came into their own in the 1920s. The decade saw them finally reach and win the World Series, build a beautiful home for themselves, outdraw every team in baseball, and start a tradition of success that would be unparalleled in any sport. After losing the 1921 and 1922 World Series bouts, the boys from the Bronx at last tasted total victory with the defeat of the Giants in the 1923 World Series. What better way to celebrate the birth of a new home?

Getting bigger: the stadium and the Babe

The 1923 World Series convinced Colonel Ruppert his new gem already needed enlarging. In October, he told reporters, "I thought when I built this stadium that it would be plenty large enough to care for the crowds, but now I am convinced that the stadium is far inadequate." He was thinking of increasing seating capacity to 85,000 patrons. [44]

In early 1924, some changes were made. The playing field was swung slightly to the right, with the baseball diamond moved out nearly 12 feet. The right field foul line extended 37 feet longer than in 1923 with the elimination of the "bloody angle." This was the short pocket section of the field where the end of the grandstand and beginning of the bleachers met. Baseballs would often take crazy bounces in this area. This section was now in foul territory. Instead of 257 feet, 6 inches, the right field foul line now measured 294 feet, 6 inches. The left field line went from 257 feet, 6 inches to 281 feet, 1 inch. In comparison, the Polo Grounds' right field line was 257 feet, 8 inches while the left field foul line stood at 279 feet. The Sultan of Swat would not be much affected by the modification, as he generally hit his memorable blasts in the right field bleachers, and not down the line.

The field change gave more room to the first and third basemen, as well as the catcher. Yankees management said the fans in the first and third base sections were happier because they had better sight of home plate. In September of 1923, people noticed the players having trouble catching infield fly balls because of shadows thrown onto the field by the stands. With the stands now being 10 feet farther away from the field and the shadows being reduced, both the fielders and spectators could now see the ball easier. Phil Schenck remodeled the diamond and nearly reduced the turtle-back hump to nothing. The streets surrounding the domicile had been paved and the subway station was enlarged. More turnstiles were installed to handle the large crowds.[45]

At 3:30 p.m. on April 23, 1924, the Yankees again faced the Red Sox and their new manager, Lee Fohl, on Opening Day at the stadium. The gates welcomed the loyal supporters at noon and New York City's Seventh Regiment Band supplied the music beginning at 1 o'clock, as did musicians from Governor's Island's Sixth Infantry Regiment. At the deep center field flagpole, the Yankees raised the American flag, and below it the red, white and blue banner proclaiming the Yanks as "Champions American League, 1921, 1922, 1923." The World Championship pennant also made its way up the pole, which was the first time an American League team in the city had such an honor.

Mayor Hylan threw out the first ball. The Babe put on another show with a three-run home run in the right field bleachers in the eighth inning off of Lester Howe. The 46,584 admirers saw pitcher Herb Pennock and the Yankees whip the Red Sox, 13-4. This was in addition to seeing the World Champion Yankees each receive a gold watch from Commissioner Landis at the pitcher's mound for last year's toppling of the Giants in the World Series. Jacob Ruppert supplied his champs with a gold watch fob and chain to hold their precious mementoes.

On May 14 the team held Babe Ruth Day at the park, in which A.L. President Ban Johnson presented the star pupil a diploma with a "Master of Swat" degree from the school of baseball. This was to celebrate the Bambino being voted the American League's Most Valuable Player of 1923 by the baseball writers. Joining Johnson in the presentation was Irving Sanborn, chairman of the Writers' Committee, and creator of the MVP honor. [46]

The day, however, didn't go as well as expected. George Sisler and the St. Louis Browns trounced their hosts, 11-1, in the homerless slugfest. The band of the USS West Virginia, along with Judge Landis and 25,000 fans, witnessed the assault. Curiously, Ban Johnson was to have attended as well, but never showed up on Opening Day or other celebrations when Landis, who he had opposed for the appointment, was present. Waite Hoyt lost the game and all the Babe could muster was an infield single.

In 1925, at the age of 30, Babe's eating and carousing were about to catch up with him. He reported to the spring training camp at 270 pounds. After training camp finished, while enroute to New York, he and the team were boarding a train in Asheville, North Carolina. He collapsed, and stayed behind to recover before going up to New York. On his second attempt to take a train up north he again buckled, this time hitting his head on the floor. This was the famous "Bellyache Heard 'Round the World." He reportedly ate about a dozen hot dogs, among other food and drink, giving him acute indigestion. Other sources said it was an ulcer that did him in, and still others said it was syphilis. He underwent an operation in New York's St. Vincent Hospital on April 5 and remained in bed until May 26.

Babe ended up playing in only 98 games that year. By the time he joined the Yankees on June 1, the writing was on the wall that a pennant was not to be. He only hit 25 home runs, knocked in 66 runs, and batted .290. In 1925, the team ended up in seventh place, making it a year they wanted to forget.

A much lower note was sounded for shortstop Everett Scott. On June 20, 1916, while with the Boston Red Sox, he began his streak of playing in consecutive games. George Pinckney, of the Brooklyn Grays/Bridegrooms (later the Dodgers), set the previous record, by playing in 577 contests, from September 21, 1885, through May 1, 1890. Scott broke the record on April 26, 1920.

Babe Ruth hits his record-breaking 60th home run on September 30, 1927, at Yankee Stadium. The Babe's victim was Tom Zachary of the Washington Senators. Photo courtesy of the NATIONAL BASEBALL HALL OF FAME LIBRARY, COOPERSTOWN, N.Y.

Yankee Stadium, 1928. Photo courtesy of the NATIONAL BASEBALL HALL OF FAME LIBRARY, COOPERSTOWN, N.Y.

The streak almost ended on August 13, 1922, when the train he was on was involved in a wreck. He ended up hiring a car for $40 so he could play against the Chicago White Sox. He reached the 1,000 mark on May 2, 1923, as a Yankee, who he joined with other former Red Sox players on December 20, 1921. The A.L. presented him with a gold medal for this remarkable achievement.

His record of 1,307 games ended on May 5, 1925, when manager Miller Huggins benched him in a shakeup of the Yankees line-up. This angered Scott, who had two hits the day before. During his record breaking feat, he had 1,176 hits, 18 home runs, and a batting average of .254. Shortly after his streak ended, the Yankees sent him to Washington on waivers.

In a twist of fate, Yankees first baseman Lou Gehrig began his streak of 2,130 consecutively played games on June 1, when he pinch hit for Pee Wee Wanninger. The next day, first baseman Wally Pipp wasn't up to playing because of a headache. Gehrig replaced Pipp, and Pipp was out of the picture. Gehrig played his 1,000th straight game on August 18, 1931, then broke Scott's mark on August 17, 1933, as the St. Louis Browns edged the Bronx Bombers, 7-6, in 10 innings.

The year 1928 marked the first expansion to "The House That Ruth Built" when, on February 1, the Yankees announced they had awarded a contract to Leopold Neckermann and Son, of 205 East 42nd Street, New York, to expand the mezzanine and upper deck in left field, with the project starting the next day. Neckermann guaranteed the job would be completed July 1 or a few days earlier.

The company enlarged this area by adding seven new sections to the stadium, ending near the foul pole and reaching the left field bullpen. The foul pole extended from 281 to 301 feet from home plate. Neckermann finished the job ahead of schedule at a cost of $282,215. The J.P Hall-Smith Electric Company, an electrical subcontractor, worked on lights on the ramps, runways, all three decks and the roof at a cost of $6,434. Osborn Engineering served as architect for the expansion. [47]

The facility now held 72,000 Bronx faithful. They could squeeze in 80,000 to view football games, and a whopping 100,000 for boxing matches. This move paid off, as a record 85,265 faithful packed the park to see the Yankees whip the Philadelphia Athletics in both ends of a doubleheader, 5-0 and 7-3, on September 9. The teams were fighting in a pennant race that year. The next year the team would be the first in the major leagues to introduce numbers on the back of their uniforms. This worked well in the minor leagues. The batting order determined which number a player would wear. For instance, Babe Ruth batted third, so he wore number 3. Lou Gehrig followed him, so he bore number 4. Below is a list of the players and their positions. The number to the left of their name is their uniform number.

1. Earl Combs cf
2. Mark Koenig 3b
3. Babe Ruth rf
4. Lou Gehrig 1b
5. Bob Meusel lf
6. Tony Lazzeri 2b
7. Leo Durocher ss
8. Johnny Grabowski c
9. Ben Bengough c
10. Bill Dickey c
11. Herb Pennock p
12. Waite Hoyt p
14. George Pipgras p
15. Hank Johnson p
15. Art Jorgens c
16. Tom Zachary p

Manager Miller Huggins had no number.

17. Fred Heimach p
18. Wilcy Moore p
19. Ed Wells p
20. Myles Thomas p
20. Julian Wera p
21. George Burns if
21. Gordon Rhodes p
22. Gene Robertson if
24. Lyn Lary if
25. Ben Paschal of
26. Cedric Durst of
27. Sam Byrd of
28. Liz Funk of
29. Al Shealy p
30. Bots Nekola p
30. Gordon Rhodes p
31. Roy Sherid p
32. Art Jorgens c

Business Manager Edward Barrow had announced on March 3, 1933, that the Yankees had planned to sign a contract with the Neckermann Company for $850,000 to expand the right field stands another 100 feet.[48] Additional work would replace the present 23,000 wooden bleachers with concrete ones. Demolition started on March 1, 1936, and construction continued through the majority of 1937. Revere Copper & Brass of New York City, supplied 20,000 pounds of copper sheets for the project.

During this project, the center field distance was reduced from 490 to 461 feet. Again, Osborn Engineering designed and supervised the job. Enlarging the seating would now let 84,000 witnesses observe the Bronx Bombers in action. Between 90,000 and 95,000 fans could cheer on their football heroes, and pugilists would hear 120,000 screaming fans. The building of Yankee Stadium and the two renovation projects cost the club almost $3.5 million.

The Yankees were once again under new ownership when Larry MacPhail, Dan Topping and Del Webb, bought the team from Ruppert's estate on January 25, 1945, for $2.8 million. Jacob Ruppert died on January 13, 1939, from phlebitis, at age 71. [49]

Under their stewardship, lights adorned the newly renovated Yankee Stadium in 1946 when the Washington Senators defeated the Yankees by a score of 2-1 on a chilly May 28. A crowd of 49,917 witnessed knuckleballer Dutch Leonard besting Clarence "Cuddles" Marshall, tossing a six-hitter and helping himself with two hits and an RBI. This historic event should have taken place one day before, but was delayed by rain. The Yankees scheduled 14 night games for the year.

The evening's festivities started with the 150-piece Hempstead High School band from Hempstead, Long Island, playing at 8:15 p.m., while Metropolitan Opera House soprano Rose Bampton sang "The Star Spangled Banner." Charles E. Wilson, president of the General Electric Company, threw out the first ball. Besides new lights, the Yankees introduced the official scorer's decisions on hits and errors for the first time on a baseball scoreboard. This was also the first year the team would broadcast the complete 154-game schedule on radio. Mel Allen announced the play-by-play.

Back on November 15, 1945, Yankees president MacPhail had announced $500,000 in improvements for "The House That Ruth Built," which included $250,000 for the installation of lights, and increased seating capacity for football games from 79,000 to 90,000. [50] The Blaw-Knox Construction Company of Pittsburgh, Pennsylvania, erected the towers, while General Electric installed the Type L-69 floodlights. Previously, MacPhail had illuminated Columbus in the American Association in 1935, and Cincinnati's Crosley Field in 1935. Ebbets Field followed suit in 1938.

The three and a quarter acre Yankee Stadium playing field now boasted a 200 foot-candle uniform illumination, whereas most infields had 100 foot-candles. Most outfield lighting decreased to the neighborhood of 40 foot-candles. The stadium's six light towers consisted of 1,245 floodlights, with each one containing a 1,500-watt lamp, making Yankee Stadium the most brilliantly-lit arena up to this time. This provided enough illumination to light a four-lane highway from New York to Washington, D.C. To give an idea of what this meant, Pittsburgh's Forbes Field, home of the Pirates, had 864 lights, the previous highest number in the major leagues. The new lights would increase efficiency and decrease costs.

Other improvements incorporated replacing all 15,000 reserved and box seats in the lower mezzanine levels with seats four to five inches wider, thus making ballgames more comfortable for the fans. A new Yankees clubhouse would be built under the stands behind the first base dugout. The press was also going to have new headquarters. The Harry M. Stevens concessionaires would now have a two-story structure on the first base side of the stadium grandstand with a 15,000-square-foot floor area, stopping at six levels. The goal was to make food storage, preparation and movement much easier for the vending giant.[51]

MacPhail's last day on the job was October 6, 1947. The Yankees had defeated the Brooklyn Dodgers for the Yankees' 11th World Series win. MacPhail quit as the Yankees were celebrating their win at the Yankees victory party in the clubhouse. MacPhail was drunk. He hurled verbal assaults, punched out a writer, then announced his resignation. He cited health reasons as the reason for quitting. This was not the first time heavy drinking caused his erratic behavior. On October 7, his co-owners, Topping and Webb, bought out MacPhail's contract for $2 million.

It took seven games for the Yankees to once again become the world champions. Besides Jackie Robinson being the first black major league baseball player to ever play in the World Series, other historical events included Yankees pitcher Bill Bevens missed pitching a no-hitter in Game 4, as Cookie Lavagetto lined a base hit to right field in the ninth inning with two outs. The ball took a strange bounce off the right field barrier, making it difficult for Yankees right fielder, Tommy Henrich, to field the ball. Two runs scored, and the Dodgers won the game by a score of 3-2.

Another play of note was Al Gionfriddo catching a Joe DiMaggio smash in front of the Dodgers bullpen at Yankee Stadium in Game 6. If the game had been played at Ebbets Field, it would have easily been a home run. Ironically, Gionfriddo, Bevens, and Lavagetto would never play in another major league baseball game after this World Series.

This was the first World Series in which receipts totaled over $2 million. The Gate Receipts added up to $1,781,348.92. The Radio Rights brought in another $175,000, while Television Rights fetched $65,000. [52]

Both Topping and Webb had the knack for making money. They were stockholders and board members in concessionaire Automatic Canteen Company of America. Its headquarters had been in Chicago. On October 17, 1963, *The New York Times* reported that Automatic Canteen would replace Harry M. Stevens as the Yankee Stadium concessionaire, effective January 1, 1964. Stevens had hawked hot dogs and other food and souvenirs since Yankee Stadium opened in 1923. They listed net profits at $1.5 million annually.

As the nation's largest vending company, Automatic Canteen had net sales of more than $2.5 million through the first week of June 1963. The company would spend $1 million in 1963 for new kitchen equipment and 27 food shops at the ball park. The catering portion of the company was known as Nationwide Food Service. Patrick L. O'Malley was the company's president and chief executive officer. Vending accounted for only 4 percent of sales. The contract would run through December 31, 1973. [53]

The age of television

The 1947 World Series was the first to be broadcast on television, and Billboard Magazine reported then that over 3.9 million people watched the games. Most of these fans saw the action in bars, as not many households had TVs in 1947. Since television was in its infancy, there were fewer than 100,000 televisions in America's homes, whereas there were 40 million radios. Only 28,000 TV sets were sold during the year.

That would change drastically, as the number of TVs in the country rose to 13 million by 1953. A decade later The Columbia Broadcasting System (CBS) would buy Topping's and Webb's controlling interests. *The New York Times* headlined the story, "CBS Buys 80% of Stock In Yankee Baseball Team." The media giant wanted to diversify its holdings. They paid $11.2 million to Topping and Webb. The team's assets appraised at $14 million. Webb and Topping each still held 10 percent interest in the team. Webb would sell his remaining 10 percent share of the Yankees to CBS for $1.4 million on March 1, 1965. Topping stayed on as team president until September 19, 1966, when he would sell his 10 percent interest in the team to CBS, then resign his position. [54]

The August 15, 1964, issue of *The New York Times* reported that "CBS now will acquire the franchise, the players' contracts, the Yankees' rights to talent in five minor league affiliates, television and radio contracts, concessions at Yankee Stadium and the lease on the stadium, which is owned by Rice University." [55] Two years earlier, Rice University Alumnus John Cox had given the stadium to the Houston university. Cox had acquired all of the capital stock of the stadium holding company in 1955.

Charles O. Finley, owner of the Kansas City Athletics, and Arthur Allyn, who owned the Chicago White Sox, disapproved of the CBS deal. Finley said, this was "just another perfect example of the shenanigans of the American League president and the New York Yankees." Allyn, in part said, "It's a hell of a way to run a league. I don't like to be called at 11:45 about something and be asked to approve it in three hours." He indicated there were days of discussion that could have been used to confer about the sale. They were outvoted by the Yankees and seven other American League franchises. Three quarters of the teams had to give approval in order for such a transaction to take effect. [56]

CBS had been paying the Yankees $500,000 a year to broadcast the rights of Yankees games on television's game-of-the-week. The broadcasting company had plenty of capital, as it earned $23 million in the first half of 1964. Otherwise, Yankee fans followed the Bronx Bombers on WPIX, Channel 11. WPIX, which was owned by the *New York Daily News*, had a contract with the team through 1966. National television revenue was $8.7 million in 1949, but jumped to almost $2 billion in 1964. WCBS radio also broadcast the games for the club.

Yankee Stadium, 1961

When asked why they would sell a team that had 28 American League pennants and 20 World Series wins under its belt, Topping responded, "We've had a lot of offers to buy the Yankees, of course, but we never had any idea of selling. But this was way too much money to walk away from, especially when we could continue to operate the club." Topping and William S. Paley, the chairman of the board of CBS, had been close friends. [57]

Topping and Paley verbally told baseball Commissioner Ford Frick that the Yankees would be operated separately from CBS under the guidance of Webb and Topping for at least five years. Frick said, "CBS would have to bid on the same basis as the other networks for either the World Series rights or the proposed [game-of-the-week] spectacular."

Arthur Allyn angrily responded, "When the hell did he ever take a position on anything? If you find one, let me know and I'll start the whistles blowing and the smoke flying." Finley criticized Frick for not stopping the sale, and condemned it as "Yankee shenanigans" and "high-handed." [58]

In Baltimore, where the third-place Yankees were going to play the league-leading Orioles, general manager, Ralph Houk, told the players the operations of the team would remain the same. He also informed them "being associated with a big outfit like this will make it possible for us to provide many nice things for baseball and our fans. But I don't think I should go into specifics now." [59]

The United States Senate got involved, as antirust questions sprang up with the sale. Webb tried to mollify those against the deal by stating, "We will continue as before, Topping as president and myself as vice president. Also, we have no idea of leaving Yankee Stadium, and, in fact, we intend to improve it and make it a better place for baseball." Talk of conflict of interest was feared by many, especially the other television networks. In the end, the Justice Department approved of the deal.[60]

Leonard Koppett, a sportswriter for *The New York Times,* wrote a story on October 18, 1964, titled, "Yanks: Healthy, Wealthy but Unwise." One segment of the article said, "Almost every move the club makes, aside from actual game activity, is met with hostility, criticism or disinterest within the more dedicated portions of sports fandom, and this public reaction doesn't seem to be affected by the intrinsic merits or demerits of the action taken." Examples he gave were attendance being at a 19-year low, the recent firing of Yogi Berra as manager after losing the World Series to the St. Louis Cardinals in seven games, and no stars of Ruth or Mantle magnitude in the farm system.

Yogi Berra added "color" to the team, but that didn't improve attendance or fans' attitudes towards the organization. Nor did another pennant and near-win in the World Series. Koppett also wrote that morale of the players had suffered. He blamed the arrogance of many years as being a key factor in turning people off. As he proclaimed in his criticism, "The first source of Yankee problems is the way of thinking that says, "We've decided that this is how it ought to be"- and then confidently expects other people or the universe as a whole to follow smoothly along the path the Yankees have outlined." [61]

He cited selling tickets at higher prices and alienating the common fans by catering to wealthier patrons. The average home fan was turned off by the Yankees aloofness, although it brought in tourists. With virtually every game on television and a poor parking situation, fans didn't have to come to the ball park. Fewer stars were on the club, or just getting older. Mickey Mantle suffered so many injuries that he couldn't be counted on by the idol worshippers who hoped to see him play in person. These reasons and the fact that the obstructed views, narrow aisles and lack of comfort compared to newer parks hurt attendance.

The hapless New York Mets, on the other hand, had been neck and neck in attendance with the Yankees since their inception in 1962, then began outdrawing them in 1964. They had a brand new ballpark (Shea Stadium) in 1964, which was a stone's throw from the 1964-1965 New York World's Fair. They had previously played in the Polo Grounds since the Yankees wouldn't permit them to play in the land of Ruth. Baseball at Shea was fun, with the Old Professor, Casey Stengel, leading the way. Marvelous Marv Throneberry, Duke Snider, Gil Hodges, Frank Thomas and a host of other colorful souls on the team brought out the love of baseball in their fans.

The Yankees were looked upon more like United States Steel – more business than fun. While the Yankees were justifiably equated with success, in the minds of the fans they lacked heart. Koppett said it was up to Manager Ralph Houk to change this trend, as he knew how the baseball mind worked. He had to reach the souls of the fans to bring them back into the seats of Babe's Place. [62] Houk was known to be tough but decisive, a real player's manager.

Year	Yankees Attendance/Finish/Record	Mets Attendance/Finish/Record
1962	1,493,574/First/96-66	1,136,016/Tenth (Last)/40-120
1963	1,308,920/First/104-57	1,080,108/Tenth (Last)/51-111
1964	1,305,638/First/99-63	1,732,597/Tenth (Last)/53-109
1965	1,213,552/Sixth/77-85	1,768,389/Tenth (Last)/50-112
1966	1,124,648/Tenth (Last)/70-89	1,932,693/Ninth/66-95

Michael Burke acted as liaison from his CBS office on the 34th floor at 52nd Street and Sixth Avenue. He kept in constant contact with the Yankees office at 745 Fifth Avenue. Part of his routine was to attend every home game at night and on weekends, sitting in the Yankees' club box in the mezzanine behind first base. He would also meet Houk at the stadium for dinner to discuss the team.

Sportswriter Joseph Durso, of *The New York Times* related in a December 26, 1965, article, titled, "CBS Tells of Plans for Yankees," that a six-man board of directors met four times a year to lead the Yankees. They were William Paley, Frank Stanton, Michael Burke and Joseph A.W. Iglehart, all from CBS. Houk and Topping of the Yankees rounded out the group. [63]

Burke took over as president of the Yankees on September 20, 1966. Two years before that he worked as vice president to explore diversification opportunities, followed by his becoming vice president for development. At a news conference at the Stadium Club at Yankee Stadium on his first day as president, he said that Houk's contract for $75,000 a year would be honored, as he had three years left on it. He also noted that Yankee Stadium was not obsolete and that it would be overhauled, although no specific plans had yet been made. He also said that a general manager would be hired after the World Series. Lee MacPhail, Larry's son, would fill that position on October 14.

As president of the New York Yankees, Burke would focus on the team and drop all other responsibilities at CBS. He would also move to the Yankees offices on Fifth Avenue within days. He made his intentions clear when he said, "I'm in the baseball business from today on." He also let it be known that he would ask Houk how to rebuild the team. [64]

Michael Burke changed the thinking of the New York Yankees, making the iconic team very fan friendly. Koppett wrote about this change in his *New York Times* column on May 21, 1967. Titled "Burke Setting Tempo for Yankees' New Image," Koppett described how Burke personally answered mail and instituted training of Yankees' employees to be courteous and pleasant. This was especially true of ticket sellers in the box office. Players would be used for public relations efforts. They had to now make two appearances as a group and three individually during the season at schools, luncheons, etc.

Burke asserted, "Fundamentally, we're dealing with attitude - our attitude, at the top. We are determined to make attendance at a Yankee game a pleasant experience. We've promised that all over the place, and now it's up to us to make good on the promise every day. You do that only by working at it." He also knew winning teams would help bring people to games. [65]

The Independent Press-Telegram, in Long Beach, California, ran a story on April 26, 1967, called "Yankee Aim: Remold Old Image." Burke said, "Rightly or wrongly, the Yankees have had a reputation of indifference and arrogance. That isn't right. Our attitude now is that the fan is a guest in the house who deserves the utmost courtesy and respect. This applies to everybody in the organization, even the man who tears the ticket at the gate." He decreed, "It's the dawn of a new era for the Yankees." [66]

The author can attest to this approach. Having had the pleasure of going to quite a few Yankees games, Michael Burke personally signed baseballs and Yankees yearbooks and programs for me. Not once did he turn me down. He was always kind. I would also request his autograph in the mail. Again, I was never disappointed. I even wrote a couple of letters of complaint. Mr. Burke would respond by sending me a response on his Yankees letterhead. As long as I live I shall always have a deep respect and love for this man because he truly cared about the fans.

During the winter of 1966-1967, CBS remodeled the stadium once more. Most of the $1.35 million transformation was spent on 90 tons of paint. The brownish concrete exterior of the park changed to white, as did the famous green copper frieze. Also, the grandstand seats were painted royal blue instead of light green.

Michael Burke was totally against color-coded seating. He felt that everyone in the stands was there to see a baseball game. As such, a single color of seat would be more unifying. After all, the fans were watching the same game, eating the same hot dogs, and drinking the same beer and soda. This encouraged subliminal unity among the fans. Blue was pleasing to the eye, and would replace the 17 shades of green painted on the wooden seats in previous years.

Burke had two sections of about 100 seats painted different shades of blue. Frank Stanton of CBS stopped by at Burke's request. They stood on the infield to look at the colors. Stanton chose the same blue as Burke. This color became known as "Yankee blue." It also became the color of the seats used in the 1970s renovation. The Hudson-Shatz Painting Company of New York City did the painting. [67]

Aside from the paint, gray fiberglass bleachers replaced the concrete benches. A telephonic Yankees Hall of Fame, located in Lobby 6 at Gate 6, behind the right field stands, featured large photos of 34 past and present Yankees stars, and tips on how to play baseball, or great thrills experienced by a player. Michael Burke and CBS creative director, Louis Dorfsman, brought this feature to the Stadium. Lou Gehrig's and Babe Ruth's farewells, and Don Larsen's perfect World Series game in 1956 were included in the lineup. Roger Maris, Charlie Keller, Red Rolfe, Miller Huggins, Roy White, Ralph Houk, Mel Stottlemyre, Stan Bahnsen and Fritz Peterson had also been included in this historic cast.

Mickey Mantle had been depicted in two displays. One highlighted Mickey Mantle Day in 1965. The other portrayed Mickey's 500th home run. Non-baseball events depicted a Joe Louis/Max Schmeling boxing match and Pope Paul VI's 1965 Mass.

By lifting up the telephone receiver, fans would hear the actual voice of one of the named players. This attraction closed on September 30, 1973, the last day of "old" Yankee Stadium's existence, and later became a souvenir stand. The hope was that this makeover would affect the fortunes of the team and the surrounding area in a positive way. Nobody knew it, but in a few short years, major changes would close and transform Babe's Place after a two and a half year overhaul.[68]

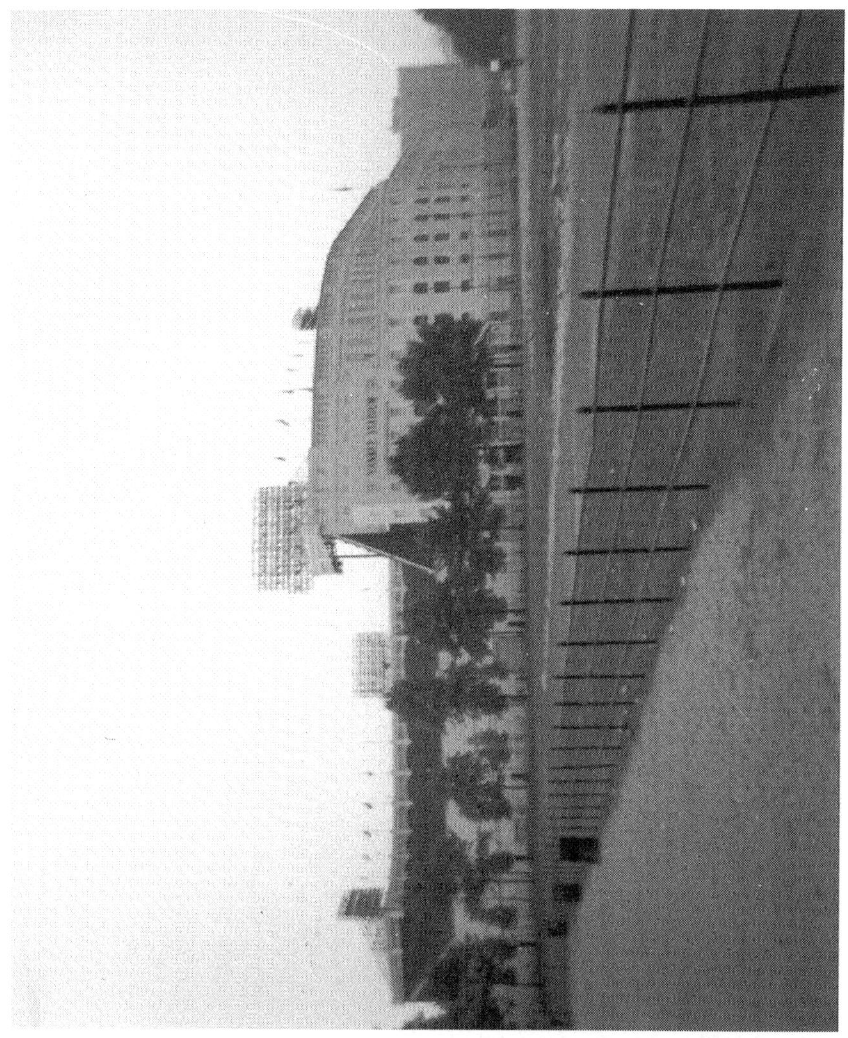

Yankee Stadium as seen from Macombs Dam Park, July 22, 1972.

View of pre-renovated Yankee Stadium scoreboard and monuments, 1973.

Yankee pitcher Waite Hoyt running onto the field after being introduced at the Old Timers' Day game, July 22, 1972.

The reality of this upheaval occurred on June 30, 1972. John Waterbury of the engineer/architectural firm of Praeger Kavanagh Waterbury (PKW), sent his company's "Comprehensive Study and Report for the MODERNIZATION OF YANKEE STADIUM" to Department of Public Works Commissioner Alfred C. Maevis. The report encompassed 69 pages detailing the current conditions at the ballpark and PKW's vision for making improvements.

The object of the modernization was to make Yankee Stadium as up-to-date as any other baseball park in the country, and let the game's spectators watch the ball game comfortably without any obstruction. This was to be accomplished by removing the 118 girders used to support Yankee Stadium. New, comfortable seats would be installed. More public toilets with greater capacity would be created. Modern lighting on the roof would improve spectator viewing. Three entrances containing escalators would allow fans to enter and exit the stadium more quickly. More parking spaces and better access roads would be added to lessen traffic congestion to and from the games. These were just some of the major plans for the home of the Bronx Bombers.

PKW estimated construction costs to total $21,677,000. General Construction had been estimated at $14,365,000. This included such items as concrete, structural steel, stadium signs and carpentry. Plumbing tallied at $1,090,000, Heating, Ventilating & Air Conditioning would cost $1,355,000, Electrical amounted to $2,608,000, and Elevators and Escalators accounted for $2,259,000.[69]*

Much of what the architects designed for the remodeled Yankee Stadium was untested. In theory, it would work. The reality would not always be so smooth, not only with respect to cantilevering the stadium, but also with the skyrocketing costs.

While not everyone who worked on the Yankee Stadium modernization knew if the plans drawn on paper would actually work in reality, time had proven that it did. Even the detractors of this venture could not escape the fact that the Bronx Bombers would successfully stay in their remodeled home for another 33 years before it was razed and replaced. Along the way, the team won another 10 pennants and six World Series. A staggering 87,578,241 fans watched the team through this time period during the regular season. This does not include playoffs or World Series games. [70]

The team's fortunes with the renovated Yankee Stadium flourished hand in hand. Attendance of 2,012,434 in 1976, to the stadium's gate of 4,247,123 in its final year of existence in 2008, spoke volumes of the success of the franchise. The leadership of George Steinbrenner, who took ownership in 1973, again brought the winning ways the Yankee fans had expected in Babe's Place.

Yankee Stadium. The name was magic. This sacred ballpark exuded history, class, dignity, and many of the greatest memories ever witnessed in sports – and non-sporting events. Just the names Babe Ruth, Lou Gehrig, Joe DiMaggio and Mickey Mantle alone bring a rush of emotional joy to fans. Then you can add other names, such as Casey Stengel, Yogi Berra, Roger Maris, Whitey Ford, Reggie Jackson, Thurman Munson, Derek Jeter, Bernie Williams…where do you stop? Perhaps Pope Paul VI, Billy Graham, Muhummad Ali, Jack Dempsey, Joe Louis, and Y.A. Tittle evoke memories more to your liking. Yankee Stadium was so immersed in history that you felt it when you stepped into this holy shrine.

Writer's note: Harry Swanson, author of *Ruthless Baseball: Yankees Purified by Fire Stadium Construction*, published by Author House, Bloomington, Indiana, 2004, was generous in allowing me to use much of the material in this chapter from his book, regarding the construction of Yankee Stadium, and the circumstances leading up to the construction of the ballpark.

*Judith Lillard, of URS Corp., New York City, was a tremendous help in helping me to receive permission from URS to use the 1972 Yankee Stadium Modernization Plan. It's a very important document that gives the reader a greater appreciation of the historic nature of what went into the renovation of Yankee Stadium. Unfortunately, permission from the New York Yankees' Legal Department to reproduce this precious document either in part or in its entirety, was denied, so I was unable to reprint the pages from that resource in this book.

Chapter Two

TO STAY OR NOT TO STAY

Decisions, decisions

The fortunes of the Yankees club and its neighborhood declined in the mid-1960s. The team's stars were getting older or retiring, their failing farm system had not produced much talent as it had in the past, and dubious trades lacked spark. Parking spaces in lots next to the ballpark accommodated only 3,000 cars, while another 3,500 parking spaces could be found in surrounding streets and garages. However, rising crime along with congested streets, and the Yankees' lackluster performance, kept people away.

Competition with the Mets added to the mix, especially after the Metsies vanquished the Baltimore Orioles in the 1969 World Series. From that magical year for the National League wonders through 1972, they led the major leagues with attendance of over two million fans each year. Shea Stadium, the Queens home of the Mets, also provided far easier highway access and more parking than that of their Bronx rivals. Previously, the Yankees posted the highest fan turnout in the American League in 16 out of 19 years from 1946 through 1964. Their gate numbers dropped to below one million in 1972. This had not happened since 1945.

CBS, the television network giant that owned the Bronx Bombers at this time, had not lost sight of the fact that other clubs had new ballparks, such as the Mets' Shea Stadium, which was completed in 1964, and Dodger Stadium, opened in 1962. The Cincinnati Reds moved into Riverfront Stadium, the Pittsburgh Pirates to Three Rivers Stadium, and the Philadelphia Phillies into Veterans Stadium–all in 1970-71. The newer baseball diamonds had plenty of parking and easy access for motorists. Municipalities built these structures.

Meanwhile, the Yankees leased Yankee Stadium from Rice University, paid real estate taxes, and were accountable for repairs and maintenance of the stadium and grounds. Across the Hudson River in East Rutherford, New Jersey, a new sports complex was to open in 1975, with the Yankees and football Giants targeted as its occupants. Ironically, many Yankees called New Jersey home over the years. Jerseyites included Yogi Berra, Elston Howard, Gil McDougald, Phil Rizzuto, Gene Michael, and Roy White, to name a few. Commuting to Yankee Stadium had been easy for them.

New York City's Mayor, John Lindsay, fearing the loss of these two institutions, spoke with Yankees President Michael Burke in 1970. Burke told the Mayor that he'd prefer the team remain in the Bronx, but he had concerns regarding lack of parking, and the area surrounding the Bronx landmark needed revitalization. The $24 million proposed figure was arrived at because that was the cost of building Shea Stadium, which opened in 1964.

As Michael Burke put it, "We've been in the stadium for 48 years, and we can't stay another 48 without some dramatic changes. Our present lease runs until 1981, but honestly, I don't know if the Yankees will be there until 1981. We have a problem to improve the stadium to satisfy the fans. We have to find some way to do that over the next several years or find another place to play." Rice University owned Yankee Stadium and the Knights of Columbus owned the land. The complete property had been appraised at $5 million. Although the Yankees repeatedly complained to Rice University about Stadium conditions, the University said they had no funds to modernize the ballpark.

According to the Yankees chief, "There are four pieces to this matter. Age and condition of the stadium, parking, the whole traffic pattern around the stadium and the total environmental situation. If something can be done about those situations, then it will be business as usual." Offers for a new home for baseball's most famous address came from New Jersey, Long Island and New Orleans. When asked about building a new stadium in New York, Burke called this idea "totally unrealistic," due to the cost that would entail. Also, New York was in a financial crunch at the time.

Sharing Shea Stadium had not been discussed with the Mets. Burke related, "Shea is out. The Mets have an ironclad, exclusive contract with the city for the next 20 years or so at Shea, and there is no chance of changing their minds." The Yankees boss also commented that the football Giants would be involved in the Yankees' decision. He proclaimed, "We've always felt our futures were linked – in effect, a partnership." [1] Burke promised to keep the Yankees in the city whether or not the Giants agreed to follow suit, as long as the city enhanced Yankee Stadium and the surrounding area. At this same time, Wellington Mara, president of the New York Giants, had been weighing his options.

On January 27, 1956, the Giants announced they would leave the Polo Grounds for a 10-year lease at Yankee Stadium. The football team played at the Polo Grounds for all of their 31 years of existence. As with the baseball Giants, the Yankees would receive 15 percent of the gate receipts after Federal and State taxes were deducted from their new tenants. This move gave birth to speculation that the baseball Giants might be leaving their home in the very near future, as well. The uncertainty of what the baseball Giants were going to do prompted the footballers to play it safe and go where they knew they would have a home.

On February 4, 1961, John V. Mara, president of the Giants, and Yankees president, Daniel R. Topping, tore up the previous contract and wrote up a binding agreement where the Giants would stay as Yankee tenants for 10 years, with an option of 10 more. The average attendance for Giants games over the past five years at Yankee Stadium was 53,431 per game, which amounted to 1,763,224 fans. This presented the Yankees with revenues of $1 million.

In May 1967, a New Jersey newspaper first suggested the idea of building a sports complex in the state's Hackensack Meadowlands. By 1970, the administration of New Jersey Governor William Cahill entered serious negotiations with the Giants in a move to lure the club away from New York. New Jersey State Treasurer, Joseph McCrane, was the force behind the event.

On March 24, 1971, Mara said he was considering moving his team to New Jersey if Governor Cahill would erect a new sports complex in the Hackensack Meadowlands. Mara told Cahill the team would commit to the state if the sports complex became a reality. It was expected to cost between $100 million and $200 million. In Palm Beach, Florida, during the National League Football owners' meeting, the Giants chief said, "If the governor can make it possible for us to take better care of more of our fans, we would certainly be prepared to enter into serious discussions about leasing the facility."

Mara added, "Two things make it attractive. It's been a pressing problem to us that we haven't been able to solicit ticket sales since 1961 and we'd be able to take care of more fans. The thought of a stadium built for football is a tremendous thing for us." [2] Mayor Lindsay believed the team would stay in New York. He told the press, "We are confident that if the city acquires Yankee Stadium and completes its plans for modernization of the stadium, the New York Giants as well as the Yankees will remain in New York City." Lindsay said if the plan didn't go through, the city would condemn the historic stadium. [3]

For the first time in their history, the Giants would have their own home instead of being tenants. The football team would pay a yearly rent of 15 percent of ticket sales, and split the concession sales 50-50 with the state. The new 76,500-seat home of the Giants would be in East

Rutherford, along with a thoroughbred horse racetrack, baseball stadium, and exposition and convention center.

The $329 million 588-acre complex would encompass 20,000 acres of wasteland, and hold 20,000 cars and 400 buses. This greatly surpassed Yankee Stadium parking. Times Square measured 6.6 miles from Yankee Stadium and 6.9 miles to Giants Stadium. Governor Cahill exclaimed, "It's a truly great day for New York Giant fans and all citizens of New York." He called this event "another bridge between New York and New Jersey." Giants Stadium alone cost $68 million.

An angry Mayor Lindsay didn't see it that way. He considered taking legal action, and asked Emanuel Celler, Chairman of the House Judiciary Committee from New York, to look into the matter as an anti-trust action. The Mayor called the Giants, "selfish, callous, and ungrateful." He also said, "I am today directing Corporation Counsel to initiate proceedings to restrict the right of the Giants to call themselves by the name of the city they have chosen to leave." He set about to find a replacement football franchise to fill the void. This event may have put the renovation of Yankee Stadium in peril.

As for Yankees President Michael Burke, he said, "We are sad to see the Giants go. It's rather like having a member of the family leave home, but we wish them good luck." He continued, "My overriding concern remains the future of the Yankees. We shall have to now take a new and realistic reading of our option." [4]

Money, or the lack of it, played a key role in choosing where people stood on this issue. In May, Sidney Siller and Edward S. Patterson, representing Chelsea Forum, a citizens group, hoped Mayor Lindsay would be able to obtain private funding for the purchase of Yankee Stadium and its renovation. They stated that modernizing the Stadium would not guarantee the Yankees would stay in the Bronx. Patterson continued, "...we do feel there are greater priorities than ball parks - hospitals, for example. And some future city administration is going to find a way to pay off the bonds." [5]

In mid-June the City Planning Commission met to approve $3.5 million for acquiring and coming up with preliminary renewal plans for Yankee Stadium. The Board of Estimate would hear the same agenda, backed by Mayor Lindsay. By not revealing the price tag or completed plans of the project, Lindsay wanted to get the ball rolling so far forward that there would be no turning back. The *New York Daily News* questioned the issues of cost, taxpayer expense, and utilizing Shea Stadium. The newspaper wrote in its editorial section, "The public has a right to expect complete answers to all these questions, and the Board of Estimate will be shirking its duty if it does not provide them." [6]

Governor Rockefeller is on board

July 6 witnessed New York Governor Nelson Rockefeller signing a bill authorizing New York City to purchase and modernize Yankee Stadium in order to keep the Yankees and Giants in New York. This same bill authorized the city to build a large exhibition and convention center along the Hudson River north of 42nd Street. Approval by the Legislature and Governor were necessary since the city planned to raise the needed revenue for the renovation by issuing bonds outside its constitutional debt limit. Richard Brown, the city's legislative representative, described Yankee Stadium as nearly 50 years old and "physically and functionally obsolescent."

From City Hall, a jubilant Mayor Lindsay exclaimed this plan meant that "big-league baseball and football can flourish as never before in the Bronx. It will stimulate the ongoing revival of the Bronx and it will help New York expand its role as one of the nation's tourism and recreational centers." [7]

In his *New York Daily News* column of July 9, "Young Ideas," sports columnist Dick Young reported the New York Giants football team was ready to sign the lease to move to New Jersey. Young wrote, "Mayor Lindsay, when he talks of retaining the Giants by refurbishing Yankee Stadium, must know he is telling a fib, must know he is speaking for political effect. Either that, or he is being misled by the boy scouts he employs as advisors, which has happened before." Young further related, "The Giants are gone. If the city goes through with the expenditure of $24 million to purchase and paint Yankee Stadium, it will be pouring money down a sewer." He also said that it would be easy for fans of both teams to see them in New Jersey thanks to better roads and parking, as well as easy train access. [8]

Some members of the New York City board and council had second thoughts about the whole renovation concept once the football Giants agreed on August 26 to move to the Meadowlands in New Jersey. Their move would take effect in 1975. It didn't help that M. Donald Grant, Chairman of the Board of the New York Mets, threatened to move the Mets to New Jersey if forced to share their home with the Yankees. The Mets' rental with the city would terminate in 1991.

On August 28, 1971, *The New York Times* reported that both the Yankees and Mets opposed sharing Shea Stadium in the event of a Yankee Stadium modernization. City Council President Sanford D. Garelik and other city officials had brought forth this idea. Garelik felt that Shea Stadium could be better utilized by adding seats and possibly a dome so it could be used year round for sports and other venues. The Mets leased Shea from New York City for about $500,000 annually. The city operated Shea at an annual loss of $300,000. M. Donald Grant said leasing the ballpark to the Yankees "would be like unscrambling an egg. We have an investment of $3 million in offices, dining rooms and many other facilities." He continued, "Two baseball clubs have never worked well in the same stadium. One club always suffers."

Likely, Grant was angry because the Mets had to pay $100,000 territorial rights to the Yankees in 1961. More insult was added when the Yankees refused to let the Mets play in the Bronx while Shea Stadium was being built. Instead, they had to play at the Polo Grounds in 1962 and 1963. Grant angrily said, "What did they ever do for us?"

Conversely, Michael Burke firmly believed the Yankees and city needed a football team as a co-tenant. The Yankees president affirmed, "It would be a very severe handicap to try to operate without a football team, and the city would find itself in the same straits. The football sub-lease represents a major portion of our income." Burke noted, "Some months ago, John Lindsay proposed that the city buy Yankee Stadium and improve it. We said O.K., if all that is done, we'll stay in the Bronx." He stressed that "We don't want to undermine the Mayor. Our first preference is to stay in the Bronx in a modernized Yankee Stadium in an upgraded environment – better streets, better parking, a better environment. We don't have any preference because so far it hasn't been necessary to consider one." Part of this upgrade was to increase motorist parking from 3,000 to 10,000 vehicles. [9]

In early September, the Board of Estimate guaranteed success in the plan when Queens Borough President Sidney Leviss hopped on board in favor of it. Originally opposing the idea, he reversed his vote, stating, "My original thoughts were that maybe some accommodation could be made between the Mets and the Yankees. But now that the Mets have made it clear that they do not want the Yankees to use Shea Stadium, I've been rethinking my position." [10] Bronx Borough President Robert Abrams, Brooklyn Borough President Sebastian Leone, and Manhattan Borough President Percy Sutton were already in favor of the renovation. William S. Paley, chairman of the board for CBS, which owned the Yankees, was a close friend of Mayor Lindsay. Paley let Michael Burke negotiate with the city relating to the Yankee Stadium transformation.

An article in the September 13 issue of *The New York Times* said the city had begun to revamp highways and streets, as well as create thousands of new parking spaces for cars around Yankee Stadium. The city also was examining ways to use federal funding for redeveloping the South Bronx. Arthur Kessler, the administration's director of the Bronx development, said up to 4,000 new parking spaces would be provided in the Bronx Terminal Market area, as that building would also be updated. Work on 1,500 parking spaces was expected to be finished by November. Another 1,000 were designed as a second level to a parking lot between 153rd and 157th Streets. The city proposed a $4 million to $5 million plan to New York State for wide-ranging upgrading of the Major Deegan Expressway between Ogden Avenue and 149th Street. This was to be financed with state and federal funds.

By the end of September, Mayor Lindsay asked the City Planning Commission to provide a package for a $3.5 million capital budget amendment to begin the task of keeping the Yankees in town. This was the beginning of the $24 million estimated endowment necessary for the rejuvenation of The House That Ruth Built and the nearby area. Ken Patton, the Economic Development Administrator, coordinated the improvements to the Stadium and immediate vicinity.

Of the four demands by the Yankees, only the request for 10,000 extra parking spaces posed a problem. City Council members felt the votes were there for this agenda. A potential problem was that Sidney Leviss was leaving his post as Queens Borough President shortly to become a New York State Supreme Court Justice. Hopefully, his two votes would still be in favor of the endeavor when Donald Manes succeeded Leviss. Manes would cast his ballot based on "what's best for Queens." However, a member of the Board of Estimate concluded, "If Lindsay wants this, he'll get it. It's as simple as that." [11]

By early October, the city's plan for the undertaking was nearly complete. Landscaping and replacement of strip stores below the elevated IRT train and street closings would give the area the feel of being in a park. Adding shrubbery and traffic lights, as well as improving roads, would create a nicer view of the area. Washington would pay for 90 percent of reconstructing the Major Deegan Expressway access improvement, and Albany would contribute the other 10 percent.

The Mayor wanted to convince the City Council that the renovation of Yankee Stadium and the area would make money, not lose it. The main problem was not convincing the politicians, but getting the newspaper writers to feel the same way, because what they printed would be taken as gospel by the readers. After all, would the public be more apt to believe politicians or their trusted news sources? Serious negotiations had begun with the National Football League and Canadian League to bring a professional football team to the Bronx to replace the soon-to-be gone New York Giants. Deputy Mayor Richard Aurelio let it be known that some college teams wanted to play at the Stadium. [12]

At an unscheduled vote at City Hall on November 3, the City Planning Commission approved a budget amendment allowing for the first $3.25 million of the $24 million required for the enterprise. This amendment still had to make it through the Board of Estimate and City Council. *The New York Times* said approval for the measure was unanimous. The official report stated, "Spending $24 million on Yankee Stadium is not a sentimental gesture. The project is economically sound. Without the stadium the nearby commercial area would decline. Commercial deterioration would spread, inevitably followed by housing abandonment. A corrosive cycle of decay would hit the communities of the Concourse, Claremont and Highbridge, among others." This vote was not listed on the 35-item board calendar. That didn't matter, as the public would not have had a say even if they were present. [13]

Mayor Lindsay "reaffirmed his total dedication" to keeping the Bronx Bombers in the city, the *Times* said on November 23. "The key date is December 7," proclaimed Michael Burke. "The Mayor plans to go before the Board of Estimate then with his program for modernizing the stadium." The Yankees' top boss continued, "One of the things he presumably will ask is for an engineering survey of the stadium to determine the feasibility of modernizing it. He also may ask $3 million to acquire the stadium. Precisely what his plan is, I don't know. But at least the program will be presented and we shall know whether it will go ahead or be halted." [14] Meanwhile, Lee MacPhail, the Yankees' executive vice president and general manager, was hunting for an infielder and left-handed relief pitcher during the winter. The team's fourth-place finish during the year didn't help its position with the public.

The December 7 Board of Estimate meeting proved fruitful, as it approved backing for the Mayor's plan. At the hearing, Mrs. Lou Gehrig, Yankees announcer Mel Allen, restaurant icon Toots Shor, and others who represented the glory years of the ballclub, helped convince the Board to allow $225,000 for a thorough six-month engineering study of required stadium repairs to establish if the arena could be "renovated in a manner and at a cost that is favorable to the city."

Mel Allen, the "Voice of the Yankees," explained, "I would love to see Yankee Stadium remain because it is a true landmark – not only in the city, but in this nation." If transportation and parking issues proved overwhelming, he would "still like to see the Yankees remain in New York City because they belong here."

Mrs. Gehrig told the members, "I never thought I'd be called upon to beg for Yankee Stadium to get a facelifting. I beg you really, to remember the great tradition: that of Jacob Ruppert who built the stadium; Babe Ruth who slugged for it, and Lou Gehrig who picked up a few bricks for it. It's a landmark. Remember the Coliseum in Rome – people go there and nasty people played in that place, but it's a great money-maker."

A letter from Michael Burke was read to the participants. He wrote, "Our preference is to remain in the Bronx. This preference was conditional on whether the city lived up to its part of the bargain, particularly in improving access to the stadium and parking facilities." [15]

Ken Patton said the renovation would most likely "include new seats with an improved layout, new private boxes and lounges, escalators and elevators, improved dining areas and locker rooms, and enlarged parking lots." At least two more Board of Estimate approvals were necessary before the modernization strategy could proceed. One endorsement would allow for the $24 million, and the other to let the city lease the stadium back to the Yankees. Opposition to the city's plan, in the 16-6 vote, included City Council President Sanford D. Garelik, who felt the money would be better spent building a new domed stadium rather than renovating the old one. He actually preferred to see money spent on items such as bus passes for school children and restoring after-school facilities.

Another disapproval came from Staten Island Borough President Robert T. Connor, who believed the money would be better spent on waning municipal services. Manhattan Assemblyman Louis Disalvo said, "People need housing, not baseball parks." Comptroller Abraham Beame called the decision an "unsound device." [16] Three young women, on behalf of the Women's Liberation, opposed the project, saying the money would be better used for child care, abortion clinics, and sports involving active women, such as tennis and bicycling. To show how much he believed in the importance of the hearing, the Mayor officiated at the five-hour meeting, rather than making his usual few minutes' appearance at such a gathering.

In a *New York Daily News* December 16 "Letter To The Editor," citizen Joe Manglione said the $225,000 the New York City Board of Estimate spent to study the feasibility of modernizing

Yankee Stadium would be better spent to save Knickerbocker Hospital. He felt the money for the study and the $25 million or so to be spent in the future should not benefit a private business. [17]

Bob Fishel, the Yankees' Director of Public Relations, let it be known on January 26, 1972, that the Yankees and Mets might actually share Shea Stadium. Negotiations were ongoing, with the goal of preventing the Yankees from moving to New Jersey. Three days later, Michael Burke announced that the Mets and Yankees had agreed to share Shea in 1974 and 1975 if the city came through on its promise to buy and renovate Yankee Stadium. M. Donald Grant made no objection to the deal. He told the press, "We want to be sure before we go through with this that the negotiations will not bog down. The Yankees, the city and we all agree that it would not be a permanent arrangement." [18] Given the politics and economics involved, once the city agreed to pay for the Yankee Stadium renovation, the Mets had no choice in the matter.

On January 31, Mayor Lindsay proposed a $1.8 billion capital budget, whereby education, transportation and environmental protection would receive 71 cents of each construction dollar in the next fiscal year. The current capital budget was $1.6 billion. The Mayor called the construction program the "tightest" in the Big Apple's modern history. He offered the 160-page manuscript to the City Council and Board of Estimate. They would hold hearings by April 15.

"Significant new projects" listed by his honor included the Board of Education idea to "move in the direction of smaller schools," a new combined police and fire-alarm voice-box system for $5.1 million, and the purchase of Yankee Stadium for $21 million. The Yankees would lease the ball park. The city budget made no provisions for new libraries or subway cars. [19]

Twenty New York City taxpayers filed a suit in Manhattan Supreme Court on February 9, with the intention of preventing the city from using $24 million in urban renewal and capital construction funds to revitalize Yankee Stadium and its environs. Patricia Wagner, a marketing executive, and George Downes, a public relations consultant, headed the group, known as "The Perspective Committee." They began the lawsuit after learning the city applied for a secret court order to condemn the property around Yankee Stadium without a public hearing.

The group felt that since CBS wanted to own a baseball team, then they should use their own funds to fix Yankee Stadium. The heart of the matter came in their statement that said, "We feel the public is entitled to know the facts now and that accountability should be had while those who are making this deal are still in office and not years later when the city is stuck with a $100 million mistake." [20]

"The Perspective Committee" also filed papers in the Kings County Supreme Court in Brooklyn in February to try to achieve this end. They also aimed to "establish proper priorities in accordance with the real needs of the city and the people." Thirty-six members of the organization brought this grievance to the court, including Wagner, Downes, real estate executive Fred Schauffler, and businessman John Limpert. The assemblage felt that the city and its citizens would not see any benefit from the expenditures, although CBS would.

Wagner echoed the sentiments of many people when she said, "With cutbacks in school budgets, the freeze on the hiring of policemen and other key city employees, and with hundreds of thousands of New York residents without housing, it is ridiculous and an outrage to take public funds for this frivolous use." [21]

Babe's Place makes the final cut - sort of

They received their answer when the March 24 issue of *The New York Times* hit the newsstands. Yankees fans reading the sports section were relieved by the article headline, "YANKEES TO STAY 30 YEARS IN PACT APPROVED BY CITY." The team committed to remaining in New York after the Board of Estimate approved of the remodeling of the legendary park – whatever the cost. Mayor Lindsay greeted the news as a "historic step." He further noted the vote "guarantees the reconstruction of a stadium whose facilities will be second to none in the United States."

Not all the news was cheery. Comptroller Abraham Beame called the accord "not sound government practice." Beame abstained from voting, citing the feasibility study for the endeavor that would not be completed until June. The city hired the architectural engineering firm of Praeger, Kavanagh & Waterbury, 200 Park Avenue, New York, to do a study for $225,000. City Council President Sanford D. Garelik opposed the measure, along with Staten Island President Roger T. Connor. Garelik criticized the pact as a series of "errors," accusing the Mayor's administration of spawning "a soufflé of nostalgia, apple pie and motherhood that clouded the issues."

Mr. Garelik further argued, "the administration, while talking of the future, has committed itself to the refurbishment of an old stadium that, when completed, will still be nothing but a glossed-over relic of the past." Although extra costs did not come up, he feared the price might climb to $40 million. The City Corporation Counsel would most likely give routine approval, although a taxpayer's suit was in the State Supreme Court, which charged improper expenditure of city funds. The next hearing for the case would be April 18 in Manhattan. [22]

As agreed by the parties, New York City was to purchase the Stadium from Rice University in Houston, which Rice owned as the Yankee Stadium Corporation. The city was also to buy the land from the Knights of Columbus. The lease called for starting the renovation in early 1974 and completing the job in time for the 1976 baseball season. During the renovation the team would play at Shea Stadium. The $24 million cost included improved parking at the Stadium's location at 161st Street and River Avenue. Detractors did not like the no-cost ceiling attached to the accord, nor did they like rising construction costs, which already had people thinking expenses could reach $35 million or more when work actually began.

Terms of the lease would bestow to the city 5 percent of receipts from admissions and concessions when attendance reached up to 750,000 yearly; 7.5 percent with attendance between 750,000 and 1.5 million; and 10 percent when the tally totaled above 1.5 million. The minimum the ball club would pay the city was $200,000 annually. The higher the attendance, the more the city would collect. Shea Stadium, on the other hand, earned the city a fixed 7.5 percent of receipts, with a minimum of $300,000 annually. The maximum would be $550,000, plus parking fees.

Michael Burke affirmed, "our decision to stay was, in a sense, a declaration of faith in the city and its future." Sebastian Leone, the Borough President of Brooklyn, who voted for the measure, agreed, "I don't think you're taking any gamble if you get the conditions you ask for. I think we're paying dearly to keep the Yankees here." [23] Several escape clauses were provided for the Yankees should the city not fulfill the terms and timetables of the contract.

By early June it appeared the Yankees would fail to reach the million mark in home attendance. This milestone had not eluded them since 1945, when they played before 881,846 fans. Their fortunes changed in 1946, since the Bronx ballpark had lights installed for night games, and World War II had ended the year before. That year saw a surge of 2,265,512 fans visit the sacred stadium. The figure stayed over the two million mark for five years, then reached a low of 1,067,996 in 1969. In fact, the Yankees home attendance totaled 966,328 in 1972. The team missed four home games due to the April 1 to 13 baseball strike.

In Queens, the Mets projected their third straight year of drawing over two million fans. The Yankees outdrew the Mets in attendance in 1962 by 571,000 fans and by 228,000 in 1963. The tide turned in 1964 when Shea Stadium opened. Even though the hapless Stengel bunch repeatedly came in last place each year, Casey's crew surpassed the Bronx Bombers in attendance when Shea Stadium opened adjacent to the New York World's Fair in 1964. The trend continued to rise, as the Mets played to almost 1,200,000 more fans than the luckless Yankees in 1971. One could only wonder what ex-Yankee and current Mets manager, Yogi Berra, was thinking about this irony. In fact, since Shea Stadium opened its doors, the Yankees had won 64 more games than the Mets, yet the Mets had sold 7,077,264 more tickets than the Yankees.

By August 14, a city official described some of the plans for Yankee Stadium. The elimination of pillars that blocked fans' views, installing elevators and escalators to upper seating, and shortened outfield fences were just part of the plan. Besides more comfortable seating, wider aisles and upgraded concessions areas, more rest rooms and a cafeteria for fans would be added. To remove the supporting structural pillars, the roof had to be removed.

On August 17, *The New York Times* heralded their sports page with the headline, "Yanks, City Sign 30-Year Stadium Lease." The previous day at a City Hall press conference, Mayor Lindsay, Michael Burke, and Bronx Borough President Robert Abrams gathered around a model of the renovated Yankee Stadium to make the official announcement. The Mayor and Michael Burke signed ten copies of the agreement, each one being the same size as an old-time bookkeeper's ledger. [24]

The city also extended the same terms of the lease to Wellington Mara, president of the New York Giants football team, as all existing leases and subleases had been voided on August 8. This was when the city received title, through condemnation proceedings, to Yankee Stadium from Rice University, and the land the Stadium sat on from the Knights of Columbus. State Supreme Court Justice George Postel had signed the condemnation order a few days earlier, in which the vesting title of the field went to the city. The Giants needed to find a temporary home for two years until their East Rutherford residence became a reality. The Mayor told reporters, "discussions have never stopped" in trying to find another football team to replace the Giants. [25]

The charter declared the renovation must start at the end of the 1973 baseball season. Mayor Lindsay praised Mets owner Joan Payson and M. Donald Grant as people "whose public-spirited

New York Yankees Inc.

MICHAEL BURKE
CHAIRMAN AND PRESIDENT

YANKEE STADIUM
BRONX, NEW YORK 10451
293-4300

Dear Mark

Thank you very much for your note expressing concern over a possible Yankee move to New Jersey. That is highly unlikely. In all probability, we will be remaining in New York.

Sincerely,

Michael Burke

Mark Ramtz
2497 Riviera Lane
Bellmore, New York 11710

February 3, 1971/b

Letter from Michael Burke to Mark Ravitz doubting the Yankees would be moving to New Jersey. Courtesy of Mark Ravitz.

cooperation was crucial to the agreement for the Yankees' two-year use of Shea Stadium." His Honor called this moment "an important day in the history of New York. It is the first step in renovating Yankee Stadium and making the 'House That Ruth Built' an even greater attraction for present and future generations of New Yorkers. This administration regards the modernization of Yankee Stadium and the retention of the Yankees as vital to the continuous strengthening of our city's recreational, economic and cultural base." He expected modernizing the stadium to cost $21 million. [26]

A new vision for Babe's Place

Praeger, Kavanagh and Waterbury, a division of URS Madigan-Praeger, Inc., was chosen to design the "new" Yankee Stadium. John Waterbury, A.I.A., a partner in the firm, became the architect-in-charge of the Yankee Stadium project. Mr. Waterbury, well-liked and respected, said there would be no blocked seat views of the playing field, the existing columns would be removed, and the mezzanine and a portion of the upper level would be cantilevered and supported by structural cables. Seating was to be reduced from 65,010 to 57,500. The primary objective of the remodeling was to provide an unobstructed view of the baseball field from every seat in the ball park. Comfort for the fans was also extremely important. Waterbury's associate, Robert C.Y. Young, served as Project Manager and Structural Designer. This was the same company that designed Shea Stadium and Dodger Stadium.

Young called Waterbury the "Father of Modern Stadium Design." Waterbury formulated the guidelines for stadium designing, which began in the 1950s and would continue well past the 1970s renovation of Yankee Stadium. These guiding principles included building a column-free structure to assure unobstructed views of the playing field, wider seating for comfort of spectators, and ring-lighting to illuminate the field instead of tower lighting in order to distribute lighting more uniformly. [27]

New York City's Economics Development Administrator, Ken Patton, predicted more income from its deal with the Yankees than the Mets, as the most the city could garner from the Mets was $550,000, whatever the attendance. The Mets also had to give the city consent for non-baseball events. The Yankees lease allowed the city to book non-baseball programs and collect the same entitlement as for baseball events. Michael Burke said the team had played for 600,000 fans, and he expected the total to be 1.1 million by season's end. He noted that this was "an act of faith in this city." [28]

Mayor Lindsay named Don Evans, one of his aides, as the city's landlord agent at the ball park. Evans had served as a political worker in the Mayor's defunct Presidential campaign, as well as other jobs for the Mayor. Ken Patton said this job was necessary to track the numerous aspects of the Stadium's transformation. This employment earned Mr. Evans an annual salary of $15,000. Richard Weston, also in the city government as sustaining City Hall's liaison, had already been involved in assignments such as street closings, redesigns, and arranging construction. The wheels of change were now starting to turn.

The Yankees announced their 1973 home schedule on December 17. They would play 36 night games during the season. The Bronx Bombers would start their home season vs. the Cleveland Indians on Monday, April 9, at 2:00 p.m. This game would be most interesting since the two teams completed a multi-player trade on November 27, which brought third baseman Graig Nettles and catcher Gerry Moses to New York in exchange for Jerry Kenney, John Ellis, Rusty Torres, and Charlie Spikes. They also obtained outfielder Matty Alou from the Oakland Athletics two days prior, in a trade for Rob Gardner and Rich McKinney. The team already had Matty's brother, Felipe, since April of 1971.

The team finished the 1972 season in fourth place, with a 79-76 record. They were six and a half games behind the pennant winning Detroit Tigers. Even with roster changes during the off-season, there was no particular reason to think that the 1973 finale in Yankee Stadium would remind spectators there of the team's glory days.

Chapter Three

1973 AND THE BEGINNING OF THE END

A new team of owners

The New Year showed itself to be ominous early on, as the Columbia Broadcasting System (CBS) sold the Yankees on January 4, to a group of 12 men, headed by 56-year-old Yankees president Michael Burke and 42-year-old Cleveland, Ohio, shipping magnate George Steinbrenner III. The $10 million bargain price tag was $3.2 million less than CBS paid for the team in 1964. Burke had been running the team since CBS purchased it. [1]

Born in Enfield, Connecticut, in 1916, Edmund Michael Burke grew up in Ireland, which he dearly loved. He also loved New York. The city was fortunate that they were dealing with him. Deep down, he never wanted the Yankees to leave the Bronx. As he once said, "You don't just pick up the team and leave the city because of a few dollar signs. What sets a baseball team apart from, say, a dry-cleaning business is that peculiar nature of a ball club. You're a citizen of the city with civic responsibilities. If you have any sense of this city, you have a commitment." He felt it was important to keep the Yankees in New York. He was an honorable gentleman and a man of his word.

He led quite a life. He graduated from Yale Law School before joining the Navy. During World War II, he was a secret agent with the Office of Strategic Services (O.S.S.). His heroics earned him the Navy Cross and Silver Star. Screen legend Gary Cooper played Burke in the movie, "Cloak and Dagger." He managed the Barnum & Bailey Circus and was also a film writer, as well as television executive. CBS hired him in 1957 as president of CBS for Europe, then transferred him to New York in 1962 as vice president in charge of development. After the entertainment giant purchased the Yankees from Dan Topping, Burke took over the daily operations of the team, as well as buying a portion of it. In July 1972, he acknowledged that CBS had been paying attention to proposals to buy the team. [2]

Steinbrenner was chairman of the American Ship Building Company and part-owner of the Chicago Bulls basketball team. These two gentlemen were the only two partners to appear at the Yankee Stadium press conference. Yankee greats Phil Rizzuto, Elston Howard, and general manager Lee MacPhail also appeared. Other members were to be announced about one week later. A delighted Mayor Lindsay happily responded that "as the landlord of the Yankees," the purchase and restoration of the ball park would "continue in full force." [3]

Steinbrenner had attempted but failed to purchase the Cleveland Indians two years prior to this acquisition. The Indians had recently sold for $10.8 million. In referring to his recent Yankees partnership, he elatedly said, "It's the best buy in sports today. I think it's a bargain. But they [CBS] feel the chemistry is right – they feel they haven't taken a loss on the team." The consortium beat out baseball man Herman Franks, who was talking to CBS about buying the Yankees for between $13 and $14 million. Franks and his friends were five days late with their offer.

A mutual friend had introduced Burke and Steinbrenner a few months earlier. On December 19, 1972, they made their proposition to William S. Paley, chairman of CBS. He agreed to their price three days later. When Burke was the CBS vice president in charge of investments, he had advised the entertainment giant to buy the Yankees.

Of this latest venture, he said, "CBS substantially broke even on this deal, taking account of investment and depreciation and things like that. Some years were profitable, some were not. The first half of last season was disastrous, but in the second half our attendance doubled. I think CBS suffered some small embarrassment in buying a club at its peak and then having it fall from first place in the league to sixth and then to tenth."

He continued, "Last summer people were tripping over themselves to buy the club, but until recently Mr. Paley was not interested in selling it. Lately he believed the Yankees did not fit into CBS's plans. He did feel that I should stay on as chief executive officer, and the club should be sold to a respectable group. Now there's $10 million on the table – and it's not a dollar down and a dollar a month." [4]

Deputy Mayor Edward Hamilton, who also came to the media event, denied that an outside group would reap the rewards of the $24 million renovation. He called the pact "an investment" in the Bronx. He further said, "Any landlord is delighted to learn that the tenant is hot property. We are delighted. . .for the Yankees, which are such an integral part of the Bronx and the whole city, we know the best is yet to come." [5]

The CBS disclosure said, "the $10 million purchase price substantially recoups the original CBS investment of $13.2 million, taking into account consolidated financial results during the period of ownership. The purchase price is well in excess of the value carried on the CBS books." [6]

For his part, George Steinbrenner decreed, "We plan absentee ownership as far as running the Yankees is concerned. We're not going to pretend we're something we aren't. I'll stick to building ships." This new partner grew up as a fan of the Cleveland Indians, his hometown team. But he liked the Yankees and held them in great esteem, even if secretly. Speaking at the Stadium Club at the Bronx ball yard, he exhorted, "When the Yankees came to town, it was like Barnum & Bailey coming to town. I don't mean that they were like a circus, but it was the excitement. They had these gray uniforms, but there was a blue hue to them. Watching them warm up was as exciting as watching the game. Being in Cleveland, you couldn't root for them, but you would boo them in awe."

He could tell his true feelings about the club now that he owned a part of them. "The Yankees are important to New York, but they're also especially important to baseball and to the whole nation. The Yankees are baseball. They're as American as apple pie. There are still great things about the past that are worth going back to and grabbing into the present. I think that's so with the Yankees." [7]

Steinbrenner had always been interested in sports. He ran track and was halfback on the Williams College football team. After a stint with the U.S. Air Force's Strategic Air Command, he became a high school basketball and football coach in Columbus, Ohio. He also spent a year each as an assistant football coach at Northwestern and Purdue Universities. He went into the family shipping business in 1957 after leaving his college position.

But sports was in his blood. He ran the Cleveland Pipers basketball club from 1959 thru 1961. The club won two championships, although losing $250,000. In 1967 he bought the struggling American Ship Building Company from his father, Henry. It was now worth $100 million. This entrepreneur became part-owner and vice president of the Chicago Bulls basketball team, as well as proprietor of the 860-acre Kinsman Stud Farm in Ocala, Florida. He was also the part-owner of a limousine service in New York City.

Besides possessing the great knack of making money, this Yankees chief had generously sent 75 students through college with his own funds. He was also well known for raising money for civic and charitable purposes. As for the Yankees, he was quoted in the January 4 issue of *The*

New York Times as saying, "I won't be active in the day-to-day operations of the club at all. I can't spread myself so thin. I've got enough headaches with my shipping company." [8]

The Yankees introduced their other partners at New York's 21 Club on January 10. This included the surprise addition of Gabe Paul, who had worked for the Cleveland Indians for the past 12 years. He had just resigned as vice president and general manager of the team although he had four years left on his contract. Paul had spent 30 years as a baseball executive, including posts with the Cincinnati Reds and Houston Astros. Steinbrenner approached Paul after receiving permission from Indians owner Nick Mileti. The 63-year-old Paul made the decision to join the Yankees after being assured that Lee MacPhail and Ralph Houk would stay with the team. Phil Seghi, who had served as the Indians vice president and director of player personnel for the last 14 months, would fill Gabe Paul's empty position. Michael Burke said he would keep his titles of president and chief executive officer. Gabe Paul would function as Administrative Partner.

The list of Yankees Leadership for 1973: (from the 1973 New York Yankees yearbook)
Michael Burke -- General Partner
George M. Steinbrenner III -- General Partner
Gabe Paul -- Administrative Partner
Lee MacPhail-- General Manager

Limited Partners:

Jess A. Bell -- Steamboat Springs, Colorado
Leslie Combs II -- Lexington, Kentucky
Lester Crown -- Chicago, Illinois
John De Lorean -- Detroit, Michigan
Thomas Evans -- New York, New York
Edward Ginsberg -- Cleveland, Ohio
Edward M. Greenwald -- Cleveland, Ohio
Sheldon B. Guren -- Cleveland, Ohio
Nelson Bunker Hunt -- Dallas, Texas
Daniel R. McCarthy -- Cleveland, Ohio
James M. Nederlander -- New York, New York
Francis J. O'Neill -- Cleveland, Ohio
Marvin L. Warner -- Cincinnati, Ohio

Charlotte L. Witkind -- Columbus, Ohio
Joseph W. Iglehart -- Consulting Partner [9]

On April 5, Mayor Lindsay advised the public that the estimated price tag of the Yankee Stadium remodeling alone was rising by $6.9 million to $27.9 million. He called it "routine – a moderate escalation." The cost of purchasing the Bronx arena was $3 million, with a $21 million outlay for the actual reconstruction.

Comptroller Abraham Beame and City Council President Sanford Garelik, both mayoral candidates, assailed the rebuilding of Yankee Stadium. Said Garelik, "The Mayor's casual admission of a nearly $7 million increase in the Yankee Stadium price tag defies belief. The administration ignored my admonitions and the public was told that the $21 million figure was a sound one which took into consideration the normal costs of escalations. Today the Mayor, without blinking an eyelid, contradicts himself when he says the increase is normal and moderate. The total stadium cost may well come in twice the $24 million cost of Shea Stadium." Garelik also stated that "the public has been had."

Beame called the almost 30 percent cost alteration "rather steep." He added, "In any event, adding the Mayor's increase of $6.9 million to my original estimate of $47 million brings the total Yankee Stadium project cost to $53 million. Brand new all-weather stadiums with retractable domes can be built for about $80 million." The original $24 million appropriation had included a built-in 15 percent escalation clause. This really meant the city pledged nearly $28 million to the remodeling. The Board of Estimate and City Council would have to approve a capital budget amendment for any funding above that. [10]

Lindsay did not want the Yankees to flee the city as the Dodgers and Giants had. He strongly felt the Bronx would suffer, as the Yankees had brought much needed revenue into the South Bronx. Fans spent millions of dollars yearly at restaurants and local shops. Building another apartment complex wouldn't bring in revenue. He no doubt kept the cost numbers low in order to gather support for his plan. That's why there was such a wide scale of costs being bandied about. Virtually everyone was kept in the dark for fear of losing support. When asked what might happen at the end of his term as Mayor on December 31, Lindsay responded, "By the time I retire, the Stadium will be gutted and the project so far down the road, it will be impossible to reverse it." [11]

As for the game of baseball itself, the Yankees wasted no time in adding to the team's role in baseball history. On April 6, Ron Blomberg became the first designated hitter (DH) in the history of the game. Boston Red Sox pitcher Luis Tiant walked Blomberg on his first at bat at Fenway Park. That was the highlight of the three-game series, as the Yankees lost all three games by scores of 15-5, 10-5, and 4-3. After such a terrible series, the Yankees were glad to leave Beantown before coming home to the Bronx.

Fifty years at Babe's Place

The last home opener at Yankee Stadium, as fans knew it, began at 2:00 p.m. on a chilly Monday, April 9, vs. the Cleveland Indians. A paid crowd of 17,028, less than one-third of the park's capacity, witnessed the two hour and 34-minute game. One of the fans was Mayor Lindsay, who sat to the left of the Yankees dugout. It must have crossed the minds of the Mayor and Yankees brass that with only 966,328 fans attending games in 1972, this turnout might seem ominous for 1973 receipts. This year would end up with a gate of 1,262,103 paying customers.

Eighty-one-year-old Herbert Bluestone had the honor of throwing out the first ball. This operator of a pharmacy at Manhattan's Plaza Hotel had attended the opening of Yankee Stadium 50 years earlier. "You couldn't get in that day," Mr. Bluestone reminisced. "They turned away about 25,000 people. I paid 25 cents for a seat in the bleachers." Nearby sat former Mayor Robert F. Wagner, who when asked how he felt about the renovation said, "I'm enjoying the game. My father took me to the 1923 opener. The city helped the Mets and I think the Yankees have to be helped, too."

The First Ladies of the Yankees, Mrs. Babe Ruth and Mrs. Lou Gehrig, also came to the historic game. Mrs. Gehrig conveyed, "They'll earn it all back. And don't worry about this year's club. We always used to say, 'Wait till the Fourth of July.'" Mrs. Ruth chimed in, "It's too young in the season to start worrying. If they want to fix up the Stadium, I'm definitely for it from a business standpoint." She added, "You know, there'll never be another one-two. . .like Babe and Lou." [12]

On the field, southpaw Fritz Peterson pitched for the Yankees against Cleveland's Brent Strom. The Indians won, 3-1. The Yanks scored the first run in the second inning when Felipe Alou doubled and Thurman Munson hit a sacrifice fly to score him. Cleveland scored single runs in the third, sixth, and ninth innings. Peterson pitched 5 1/3 innings, giving up two runs and six hits. Lindy McDaniel relieved him and yielded one run and three hits. Strom pitched all the way for the Tribe.

The official celebration of the 50th anniversary of the historic stadium's opening took place on Sunday, April 15, against the Boston Red Sox. The golden anniversary celebration included each fan receiving a specially wrapped chocolate Hostess cupcake. The wrapper had a label that featured the 50th anniversary logo of Yankee Stadium. Besides 40,000 of these cupcakes being delivered to the Stadium, a six-foot-high by six-foot-diameter white frosted cake was created in the shape of Yankee Stadium. The cake featured the infield, the scoreboard, and the lights and flags on the upper deck. The inscription said, "Yankee Stadium, 50th Anniversary." The cake was cut in pre-game ceremonies.

On April 15, 1973, in celebration of Yankee Stadium's 50th Anniversary, fans received a chocolate Hostess cupcake. This is a copy of the label that came on the cupcake's cellophane wrapper. The actual label size was 1 ½"x 2 ¼". Permission to use this label is courtesy of Interstate Bakeries Corporation, Kansas City, MO.

Gate 6, July 22, 1972.

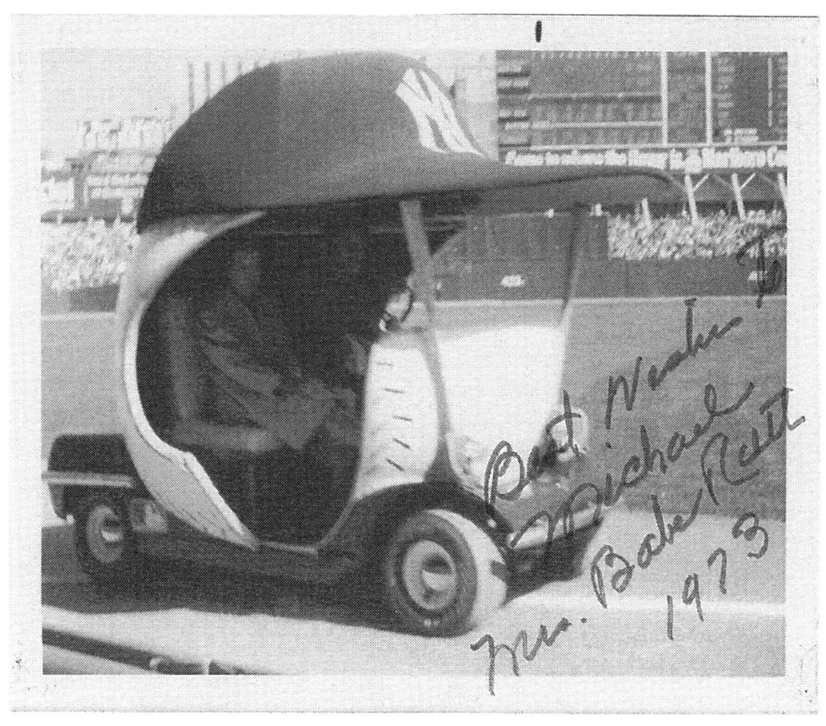

Mrs. Babe Ruth riding in Yankee cart, April 15, 1973.

Bob Shawkey, who had pitched the inaugural game at Yankee Stadium on April 18, 1923, threw out the first ball from the pitcher's mound, while Whitey Witt, the first Yankees batter in the 1923 opener, stood in the batter's box. The Knickerbocker band played tunes, and the New York All-City High School Chorus sang old-time tunes. Each fan received a reproduction of the 15-cent program sold at the Opening Day game a half-century earlier.

Famed postmaster James A. Farley, who had attended the first game, was here, too. The long-time Yankees fan recalled, "I was there the day it opened. I don't remember much about the game, but I was there – and have been for many years since." He reminisced, "Why did the stadium become the showplace? It was partly the city: New York's the place. Partly the team that played there: the Yankees. Mostly, it was Babe Ruth. He came in during John McGraw's heyday with the Giants and took over." [13]

The crowd of 35,700 sat through the two hour and 14-minute contest, in which Mel Stottlemyre led the Yankees to a 6-2 win over John Curtis, who pitched for the visiting rival Boston Red Sox. The local heroes scored all of their runs in the fourth inning. The Fenway group gained their pair of runs in the sixth inning.

The face of management changed on April 30, when Michael Burke stepped down as chief executive officer of the team. George Steinbrenner and Gabe Paul effectively dissolved Michael Burke's responsibilities in an evident power struggle. Paul's many years in baseball clinched the deal. Burke had the CBS and New York contacts needed by Steinbrenner and Paul.

Disagreements between the two general partners ranged from the length of players' hair, to television issues, pre-game entertainment, and pledges made to each other. Perhaps the greatest disparity was the disagreement concerning the financial operation of the ball club. With Burke out of the picture, Steinbrenner and Paul could run their new team freely. With Burke's future now uncertain, several people thought the charismatic entrepreneur should run for public office.

Before the May 13 doubleheader vs. the Baltimore Orioles, Burke and Steinbrenner appeared at a news conference in an effort at public resolution. Burke could not conceal his regret at not actively taking part in operating the team he loved. He was to remain with the Yankees as a limited partner and paid consultant, under a ten-year agreement. Steinbrenner commanded the assembly, as he said a big contrast came from "which persons fit best in which areas." This referred to Gabe Paul's presence into the front office. Burke said, "With Gabe's background and experience, he couldn't join an organization like this without getting involved." [14]

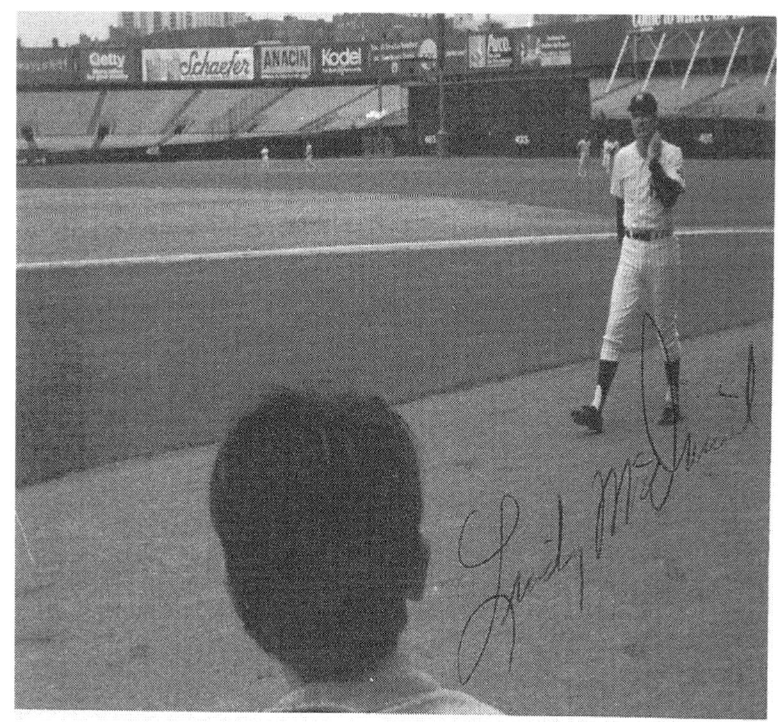

Lindy McDaniel, June 19, 1973.

Ron Blomberg, August 11, 1973.

Steinbrenner, who sat next to Burke, said, "Mike didn't agree with everything I wanted to do, but he was a big man about it." Burke interjected that the sale to his group from CBS happened so quickly "we didn't get to know each other better before we got the club. Before long, we were facing a certain degree of incompatibility. We were two strong-minded independent individuals and we had a clash. We considered the possibility of trying to put ourselves back where we were six months ago. Could we start all over again and try to work it out? But we decided this was the best way to do it." He added, "When you're so totally immersed in something like the Yankees, there's a lingering sadness or disappointment that things didn't turn out well. But one has to be pragmatic."

A couple of days before this meeting, they resolved their differences through a number of meetings. They agreed on Burke's position with the Yankees. "A lot of times making someone a consultant is putting him out to pasture or a settlement," said Steinbrenner. "This isn't the case here." The two gentlemen felt Burke had practical wisdom in specific areas, such as the upcoming renovation. Burke retorted, "I'm interested in contributing as much as I can to the success of this ball club. The Yankees have become part of my chemistry and perhaps, I theirs." [15]

Burke had been contacted by "a whole slew of people" about numerous job prospects. He did, in fact, speak to sports impresario Sonny Werblin, who was searching for somebody to operate the New Jersey Meadowlands sports complex. Burke said he would make no career decisions for at least two months. Steinbrenner commented, "Some people may find it hard to believe, but I don't intend to project myself into it. They'll see no interference from me. I think we have it working now in a way that will be best for the Yankees." [16]

A new challenge awaited Michael Burke, when on July 26, he was named president of Madison Square Garden. Irving Felt, the board chairman of Gulf and Western, the major stockholder of this site, wanted Burke to improve its corporate image and the value of its stock. Six years earlier, shares sold for a high of 14¼. Now it sold at less than $2 per share. Stockholders roared about mismanagement. New Yorkers liked, respected, and trusted Michael Burke. Madison Square Garden counted on him to transfer these qualities to them in order to raise their stock and trust in the eyes of Knicks and Rangers fans, and others who had a stake in the company.

Starting on July 8, Yankee Stadium hosted 70,000 Jehovah's Witnesses for a five-day "Divine Victory" assembly for their faithful in the Atlantic Seaboard states. The packed venue held 63,700 in regular seating, 5,000 in folding chairs around the track, and 2,000 sitting below the bleachers. Another 5,000 people listened to speeches via the public address system piped into a temporary tent bordering the Stadium. Even in the stifling early July heat, the sect believed that divine intervention was the only means to solving troubles currently facing humanity. [17]

Another big, but different crowd arrived on Saturday, August 11. This celebration brought the 27th annual Old Timers' Day Game to the historic ball park. The Yankees hosted the Oakland Athletics on this day, which paid tribute to the 50th anniversary of Yankee Stadium. Representatives from 50 Yankees teams included Whitey Witt, Waite Hoyt, Joe Dugan, Bill Dickey, Joe DiMaggio, Johnny Lindell, Casey Stengel, Bill Skowron, Mickey Mantle, Whitey Ford, Tom Tresh, Horace Clarke, and Bobby Murcer.

Approximately 65 Yankees were on the guest list, along with the newest National Baseball Hall of Fame inductees, Monte Irvin and George Kelly. Mrs. Babe Ruth, Mrs. Lou Gehrig, and Mrs. George M. Weiss were Special Guests of Honor. Frank Messer served as Master of Ceremonies and introduced all the guests. Mel Allen acted as Master of Ceremonies for the Old Timers' baseball game. Introductions began about 1:15. This was followed by the playing of the National Anthem by Guy Lombardo and the Royal Canadians at 2:00. The two-inning Old Timers' game started about 2:05. The Yankees then played the A's after the Old Timers' Day festivities ended. The 46,293 cheering fans could not help the current Yankees overcome a few errors and lackluster hitting, as Vida Blue led the A's to a 7-3 win over Mel Stottlemyre and the home team.

Besides commemorating the golden anniversary of America's most historic baseball stadium, 1973 had a couple of surprises under its belt. The incomparable Willie Mays announced he would hang up his spikes for good at the end of the season. He broke the news on September 20. His 22 years of exciting baseball began with the New York Giants in 1951 and ended in New York with the New York Mets. Willie, at age 42, played in only 66 games and batted only .211. The great legend hit the last of his 660 home runs at Shea Stadium on August 17 against Don Gullett of the Cincinnati Reds. The "Say Hey Kid" last played center field on August 24 against the visiting Giants. By September 20 he was nursing a sore arm and bruised ribs, which occurred while playing first base on September 9, after hitting a railing while chasing a foul ball in Montreal. That was his final regular-season game as a major leaguer.

With the Mets now in a heated pennant race, the beloved idol said, “I had a love affair with baseball, and now we’re parting.. . .I wish I could help them, but I know I couldn’t. Hitting .211, it’s not fun going out there.” Baseball Willie did play in three World Series games against the Oakland Athletics. In seven at-bats he had two hits, scored one run, and batted .286. The A’s won four games to three. Thus came the end for one of the game’s brightest stars. [18]

Another National League superstar was on the verge of setting one of baseball’s most sacred records on its ear. Hank Aaron was closing in on Babe Ruth’s sacred record of 714 lifetime home runs. During the September 29 game in the fifth inning, the quiet 39-year-old Atlanta Braves outfielder smacked a slow curveball near his knees over the left-center field fence for number 713. Jerry Reuss, pitcher for the Houston Astros, gave up Hammerin’ Hank’s latest blast. Carl Morton pitched a six-hitter in front of 17,836 fans at Atlanta Stadium for the Braves’ 7-0 victory. Hank had one more game to play, but registered no home runs. He had to wait until next year.

On Monday, September 24, representatives from the National Baseball Hall of Fame, the Smithsonian Institution, the Babe Ruth Museum in Baltimore, and Manny from Manny’s Baseball Land, across the street from Yankee Stadium, were allowed to carry away items from the Stadium before the demolition phase of the renovation a week later. The Hall of Fame took a ticket booth, an old wooden staircase near the visitors clubhouse below the third base stands, a dozen seats from the special guest section, and a turnstile. The Babe had used the wooden stairway as a private exit from the Stadium while the Yankees used the third base dugout. The Smithsonian received the Yankees bat rack and a ticket booth. [19]

Last day of the old park as we knew it

Sunday, September 30, spelled the last game for Yankee Stadium as we knew it. Fans received a 33 1/3 RPM record, “YANKEE STADIUM, The Sounds of a Half Century.” The Voice of the Yankees, Mel Allen, narrated the 32-minute album, which relived some of the greatest moments of Yankee Stadium. The grand old park hosted the Detroit Tigers for the 2:00 p.m. finale. Mayor Lindsay threw out the first ball. Fritz Peterson started the game for the Yanks, and Fred Holdsworth pitched for the Tigers. The Yankees lost, 8-5, in front of the 32,238 faithful. Detroit reliever John Hiller won the game and Lindy McDaniel recorded the loss for the Yankees. The Yankees finished in fourth place, with an 80-82 record and a .494 winning percentage. The league-leading Eastern Division Baltimore Orioles finished a whopping 17 games ahead of the Yankees.

The highlight for the Yankees was that Duke Sims hit the last Yankees home run into the right field bleachers. Before the game Jerry Moses and Sims tossed a coin to see who would be the catcher for this last game. Sims won the toss. The crowd heartily booed manager Ralph Houk when he pulled Lindy McDaniel in the eighth inning after McDaniel pitched to eight batters and only got two of them out. A couple of banners in the stands declared, "Houk Must Go," and "Fire Houk." Wayne Granger pitched the final 1 1/3 innings for the pinstripers. At 4:41 p.m., Mike Hegan flied out to Mickey Stanley in center field for the final out at the old ballpark. Instead of Sparky Lyle's theme of "Pomp and Circumstance," organist Toby Wright played "Auld Lang Syne."

Nine-year old Larry Wiederecht of Westchester went to the game with his dad and two brothers. They sat in the left field upper deck. To their surprise, Michael Burke was only a few rows away. Young Larry also remembered seeing a small number of plastic seats similar to what would be found in the Stadium in 1976. [20]

Some 20,000 fans poured onto the field after the last out. Security officer Harvey Levene protected home plate from souvenir hunters. He refused a $20 bribe from a fan who carried a shovel in hopes of making off with the historic piece. [21] First base coach Elston Howard snatched first base before the fans could, although at least one tried to grab the prized trophy. Everything was up for grabs as far as the souvenir hunters were concerned. The center field monument plaques of Miller Huggins, Lou Gehrig, and Babe Ruth had been removed a week earlier in anticipation of such an event. Fans did manage to grab second base. *The New York Daily News* reported that Detroit third baseman Ike Brown took third base. [22]

Prowling fans kicked seats out of their cement anchors and carried them away, with many having to leave them behind as police officers confiscated them as the souvenir hunters were leaving the stadium. Others took signs. One fan yelled to the press box, "Hey, any of you guys got a screwdriver?" Larry Wiederecht's brother took sod, put it in a dish at home and tried to water it. The divot died in November.

The author brought a half-gallon Carvel plastic ice cream container and put dirt from the area where the second baseman played into it, along with some sod. Someone even tried to pickpocket him on the field. All this mayhem occurred despite the fact that the Yankees let it be known that anyone taking anything from the Stadium would be arrested for theft and prosecuted. Hardly any damage actually occurred.

Roy Slezak of Passaic, New Jersey, recalled a number of ushers armed with screwdrivers, charging $3-5 to take brass plates off railings that had section and seat numbers on them. Some fans also brought hammers and screwdrivers to salvage souvenirs. [23]

Unbeknownst to Yankees fans, Ralph Houk tearfully bade his team goodbye, then made his official resignation announcement at a news conference shortly after the loss to the Tigers. He had two years left on a three-year contract, which reportedly paid him $75,000 annually. Still in

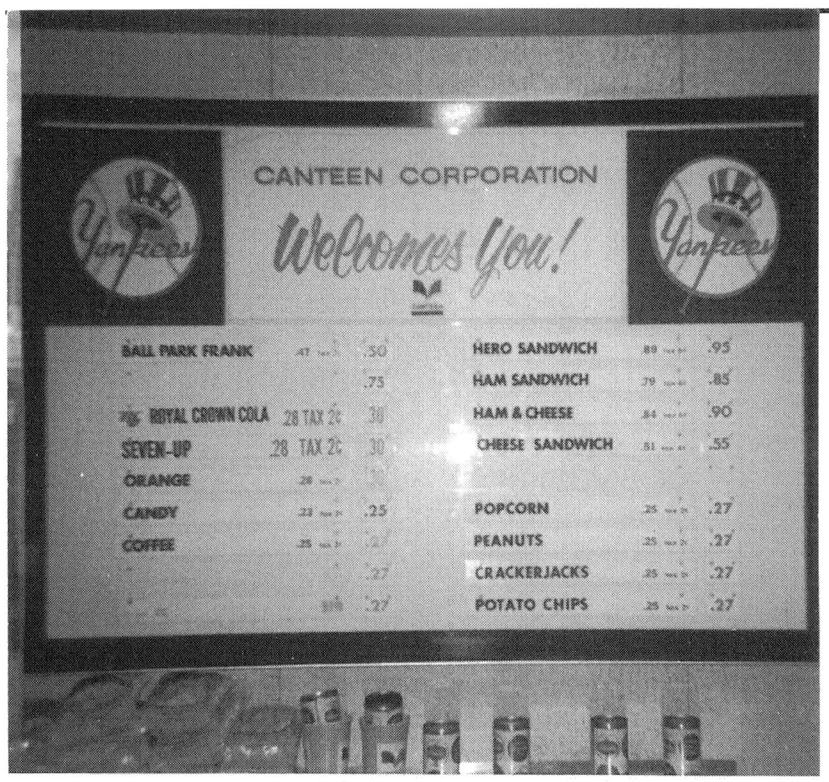

Concession stand price list from September 30, 1973.

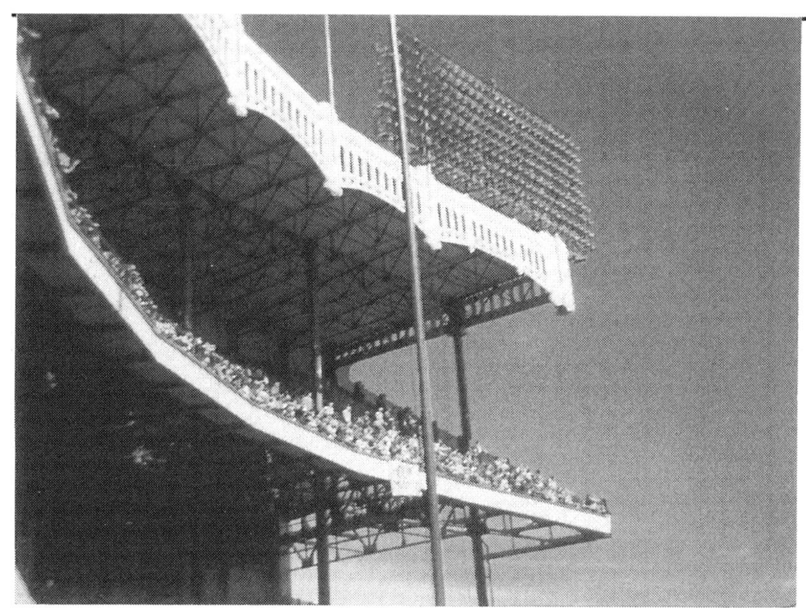

Left field upper deck as seen from field level.

View behind the frieze taken from the left field upper deck grandstand. Photo taken at the last game before the renovation, September 30, 1973.

View of metal truss supports for roof and frieze from left field upper deck, pre-renovated Yankee Stadium. Photo taken last game before renovation, September 30, 1973.

Fans milling around the field after the last game in the pre-renovated Yankee Stadium, September 30, 1973. Photo taken by Tom Langan and provided by Dennis Concepcion.

Looking for souvenirs at ticket booths after the last game before the renovation, September 30, 1973.

his beloved pinstripes and choking back tears, he said, "Sometimes when you've been with somebody as long as I've been here, and when you don't accomplish what you are after, you get the feeling it is better off for the Yankees, who have done so much for me and my family, to resign. I believe I'm making the right decision. I decided four or five days ago to resign. This has been a rough year. We really thought we had a winner. We've won some pennants. But it's been a little rough since 1966. A man has to go with his convictions. I blame no one but myself. It will be better for the Yankees to have a new manager." [24]

What really happened was that the Yankees were in first place for six weeks, including the whole month of July. Then things went downhill after the All-Star break late in that month. Sparky Lyle pitched brilliantly until August, but then fizzled out. The defense did poorly, giving away a number of games. The starting pitching rotation stumbled; Steve Kline was hurt. New hurlers Sam McDowell and Pat Dobson didn't pitch as well as hoped. By August there was gossip that the players stopped caring about whether they won or lost.

So ended Houk's 35 years as a Yankee, which was also his uniform number. The long-time Yankee had no immediate plans for the future. He concluded, "I'm going down to Florida, put out some lines without hooks and just sit there for a while." The Yankees brass tried to talk him out of leaving, but failed. Sometimes you just need a change in life. [25]

Out with the old, in with the new

At noon on Monday, October 1, the beginning of the end dawned at home plate at Babe's Place. Mayor Lindsay, Lee MacPhail, Gabe Paul, and Bronx Borough President Robert Abrams presided over the official ceremony that would begin the renovation of Yankee Stadium. Elston Howard and pitcher Sam McDowell were among the 25 or so people in attendance. The Mayor would present home plate to Mrs. Babe Ruth and first base to Mrs. Lou Gehrig. The two female icons of Yankees tradition arrived half an hour before the Mayor and reminisced. They were sorry to see Ralph Houk leave as the Yankees manager, as they agreed that he was a nice man. His Honor, dressed in a gray business suit, received the first set of seats removed from the Stadium. He would donate the box seats to Gracie Mansion, the home of the Mayor of New York City.

When the Mayor presented home plate to Mrs. Ruth, he said, "I am happy and honored to present you this home plate from The House That Ruth Built. I want to assure you that there always will be a House That Ruth Built." Mrs. Ruth responded, "Thank you, Mr. Mayor, for your hard work and determination." He then offered first base to Mrs. Gehrig, saying, "Mrs. Gehrig, I am happy to present to you this first base from Yankee Stadium. Lou was first in everything he did." Dressed in blue pants, red blouse, and a mink vest-like cape, she replied, "Thank you, Mayor Lindsay, and I want to wish you a very successful future – after all, you're still a kid." Mrs. Gehrig later presented first base to the National Baseball Hall of Fame in Cooperstown, New York.

During the ceremony Lindsay said, "Nothing could be more important to the economic vitality of our city than to assure that The House That Ruth Built and the New York Yankees remain here in the Bronx for future generations of New Yorkers. That commitment has been made and today we not only honor the past, but look with great expectation to the future."

Mrs. Ruth was asked why nobody was crying. Her response: "Why should we? It's just like changing coats. When your fur wears out, you get a new one. There's nothing I hate worse than a ratty fur coat." Mrs. Gehrig echoed, "You can't stop progress. I am happy to see progress." [26]

Ross Lewis, destined to become a renowned photographer for the National Football League, was one of many Americans who had grown to love Yankee Stadium. He was one of the photographers on hand for this bittersweet event. From this date through April 15, 1976, Lewis would shoot a staggering 13,000 museum-quality photos of the renovation of Yankee Stadium. He was the only photographer granted special credentials by the City of New York to photograph this project.

After the ritual, Roy Slezak accompanied Mrs. Gehrig from the Yankees dugout to second base so she could visit with Mrs. Ruth. During this stroll, Mrs. Gehrig proudly showed Slezak the charm bracelet on her wrist. The widow proclaimed, "the charms were cut from Lou's World Series and All Star rings." Mr. Slezak was kind enough to send me his poignant, yet fascinating story, which follows:

MEMORIES OF A TRUE BASEBALL FAN
MEETING THE WIDOWS OF THE LEGENDS

It was the House That Ruth Built; a magnificent sight on 161st Street in the Bronx.

I arrived at the stadium quite early and was able to take in the view from the pitcher's mound; the famous right field façade where the Mick came within feet of clearing and putting the home run out on the street, the short right field line, where 5 years earlier I "accidentally" hit one into the seats during a tryout.

I walked around, as I did once before, standing where my heroes stood and walking on the hallowed ground where the Yankee Legends had practiced their craft.

This was a special event in many ways. The stadium in which The Bambino, The Iron Horse, The Moose and the Yankee Clipper played would be updated to reflect a more modern look with a longer right field line and a shorter centerfield. There would be a new picnic area behind the center field fence that would house the monuments that were once in play honoring heroes of long ago.

The ceremony was taking place one day after the last game of the season's finale and was attended by many celebrities of the day; including New York Mayor Lindsay, Elston Howard, the Yankees catcher and "Sudden" Sam McDowell, a fireball pitcher who looked dapper as usual in his hounds tooth jacket. There were more Yankee executives than I knew existed, including Yankee GM, Lee MacPhail.

But there were no guests more prominent than the two elderly ladies who were the widows of The Iron Horse and The Bambino. I also remember a gentleman whose name escapes me. This man started work at Yankee Stadium on the first day it opened and 50 years later was still there. Just imagine what he saw; he saw it all.

As the time for the ceremony drew near, the Yankee execs brought out a home plate and a base. They told me that they were the home plate and first base used in the last game, and they would be given to Mrs. Ruth and Mrs. Gehrig.

With the speeches and presentations over, there was some time for mingling. Mrs. Ruth was out toward second base, and I was near the Yankee dugout with Mrs. Gehrig close by.

Not being too sure on her feet, Mrs. Gehrig asked me to escort her out to the second base area so she could talk with the Babe's wife. I obliged, and there I was walking arm in arm with the wife of one of baseball's greatest players. The slow walk turned into a stroll, and then Mrs. Gehrig stopped and wanted to show me something. She held up her hand and showed me a gold charm bracelet on her wrist. "The charms," she said proudly, "were cut from Lou's World Series and All-Star rings;" a gift from her husband. She insisted that I look at each and every "charm" on the bracelet before we continued our stroll out to second base.

I stood by as the ladies chatted and then escorted both ladies to home plate, where Mayor Lindsay was "holding court." I just couldn't believe it, here I was again, walking arm in arm with the wives of baseball's most recognizable figures.

I couldn't help notice that the ladies seemed to take on the personalities of the men they were married to. That is from what I knew about their husbands. Mrs. Ruth was fiery, even in her frail and elderly state, and Mrs. Gehrig was a more demure and calm, gentle lady.

Mrs. Ruth showed how fiery she could be as she proceeded to "chew out" Mayor Lindsay because no one had arranged to take the two ladies to lunch. The mayor was lost for words, and all I could do was smile as this frail, fiery lady continued to give the most powerful man in NY a piece of her mind. And yes, the mayor did take the ladies to lunch after that.

I kindly asked Mrs. Ruth and Mrs. Gehrig to sign something for me, and they both happily signed their names with the year 1973. As the mayor asked the ladies to come with him, Mrs. Gehrig gently grabbed my hand, looked at me and said, "Thank you for being such a gentleman." As they disappeared into the tunnel to get into the mayor's limo, I felt the goose bumps rise on my arms at what I had just experienced.

In 1976 the "new" Yankee Stadium opened with a lot of hype and fanfare. But nothing will ever match that day in the fall of 1973 when I met the wives of The Bambino and The Iron Horse.

That's a day I will cherish forever. Roy Slezak 2008 [27]

Shortly after the ceremony, the Mayor began the official demolition by sitting in the cab of a bulldozer and scooping up dirt in short right field. In reality, even before the day's ceremony began, workers had begun ripping seats from their anchors. A bulldozer was also tearing up the field.

The beginning of the end of Yankee Stadium as we knew it had transpired on August 24, when Herbert T. Simins, the city's Commissioner of Public Works, awarded contract ED-98 to a joint venture between Invirex Demolition Inc., and Cuyahoga Wrecking Corp. They submitted a $988,000 bid to furnish all labor and material for the demolition work of Yankee Stadium. Cuyahoga Wrecking Company was located in Hazelwood, Missouri, and Invirex Demolition, Inc., was located at 2-01 55th Avenue, Long Island City, New York. Cuyahoga was a subsidiary of Diversified Industries, Inc., of Hazelwood, Missouri. Ray Berke, a demolition expert, ran Cuyahoga. Berke taught Jay (L.L.) Schwall, who would head the demolition phase of the Yankee Stadium Modernization, the art of estimating, as well as Schwall's son 20 years later. The proposition by Invirex-Cuyahoga bested the following three competitors for the demolition phase of remodeling Yankee Stadium:

Company	Bid
1. Invirex-Cuyahoga	$988,000
2. Akron Wrecking Co., New York City	$1,058,000
3. Associated Wrecking Co., New Jersey & Alpine Wrecking Co., New Jersey	$1,778,000
4. DeFoe Construction Co., New York City	$4,879,025

The lowest bidders for modernizing Yankee Stadium tallied at:

Number of Bidders	Job	Lowest Bid
4	Demolition	$988,000
4	General Contract	$22,220,000
13	Electrical	$2,849,000
15	Heating, Venting, A/C	$2,431,000
10	Plumbing	$1,650,000
8	Elevator & Escalator Work	$1,580,731 [28]

Bids for the reconstruction of Yankee Stadium were released on December 4. They were $5 million more than estimated by the architects, Madigan-Praeger. Instead of costing the $50.7 million allocated in the 1974-1975 capital budget, the expense for the money-gobbling undertaking went up to at least $55 million. Herbert T. Simins, the city's Commissioner of Public Works, opened the proposals. Law required separate contracts for bidding on public works projects. They were for general construction; electrical work; heating, venting and air conditioning; plumbing; and elevator installation. The five bids totaled $30,730,731, or 22 percent more than expected. Madigan-Praeger had predicted that the bids would come in at $25,129,000.

Mr. Simins was pleased with the number of bidders. Advertisements for these submissions had been published six weeks earlier. He explained that the lowest bidders would not necessarily get the job. They also had to prove competence and be bonded. The architects estimated the bare construction costs to be about $32.7 million. [29]

Invirex-Cuyahoga began selling items from the Stadium to the general public on October 1. Some relics for sale: the electric scoreboard, chairs, uniforms, the city's longest bar, flag poles, and bricks. The company placed ads in *The New York Times* listing other items for sale, such as refrigerators, ice cream freezers, cash registers, mechanical equipment, and other kitchen paraphernalia. Invirex-Cuyahoga hired a few Yankees groundskeepers, who greatly aided the operation, as they intimately knew the Stadium. At this time the estimated cost of the renovation was $27-50 million.

The salvage rights for the New York Yankees lasted only five days. The team could take whatever they wanted during that time. After that, Invirex-Cuyahoga took possession of everything at the site. This included food in the freezers the Yankees were not able to dispose of. Nothing was handled by New York City. The demolition took on urgency.

Time was greatly constrained, as the main focus was to complete the job on time. Collecting baseball memorabilia was in its infancy, so many treasures ended up in the garbage dump. This included the medallions above Gates 2, 4, and 6, for instance. They were demolished mechanically. Three or four did survive. A public works person traded for one of them. The fate of the rest are unknown. Many black and white taped Yankees games ended up in the heap as well. There was far more memorabilia than Schwall knew what to do with. Also, Schwall did not have the finances that was necessary to market Yankees collectibles at that time. There were two totally different worlds with respect to the value of baseball merchandise, when you compare 1973 to 2008. Schwall started his company almost a year before the demolition.

A safe used by the Yankees since 1903, when they were known as the Highlanders, was sold as scrap. Schwall couldn't give it away. Nobody wanted it. Cast iron sculptured water heaters from the Stadium were also sold as scrap. They had the Yankees logo on them. Again, nobody wanted them. Most of the scrap went to Schiavone Bonomo, a scrap outfit in New Jersey. Virtually all of it would be melted down. [30]

Forty-one-year-old L.L. "Jay" Schwall, a civil engineer graduate of the University of Kentucky, was president of Invirex. He gained demolition experience with the Cuyahoga Wrecking Co., Cleveland, Ohio; Cleveland Wrecking of Chicago, Illinois; and Wrecking Corp. of America, (WCA), New York City. He was a Chicago Cubs fan who worked on razing the Polo Grounds, the Metropolitan Opera House, and Belmont Park. His general manager at WCA knocked down Ebbets Field. Schwall assured fans, "the Stadium isn't really being destroyed. I'm a baseball fan and I'd much rather go to Yankee Stadium than Shea Stadium. It's more of a ballpark. The changes that will be made will be for the fans' comfort. If the change is good enough for Mrs. Ruth, it's good enough for me. The history will still be there." Jay Schwall, a baseball fan and sentimentalist, had a wonderful respect for the history of "The House That Ruth Built." [31]

Mr. Schwall called this particular job "selective demolition." This was because certain items would be saved, such as lights, chairs, and other equipment. Also, rather than completely knocking down the Stadium, his workers had to be careful, as most of it would be preserved. With about a dozen men clocking in for work on the first day, the figure would rise to about 50 on a daily basis. Roughly 1,000 chairs would be moved every day. A 20-foot-high wire fence surrounded the perimeter of the site. A covered sidewalk protected pedestrians from debris. May 1 was the target date for ending the demolition phase of the renovation.

Invirex-Cuyahoga sold the floodlights to the Booster Club of Saddle Brook, New Jersey, for $20,000, which in turn sold them to various Little Leagues in the area. A baseball fan in Detroit doled out $500 for a ticket booth. A Japanese department store chain procured more than $10,000 worth of keepsakes, such as groundskeepers' garments, pictures and paintings of Yankees teams and players, which they would display in their Osaka department store. Invirex-Cuyahoga donated numerous items to the National Baseball Hall of Fame and Museum in Cooperstown, New York, as well as the Smithsonian Museum in Washington, D.C. They each received a red ticket booth, located outside the Stadium's gates. Five thousand box seats went back to the Yankees to give to Box Seat ticket holders.

The other booths were taken apart and scrapped, although Schwall saved the roofs from all of them. One of his friends in Cold Spring Harbor, New York, had one of the roofs put onto a gazebo he had made. Another friend had a bed and breakfast in Maine. He used the roof to cover a salad bar at the establishment. [32]

Schwall said 40,000 seats from the demolition would be sold at $20 per box seat and $10 per grandstand seat. Michael Burke received a pair of seats. Stan Musial acquired seats for his restaurant in St. Louis. Former Yankee Jim Bouton bought a turnstile and wicker chair from the manager's office. Billy Martin came away with two stairs and a banister from the dugout. He said, "I own two stairs and a banister from the dugout. I got it when they tore the place down. I'm going to build a bar in my house and have those stairs to stand on and that banister to hang on." [33] Fritz Peterson kept the black stool he used in the locker room, as well as some seats. [34] He later gave the seats away, but kept the stool. Manny's Baseball Land, across the street from the Stadium on River Avenue, bought 3,000 Mickey Mantle brochures. [35]

Fans purchased box, grandstand, and bleacher seats, uniforms, signs, bricks, papers, and whatever else the recesses of Yankee Stadium may have held. They entered the area via the club's former executive offices, which were located at E. 161st Street. Willie Kowal, a Superintendent for Invirex-Cuyahoga, managed sales for the precious memorabilia. Turnstiles sold for $100; $15 for an usher's cap; $100 to $500 for photos of Yankees teams or scenes; bricks for $1 each; Joe Pepitone's duffel bag for $50; "IN" and "OUT" rest room door signs for $3; $10 for a groundskeeper's uniform; hot dog vendor tray for $5; a locker room scale for $75; a Gate A sign for $300; and unused 1972 playoff tickets for $2 each. [36]

Mark Forgione of Bernardsville, New Jersey, purchased seats, as did Dolores Bickenberger of Nanuet, New York. Rosalie Negrini of Ridgefield Park, New Jersey, bought a seat for her husband's anniversary present. Anthony and Popy Guarente spent $200 on a large photo of Joe DiMaggio swinging a bat. NBC bought 500 seats and installed them for the audience of "Saturday Night Live." A few dozen seats made their way to War Memorial Stadium in Greensboro, North Carolina. Sandy Ackerman, who was once a Yankees batboy, glumly visited the site. He said, "This place is nude. It doesn't look the same. This has to be, or was the best field in baseball. Now look at it. Well, this is one beautiful place, no matter what they do to it. This is still Yankee Stadium." [37]

E.J. Korvette's, a New York area department store, was selling Yankee Stadium grandstand (Reserved) seats for $7.50 and five empty Winston Crush-Proof Boxes, or one Winston Cigarette Crush-Proof Box Carton End Flap. The offer was good May 11 thru May 25 at the Korvette's Sporting Goods Department. Seats had to be picked up at the Winston Garage, 622 West 57th Street, New York City. This offer was good for people 21 years of age or older. [38] Korvette's did not obtain their seats from Invirex-Cuyahoga, but rather through a private entrepreneur. A few years later, Stamford House Wrecking, in Stamford, Connecticut, had Yankee Stadium seats for sale.

The Reserved seats weighed about 45 pounds each, and measured about 19 inches wide and 31½ inches tall. The seats were 13¼ inches deep, and 15 inches off the ground. The bottom of the seat had six slats, and the back contained three.

The gray fiberglass bleacher seats were cut into sections weighing about 40 pounds each. They measured 10 inches wide and stood 14 inches above the ground on metal legs. The trouble was that virtually nobody was interested in the bleacher seats. Schwall related that Invirex-Cuyahoga sold no bleacher seats to Korvette's due to the lack of interest by fans. The bleacher seats just stayed in the demolition company's yard.

Ron Swoboda came away with four seats, which he gave to announcer Don Criqui. The famous boxing author and owner of the magazine, *Boxing Illustrated*, Bert Randolph Sugar, handled some promotions for the Yankees. He took advantage of the offer from the Yankees to take virtually anything he wanted, as he seemed to be one of the few people at the time who realized what valuable treasures these were. He paid the Yankees with two checks and loaded 17 U-Haul trucks with memorabilia such as lockers, chairs, plaques, uniforms, documents, Jacob Ruppert's original stock certificate, and even a copy of one of Babe Ruth's contracts. He donated numerous items to the Baseball Hall of Fame. [39]

John Peterman, known as J. Peterman, purchased a treasure trove of Yankee Stadium items from Jay Schwall in 1998. Peterman put these items in his December 1998 Catalog, including the Longines scoreboard clock, which listed at $20,000 and measured 9" thick x 49.5" high x 40.25" wide; the famous walnut Hammond organ played by Toby Wright, measuring 27" wide x 51" long x 42" high historical artifact and marked at $7,500; two red and chrome Perey turnstiles, measuring 27" x 32" x 22", for $5,000 each; 24" x 36" reproduction blueprints of Osborn Engineering Company's plans of Yankee Stadium for $100 each; a cracked Elston Howard baseball bat for $2,500; four pine chairs that were the original box seats from Yankee

Stadium in 1923 at $2,500 each; two pitching rubbers at $2,000 each.; two big pieces of the copper frieze; 12 small circles of the copper frieze; a replica of home plate signed by Mayor Lindsay and the 1974 team; a 1925 team picture; a 1948 Yankee Corporate Book; 10+ four-foot-tall copper letters from the outside sign that spelled "YANKEE STADIUM"; a kiosk top from a ticket booth; and a bronze 200-pound Babe Ruth Plaza marker. The original Babe Ruth Plaza marker was stolen and later returned. It was found under some trash found under the stands. A new one had already been cast to replace the original. [40]

By early 1974, seven construction contracts had been agreed to by the city. Walsh Construction Company of New York City acted as construction manager for the whole project. Walsh Construction was a division of the Guy F. Atkinson Company of California. Frank McLasty, the project manager for the joint venture, said all non-structural objects from the Stadium would be torn down.

Invirex-Cuyahoga used a Manitowoc 4000 crawler to lift the facade and roof sections to the ground. Wrecking balls demolished concrete decks and partitions in the lower levels and accessible areas of the ballpark. Crews used jackhammers to dismantle covered and upper elevations of the structure where heavy equipment bore too much weight for the area or was too large to be accommodated. They also used two Melroe Bobcats (Models 371 and 600) with hydraulic hammers on the low roof between the two walls to accomplish this feat. Caterpillar Model 977K loaders were among those used to transfer debris from the field to dump trucks.

To lower the inside top wall by five feet, a panelization method was used. Jackhammers broke the concrete and cut the rebars into nine-ton sections. The Manitowoc 4000 lowered these portions to the ground, where crews separated the steel and concrete. Completion of the roof dismantling occurred in November.

Farewell, copper trademark and iconic scoreboard

Invirex-Cuyahoga started removing six-ton sections of timber and steel from the roof in October 1973, with a Lorain 9115 tower crane. The Manitowoc 4000 took over and finished the task, as it was more mobile. The insulated lumber was in fine shape, so it was resold. The steel went for scrap, as did the famous copper frieze. Schwall remembered seeing two indentations on the downed frieze, caused by Mickey Mantle's two left-handed mammoth home runs. [41] One blast came against the Washington Senators' Pedro Ramos on May 30, 1956, the other towering shot off Bill Fischer of the Kansas City A's in the 11th inning of a game on May 22, 1963. Both of these segments were also lost to history. Once on the ground, the prominent icon was taken apart with an axe and blow torch. Arnold Kahn, who owned All State Metal in Albany, New York, purchased all the copper and brass for $75,000 and melted it down. [42]

Nothing defined Yankee Stadium more than its copper scalloped frieze, which many fans called the façade. The length of each panel measured 26'1 15/16" or 42'. Not long after being installed, oxidation caused the copper to turn the same green color as the Statue of Liberty. *The Olean (NY) Evening Herald* published a photo and story titled, "New Yankee Baseball Stadium Topped By Copper Cornice Weighing 15 Tons." The January 16, 1923, article stated, "One of the most striking features of the new stadium will be the copper cornice weighing 15 tons that will surmount the roof. . . .The Yankee management wanted a frieze of soft green color to blend with the green of the grass, and planned galvanized metal at first. But when they found how much it would cost to paint it often enough to keep it from rusting, they turned to copper, which will be as permanent as the concrete on which the stadium is built."

An October 9, 1923, article in *The Mansfield (Ohio) News* declared, "Both the cornice and bat were done in copper because of the permanency of that metal and the fact that both its perfect resistance to the weather and in lightness preclude the possibility of repairs ever having to be made." The bat they referred to was the three-foot-long copper baseball bat that served as a weather vane. A copper baseball sat above the bat. [43]

The rival New York Giants had a frieze or decoration that ringed their Polo Grounds grandstand. Since the two teams were not on the friendliest of terms, maybe the American League upstarts wanted to outclass their National League counterparts by displaying a more prominent one that was unlike any other.

Finding out who designed the frieze or how the design was arrived at has been elusive at best. Possibly the idea came from the airiness and dignity of an opera house, such as the Arena di Verona in Italy, the Komische Opera House in Berlin, Germany, or New York City. Jacob Ruppert was a big opera fan. Or, perhaps, one of the numerous viaducts or railroad trestles that dot the east coast of the United States. Quite possibly, Jacob Ruppert or one of the engineers who designed Yankee Stadium felt such an expression of art would lend an air of dignity to baseball's grandest arena.

The plans from Osborn Engineering, the firm that designed Yankee Stadium, called for the frieze to be made of 22 gauge Toncan copper. The idea of a wooden frieze was bandied about, but it would have to be painted yearly. A 1923 ad by United Alloy Steel Corp., of Canton, Ohio, ran the headline, "Tons of Toncan went into this stadium." The flyer said, "Toncan is commercially pure iron, alloyed with just the right amount of copper, which gives it the greatest possible resistance to rust." Molybdenum alloyed with the copper made the iron non-corrosive.

In part, the ad also claimed, "Toncan is anti-corrosive and rust resisting." [44] Copper's green patina also resisted glare from the sun. Harry Swanson, in his book, *Ruthless Baseball*, credited Kinnear Manufacturing of Columbus, Ohio, with installing the original 1923 frieze.

The October 1937 issue of the "Bulletin of Copper & Brass Research Association" in New York called the ballpark's topper the largest copper frieze in the world. The extension of the right field grandstand for several thousand fans also added more copper frieze. The story said the Stadium's frieze now contained 43 tons of 16-ounce copper. The narrative went on to say the Hermann & Grace Co. installed 36 tons of copper in the Stadium in 1923 and that A.E. Carlson used 50,000 pounds of copper to extend the 1937 frieze expansion. [45]

According to Jay Schwall in a June, 2011 interview with the author, all of the frieze that ringed the grandstand roof of Yankee Stadium was 100 percent pure copper. No alloy was mixed in. There was no iron or molybdenum in the frieze. He emphatically stated to the author that there was no iron or any other material in the famous frieze. There may have been in other copper to be found around the famous ballpark, but the iconic trademark of the Bronx Bombers was only made of only pure copper, as were the large letters on the outside of the arena that said "YANKEE STADIUM." [46] He remembers popping out about 20 round discs from the frieze by hand. They were not soldered, but were placed hand tight on the frieze.

Jay Schwall provided information about demolition figures to the author over the telephone.

As of September 1973:

Scrap Iron -- 1,600 tons

Copper Scrap (non-frieze)-- 60+ tons

Copper Frieze -- 70 tons (Approximately 120,000 square feet). The frieze was tacked on with solder, and was less than 1/16 of an inch thick. The frieze was #2 thin copper.

Total Copper -- over 100 tons. Over half of it was wiring.
Non-Ferrous (no iron) Scrap -- 112 tons -- copper, stainless steel, brass, etc.

Recycled Steel Beams -- 115 tons

Wood Scrap -- 400,000 board linear feet

Recycled Lumber -- 100,000 board linear feet

Total Trucking and Disposal Cost -- $101,322

Labor Man Hours -- 30,000 Man Hours

Approximately 3,700 quarts of milk for Union Burners (Torch Men). Men cutting steel got 2 quarts of milk a day. This was supposed to counter all the lead fumes they inhaled.

Approximately 15,000 tons of concrete.

7,300 cubic yards of dirt -- the field was lowered five feet so that lower box seats could be tilted for better viewing.

Contract with City of New York -- $984,040 and $75,645 for extras. Extras referred to hidden items that were found in the construction of Yankee Stadium or the field that were not found on blueprints.

Income from scrap and useable materials -- $205,804

Income from chairs, signs, uniforms, etc. -- $97,515

Total Income - $1,363,006

Total Cost - $1,304,485 [47]

The iconic electric Yankees scoreboard was erected in early 1959. At 113 feet wide by 45 feet high, it was the largest scoreboard in the major leagues. The tower in the center rose to 75 feet. Henry (Lon) Keller, a well-known American artist, designed the $300,000 mammoth. He also produced the official Yankees top hat logo, which made its first appearance in 1946.

The Spencer Display Corporation, 271 Madison Avenue, New York, constructed it. With 11,210 bulbs and 115,000 watts, it contained 619,000 feet of electric cable, 4,860 push buttons on the master control console, and weighed 25 tons. This did not include the steel support structure. The front of the non-glare black enamel scoreboard contained 4,872 square feet. Letters and numbers measured 22 inches high.

The message board, located in the middle, had seven lines at the bottom of the tower that could flash messages. Each line could flash up to eight characters. The left side of the scoreboard carried information about the Yankees game, such as the score, balls, strikes, and outs. The right portion told the time, scores of the other American and National League games, and the umpires. In the end, this famous feature was sold for scrap, as was the electronic Longines time sign above the Gate 4 entrance. [48]

Ball field dimensions were part of the planned changes for the upcoming structure:

	1973 Yankee Stadium	1976 Yankee Stadium
right field foul line	296 feet	310 feet
left field foul line	301 feet	312 feet
deepest center field	461 feet	417 feet
seating capacity	64,644	52,671

The newly remodeled Stadium field slope would incline from outfield to infield. The current field was just the opposite. Sodium vapor lights would encircle the new roof instead of the present group of six floodlights.

New homes for Houk and MacPhail

A stunning press conference at Tiger Stadium on October 11 occurred when the team announced the hiring of Ralph Houk as manager for $75,000 a year. The word was that George Steinbrenner had undermined Houk's job as Yankees skipper by making disparaging comments about certain players and about how things should be handled on the field and off. People close to the situation thought this contributed heavily towards the downfall of the Yankees in the last couple of months of the season. Detroit's General Manager, Jim Campbell, would allow Houk the freedom to run the team as he saw fit – just as Michael Burke had done. George Steinbrenner's constant interference apparently was a major factor in Houk's surprise resignation as Yankee manager.

As Houk put it, "I went fishing for a few days after Campbell called me last Sunday [October 7] and I couldn't quit thinking about it. And the more I thought about it the more excited I got. I had been with the Yankees 35 years. I think I had just been there too long. I was tired of saying the same things to the same players every day." Houk replaced interim manager Joe Schultz, who had taken over the managing responsibilities after Billy Martin was fired on August 30. Since the Tigers were an older team, Houk knew he'd have to rebuild the lineup with younger players. [49]

The Yankees shook things up as well when they hired executive vice president Talbot Smith from the Houston Astros on November 1. He replaced Lee MacPhail, who had been elected president of the American League. Gabe Paul, president of the Yankees, had worked with Smith during a stint with the Cincinnati Reds 16 years earlier, and with the Astros 12 years earlier. Paul said if MacPhail had not attained his new rank, he would currently be the Yankees' president.

The current adminstration terminated the position of general manager, as they deemed it an "outmoded concept." Running a baseball club was too complicated now. Smith knew the importance of being the third-highest member in the Yankees organization. As he explained, "The Yankee image and tradition are number one among the 24 teams in the big leagues. I feel the Yankees have talent and are making strides. To join them is a real tribute, and I'm excited by the challenge." [50]

New York City Mayor, John V. Lindsay, above, and New York Yankees president, Michael Burke, below, were responsible for the renovation of Yankee Stadium. Photo of John Lindsay is courtesy of the LBJ Museum, Austin, TX. Michael Burke sent me the signed photo below.

This ad appeared in "Wrecking and Salvage Journal Magazine." Printed with the permission of Jay Schwall and Mack Maloney.

AVAILABLE END OF BASEBALL SEASON FROM

YANKEE STADIUM

Modernization of THE HOUSE THAT RUTH BUILT Makes the following available:

60,000 Stadium Seats...Complete field lighting system... Modern electric score board...Bar, Restaurant & Concession Equipment...All mechanical equipment and Auxiliaries... Half-million board feet of 2 x 6 T & G Lumber.

For additional information and detailed list
CONTACT:

Jay Schwall or Ray Berke

INVIREX - CUYAHOGA

Joint Venture

2-01 55th Avenue L.I.C., NY 11101 (212) 937-8104 (314) 731-3060

Jay Schwall and family during the renovation. Courtesy of Jay Schwall.

This was my first visit to the Stadium after the renovation began. I had easy access onto the field. This view is from the outfield looking towards the infield. The view below is from the visitors bullpen in left field, October 20, 1973. (Mickey Mantle's birthday).

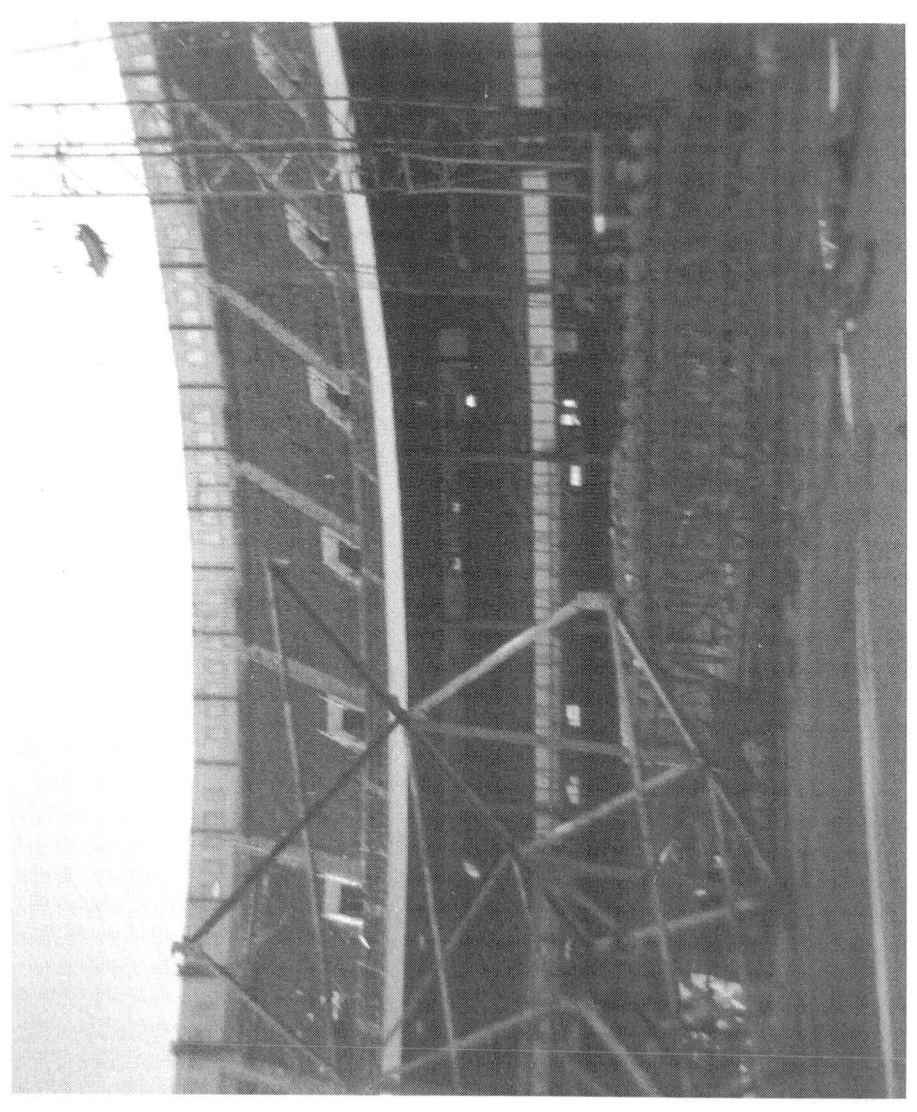

Parts of seating, lights, metal skeleton, and the trademark frieze lay on the field, October 20, 1973.

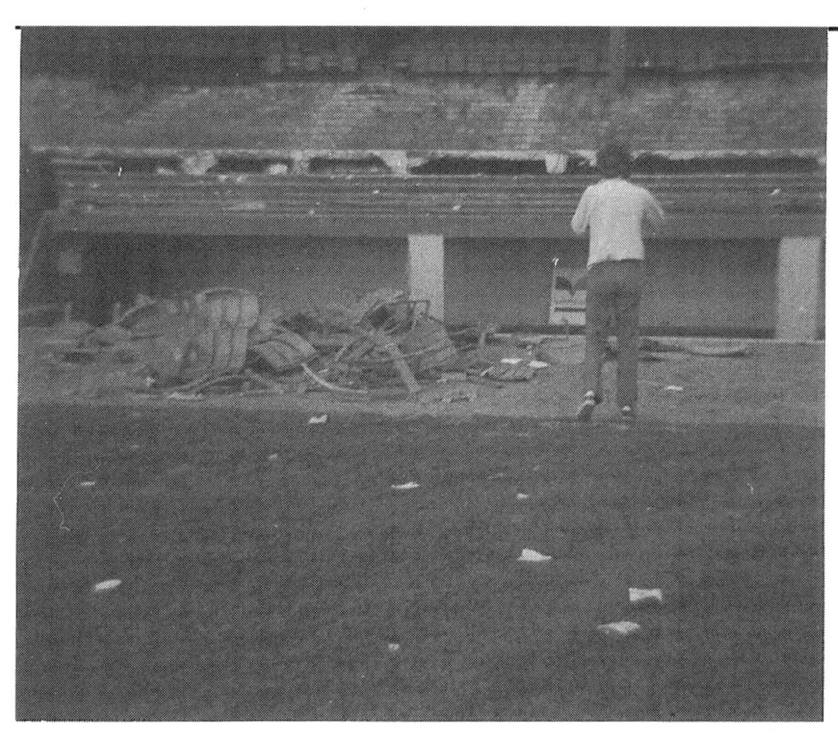

Broken seating in front of dugout, October 20, 1973.

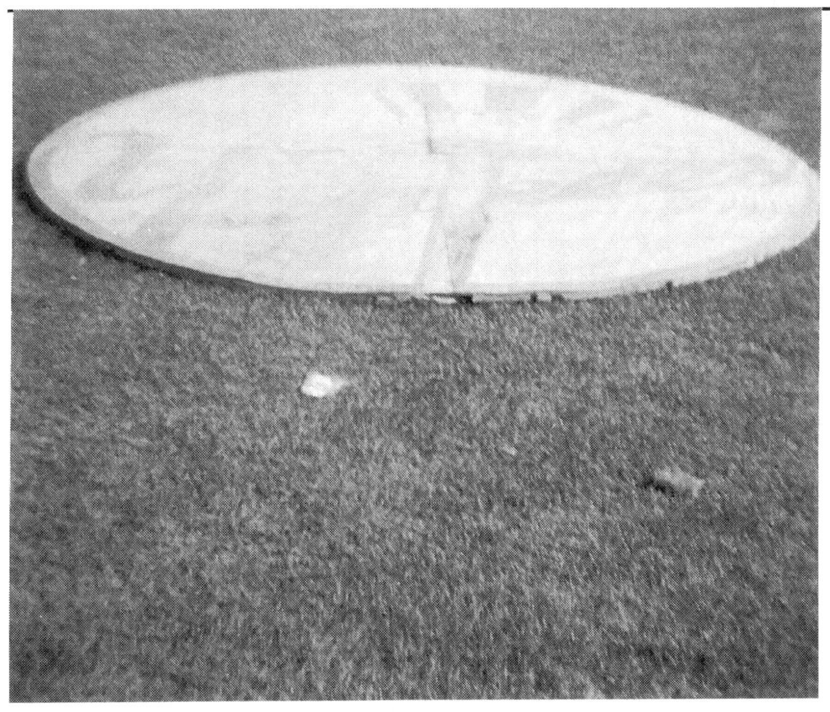

The famous Yankee logo sitting on the field, October 20, 1973.

Much of the frieze is still adorning the stadium, while some seats lay on the field with mounds of field dirt, October 20, 1973.

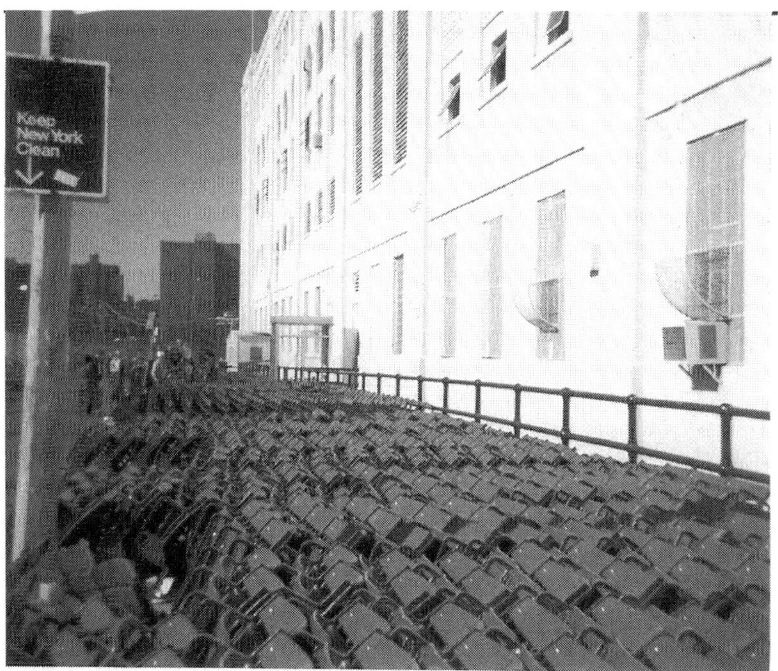

Rows of seating lined up outside the stadium wall, October 20, 1973.

Yankee Stadium at sunset. Courtesy of Jay Schwall.

Renovation frieze removal. Photo courtesy of Jay Schwall.

A crane at work during the Yankee Stadium renovation. Photo courtesy of Jay Schwall.

We still had our beloved voices

Yankees fans were glad that some things would not change during the Stadium's upheaval. While growing up, we always felt closer to our heroes on the diamond because of the friendly banter of the men in the radio or TV booth. We connected with them. They were all part of our family. I can still hear Phil Rizzuto calling Bill White, "White." Or wishing someone a speedy recovery from a recent illness. We also learned a lot about baseball strategy from their experience as ballplayers and the many baseball stories they'd tell. They liked each other, and that came through. The Yankees would continue their broadcasts with our TV and radio friends.

The team had quite a long history of communicating with their fans. KDKA radio in Pittsburgh, Pennsylvania, broadcast the first-ever baseball game on radio in 1921, when the Pirates thrashed the Phillies, 8-0. That same year, the first radio broadcast of a World Series game occurred, when the Yankees beat the Giants, 3-0. Baseball was on its way into the homes of America when WJZ radio, out of Newark, New Jersey, and WGY from Schenectady, New York, transmitted the complete 1922 World Series over the airwaves.

The next year, when Yankee Stadium opened, Graham McNamee began his baseball announcing career. He enthusiastically broadcast the 1923 World Series on New York radio station WEAF, which was the predecessor of WNBC.

The Yankees first broadcast games on a regular basis in 1939. Arch McDonald, Garnett Marks, and a youngster named Mel Allen announced the games on radio. Other names that would bring listeners play-by-play of the Bronx Bombers through the years up to the 1970s remodeling of Yankee Stadium included the likes of Connie Desmond, Russ Hodges, Bill Slater, Jim Woods, Red Barber, Jerry Coleman, Phil Rizzuto, Frank Messer, Bill White, Joe Garagiola, and Bob Gamere. Not all of the famous Yankees lore came from the field. Much of it also came from the supporting cast.

Mel Allen, the legendary Yankees announcer, was famous for exclaiming, "How about that!" and "That ball is going, going, gone." These words became Allen's trademark signatures. Mel also called a home run a "Ballantine Blast." "The Voice of the Yankees" stayed on for 26 years, through 1964. The Alabama native, educated as a lawyer, introduced Lou Gehrig to the packed Yankee Stadium throng on July 4, 1939, for the tearful Lou Gehrig Day ceremony. He also introduced Babe Ruth to the fans during the Bambino's last Stadium appearance on June 13, 1948. To be sure, Mel had many happy memories from his post, such as Joe DiMaggio Day, held October 1, 1949. He dubbed the great DiMag “Joltin’ Joe,” and Tommy Henrich “Old Reliable.” He called many Yankees Old Timers’ Day games from the ball field. He even came out of retirement in 1978 to broadcast Yankees games on cable TV.

Another legendary broadcaster, Walter Lanier "Red" Barber, announced games for the Cincinnati Reds from 1934-1938, the Brooklyn Dodgers from 1939-1953, then joined Mel Allen in the Yankees broadcast booth in 1954. Perhaps his most famous call was when Dodgers left fielder Al Gionfriddo robbed Joe DiMaggio of a double or triple in game six of the 1947 World Series. Snuffy Stirnweiss and Yogi Berra were on base at the time. The Yankees won the World Series in seven games. Barber was famous for such country expressions as, "the catbird seat" and "tearin' up the pea patch." "The Ol' Redhead" ended his term with the Yankees in 1966 after he let it be known on TV that only 413 people attended a game on September 22 of that year. That was the year the team finished in last place. It's funny that two southerners, Allen, from Alabama, and Barber, from Mississippi, both ended up in Yankee Stadium. And both were loved!

Phil Rizzuto, Bill White, and Frank Messer dominated the play-by-play during the 1970s, on WPIX-TV, Channel 11, and WMCA radio, 570 AM. This team spent 15 seasons upstairs for the Yankees.

Rizzuto, who would be elected to the National Baseball Hall of Fame in 1994, had a spectacular career as the Yankees shortstop from 1941-1956. The Dodgers had turned down the Brooklyn-born “Scooter” because they said he was too small. They ate crow many a time, especially when he was voted the American League’s MVP in 1950. In 1957 he joined the broadcast team, and excitedly called Roger Maris’ 61st home run in 1961, which eclipsed Babe Ruth’s mark of 60 for a season, set in 1927.

Phil permeated the broadcast scene with his catchphrase, “Holy Cow!” and, if someone did something he didn’t approve of, that person became a “Huckleberry.” He brought warmth and humor to the booth. He was a Yankee through and through. His record 40 years broadcasting Yankees games is a testament to his legacy.

Frank Messer called games for the Baltimore Orioles starting in 1964, before landing in New York in 1968, when he replaced Joe Garagiola. He’ll be remembered for his warmth, smooth voice, and dignity. While Rizzuto and White would often engage in antics, Messer focused on the game. He also served as master of ceremonies for the memorable Yankees Old Timers’ Day games. I still remember one year he did so on crutches on the field. Another memory I have was on September 30, 1973, the last game before the renovation. Messer was walking on the warning track from left field and saw I wanted to take a picture of him. He stopped to pose and smile. I still have the photo.

Frank Messer will always have a very soft spot in my heart because he was always a kind, dignified gentleman. He left the Yankees in 1985. He retired after spending 1986 and 1987 broadcasting Chicago White Sox games with Don Drysdale. Messer continued to act as Master of Ceremonies for the Old Timers' games through 1997, well after he was done broadcasting games.

Bill White had a fine career playing first base for 13 years for three National League teams, most notably the St. Louis Cardinals. The Gold Glove winner joined the Yankees broadcast crew in 1971, becoming the first black person to broadcast for a major league team. He and Phil Rizzuto had many funny exchanges on the air. White also brought a seriousness and dignity to the game. He analyzed games and explained it to viewers in language they could understand. Fans liked and respected him in his 18 years in the booth. The same could be said for Major League Baseball, as he served as president of the National League from 1989 thru 1994.

Of all the eminent people manning a microphone at Yankee Stadium, perhaps the top position goes to Bob Sheppard, the public address announcer. Dubbed "The Voice of God," by Yankees slugger Reggie Jackson, Sheppard opened games by saying, "Good afternoon (or evening) ladies and gentlemen, and welcome to Yankee Stadium. Here are the starting lineups..." During the game, the crowd would then hear the booming voice enunciate, "Your attention please, ladies and gentlemen, now batting for the Yankees. . ." since April 17, 1951. Mr. Sheppard retired in 2008 due to illness and died in 2010 at the age of 99. His spectacular career spanned 53 years and over 4,200 games.

Born in Richmond Hills, Queens, the former high school speech teacher also stayed on as a speech professor at St. John's University, in Queens. Scheduling classes around his public address schedule, he said simply, "I think my teaching has been, or was, more important in my life than public address, [because] teaching was more important than public address announcing in its value to society." He laughed when adding, "I have received many, many letters, phone calls and visits from former students. I've never received a visit, a phone call or a letter from any athlete that I've introduced." [51]

The distinctive voice of the New York Yankees began his career at a New York Yankees football game vs. the Chicago Rockets in Freeport, Long Island. He also did a stint for the Brooklyn Dodgers football team, and missed only about five Yankee games during his illustrious career. This was quite an impressive record for someone who was a Giants baseball fan before the Bronx Bombers came calling.

Sheppard's favorite baseball moments included Don Larsen pitching baseball's only perfect World Series game vs. the Brooklyn Dodgers on October 8, 1956; Roger Maris hitting 61 home runs in 1961 to eclipse the record of Babe Ruth; Chris Chambliss hitting the game-winning homer in the bottom of the ninth inning of Game 5 of the 1976 American League Championship Series against the Kansas City Royals to propel the Yankees into their first World Series in 12 years; and Reggie Jackson blasting three consecutive home runs against the Los Angeles Dodgers in Game 6 of the 1977 World Series.

Sheppard routinely arrived at the Stadium three or four hours before the first pitch. Of all the names he called, Mickey Mantle's remained his favorite because of the double "M" and its strong ending. It had a nice rhythm to it. Mickey said he'd get shivers when Sheppard said his name, and Bob said he'd get shivers saying it. [52]

Toby Wright was the first Yankee Stadium organist from 1965 to 1966. He played a Lowery organ. Wright was a local pianist and Lowery demonstrator. Eddie Layton took over and played the new 50,000-watt Hammond organ at Yankee Stadium from 1967 thru 1970. Both talented gentlemen also played at Madison Square Garden for the New York Knicks basketball team and New York Rangers hockey team.

Toby Wright returned in 1971 and left this post in 1977, when Eddie Layton returned to serenade the Yankees masses. Wright was best known for playing "Pomp and Circumstance" when ace lefty reliever Sparky Lyle came in from the bullpen to extinguish many opposing rallies.

Robert Merrill, the great baritone opera singer, regularly sang at New York's Metropolitan Opera House at Lincoln Center. He also honored Yankees fans by frequently singing the National Anthem at baseball games, starting in 1969. He normally did so on Opening Day and many Old Timers' Day games, when he wore his pinstriped uniform, with the number 1 ½ on the back.

Pete Sheehy - the luckiest man behind the scenes

Perhaps the greatest non-playing Yankee of all was Michael "Pete" Sheehy, who was every inch the Yankee that Babe Ruth was. Perhaps, even more. This unsung hero was the clubhouse man for the New York Yankees from 1927 thru 1985. He began his career as one of the luckiest men on the face of the earth, when, at age 15, Fred Logan, the Yankees equipment manager, asked Sheehy, "Son, will you help me with some equipment?" Pete had been waiting for the gates of the grand ballpark to open. Later, while sitting on a trunk, Logan asked "Silent Pete," as he called the lad, to come around the next day. The next day turned into 58 years.

Pete's military service in the Pacific from 1942 to 1945 carried over into the way he worked the clubhouse. Fred Logan was still in the clubhouse when Pete left, but retired by the time the war veteran returned. As Nick Priore, assistant to Sheehy since 1971, related, "I don't know if you've ever noticed, but the shirts would be hanging on the left side of the locker, and the pants would be hanging two hooks away. Pete was very military-minded. He liked things to be orderly." Before Priore, "Little Pete" Previte had been Pete Sheehy's lucky assistant since 1942.

While Pete Sheehy enjoyed Babe Ruth, he loved Lou Gehrig. The Babe would frequently ask Pete to get him a "bi," short for bicarbonate. "The Babe was a big, lovable fellow–always a kid. The Babe never had a uniform fitted in his life. He had to take it right off the shelf." As for Lou Gehrig, Pete said, "What a sweet man he was. He became one of my best friends, a quiet gentle fellow, no conceit, no bombast at all."

"DiMaggio was a shy man," said Sheehy. Joe DiMaggio would always have the trusted Sheehy get him a "Cup of coffee, Pete, but only half a cup." Pete said that of all the players, DiMaggio was the most perfect. "DiMaggio never made a mental mistake, he was the greatest all-around player of them all. I rate him with the greatest."

"No man ever swung a bat with more power" was his assessment of Mickey Mantle. "He was a powerful man. Too bad he didn't have stronger legs."

Whether getting coffee, Coca Cola, more boxes of baseballs to autograph, picking up clothes the players dropped on the floor, polishing shoes, or washing and hanging up uniforms, Pete was there. Of the famous pinstripes, Sheehy once said, "I think it's a beautiful uniform. It's conservative, but it's beautiful. I don't know. It does something to you." While he was mostly in the clubhouse during the games, he said, "I sneak out for an inning or two, but it's before and after the games that I get to see the players most. And that's when you really get to know them." [53]

The Yankees honored Pete Sheehy by renaming the renovated Stadium's clubhouse, "The Pete Sheehy Clubhouse." It came complete with a plaque that was adorned with Pete's face on it. This beloved friend of the Yankees died of a heart attack at age 75 in a New Jersey hospital on August 13, 1985. With him went many memories and secrets that we can only dream about. Players wore a black armband in Pete's honor. [54]

Costs, costs, and more costs

New York City officials may have thought about wearing them as well when *The New York Times* reported in its November 16 issue that the cost of renovating the Stadium and surrounding area had risen to $49.9 million. This came about after the City Planning Commission approved an appropriation for another $15.9 million to cover increasing labor and construction costs, as well as design modifications. Another $10 million was added to the 1974-1975 capital budget to upgrade the neighborhood around the Stadium, thus bringing the total cost up to the latest tally. The Board of Estimate and City Council still had to endorse the increase. Budget Director David A. Grossman said the final cost would be higher or lower, based on bids by construction companies for work to be performed. Grossman declared these funds were needed to cover contracts already committed, additional agreements to be bid, and revisions of the original reconstruction plans.

He explained that the extra money would be used for upgrading subway stations, landscaping, street lighting, an entrance plaza to Yankee Stadium, and a pedestrian footbridge from a parking area in the nearby Bronx Terminal Market to the stadium plaza. [55]

Mayor-elect Abraham Beame, who had initially opposed Mayor Lindsay's plan of rehabilitating Yankee Stadium and environs due to so many unanswered questions from Lindsay, had now committed himself to the project. He really had no choice. It was just as Lindsay said. The project was so far along by now that to abandon it would make the whole undertaking a white elephant. How could the city now stop the progress dead in its tracks? They would have an expensive eyesore in its wake. It was either that or complete the job, and hope for a nice return on the investment once the Yankees returned to the Bronx.

Matthew Troy, Jr., chairman of the City Council's Finance Committee, threatened to stop further financing of the renovation. He called the project a "bottomless pit." Troy, the Democratic leader of Queens County, sent a letter to the Mayor, stating, "It is my intention now to ask for an immediate halt to this project until we get some concrete answers about projected costs and projected value to the city." He angrily went on to say that the Mayor "has deliberately deceived us as to the costs. I sometimes wonder why we do not tear the entire Yankee Stadium down and build over again rather than do what we are doing now." [56]

Troy was fully aware the Pittsburgh Pirates had built a new stadium for $45 million and the Cincinnati Reds had erected a ball park for $25 million within the past decade. New York City's Economic Development Administrator, Ken Patton, asserted that replacing Yankee Stadium with a new stadium on the present Yankee Stadium site would cost $80 million. This figure came from three architectural-engineering firms, who calculated costs based on the expenditures of the Pittsburgh and Cincinnati stadiums, as well as New York's construction costs. A spokesman for the Mayor said, "all cost factors on Yankee Stadium are publicly known and have been fully explained to the Board of Estimate." [57]

On November 16, the Board of Estimate reluctantly approved the $15.9 million funding requested earlier in the month for the renovation. The vote was 14 to 8. Among those voting against the modernization were Manhattan Borough President Percy Sutton, Staten Island President Robert T. Connor, and City Council President Sanford Garelik. Although administration bureaucrats contemplated that delaying the vote would further hike the cost of the Stadium modernization, they thought the city was too far into the project to abandon it. The City Council and Matthew Troy, Jr., still had to approve the appropriation. Troy proposed that a new football stadium be built next to Shea Stadium at a cost of $25 million, rather than continuing to pour money into Yankee Stadium and its never ending mounting costs. At the meeting, Ken Patton said there were still a "large number of unknowns" with respect to inflation and letting of contracts.

This came after a $50 million capital budget amendment was okayed to begin building a controversial $200 million convention center on the Hudson River, between 43rd and 47th Streets. That poll was 18 to 4, with Bronx Borough President Robert Abrams and Brooklyn Borough President Sebastian Leone voting against the measure. [58]

When the City Council met on November 20, they agreed to wait one week before choosing whether or not to approve these two quarrelsome issues. For one thing, Troy wanted Kinney

Systems, Inc., to explain the costs of building two parking garages near the Stadium, as the city had the option of buying them once completed. The estimated cost was $22 million. The hearing lasted from 10 a.m. to 6:50 p.m. Three hours were dedicated to Yankee Stadium.

Officials from the Mayor's office said that canceling the Stadium project would cost the city over $16 million. Sanford Freeman, special assistant corporation counsel for the city, explained that the requested $15.9 million was necessary to complete the renovation, or it would have to be dead in the water. The city would have to pay $10.5 million in existing contracts and at least $3 million for the land. With those facts, the Board of Estimate grudgingly approved more money. They also agreed to fund the convention center. [59]

Also in November, the city asked the Board of Estimate to allow the Yankees to rent Shea Stadium for $1 a year for the next two years to help compensate revenue losses on the sale of concessions. The Mets refused these earnings to the Yankees, as such earnings were guaranteed to the Mets in their contract with the city. The Mets argued that they would lose some of their fans to their Bronx rivals. Apparently, revenues from the sale of concessions meant the difference between profit and loss for the season.

The estimated loss to the Yankees would be $1.4 million over the course of two years, according to Sanford Freeman. Consequently, the city wanted to let the Yankees keep the parking fees when they played at Shea. Freeman projected the Yankees would collect $556,000 in parking fees over this time period. The team would save $374,624 in rent payments to the city, but still be $500,000 in the red due to concession earnings lost over the two years. [60]

At the City Council meeting of November 27, the group approved funding for the Yankee Stadium and West Side Convention Center projects. They voted 27 to 9, with one abstention, to budget the $15.9 million for Yankee Stadium and $50 million for the convention center.

Matthew Troy, Jr., led the opposition against funding for Yankee Stadium. The Finance Committee overrode his vote. This was the first time he could remember this event happening. Besides Troy, those who voted against backing the Yankee Stadium modernization were: Edward V. Curry, Anthony Gaeta, and Frank J. Biondolillo. They were Councilmen from Staten Island. Thomas J. Manton, Walter Ward, and Arthur J. Katzman, all from Queens, did so as well. Eldon R. Clingan and Charles Taylor rounded out the group. Manhattan Councilman, Theodore S. Weiss, abstained.

Troy had previously threatened to block any action regarding Yankee Stadium unless Mayor Lindsay gave him the total amount the restoration would cost. Although Lindsay said it would come to $40 million, after two long hearings, Troy felt that $72 million would be a far more accurate number. This would prove to be a never ending battle. [61]

The city gave the Yankees a nice holiday present on December 28, when the Board of Estimate unanimously voted to let the team lease Shea Stadium for $1 per year and pay a mere $760 per game for operating expenses. This came to $61,800 annually. The club would also be able to keep up to $450,000 in parking fees. Anything above that would be divided equally with the city. This was the last board meeting in Mayor Lindsay's administration. Democrat Abraham Beame had defeated Republican State Senator John Marchi, and would become the next Mayor of New York City on January 1, 1974. He would face the city's worst financial crisis in its history, in which the threat of bankruptcy was an ever-looming threat. Yankee Stadium's escalating costs didn't help matters. [62]

Chapter Four

TWO YEARS ON THE ROAD

Charles Finley and free agency

Abraham Beame took over the reins as Mayor of New York City on January 1, 1974. John Vliet Lindsay spent his last day as Mayor with his family at the Plaza Hotel, where they had lived the past few days. The day before proved to be crammed with events. One thing he did was to appear on a CBS morning news show, which explored his successes and disappointments as Mayor for the past eight years. He also rode the subway, gave medals to the City Hall policemen's softball team, and met with 20 City Planning Commission planners. Lindsay reappointed John Zuccotti as chairman of the Commission. The Mayor signed the documents allowing the Yankees to play baseball at Shea Stadium for 1974 and 1975. Lee MacPhail, the outgoing general manager of the Yankees, signed the agreement on behalf of the team. Well-wishers threw Mayor Lindsay a farewell party at City Hall.

Upon leaving office, he and his wife, Mary, flew to the islands of Puerto Rico and St. Vincent. They rented a 40-foot sailboat and cruised the Caribbean for one month. After returning to New York for a short time in February, the couple planned to travel in Europe for six or seven months, then reside in New York. Part of that plan would no doubt be to catch some baseball games. [1]

On January 3, the Yankees signed Bill Virdon to a one-year contract to become the 19th full-time manager of the team. This news conference occurred at the Yankees club offices in the Parks Administration Building, located near Shea Stadium. The new skipper had managed the Pittsburgh Pirates until being released late in the 1973 season.

The Yankees originally signed Dick Williams for the managerial position on December 13, 1973. However, American League president, Joe Cronin, rejected the deal, saying Williams still remained property of the Oakland Athletics. Williams quit the A's at the end of the 1973 World Series because he was fed up with the never ending meddling of team owner, Charles O. Finley. Oakland beat the Mets in seven games. Williams had led the A's to two World Series wins in the previous two years.

Part of the soap opera that was the A's was that second baseman, Mike Andrews, committed two errors in a row the twelfth inning of Game 2 of the World Series. With the score tied at 6-6 and Bud Harrelson on third and Tug McGraw on first with two outs, Willie Mays singled in Harrelson. This was to be the legend's last hit and RBI of his storied career. Cleon Jones then walked, which loaded the bases with Mets. John Milner hit a ground ball that went through Andrews' legs, scoring McGraw and Mays. The score was now 9-6. The next batter, Jerry Grote, then hit a grounder to Andrews, who threw the ball wildly past first baseman Gene Tenace. Jones then scored, making it a 10-6 ballgame.

In the bottom of the inning, Reggie Jackson hit a triple on a ball that Mays lost in the sun. Jesus Alou singled to score Jackson. The final score was 10-7. The Mets won the game and Finley lost his temper. He would eventually lose much more than that. To punish his second baseman, the furious Finley placed Andrews on the disabled list, citing a fake shoulder injury to prevent Andrews from playing in any more World Series games. Finley pressured Andrews into signing a statement saying he had this injury after being examined by Dr. Harry Walker, the team's physician. Finley said it was for the good of the team, and threatened to destroy Andrews and his career if he didn't sign the affidavit. Andrews flew home. Finley wanted minor league infielder Manny Trillo on the team, but since the post-season rosters were set, he was unable to do so. The Mets and baseball Commissioner Bowie Kuhn objected to Finley adding Trillo to the A's. Finley was livid with the Mets and Kuhn.

Word got around to Andrews' teammates when they saw Andrews was not on the airplane on the trip to New York. It was their turn to become irate. They wanted to literally throw Finley out of the plane. They knew de-pressurization of the airplane was not a healthy choice, so that prevented that action. Manager Dick Williams, however, became so disgusted with the owner, that he said he'd be quitting after the World Series ended. The A's wanted to go on strike, but knew it would hurt baseball and their loyal fans. They wore Andrews' #17 on their uniform sleeve in support of their comrade. Finley had become the pariah of baseball.

Finley held a press conference the next day, saying he hoped he could add another infielder to the roster to replace Andrews. Along with his teammates, baseball fans supported Andrews. Kuhn reinstated Andrews to the A's roster immediately, and blasted Finley for "unfairly embarrassing a player who has given many years of service to professional baseball." Andrews appeared in Game 4 of the World Series. He received a standing ovation from everyone except Finley. Andrews grounded out in the eighth inning, as a pinch hitter. Finley then ordered Andrews benched for the rest of the series. After eight years in Major League Baseball, Andrews' career was over. The team released him on November 31. He spent 1975 playing baseball in Japan. After the 1973 World Series, Dick Williams did quit the team. Kuhn fined Finley $6,500 for his World Series behavior, and another $4,500 for what he did to Mike Andrews.

The Yankees and Charles O. Finley, the A's owner, could not agree on compensation for the manager. Finley hated the Yankees and wanted them to pay heavily for Dick Williams. A big reason for his disdain of the Bronx Bombers was that before Finley owned the Athletics and the team was located in Kansas City, they would trade many players to the Yankees, and the Yankees kept winning pennants and World Series games with former A's players. Finley hoped to get Yankees center fielder Bobby Murcer or catcher Thurman Munson in reparation. The Yankees rejected this idea, along with the Yanks giving up two future prospects--outfielder Otto Velez and pitcher Scott McGregor.

Fighting the legal battle over Dick Williams would have been a long, drawn-out process, so the Yankees opted to go with Virdon. Not a bad choice, given the fact that he was a solid player and dignified gentleman of esteemed character. Yankees legend Whitey Ford replaced Jim Turner as the new pitching coach upon the latter's retirement. Former catcher Elston Howard and infielder Dick Howser had been announced as the team's first and third base coaches for the year. Jim Hegan again served as bullpen coach. Besides changes to the team, the Bronx was also undergoing a transformation. Only a few months earlier, despondent local businessmen began to believe the economic and social decay in the borough could be stopped and reversed. This led the Bronx Chamber of Commerce to commit itself to a program of action that would bring a new vitality to the 1.5 million residents of the Bronx by focusing on creating jobs. Such efforts had failed previously because the varied ethnic and racial groups were distrustful of each other. The common goal of providing employment at places such as industrial parks, became a top priority for city spending. Previously, libraries, housing, schools, and parks normally became the focus for disbursement.

The area still had the problems of crime, poverty, drug addiction, building abandonment, and other social ills. Construction projects optimistically would bring businesses and families to the Bronx, along with hope to the hopeless. Besides the renovation of Yankee Stadium, other business ventures sprang to life. The new Lincoln Hospital at 149th Street and Morris Avenue would provide hundreds of medical jobs. Thousands of jobs at Zarega Avenue and Lyons Avenue in the eastern section of the Bronx were created through new industrial parks. Another 2,000 slots would be produced on the Hunts Point peninsula with the construction of a 40-acre deep-water facility that would handle 65 percent of the meat imported into the United States.

Other such endeavors were on the board to aid the Bronx, which ranked as the fourth largest borough in New York City. This amounted to a population surpassing 15 states. Sections of the South Bronx were hindered by a 10 percent unemployment rate, which was double that of all of New York City. Even though New York City spent about $1 billion yearly to subsidize the South Bronx, at least 30,000 people in the borough were known to be jobless. It could be that Yankee Stadium was the symbol of the Bronx. The ballpark represented a community that needed a facelift and optimism. Revitalization was at long last on its way. [2] So was the crowning of a new home run king.

Hank Aaron tops The Babe

The baseball season began with a bang when Hank Aaron blasted his 714th home run in his first at-bat of the season off Cincinnati's Jack Billingham on April 4. Billingham threw a fastball in the first inning that Hank promptly drove over Riverfront Stadium's left-center field wall. Not only did that shot score three runs, but it tied one of baseball's most sacred records – tying the mighty Babe Ruth for the most lifetime home runs. Even though the Braves lost 7-6, in 11 innings, baseball fans were abuzz with the news. Naturally, the big question was when Hammerin' Hank would hit the magic #715 to break the record.

Claire Ruth, the Babe's widow, had expected Hank to do it in 1973. She felt no excitement or regret. She did not send a congratulatory telegram. "Why should I? I just wish him luck, health and no injuries." Mrs. Ruth graciously stated, "I'd like to remain out of this completely. This is Henry Aaron's day, not mine. I want Aaron to have it all." She knew that the Babe's memory and place in baseball lore would never be diminished. You can't fight a ghost.

Followers of the national pastime didn't have to wait long for the response. Atlanta Stadium's 53,775 faithful rocked the stadium on April 8, when Hank hit number 715 off Dodgers veteran pitcher Al Downing. The fastball propelled off the potent slugger's bat at 9:07 p.m. The momentous souvenir was caught by Braves relief pitcher Tom House after it sailed over the left field fence and into the bullpen. Hank Aaron, the dignified gentleman of baseball, was relieved to have the pressure behind him. He even had to worry about death threats. As Hank related, "I'm happy it's over. I feel now I can relax, my teammates can relax, and that I can go on and have a great year." [3]

The Queens Bombers

Up to the north, the Bronx Bombers inaugurated their first home season at Shea Stadium on April 6. Mayor Abraham Beame and his wife attended the event. Senator Ted Kennedy brought his son, 12-year-old Ted Kennedy Jr., to the game. The younger Kennedy, who had part of his left leg removed due to cancer, had the honor of throwing out the first ball. He delivered a high strike to catcher Thurman Munson from the pitcher's mound. Principal owner George Steinbrenner, a friend of the American royalty family, arranged for the Senator's son's Opening Day thrill. Steinbrenner couldn't attend the game, as he was indicted the day before for allegedly giving illegal contributions to political campaigns. He didn't want to detract from the historic day. The players supported their new owner and hoped he would be found "not guilty."

The Yanks used the New York Jets football team locker room, which contained items recently brought in from Florida, such as trunks, cartons, golf bags, and bicycles. The team had no real indication that they were the home team, as the large Mets logo was still at the top of the scoreboard. This was remedied a few hours before the game when workers at the park covered the Mets logo with a Yankees emblem. The previous day, the Yankees worked out on the field in their gray road uniforms rather than their home garb. Rookie pitcher Tom Buskey had the honor of using the same locker as Jets quarterback Joe Namath. [4]

Mel Stottlemyre led the home team vs. the Cleveland Indians in the game, which began at 2:15 p.m. Stottlemyre gave up seven hits vs. the nine given up by Cleveland's starter, Gaylord Perry, and two relievers. The New Yorkers won, 6-1. Yankees third baseman Graig Nettles hit a two-run homer and made a great catch into the stands of a Charlie Spikes foul ball. The fans also cheered when the scoreboard displayed the Mets' 5-4 loss to the Philadelphia Phillies.

Gaylord Perry was in hot water after umpire Marty Springstead warned him about throwing an illegal pitch in the sixth inning. Perry was well known for purportedly pitching spitballs. The Yankees had complained about it since the fourth inning, with Bobby Murcer and Thurman Munson being the loudest critics. Before the fifth inning began, Yankees manager Bill Virdon came onto the field to discuss the problem with Springstead. A new rule said an umpire didn't have to find a "foreign substance" on the baseball. The umpire could only have a suspicion of such an offense. He could then warn the pitcher about throwing such a pitch. Two warnings would eject the pitcher from the game.

Only 20,744 fans braved the cold, drizzly day to witness the game. Apparently, the teams made up later in the month when they completed a big trade on April 26. The Tribe sent first baseman Chris Chambliss and pitchers Dick Tidrow and Cecil Upshaw to the Bronx for pitchers Fritz Peterson, Steve Kline, Fred Beene, and Tom Buskey.

Another realm of sports made headlines in The Big Apple that spring. On Wednesday, May 23, Madison Square Garden Corp. announced that Edward "Ned" Irish, the head of the New York Knicks basketball team, would be retiring on July 1. "Mr. Basketball" would be replaced by Michael Burke, who took over as president of Madison Square Garden Center in July 1973. Irish became the honorary chairman of the Knicks. [5]

The two home baseball teams played each other in the 12th annual Mayor's Trophy Game on May 30. The Yankees defeated the Mets by a tally of 9-4. The night game attracted 35,894 fans and raised $100,000 to help fund city sandlot teams. A fan in right field held up a sign that read: "Beat New York." He got his wish.

The big blow came when Yankees third baseman Fernando Gonzalez hit a grand slam off Mets starter Mike Wegener in the third inning. The Yankees had 11 hits and the Mets scattered ten safeties. The Yankees used 18 players, while the Metsies utilized 19. Dave Pagan won the pitching duel for the Yankees. Wegener was the losing pitcher.

Joltin' Joe DiMaggio visits

Joe DiMaggio visited his old stomping grounds on July 2. He toured the field, which had mud and puddles from a recent rain. He didn't seem to mind that his black leather shoes had mud on them, as he inspected the torn-up shell of the place he had called home for 13 years. He said, "It looks more massive to me now than when it was complete." One workman yelled, "Hey, Joe, you coming back here to play baseball again?" The instantly recognizable Yankee icon replied, "No, just visiting," as he waved to the fan. Most likely, Joe was in town to film a commercial for The Bowery Savings Bank, as he was their spokesman. Hopefully he met the laborer who shared the same magic name as his. [6]

Certainly, the fabled star's visit would stay with Larry Rosselli, Mike Foley, and Ralph Rillero through the renovation, as well as the rest of their lives. They, along with many other workers on the site, would never tire of telling everyone about Joe D's stopover. Joe kindly gave autographs to all the kids and construction workers who asked for the prize. Not even Yankees architect Perry Green would mind. As he said, "The company may have lost an hour or so, but now that these fellows have seen Joe DiMaggio, they'll probably work harder. Human nature is funny." [7] Even though Joe left baseball in 1951, he never lost the dignity or charisma that kept him in the spotlight as a great American hero.

Changes in the works

About September, iron workers, such as Richard Muller, and laborers, such as Gene Marconi, finished splicing the new red steel trusses to the old gray steel. The next step would be to pull three-inch steel cables like the top of a tent to lift the weight off the inner columns that had blocked the view of fans for the past 50 years. Crews were also digging drainage traps. With 400 construction workers on the job, Municipal Service Administrator John T. Carroll confidently said, "nothing, but nothing, is going to interfere with Opening Day in April 1976." Mike Aquino, who managed the stadium's overhaul for the Walsh Construction Company, vowed, "This is not an alteration job. I don't know what to call it. It's like putting an artificial heart in a guy. He may look like the same guy, but he won't be."[8]

The bronze plaques on the center field monuments dedicated to Miller Huggins, Lou Gehrig, and Babe Ruth went back to the U.S. Bronze Sign Company for safekeeping. The company had manufactured the hallowed tablets. Each of these metal reliefs weighed about 125 pounds. The company was located at 101 West 31st Street in Manhattan. A wooden box was built around the memorials to protect the stone shrines from construction damage. While plans called for a grass field, the city still had the right to install artificial turf for easier maintenance in the event that a professional football team were to sign a lease to play in the renovated stadium. [9]

Formidable changes would drastically change the playing field, which would be lowered five feet. A steeper deck of seats would shorten the 407-foot power alley to about 385 feet. The right field foul line would extend from 296 feet to 310. The left field line would expand to 312 feet rather than the pre-renovation's 301.

The arena would seat fewer fans, as the 64,644 wooden seats would be replaced by 52,671 Yankee blue plastic molded chairs. The bleachers' capacity would be greatly reduced from 11,000 to 2,500. The white copper frieze which had ringed the Grandstand was now no more than a precious memory. A reincarnation would reappear as white pre-cast concrete above the new outfield scoreboard. The 560-foot scoreboard would be the biggest ever built. Its 100 rows of lights, totaling 23,272 bulbs, would display cartoons and let fans view instant replays. The

Conrac Corporation of Baldwin Park, California, was to integrate a computer, two operator consoles, six videotape decks, and a television camera into the system. [10]

Three escalator towers would be built outside the stands at the rear of first base, third base, and home plate. They would serve as entrances and exits for the Bronx devotees. River Avenue was to be widened northward from 153rd Street. Yellow and white lights had been planned along the elevated subway route along the area as well. This area would become known as Stadium Plaza. Land by River Avenue and the Harlem River was to be used for three new city garages and 12 parking lots providing 6,900 automobile parking spots.

Tom Blasso, a concrete worker, said, "It's going to be a nice stadium when it's done. I look down there and I imagine Ruth and Gehrig warming up. I never saw them play, but I used to have a season ticket for the football Giants right over there, in Section 12." Gene Marconi exclaimed, "You know what's special about working on this job? I'm making a hell of a lot of money at a time when there's very little construction work around. Joe DiMaggio was down on the field the other day making a TV commercial, and a lot of guys ran down to get his autograph. Me, I'll go down there when he's putting his name on checks."[11]

Richard Muller worked as a "connector" on the top of the grandstand. He and co-workers would spend the next six weeks shifting the weight of the grandstand to create a cantilevered system that would allow the grandstand to stand without the well-known iron columns that had blocked the view of many a fan. With the roof and trademark frieze gone, new steel columns had been mounted behind the grandstand seating sections. These would be used to shift the weight of the stadium outward onto the new posts, which had been built to support ten new rows of seats in the ballpark's top deck. One hundred and six precast concrete brackets, known as "stringers," would hold the weight of the new seating areas. Each stringer, shaped like the stoop of a New York brownstone, weighed 30 tons.

A crane positioned each stringer in place behind every new column. A galvanized steel cable slanted out from anchor points on the new structural steel used for the upper deck framing behind each stringer. Weeks later, when the last cable was secured, all the steel wires would be tightened equally by hydraulic jacks and turnbuckles. The concrete counter weight beam was the mass weight that held the tie back cables in place. Thus the weight-shifting part of the project would be completed. Problems occurred due to the stadium settling unevenly into the ground over the past 50 years. Each seating section extended across four supports. This caused some trembling during the renovation. Inserting lead into the loose areas solved the problem. [12]

To improve traffic flow, the Federal government was footing the bill for 90 percent of the Major Deegan Expressway ramps. The Yankees wanted blue traffic signs in the area and blue lines on Stadium Plaza walkways. The Federal authorities won the battle to have traffic signs green and crosswalks white, as those were the standard Federal colors. [13]

Race to the pennant

In September the Yankees led in the American League East standings for about two weeks. Yet first place didn't mean too much to the fans at their temporary home. As of September 5 they were still shy of having one million fans see them for the year, a drop in attendance by 164,000 from the 1973 total. While the Mets languished in fifth place in the National League East race, they still outdrew the Yankees by half a million fans. The last time the Yankees had won the pennant was in 1964.

On September 17 they were about to start a ten-game home stand, which would begin with a three-game series vs. the second-place Baltimore Orioles. In spite of that, there were advance ticket sales of only about 12,000 per game. The Queens Bombers didn't have the same magnetism as the Bronx Bombers. Manager Billy Martin said of Shea, "Every time you mention the name, I think of how horsebleep the park is. Worst clubhouse in baseball. They have flies bigger than bumblebees." [14] Bobby Murcer didn't like Shea Stadium because it cut down his home run production. Roy White disliked his role as designated hitter, which he performed in 53 games that season. White was so unhappy that he asked to be traded. Murcer didn't hit his first home run at Shea until September 21 against the Cleveland Indians. White belted a three-run homer and stole home in the first inning in the Yankees' 14-7 rout of the Indians. Graig Nettles also hit a homer against his former mates. A national TV audience saw the game along with the 14,648 spectators.

Meanwhile, 40 guests in hard blue hats, including a forlorn Phil Rizzuto, toured Yankee Stadium. "I was sick when they dug the first hunk of dirt out of the infield," said the Yankee great. "After all," he continued, "it will be an entirely new ball park. The outfield distances won't be the same. There will be no way to make comparisons with Babe Ruth, Joe DiMaggio and Mickey Mantle. That is what is regrettable to old-timers like myself. But the Stadium is being built for a new breed of fans who aren't as concerned over the Yankee tradition. At least they won't have to strain to look around those columns anymore." [15]

Toward the end of the month, the Baltimore Orioles gained more steam than the Yankees. Consequently, the Yankees finished the season in second place, with an 89-73 record, landing two games behind the O's. The Birds won 28 of their last 34 games, including a three-game sweep of the Yanks from September 17-19.

Perhaps the finest event for the team during the year was the election of legends Mickey Mantle and Whitey Ford to the National Baseball Hall of Fame in Cooperstown, New York. This was Mickey's first year of eligibility and Whitey's second. These long-time friends had hoped to be inducted into the shrine together.

Baseball and the New York Yankees were about to embark on a new era that would dramatically affect the sport forever. On December 16, Peter Seitz, a professional labor arbitrator, declared Oakland A's pitcher Jim "Catfish" Hunter a free agent. Seitz ruled that Oakland owner Charles O. Finley breached Hunter's contract when he failed to pay a $50,000 insurance annuity, as stated in the pitcher's contract. Thus, Hunter, a mainstay of Finley's championship dynasty, was now a free agent. With more than 20 teams bidding for Hunter's services, the Yankees anted up a contract for $3.75 million over a five-year period. This 1974 New Year's Eve agreement included a $1 million signing bonus. Salaries would never be the same.

Bleachers and right field grandstand, January 3, 1974.

Bleachers and left field grandstand, January 3, 1974.

Gate 4 is gutted, January 3, 1974.

Pedestrian walkway behind the bleachers on River Avenue, January 3, 1974.

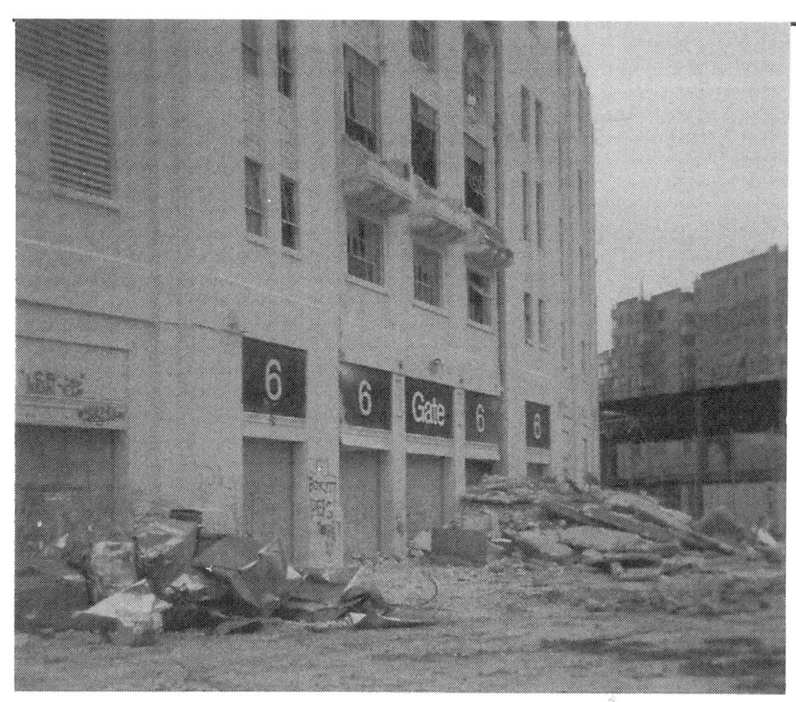

Debris at Gate 6, January 3, 1974. The el train tracks on River Avenue are in front of the apartment houses in the background.

A haunting vision of Gate 6, January 3, 1974.

Relatively untouched exterior walls, January 3, 1974.

The uprooted field is a beehive of activity, January 3, 1974.

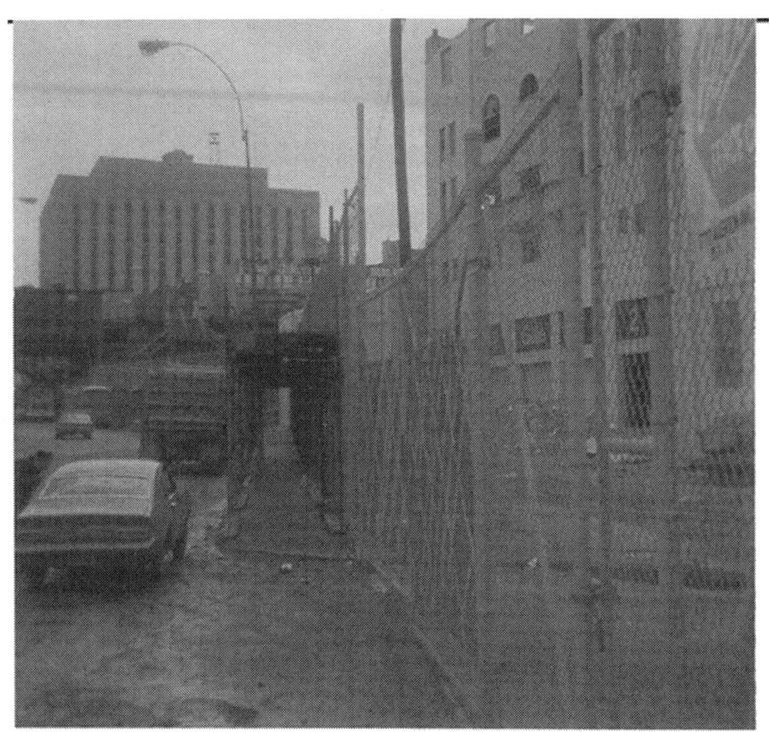

View of Gate 2 and Bronx County Courthouse on 161st Street, February 20, 1974.

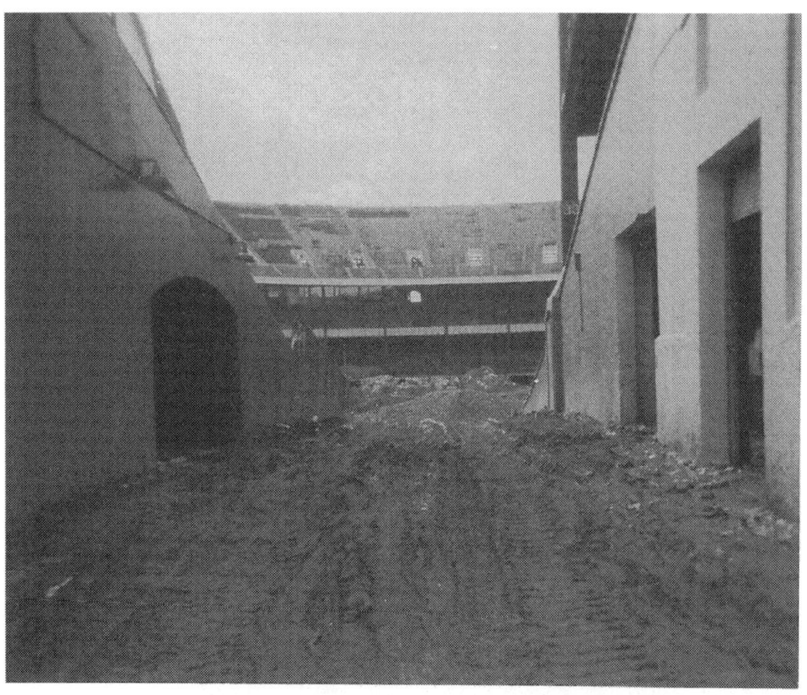

View from the visitors bullpen in left field, February 20, 1974.

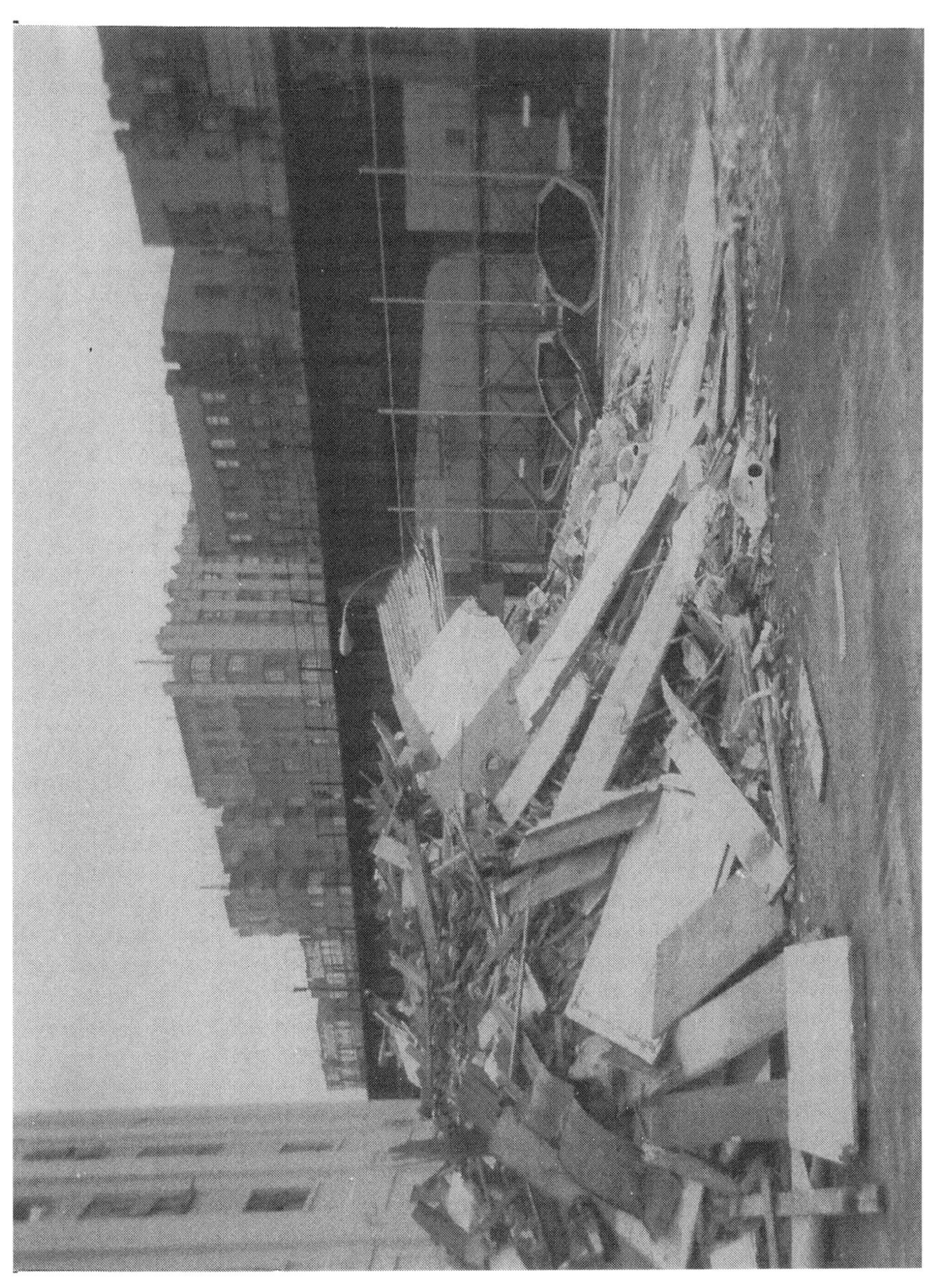

Debris at Gate 6 at River Avenue & E. 157 Street. Note the ticket kiosk tops leaning against the fence, February 20, 1974.

Bleachers and right field grandstand, February 20, 1974.

Bleachers and left field grandstand, February 20, 1974.

The field from center field subway station photo, February 20, 1974.

The stadium speaker and flagpole are still standing before the bleachers, as is a shack for workers, February 20, 1974.

A guard at Gate 2, February 20, 1974.

The left field side of the stadium, February 20, 1974.

Gate 2 with balconies and broken glass, February 20, 1974.

Lots of rubble surrounding what's left of Gate 6, February 20, 1974. Gate 4 suffered the same fate, whereas Gate 2 was relatively unscathed.

Much of the exterior walls remained untouched, February 20, 1974.

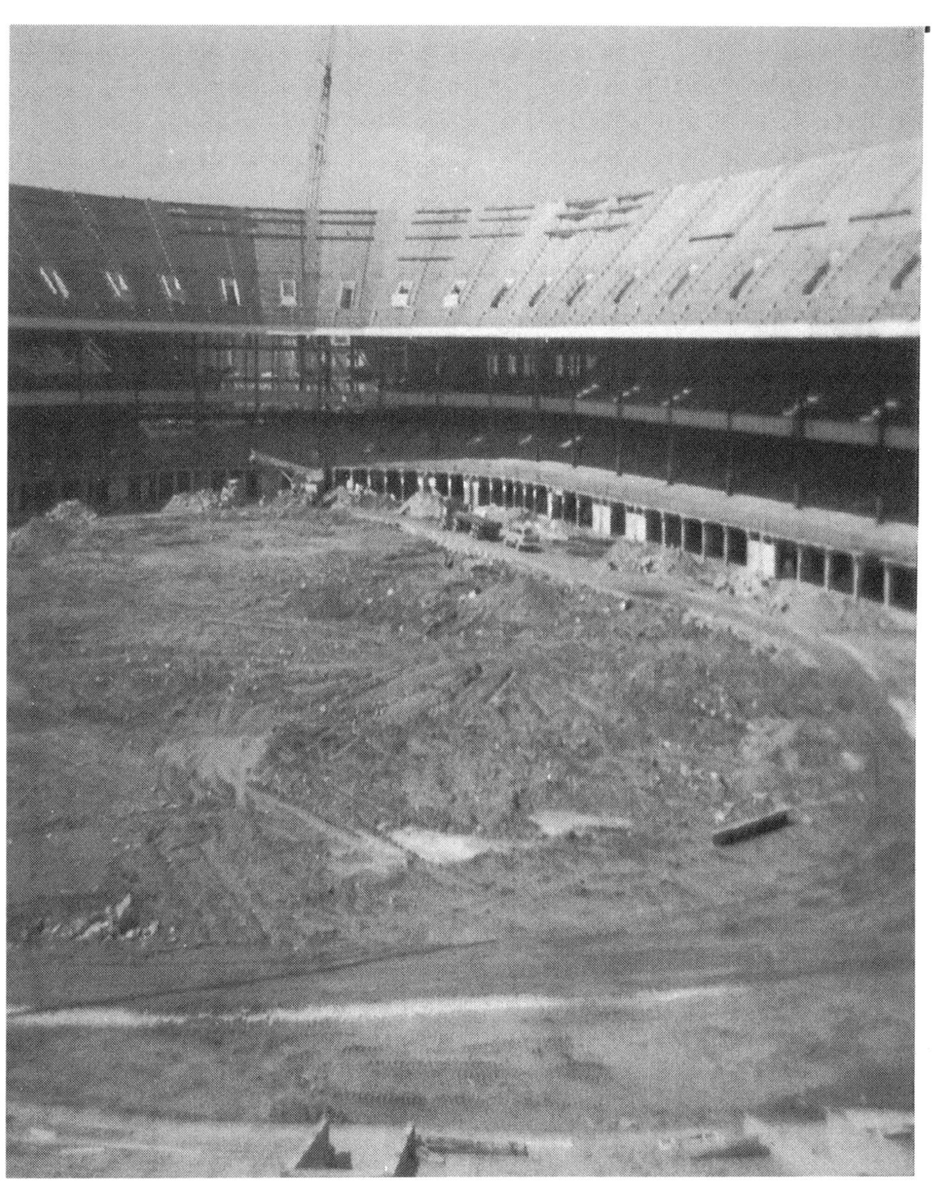

View from subway station towards home plate, April 3, 1974.

Bleachers and right field grandstand, April 3, 1974.

Bleachers and left field grandstand at E. 161st Street, April 3, 1974. The white cement structure near the street is Gate 2, one of the entrances into the stadium.

Excavating outside the stadium, April 3, 1974.

Gate 6, April 3, 1974.

Workers standing in front of Gate 4, May 8, 1974.

Macombs Dam Park and Yankee Stadium, May 8, 1974.

East 157th Street looking towards the Harlem River (West). The above photo is a close up view of concrete and rebar debris, May 8, 1974.

Wood pilings were used to support construction of the stadium's soon to be built escalator towers. The above view is from the left field visitors bullpen area. The bottom photo is from the el train platform overlooking the center field area looking towards home plate, May 8, 1974.

A security guard walks past escalator tower wood forms at visitors bullpen area. Stringers could be seen rising behind the grandstand, August 3, 1974.

Behind the bleachers on River Avenue, August 3, 1974.

Scaffolding and wood forms in Yankee bullpen area, August 3, 1974.

Bleachers and right field grandstand. Bleacher seats are evident and so are grass or weeds on dirt piles. Photo taken August 3, 1974.

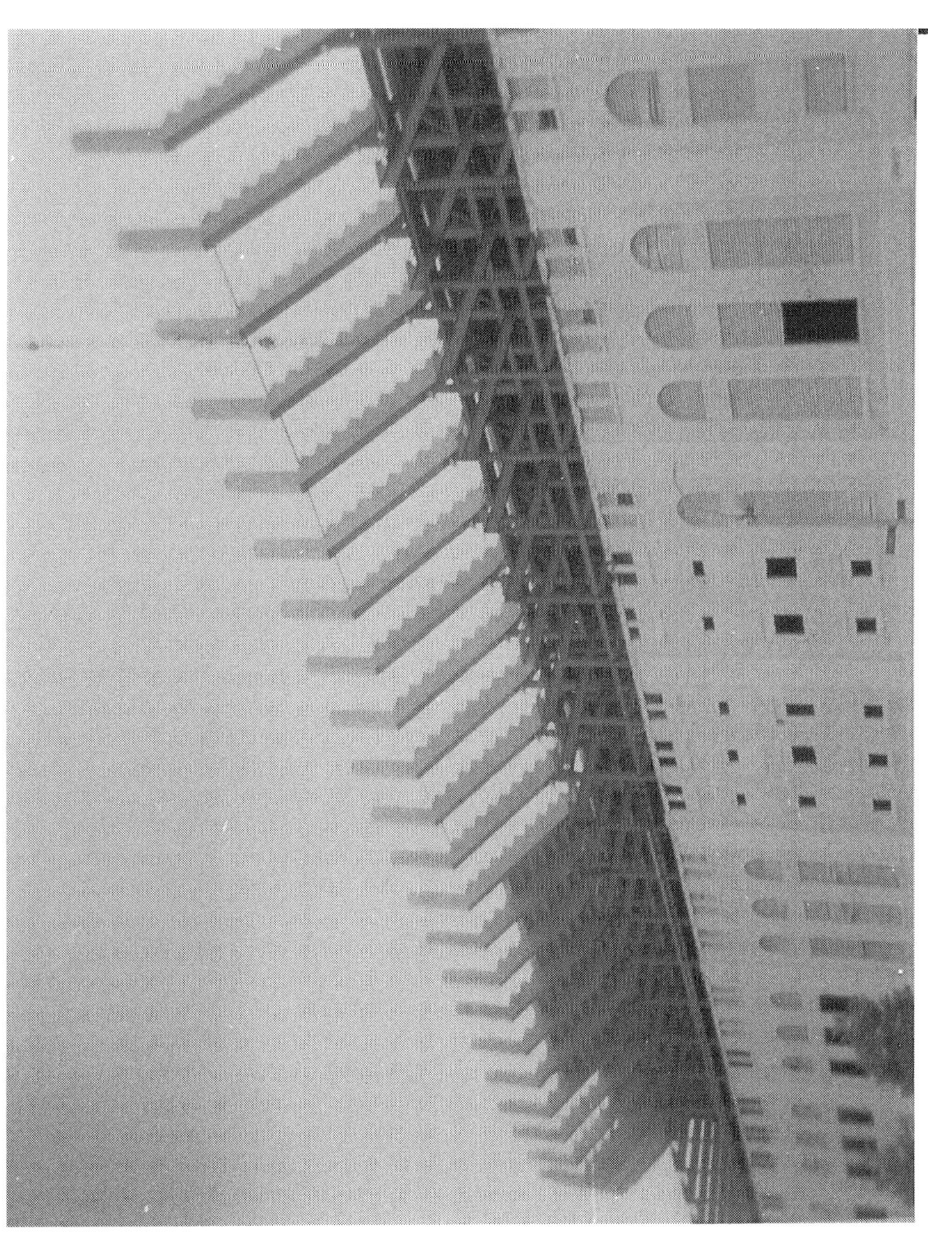

Close up photo of stringers and underside of new upper deck, August 3, 1974.

View of field with many stringers outside of stadium and mountains of dirt inside, August 3, 1974.

Gate 6, August 3, 1974.

Gate 2 and East 161st Street, August 3, 1974.

Bleachers and left field grandstand, August 3, 1974.

Shea Stadium, home of the New York Mets, 1964 to 2008. The Yankees played at Shea from 1974-1975, while Yankee Stadium underwent its renovation. Photo courtesy of the NATIONAL BASEBALL HALL OF FAME LIBRARY, COOPERSTOWN, N.Y.

Shea Stadium scoreboard featuring the Yankee emblem, April 7, 1974.

August 3, 1974 Yankees Old Timers' Day game at Shea Stadium. A view of the outfield.

Shea Stadium, August 3, 1974. New York Yankees Old Timers' Day.

The one and only Casey Stengel coming out of the Yankee dugout during the Old Timers' Day game, August 3, 1974. Joe DiMaggio is sitting behind Casey.

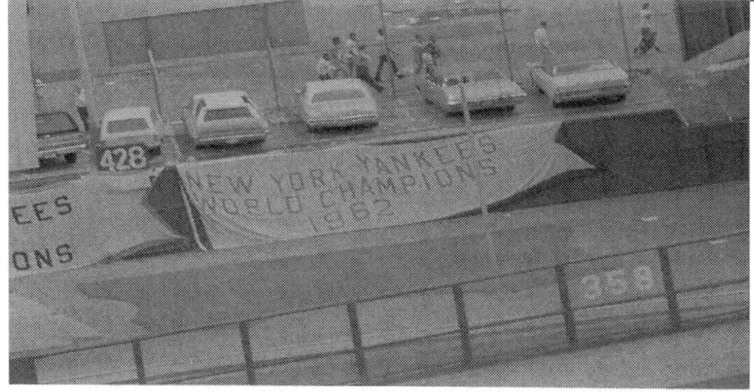

Yankee World Series banners adorn bullpen wall, August 3, 1974.

Joe DiMaggio greets Old Timers' already introduced (L-r), Marty Appel, Bob Fishel, Casey Stengel, Mickey Mantle, Whitey Ford, Jocko Conlan, Gabe Paul, Paul Kerr, Warren Giles, Joe Cronin, Lee MacPhail, Bowie Kuhn (Baseball Commissioner), Mrs. Lou Gehrig, and Mrs. Babe Ruth.

Gate 6, located at River Avenue, with wood pilings in the ground, to be used as footings for the right field escalator tower, May 8, 1974.

Right field grandstand as seen from the field, with wood pilings to be used as footings for the left field escalator (above), and as viewed from the el train platform, (below), May 8, 1974.

Left field bleachers and grandstand, May 8, 1974.

Yankee catcher, Thurman Munson, at bat (above). Dick Howser (34) is the Yankee 3B coach. Centerfielder, Bobby Murcer, is at bat (below). Graig Nettles, the Yankee third baseman, is standing next to the dugout with his bat. The Yankees won the first game of the doubleheader from the Milwaukee Brewers, 3-1, but lost the second game, 3-2, September 2, 1974.

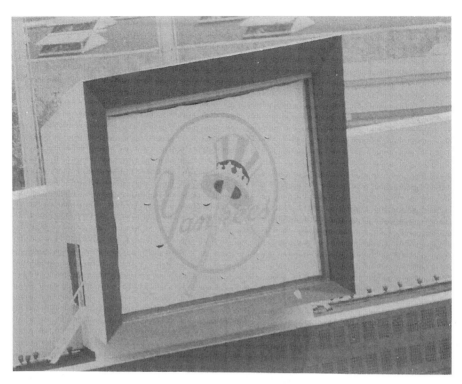

The Yankee logo graces the Shea Stadium scoreboard when the Yankees are at home. Graig Nettles stands ready to make a play at 3B vs. the Milwaukee Brewers, September 2, 1974.

Upper portion of Gate 6 remodeling, September 19, 1974.

Action on the exterior wall on Ruppert Place, September 19, 1974.

The photo above shows Falsework and other renovation on the upper section of Gate 4. The bottom image illustrates excavation at Gate 4 September 19, 1974.

Extensive renovation work at Gate 6 is also taking shape, September 19, 1974.

Colonial Stone and Sand Company delivering cement on E. 157th Street, September 19, 1974.

The bleachers and right field stands, September 19, 1974.

The bleachers and left field stands. The escalator tower is rising in front of Gate 2, September 19, 1974.

Looking at the interior left field side of the stadium, September 19, 1974.

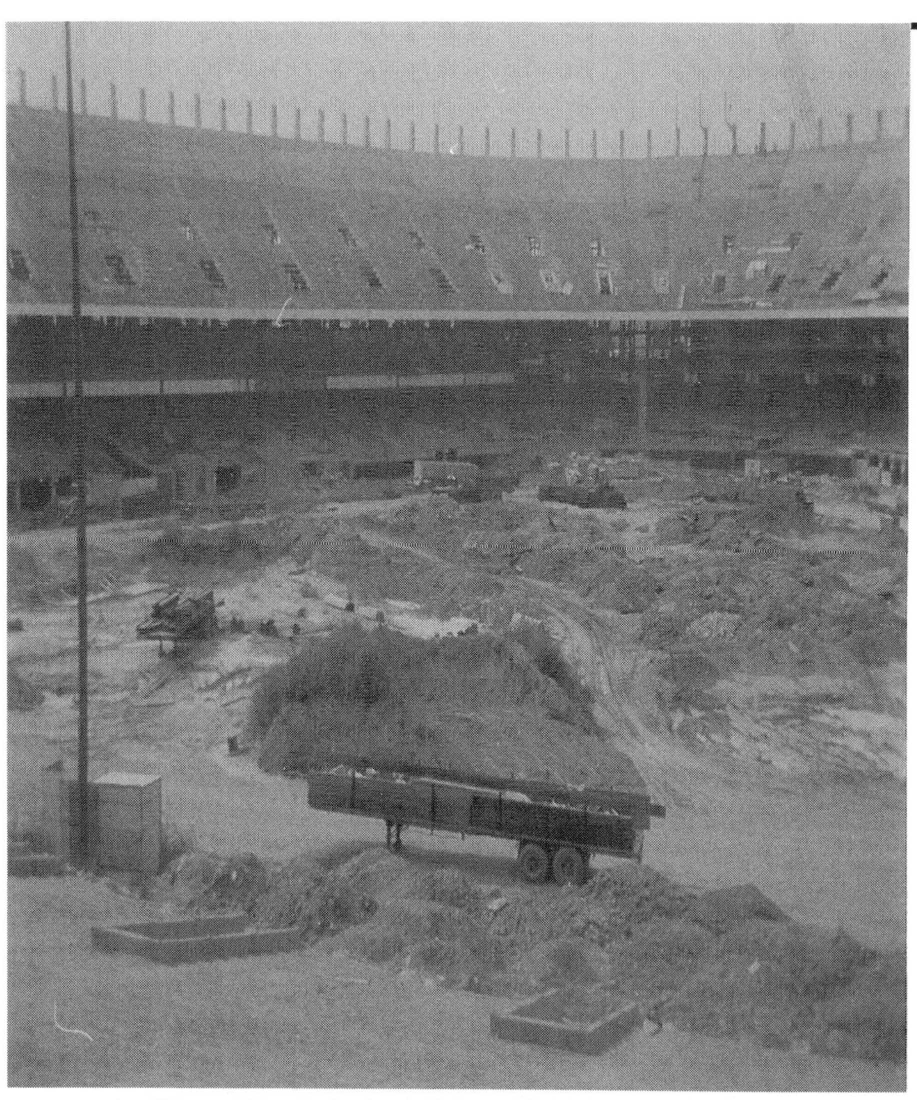

They won't be playing baseball for a while! September 19, 1974.

Wood forms being prepared for pouring of cement at Gate 4. The view above is looking towards River Avenue, October 29, 1974.

Yankee Stadium as seen on its East 157th Street (right field) side. Gate 4 is above, with the newly poured cement counterweight beam wrapping around the stadium. Gate 6, next to River Avenue, is below, October 29, 1974. The banner on the crane says "P&H". The crane boom says "DeFILIPPIS."

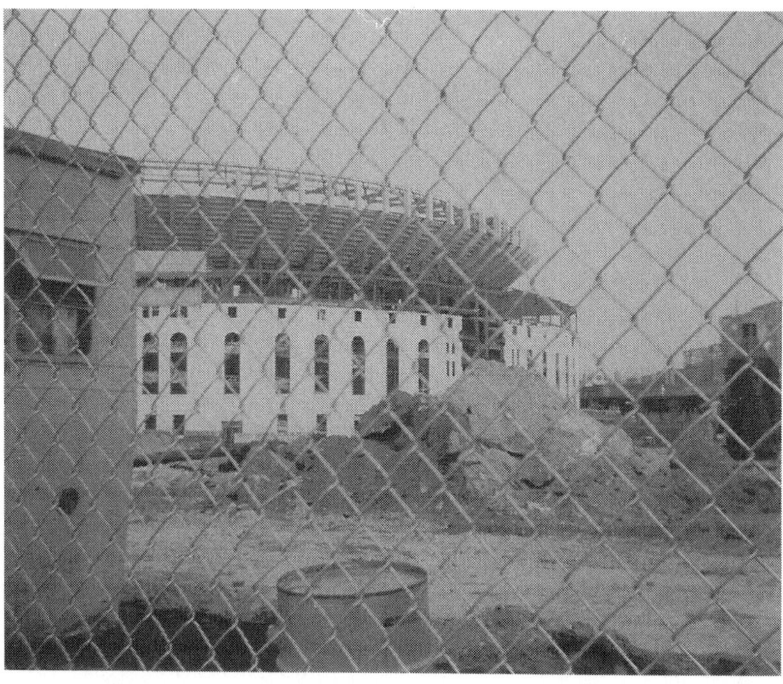

Gate 6, close up and looking down East 157th Street, October 29, 1974. The apartments seen past the crane are part of the Polo Grounds Towers, a housing project that opened on the site of the Polo Grounds in 1968. The Polo Grounds, home of the New York Giants, and temporary home of the New York Yankees, was demolished in 1964.

Ground level at Gate 6 showing wooden forms and metal scaffolding being prepared to receive concrete for escalator pod, October 29, 1974.

View of right side of field, October 29, 1974.

Progress being made of the left field side escalator pod and grandstand, October 29, 1974. Karl Koch installed precast concrete in the upper deck.

The right field stands (Gate 6) as seen from the elevator train platform on River Avenue (above) and from the left of the escalator pod near Gate 2 in left field (below), October 29, 1974.

View of the left field side of the modernization of Babe's Place, October 29, 1974. Most of the earth came from the footing excavation for the new row of columns at mezzanine level of the stadium. Excavated dirt and rock that came from the basement level was stored on the playing field.

Jim "Catfish" Hunter pitched the Yankees' opener at Shea on April 11, 1975, against Ralph Houk's Detroit Tigers. The Tigers' Willie Horton hit a two-run homer in the first inning. Nate Colbert slugged a three-run shot off the millionaire pitcher in the sixth. The Yankees lost 5-3 before 26,212 fans. Mickey Lolich picked up the win.

On the other side of the city, Crouse-Hinds announced, in February, that they would supply 855 metal halide vapor variety lights to Yankee Stadium for the renovation. Each light used 1500 watts of power. The Syracuse Chiefs, the Yankees' Triple A farm club, would receive 264 such lights for their field. [16]

By mid-July, the cost of the modernization rose to $57,088,000, or 137 percent above the original $24 million figure. A new contract amendment totaling $1,109,969 had been added for the purpose of repairing damaged concrete that occurred during the removal of seats from the stands. Municipal Service Administrator John T. Carroll, said the rise in expenses included work in adjoining areas, such as a parking lot, footbridge, and two garage remodelings. These tasks added $7,125,971 to the previous figure. Carroll said inflation elevated the costs 25-30 percent since 1972. Still, he called the job "a marvelous engineering project." [17]

URS/Madigan-Praeger, which held the simple $1,529,960 architectural contract in January 1973, gave a preliminary opinion that construction by itself would cost $27,969,390. Nab-Tern Constructors won the general construction contract worth $22,220,000 in December 1973. They also sought the contract amendment for the current concrete repair. Other agreements included:

Contractor	Amount
Mansfield Electrical	$2,849,000
Wachtel Plumbing	$2,520,000
Gotham Heating, Ventilating and A/C	$2,431,000
Otis Elevator	$1,580,731 [18]

The world's biggest bat

One of the most famous trademarks of the renovation was set up on July 26. According to Robert Young, PKW's Project Manager and Structural Designer for the renovation, the 138-foot-tall baseball bat was the brainchild of Michael Burke. It was placed on the plaza outside the Stadium behind the home plate area, behind Gate 4. The 45-ton Babe Ruth Louisville Slugger model bat was constructed of stainless steel and fiberglass. The world's biggest baseball bat measured ten feet in diameter. The handle's diameter came in at six feet.

Joe Garagiola Jr., the Yankees' General Counsel, noticed the top of the bat lacked the knob a baseball bat has. He asked architect Perry Green if putting a ring around the top to make it look like a real bat was possible. Green said it would not interfere with safety or function. The edifice now looked the way a bat should. Garagiola also suggested to George Steinbrenner that the bat be imprinted with the Louisville Slugger emblem, as well as Babe Ruth's name. The Boss liked the idea, so the Babe's bat greeted Stadium visitors and became a choice meeting spot for them.

In reality, the bat was a smokestack that was connected to a boiler system that heated offices in the historic ball park. The location of the bat was dictated by practicality due to the proximity to the boiler room and the emergency generator room. Mariano Molina, an engineer with the engineering firm of Slocum and Fuller, was a sub-consultant to PKW architects John Waterbury and Richard Fisher. Molina said he and the two PKW architects thought of the generic concept for the bat. Robert C.Y. Young said Michael Burke insisted the chimney be in the form of a baseball bat. [19]

The purpose of this bat smokestack was to find a place for the boiler flue, and for the exhaust of the emergency generator diesel fumes to escape. The large vents at the bottom of the bat were the fresh air intake for combustion of the boiler room needed to introduce fresh air into the building. Inside the bat was a heating plant chimney for the boilers and diesel engine exhaust pipe, which served the emergency generator. Molina was the Project Manager engineer who designed all the mechanical systems serving the Stadium.

Airtek Corporation, of Newton, Massachusetts, designed and made the masterpiece. Earl Wright drove the 170-foot-long truck that carried the behemoth from Massachusetts. The $100,000 edifice allowed the Yankees to burn lower quality, less expensive fuels since the bat expelled hot gases rather than liquids. The high-temperature emissions reduced air pollution. The fans were happy that the Sultan of Swat's calling card figured prominently in the design of the "new" Yankee Stadium. Twelve-year-old Michael Frank said, "I think it's really fantastic. I'm a Yankee fan, and this is the best thing the Yankees ever did." [20]

As for the field, Larry Fox, a reporter for the *New York Daily News*, wrote in his July 29, 1975 column, that the city could install either real grass or artificial turf at Yankee Stadium.

Henry Gavin of the city's Economic Development Administration, said real grass was chosen to be used months ago. As he so aptly stated, "We think God meant that you should play on natural grass." While athletes preferred normal sod, synthetic turf did not reduce injuries to athletes, as predicted. The latter would also cost $1.5 million extra than the real thing. [21]

The next week, Yankees fans received a shocking surprise during the 29th annual Old Timers' Day game, which was held on Saturday, August 2. Forty-seven-year-old Billy Martin was rehired to replace manager Bill Virdon. Most of the crowd of 43,968 gave Billy a standing ovation. The Yanks had a 53-51 record, and were 10 games behind Boston. Virdon arrived at the Stadium at 7:10 a.m. to clean out his possessions, and left about 20 minutes later. He'd find a job managing the Houston Astros two weeks later. The Yankees paid Virdon for the year left on his contract.

Gabe Paul said, "We're not blaming Bill Virdon for a thing. This is just an exciting move that became possible when Martin became available." [22] Billy had just finished a stint managing the Texas Rangers when he was fired on July 21. Paul tracked him down when Billy was on a fishing trip with his family in the mountains near Denver, Colorado. The Yankees won the two-inning Old Timers' Day game, 2-0. The Yankees also let it be known that the clubhouse in the renovated Yankee Stadium would be named the "Pete Sheehy Clubhouse." Sheehy had worked as the equipment manager in the Yankee clubhouse since 1927, when he was 16.

Even with Billy Martin at the helm, the Yankees ended the season in third place with an 83-77 record, 12 games behind the Red Sox. The Orioles came in second, 4½ games in back of Boston.

Spiraling costs of the renovation continues

Costs for the renovation kept going up. The October 11 issue of *The New York Times* reported $66.4 million as the latest estimate, as detailed by the city's Budget Bureau. John T. Carroll blamed the rise on unforeseen engineering difficulties and inflation. He put a positive light on it by explaining, "The actual cost of construction of the stadium based on the prices at the time of bidding are in line with our general experience in massive rehabilitation projects." He also claimed the cost to be a "bargain at this price when you consider the effect it will have on rehabilitating the area and the impact on the city's economy in expanding major sports activities." Carroll added, the project "is on target," claiming the job should be completed by March 1976.

The column reported that an informant said, "This was totally unrealistic." In addition, you will remember we were having fiscal problems even then and it was important to make the take-over of the stadium palatable not only to the Board of Estimate but also to the public." [23] It was obvious that Carroll tried to put a positive spin on a situation that kept spiraling out of control. No doubt city officials knew how bad things were. They didn't want the public to find out so they wouldn't feel the wrath of the people.

Budget Director Melvin N. Lechner said Mayor Beame's spending fiscal plan would go before the State Emergency Financial Control Board in mid-October. One issue would be to discuss allocating $1.5 million in 1976 to build a 1,000-car parking lot on an area currently being used by the state, while building a ramp from the Major Deegan Expressway to the stadium locale. Lechner said the city appropriated $56.5 million for refurbishing the ball park and upgrading the neighboring area. The costs did not quite add up, as frequently happens with government schemes.

The city had previously assigned $4.5 million for purchase of the Stadium property. The Budget Bureau felt completion of that facet of the renovation might take another three years, and $6.9 million would be needed in 1977 to settle the final cost, plus interest. Former Mayor, John Lindsay, said 75 percent of the financing would come from parking lot revenues. Also, he planned on financing 25 percent of the project with capital or construction budget funding to cover these extra costs. Local finance laws stated that the city had a 75 percent exclusion from debt limit loans for projects that would produce income. [24]

In his syndicated newspaper column, George F. Will wrote a story on October 23. Titled, "Absurd, But Ah, New York Will Have Its Stainless Steel 'Bat'," he exclaimed how New York's most complicated jokes came from the city government. He ranted about how strapped New York City is, but that costs for modernizing Yankee Stadium keep escalating out of control. Yet, at $64.4 million, the public was told it's still a "bargain at this price," even though it was a bargain at $24 million four years ago. All the while, the city was trying to get federal funding from Congress so as not to default on its financial obligations. "Some cities would be dismayed by this evidence that their estimates are jokes," he marveled.

Will made fun of the $100,000 stainless steel 138-foot smokestack bat, saying that a contractor declared, "A bat-shaped stack gives this neighborhood some class." Will wondered how money could be spent on this project when the city would cut jobs of policemen, firemen, and teachers to save $200.7 million, or two percent of the city's budget. Part of the savings would be the $1,422 saved monthly by having 14 city officials giving up their limousine telephones. [25]

Also in October, the neighborhood upgrade plan fell victim to the city's budget crisis. The $2 million program was abandoned. City officials hoped locals would take it upon themselves to remodel their own homes and businesses. The bureaucrats said it now "makes sense" to spend $300,000 on the Yankees since money would be saved by not spending it on the neighborhood. The city spent $301,000 to purchase equipment for the team; a new $215,000 tarpaulin to cover the field; $65,000 in various security devices; $14,000 to strengthen supports for the scoreboard; and $7,000 for a carpet or terrazzo floor for the team's general offices. The city accepted responsibility to pay for nine private executive toilets and catering facilities in Yankees V.I.P. boxes. These costs had yet to be determined. Workers began laying sod in the infield on October 27. Phil Lagana and Sons, College Point, New York, supplied the turf. [26]

The Sporting News reported in its November 8 issue that buying and refurbishing Yankee Stadium now rose to $86.4 million. John Carroll blamed the extra cost on inflationary construction costs and unanticipated engineering difficulties. He did say, however, that work on the project would be completed by March of 1976. [27]

In his *New York Daily News* commentary of November 13, Dick Young gave a description of the now $66 million Yankee Stadium. He called it "beautiful." He described various aspects of the project, such as the new 2,300 car four-story parking garage across the street, not one pole being in the way of fans viewing games, and the blue seats, with 2,000 to 3,000 being added weekly. He also spoke of the new white cement valance (frieze) running from one end of the bleachers to the other. In speaking of the 138-foot tall smokestack baseball bat outside the Stadium, Young claimed, "Only Ron Blomberg could swing it."

On Young's tour of the new creation, Carroll Sinksen, who ran the project for the Walsh Construction Company, replied to Young's fear of collapse without the girders that held up the grandstand that were now replaced by cables, stating, "there are tension cables threaded from the stands to the basement to take up the load." [28]

In a letter to the author, dated June 29, 2011, Robert C.Y.Young, the Project Manager and Structural Designer for the renovation of Yankee Stadium, wrote, "The renovation of the Stadium entailed the removal of the front supporting columns of the stands in order to offer unobstructed view for all the seats. This modification resulted in an innovative design to accommodate the reversal of stress patterns in many of the supporting members. Thus the cables in the back of the Upper Deck were added to counter-balance the long cantilevered Upper Deck structure. The cables were added not to make the renovated structure stronger, but to accommodate the "new and rerouted" stress flow pattern." [29]

By November 15 the infield and outfield had been graded and the three acres of sod was laid and manicured. Ceilings now separated the decks of the Stadium. A four-deck parking garage across the street from the nearly finished ball park would accommodate 2,300 cars. Two-thirds of the bleacher seats would be gone. The 2,500 that remained would be in right and right-center field.

Steven L. Koch, assistant manager of Walsh Construction Company, declared, “We’ll have no problem completing the work. We’re on or a few days ahead of schedule.” The contract called for completion of the renovation by February 6, 1976. Most of the lights on the roof were now in place. The 118 columns that obstructed views of many fans had been removed and 106 2½-inch steel cables ran down the Stadium and were anchored in the ground. Koch called it “a cantilever effect. We just shifted the load from the poles to the cables.” In a June 30, 2013 interview with Mr. Koch, he related to the author that the last column had been removed from Section 5 in right field on March 10, 1975. This was Column 33. He also revealed that the renovation had been completed sometime in June of 1976. Mr. Koch also said that many contractors felt that Yankee Stadium should have been leveled and a new one rebuilt due to practicality more than deterioration. While it is true that decay was present, it would have been more cost and time effective to build a new stadium from scratch. [30]

The seats would now be 22 inches wide, which was about 20 percent wider than the original ones. Seating capacity before the renovation was 65,010. It now dropped to 57,500. The once spacious outfield changed from 301 feet down the left field line to 313; 296 feet from the right field foul line to 310; straightaway center reverted from 463 feet to 419. The deepest part of the new dimensions was now 430 feet to left center field. Gone was the famous 457-foot sign of the old days.

The December 1 issue of *The New York Times* contained an article titled "Yanks Get Windfall As City Shifts Plans." The author, Martin Waldron, wrote that the direct costs of the renovation had risen to $75 million. Indirect costs, such as parking facilities, tax exemptions, and interest could add another $150 million to the tab over the next 31 years. John T. Carroll claimed the costs had risen only 10 percent after the bids were accepted.

Economic Development Administration lawyer Henry Gavan, however, said the original $24 million amount estimated to be the cost of the project was "picked out of thin air." This 1971 estimate was based on what it took to build Shea Stadium, which opened in 1964. Gavan noted that if anyone had truly felt Yankee Stadium could be renovated for $24 million, this would have been founded on "a deliberate lie" or "gross stupidity." He did, however, say the renewal of Yankee Stadium was a "necessary luxury" for civic pride and was critical to the revitalization of the South Bronx.

Local merchants still favored the project, believing it to be essential to stabilizing the area. It gave the community hope for a better tomorrow, as they believed a better Stadium would bring in more fans and economically boost their locality. They also hoped crimes such as vandalism, robberies, and muggings would soon be a thing of the past. Since the city wouldn't be aiding the neighborhood to upgrade, the city hoped businesses in the area would take it upon themselves to do such things as painting and remodeling their stores. [31]

The city, Knights of Columbus, and Rice University had still not settled on a price for the city to purchase the Stadium and the land it sat on. The city hoped to pay $8 million for both, while the two owners asked $9.5 million. The city would have to borrow all of the money to pay this expense. Interest would be at least $5 million annually, which would equate to the salaries of 400 average city employees. That would be a very bitter pill to swallow. In 1971-1972, Yankee Stadium and the land it sat on were valued at $2,875,000. The Bronx tax rate at that time was 6.032 percent. Taxes on the Stadium were $173,420. [32]

Another tough dose for the city was that it had promised to provide 6,900 parking spaces at the ballpark, costing the metropolis $60 million over the next 31 years. Since parking spaces would be occupied publicly, the city would lose $25 million in real estate taxes over the same time period. Waldron wrote that on the other side of the coin, the city could offset the $25 million figure and earn up to $2.4 million annually from rent and concessions at the arena, and another $1.7 million from parking. The sum would depend on the number of fans coming to the stadium. Such numbers would be achieved if many more fans attended games than in the recent past. The city lost out on advertising income from ads used on the Stadium's scoreboard, as the team decided to buy the scoreboard from the city in 1973. The Yankees would keep all the income earned from the advertising displays. [33]

Amazingly, with the commitment New York City made to the team, the Yankees wanted the courts to force the city to pay for damages the team claimed it lost due to the renovation. In a State Supreme Court suit, the Yankees sought payment from the city for such things as batting cages, ice makers, therapy tables, goal posts, field lights, the Stadium organ, washers, dryers, and air conditioners. The list itemized 1,096 categories, including the 64,850 seats torn from the old Stadium so new ones could be installed. This stunned city officials, given the fortune being spent on the renovation.

Luis M. Neco was handling negotiations for New York, and felt the team had no legal or moral right to any payment. Neco observed that Rice University owned the Stadium when the city condemned it in August 1972, so Rice was most likely the owner of most of the property the Yankees claimed damages for. Rice University filed an identical grievance. The Yankees actually had filed the lawsuit three years before, but it remained inactive until November 1975, when the team wished to have the claim paid quickly. A representative of the club said the Yankees were not aware the claim was pending, and that it was filed before the current owners purchased the team.

On another front, negotiations had been ongoing to bring the New York Cosmos soccer team to Yankee Stadium in 1976. The North American Soccer League team was currently playing at Downing Stadium on Randall's Island. If the Cosmos changed addresses, the city would receive 12 percent of the first $1.5 million in admissions and 13½ percent above that. Concession sales would bring in another 7½ percent. [34]

Warner Communications, Inc., hoped the Cosmos would change addresses. Warner owned Kinney Systems, Inc., which built and owned several parking garages at Yankee Stadium. Kinney would earn $2 million a year in rent from the city, and about another $2 million for tax exemptions on these properties. The 1973 city agreement with Kinney mandated that the city would pay $1.3 million a year in rent until 2007 on two main garages Kinney was to erect. These edifices were to provide 2,950 parking spots. In October 1975, however, these were increased to 3,501 spaces, and the rent went up to $1.5 annually. Kinney also agreed to modernize a third garage owned by the city, with the city shelling out $446,000 in rental fees over the next four years, then $1 a year after that.

The same agreement would have the city pay all repair and maintenance costs. Kinney would manage all the lots. Besides rental income, Kinney would also be given 20 percent to 95 percent of the parking fees, depending upon how much was brought in. Henry Gavan called the parking pact "excellent" for the city, as the city had the opportunity to make money. Gavan said the city needed $1.7 million to break even with Kinney. Such revenues could be obtained with proceeds from 16 Cosmos games and special events, such as boxing matches. Besides Kinney Parking Systems, Warner Communications owned Wachtel, Duklauer & Fein, which had won the plumbing contract for the renovation of Yankee Stadium with a bid of $2,520,000.

Part of the accord to keep the baseball team in New York for at least 31 years was an agreement in which the city would get 5 percent annually of the gross revenues of ticket sales of the first 750,000 baseball fans, 7½ percent of the next 750,000, and 10 percent over 1.5 million supporters. This same rate was to apply to concessions. Gavan said the city expected more than two million fans to attend Yankee Stadium in 1976, thereby earning the city an income of $661,250. [35]

Yankees fans were delighted on December 5, when the team signed favorite hero Yogi Berra to be one of Billy Martin's coaches for the 1976 season. Yankees veteran Elston Howard returned as first base and batting coach. Dick Howser again would coach third base. Bob Lemon came on board as pitching coach. Yankees president Gabe Paul made the announcement at a press conference at the Americana Hotel.

He was immediately inundated with questions about the expensive tarpaulin, terrazzo floors, security devices, and executive toilets. He gritted his teeth and answered as best he could. Paul stated, "The Yankees have nothing to apologize for, and some of the reports about expenditures were simply inaccurate. In fact, we are trying to set up a meeting with the city to see how we can be of help in some of the surrounding areas, particularly Macombs Dam Park." Paul said the Yankees asked Commissioner Bowie Kuhn if George Steinbrenner would be permitted to attend such a gathering. His suspension from baseball for being convicted of making illegal campaign contributions was supposed to run through the end of the 1976 season.

As for the $215,000 tarpaulin, Paul said, "It would have to be hand embroidered." He continued, "The actual cost, at most, is $10,000, and is an item that goes with the Stadium, which will be rented by the city to other users as well as to the Yankees." He addressed other issues. "An item for terrazzo floors, which did appear at one time, was removed at our request as soon as we saw it. Toilets are part of the whole facility, and I'm sure there will be toilets in the executive facilities, too."

With regard to the Yankees suing the city, "First of all, that was all done before the present owners acquired the team. It is simply a dispute over what the condemnation price should be, and is proceeding through the normal process of settlement. It was instituted by Rice University, which owned the building, and CBS, which owned the team."

He defended the scoreboard support expenses, saying, "The electronic scoreboard, originally to be supplied by the city, is now being built by the Yankees at a cost of $2.8 million. It will be 562 feet wide, the best of its kind and will be available to all other users. Since it was ordered, a new instant replay feature has been developed, and additional support for the weight of it will come to $14,000. That's the part the city is paying, since it adds to the value of the rentable stadium." [36]

The December 7 edition of *The New York Times* printed the 1976 home schedule at Yankee Stadium. The April 15 Opening Day contest would pit the Yankees against the Minnesota Twins. The article said, "The only thing Yankee fans will recognize in the former ballpark will be the natural grass on the field. There will be improved parking facilities, new escalators, unobstructed seating, a public restaurant, a new Stadium Club and a new scoreboard capable of showing instant replays." [37]

On the same day, the *New York Daily News* published an article, "Stadium Cost, Like Topsy...Keeps Growin,'" in which the city's Planning Board confirmed that the Yankee Stadium bill now reached $58 million. The story went on to say that New York was not alone in high sports arena costs. In August of 1974, the New Orleans Superdome cost between $163 million and $178 million, when the taxpayers were told the cost would be $35 million. The Houston Astrodome, which opened in 1965, was supposed to have cost $15 million. It ended up costing between $31.6 million or $40 million, depending on which report you read. Yankee Stadium had some pricey company. [38]

The December 14 issue of *The Coshocton (Ohio) Tribune* included an article titled, "Pontiac Dome Revives Fever." It began, "A new stadium at Pontiac, Mich. cost $55.7 million, including an air-supported dome." The article noted that Yankee Stadium had cost $57 million so far, just for refurbishing. The piece continued, "Projects such as the rebuilding of Yankee Stadium, new Astrodomes, Superdomes, or Kingdomes of more or less traditional construction may be growing too costly for most potential buyers. Major sports as well as smaller operators are looking at air-supported fabric domes such as the new 80,000-seat home of the Detroit Lions at Pontiac, Mich., which was brought in on schedule–and within the original budget." [39]

This did not sit well with New Yorkers, as the media kept reporting the skyrocketing costs associated with Yankee Stadium's modernization. With terrible budget worries, job layoffs, no money for improving Macombs Dam Park or other sections of the Bronx while Yankee Stadium was given a blank check, angry taxpayers wondered when the financial hemorrhage of cost overrides would stop.

Work continues on the East 157th Street side of the stadium, January 15, 1975.

The escalator tower for Gate 6 is getting higher, January 15, 1975.

Close up view of Gate 6 escalator tower, January 15, 1975.

Looking west from Gate 6 area on East 157th Street, January 15, 1975.

Right field view of bleachers and grandstand, January 15, 1975.
NAB TERN worked on the cement for the bleachers.

View of right field side of stadium, January 15, 1975.

A work crew working on Gate 4, January 15, 1975.

Top portion of Gate 4, January 15, 1975.

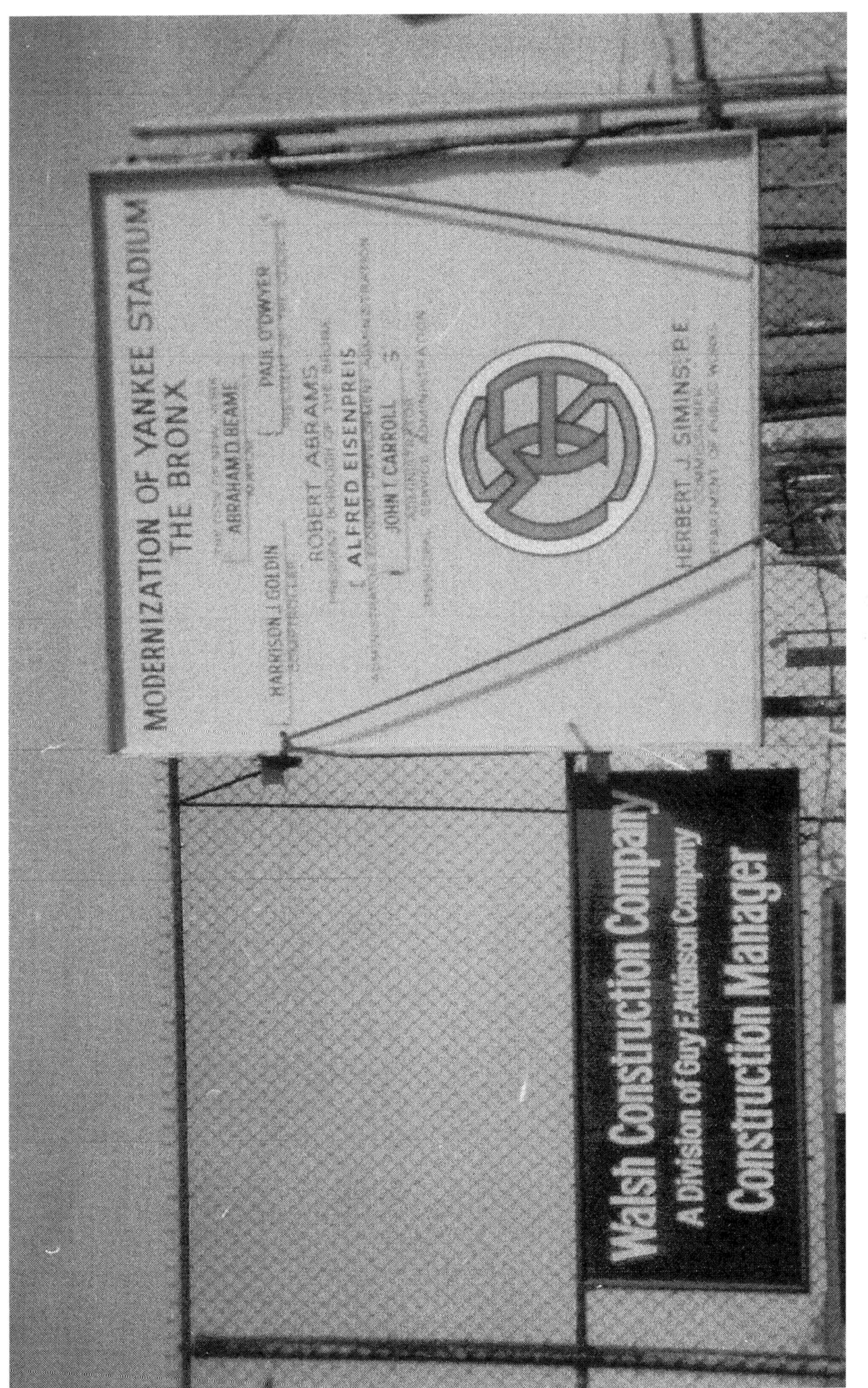
MODERNIZATION OF YANKEE STADIUM
THE BRONX
ABRAHAM D BEAME
PAUL O'DWYER
HARRISON J GOLDIN
ROBERT ABRAMS
ALFRED EISENPREIS
JOHN T CARROLL
HERBERT J. SIMINS, P.E
Walsh Construction Company
A Division of Guy F. Atkinson Company
Construction Manager

DeFilippis Crane Service crane in left field of stadium, January 15, 1975.

Left field escalator tower taking shape. Notice workers near edge of the left field grandstand, January 15, 1975.

Yankee Stadium as seen from East 157th Street near the Major Deegan Expressway, February 3, 1975. Gate 4 is still being built behind the streetlight. This area is located behind home plate.

Construction on Gate 4 (above), and looking west on East 157th Street from Gate 6 (below), February 3, 1975.

The right field bleachers, grandstand, and field, February 3, 1975.

Exterior view of Yankee Stadium Falsework progress. Photo courtesy of Structural Contours, Inc., Greenwich, Connecticut, 06831 USA

Photo of Falsework below concrete stringers. Courtesy of Structural Contours, Inc., Greenwich, Connecticut, 06831 USA

This February 3, 1975 photo is blended together thanks to the skills of Matt Visco. The Upper Deck Concourse exterior wall is substantially complete. It's clear that most of the exterior 1923 wall is original. It's also easy to recognize where the renovated upper section of the stadium begins. This is the 157th Street side of the stadium. Gate 6 is on the right side of the photo.

The giant Babe Ruth bat in its final stage of production, above. Below, the 120-foot behemoth is so tall that the trailer had to be split in half. The bat served as part of the trailer. Photos courtesy of Corbett, Inc., Somerset, N.J.

Two cranes lift Babe's mammoth club into position onto its 18-foot anchor. Photo courtesy of Corbett, Inc., Somerset, N.J.

Workers tying rebar in the bleachers to prepare wood frames for pouring of cement, February 3, 1975.

The field as seen from centerfield from the elevated train station, February 3, 1975.

Left field escalator frames are in place inside Gate 2 escalator tower, February 3, 1975.

Two supervisors or workers survey the scene from left field, February 3, 1975.

The stadium is coming along very nicely, April 21, 1975.

On this view facing west on East 157th Street, the metal frame of a parking garage is being built using an Interstate Crane Corp. crane. The storage pod across from it says, "Ship by Hecht." Below is a close up photo of the parking garage, April 21, 1975.

Looking at Gate 6 from River Avenue. Sewer pipes are next to the fence. The parking garage being built is seen past the escalator pod, April 21, 1975.

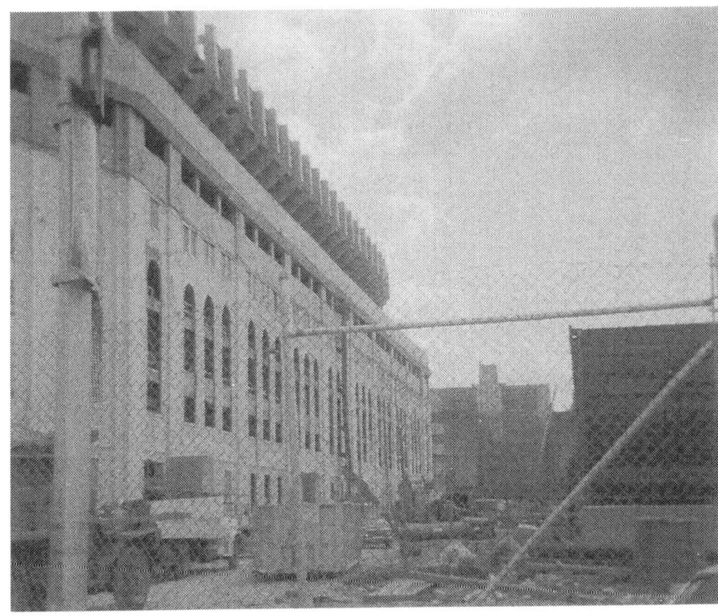

The view looking east down East 157th Street, toward River Avenue, April 21, 1975.

Gate 4 from a distance (above), and close up (below), April 21, 1975.

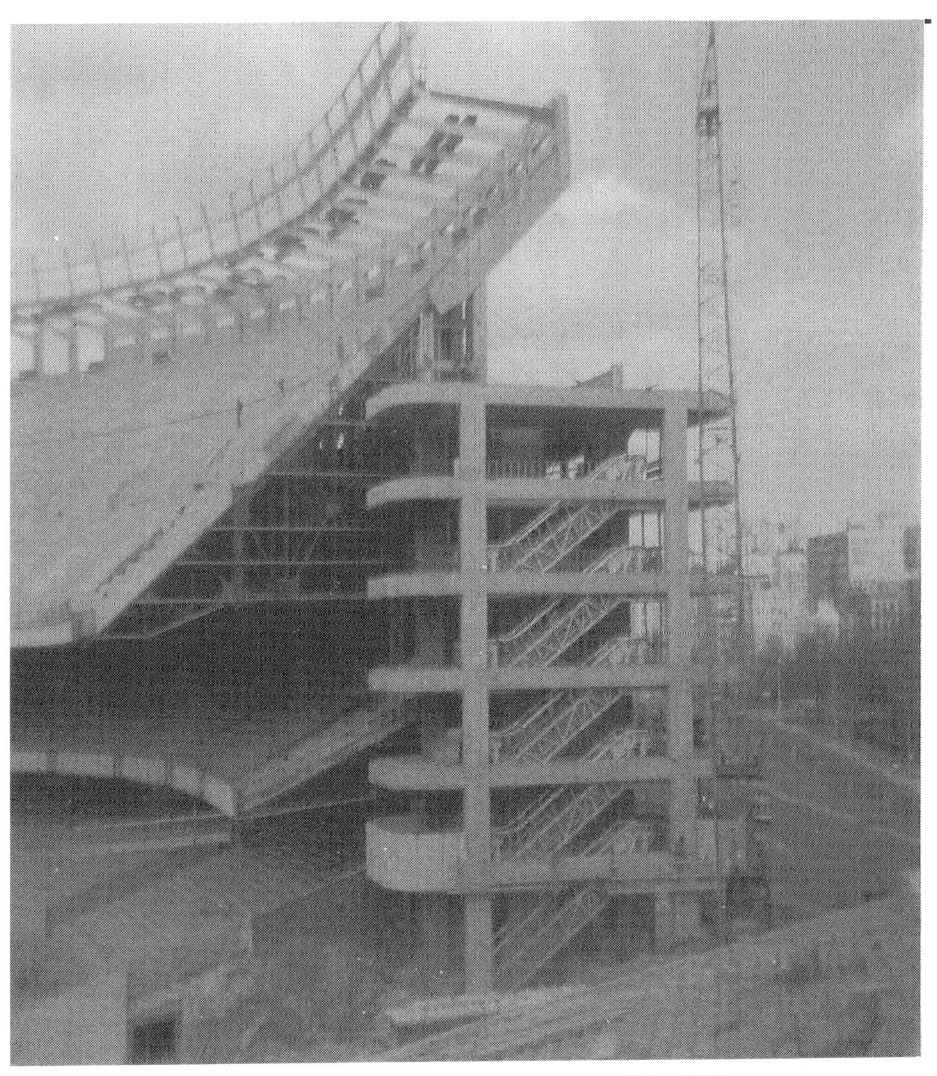

Left field escalator tower and grandstand, April 21, 1975.

The bleachers and looking toward home plate, April 21, 1975.

The bleachers and right field stands, April 21, 1975.

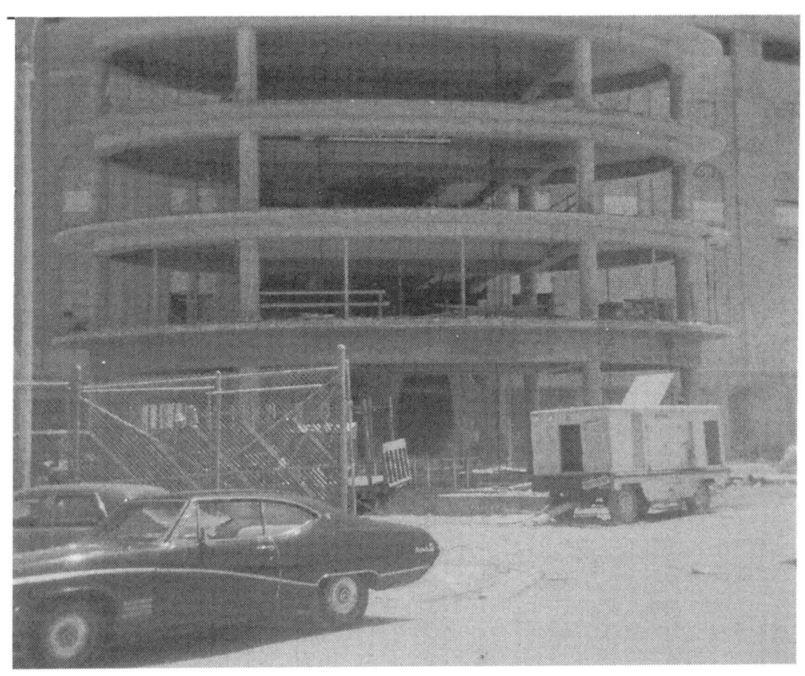

Gate 4 and some of the men working on it, May 28, 1975. The white curtains reduced sandblasting debris by helping to contain the loosened sandblasted dust in a localized area.

Gate 6 (above), and the view from the Gate 6 area on East 157th Street when looking west, (below), May 28, 1975.

A lonely hot dog vendor stands near Gate 4. East 153rd Street and East 157th Street merged at Gate 4, May 28, 1975.

This photo of the bleachers and the field shows the field to be on its way to becoming a baseball field again, May 28, 1975.

Bleachers and right field stands taken from elevated train (above), and photo taken from field level (below), May 28, 1975.

Left field escalator tower and surroundings, May 28, 1975.

The field as seen by the base of the escalator tower near Gate 2, May 28, 1975.

Hank Aaron sliding into home plate. Hank was safe. The Yankees played the Milwaukee Brewers. The Bronx Bombers won the game, 10-7, June 16, 1975.

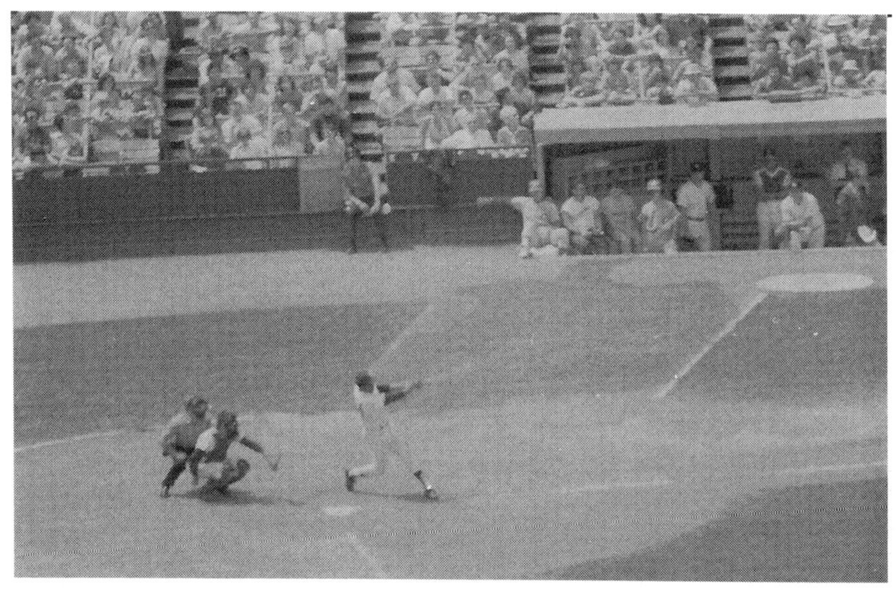

Yankees Old Timers' Day game at Shea Stadium, August 2, 1975. Willie Mays hits the ball solidly (above), while the Yankee Clipper, Joe DiMaggio, fouls one off.

Yankees Old Timers' Day game at Shea Stadium, August 2, 1975. Above is the Yankee dugout. Icons Joe DiMaggio is standing in the on-deck circle and Mel Allen is sitting at the table next to the dugout. Allen announced the Old Timers' game. In the bottom photo, another Yankee legend, Mickey Mantle, prepares to take a healthy cut at the ball.

View from near the Major Deegan Expressway. Macombs Dam Park is in the foreground. Below is Babe Ruth's 138-foot tall baseball bat, which would become a meeting place for many fans. Gate 4 is to the left of the bat, August 28, 1975.

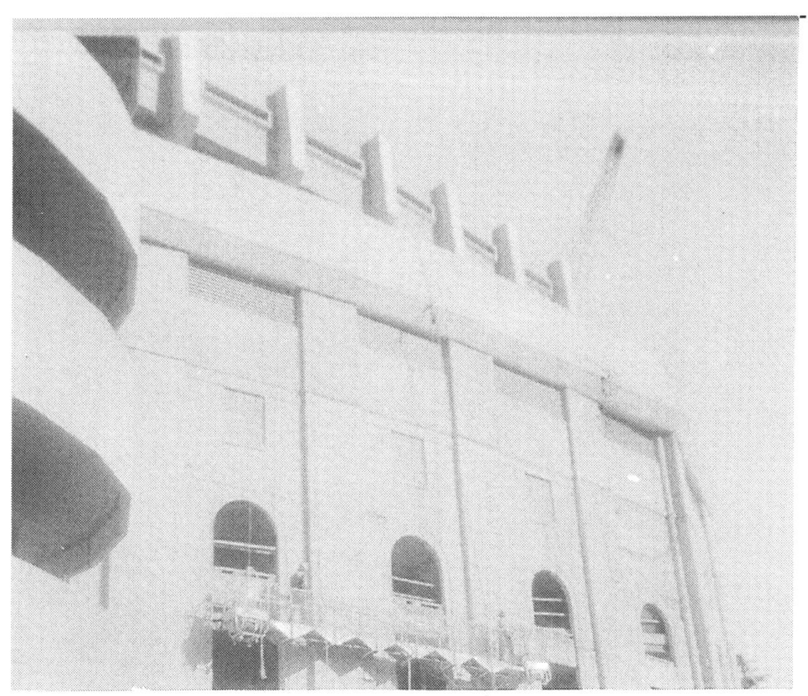

Workers on scaffold to the right of Gate 6, August 28, 1975.

This view on East 157th Street shows rubble at Gate 6 and Babe's bat near the parking garage. Cement ramps for the fans to walk to different seat levels are clearly visible inside the stadium, August 28, 1975.

East 157th Street looking west. Work is being done around the parking garage, August 28, 1975.

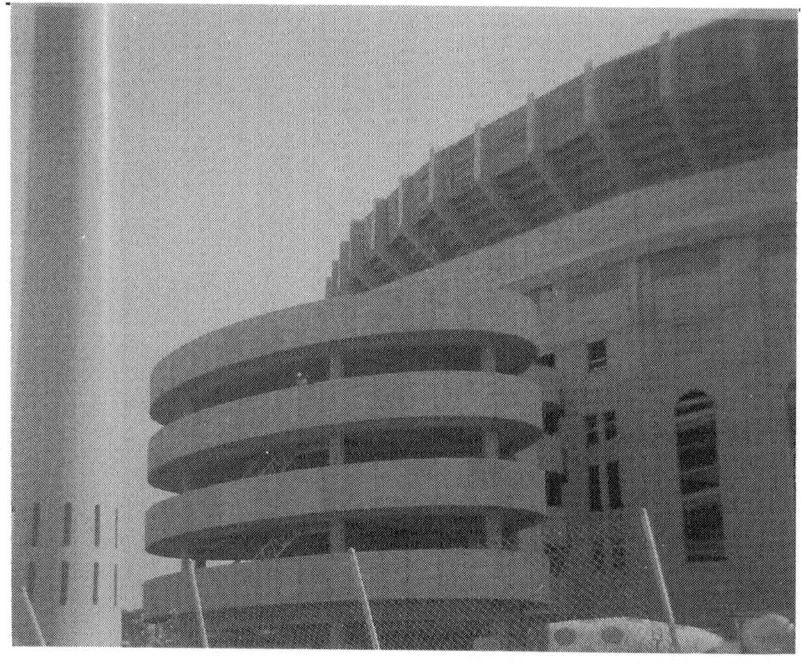

A Colonial cement truck is at Gate 4. Babe's bat is to the rear on the left. It served as a smoke stack for the boiler room. Blue letters saying "YANKEE STADIUM" are in place, August 28, 1975.

Ruppert Place as seen from East 161st Street, looking south, on 3B side of Stadium, August 28, 1975.

Babe's bat in front and workers and cement trucks working on the parking garage on East 153rd Street, where it meets East 157th Street, August 28,1975.

Right field stands as seen from base of Gate 2 escalator, August 28, 1975.

Steel framing is seen in the bleachers. This will be used to house the future scoreboard, August 28, 1975.

Workers amidst the rubble behind the bleachers on River Avenue, below the elevated train station, August 28, 1975.

The field as seen from the escalator tower near Gate 2 in left field, August 28, 1975.

The steel skeleton of the scoreboard from the elevated train platform on River Avenue.
The two flatbed trucks hold parts of the frieze, which will be mounted above the bleachers, August 28, 1975.

Views of steel frame for scoreboard in the right field section of stadium. Below, the tall structure will house the speakers for the new sound system, August 28, 1975.

Elevated train platform view of the field looking toward home plate, August 28, 1975.

The same vantage point showing the left field stands and escalator tower, August 28, 1975.

Bleachers and Gate 2 escalator area at East 161st Street, August 28, 1975. This would be my last trip to the stadium during the renovation.

Chapter Five

1976 – ROUND TWO

We're almost there

Along with America's 200th anniversary, the showplace for the Bronx Bombers was well on its way to its scheduled April 15 opening. To some it would be known as "The House That Lindsay Rebuilt," to others "Yankee Stadium II." By the end of February, the city had spent $46 million to refurbish the 873,163 gross square foot stadium. It's amazing that the original Yankec Stadium took only 284 days to complete, and cost $2,308,000 in 1922-1923.

Fixing up the surrounding area, including building two large parking garages, brought the renovation bill up to $54 million, $65 million, $101 million, or $160 million with debt service. It depended upon which newspaper you read. According to Edwin H. Brunjes, the Director of Design, Department of Public Works for the City of New York, the true cost totaled $110 million. The actual renovation of Yankee Stadium tallied $59 million. Purchasing the land from the Knights of Columbus, the Stadium from Rice University, and the rest of the environs accounted for the remaining $51 million price tag. [1]

Approximately 6,900 vehicles could now be parked for Yankee Stadium events. These spaces would generally be full when attendance reached 15,000. The ramp from the Major Deegan Expressway would be completed in the next year. Over time, New York State relieved the city by paying for the cost of the project.

These expenditures were hard for many people to swallow, as the city had a $1.5 billion budget gap. All the while, teachers, firemen, and policemen were among the groups of citizens losing jobs. Many city services suffered cutbacks. Even with the loss of 50,000 city workers through layoffs and attrition, Mayor Beame's budget ran to about $12 billion. [2]

Walsh Construction Company, 711 Third Avenue, New York City, a division of the Guy F. Atkinson Company, served as Construction Manager for the renovation of Yankee Stadium. Walsh deserves much credit for the Stadium opening on time. As the official representative for the New York City Department of Public Works, it managed the key contractors in the renovation. It acted as consultant to the Department during the final design phase of the job, for a $767,000 fee. [3]

Praeger, Kavanagh, and Waterbury used computer-generated drawings for this undertaking, years before other architectural firms began this practice. Jacqueline Thompson worked on the sight lines, dugouts, locker rooms, restaurant, and toilets. The computer was enormously helpful to the architects in setting up the geometry of the complex, "splayed U" configuration of the existing building. The labor force created 140 viewing areas and ramps for wheelchair-bound fans. These spectators would also find easily accessible drinking fountains and toilets. Men would use bathrooms painted blue, and women's rest rooms were painted red.

Exact reproductions of the louvers cost $1.5 million, as the originals couldn't be saved. Yankees architect Perry Green proudly said, "The Yankees' main concern was that the ball park be modernized while retaining its historical aura. That was my assignment." He also asserted, "It's like the old Yankee Stadium. It's got character and charm. Old Timers will feel as if they're in the old Yankee Stadium."

Green knew the importance of Yankee Stadium when he declared, "This is Yankee Stadium, in the middle of New York City. We didn't want one of those cookie-cutter stadiums, these perfectly round nothings they've been putting in every city. Go into any one of them and you don't know whether you're in Pittsburgh, Cincinnati, St. Louis, Philadelphia, or Atlanta. You have to call an operator to find out what town you're in." He proudly exclaimed, "You always know where you are in Yankee Stadium. That the original odd-shaped contour of the stadium had been left undisturbed, it was like no other park and we wanted to keep it that way." [4]

NAB-Tern Constructors, a Joint Venture of NAB Construction Corp., and Tern Construction Company, held the largest contract of all, worth $22,220,000. NAB was located at 11220 14th Avenue in College Point, New York, while Tern had been situated at 223 North 8th Street in Brooklyn, New York. NAB-Tern functioned as the contractor for the General Construction work for the endeavor. They were responsible for the major part of the venture, such as piling, concrete, masonry, waterproofing, carpentry, miscellaneous iron, sod, landscaping, and all finishing crafts. Nearly 50,000 cubic yards of concrete went into the Stadium's renovation.

NAB worked on most of the finish work, such as sheetrock. Tern did most of the concrete and heavy work. Colonial Sand and Stone supplied several thousand cubic yards of concrete for this venture. The company later went out of business. The NAB-Tern partnership lasted a number of years after the renovation, but then dissolved.

Their iron workers fabricated aluminum railings, ramps, canopy roofs, and the copper-clad frame that held the scoreboard. Although a six-month iron shop workers strike did occur at one point, NAB-Tern finished their tasks in time for the 1976 baseball season. Throughout the renovation, workers usually showed up at 5:30 or 6:00 a.m. to start their labors. [5]

A.J. Pegno Construction, College Point, New York, constructed the footbridge that would be located near the 138-foot-tall Babe Ruth baseball bat. Edwin H. Brunjes designed this walkway, as well as the parking garage next to the Stadium. This concrete and plexiglas skywalk went over the railroad tracks and allowed patrons to walk from the parking garage to the Stadium. This year-and-a-half project received the New York Concrete Industry Board Award for Aesthetics expression, as it was recognized as one of the best architectural concrete jobs in New York City at the time. Public funding supported the cost of the bridge. Pegno's workers also renovated the River Avenue subway station, as well as the River Avenue elevated train line.

In fact, in 2006 and 2007, the American Institute of Architects (AIA) conducted a poll of people's favorite buildings in the United States. The survey commemorated AIA's 150th anniversary in 2007. The connection was more emotionally based than anything else. Yankee Stadium ranked number 84. The Empire State Building came in as number one. A total of 248 structures were rated by 2,448 AIA members. A second survey of 2,214 people in the general public then cast their ballots. All voted on up to 20 buildings per person. New York City led the group with 32 buildings on the list. Washington, D.C., came in second with 17 structures. [6]

The team's fans would take escalators or ramps to their seating levels. NAB-Tern constructed the concrete escalator towers, which took patrons to the upper levels of the arena. These three structures, containing 21double-width Otis Elevator Company escalators, replaced the original entrances, located at Gates 4 and 6 as well as the top five feet of Gate 2. Escalators could travel between 90 and 120 feet per minute, and were reversible to handle large crowds. Otis spokesmen said the reason for the escalators being outside the Stadium was to handle large volumes of people without congestion. Yankee Stadium proper housed five elevators for staff, handicapped spectators, and deliveries. The contract with Otis cost $1,580,731.

The ramps that fans originally used to reach the various elevations of the ball park were "grandfathered" under the old building codes by the city, since their slope exceeded the modern building regulations. These ramps could not be rebuilt due to space restrictions, so they continued to be used as they had been since the Stadium opened in 1923.

Karl Koch Erecting Company, Inc., located in Carteret, New Jersey, fabricated and erected most of the structural steel. Their Local 40 union ironworkers also constructed all of the precast seating floors and their supporting structure. Koch had a second contract awarded in September 1973. Work began in December of that year and had been completed on time in March 1975. The $6,669,500 contract was the second biggest awarded for the remodeling.

The 500 renovators saved approximately 65 percent of the original outer walls, as estimated by Ralph Drewes, who was NAB's Contractor Superintendent. They also retained virtually all of the foundation work and basic structure of the Stadium. The Field Level stands stayed roughly 50 percent original, as did the Mezzanine (now Loge). A lot of dirt and debris was left under the stands. Usable earth backfill was used, recycled, or sent to landfills throughout the New York City area.

The Upper Level remained about 90 percent preserved, although the roof was now gone. The bleachers stood nearly 75 percent intact. NAB-Tern worked on the cement bleachers. Workers removed the front portion of the bleachers to make room for Monument Park and the bullpens. Several sections in left field were eliminated to erect a loading dock. In addition, the middle of the bleachers had been painted black to reduce glare for the hitters so pitched balls wouldn't blend in with fans' white shirts. [7]

Monument Park, a new addition to the Stadium, once again memorialized Miller Huggins, Lou Gehrig, and Babe Ruth with their familiar monuments, previously erected in center field before Yankee Stadium's transformation. Wall plaques honored Ed Barrow, Jacob Ruppert, Joe DiMaggio, Mickey Mantle, Joe McCarthy, Casey Stengel, and Pope Paul VI. His Holiness had celebrated Mass here before 80,000 followers on October 4, 1965.

Workers installed a new flagpole and baseball bat weathervane on February 27, 1976. They also built a wall behind the bleachers to prevent the public from viewing games from the subway platform, as had occurred in the original ballpark.

Specially furnished suites on the Loge Level behind home plate appeared in the new stadium. Two larger ones, built with 30 seats, cost $30,000 for the season. Seventeen 14-seat luxury boxes came with a price tag of $19,000. Thick carpet, a five-piece leather sectional, desk, refrigerator, and extra chairs came with each suite. Both larger boxes came with paintings that captured the team's past glories. Each suite boasted upholstered, self-raising, theater-type seats, a TV, wet bar, and bathroom. More than half of the boxes were sold by early March.

Some companies that leased these suites were Magnavox, the American Broadcasting Company, WPIX TV, New York Bus Service, Cue Magazine, Schaefer Beer, Ingersoll-Rand, Cabot Corp., and Edward Mosler of Mosler Safe Company fame. Celebrities such as Cary Grant, Frank Sinatra and Henry Kissinger also used these rooms for privacy.

George Steinbrenner's personal 14-seat luxury box, located on the Press Level, boasted a gray couch and four blue chairs, parked on a gray carpet. Besides a wet bar and closed-circuit TV, the lounge featured Tampa artist Phil Brinkman's paintings of Babe Ruth and Lou Gehrig on one wall. Casey Stengel was portrayed arguing with an umpire on another canvas. Another wall displayed photos of Catfish Hunter, Thurman Munson, and Bobby Bonds. Other photos included Billy Martin signing autographs and "Bat Day" at Shea Stadium. Four paintings not associated with baseball hung in the bathroom. [8]

The original Upper Deck, which became the Mechanical Level concourse, located above the Loge Level, was now closed in and hollow. It would be used for storage and seat repair. The concourse stayed in its original state.

To provide structural integrity for the great weight of the newly created Upper Deck structure, the structural engineers had designed a counterweight beam system which extended throughout the extent of the Upper Deck. Structural Contours, Inc. (SCI), of Greenwich, Connecticut, designed, engineered, and furnished a custom fiberglass reinforced plastic (FRP) Formwork System & Heavy Duty Falsework System for this massive concrete element, which would serve as the counterweight for the Upper Deck seating.

Heavy Duty Wall Mounted Jacking Brackets were thru-bolted through the exterior concrete walls below the proposed Counterweight Beam. Known as falsework equipment, these Brackets served as temporary supports for the FRP Formwork System. A sufficient quantity of Heavy Duty Wall Mounted Jacking Brackets were furnished that would allow the temporary falsework system to be set in advance, plus an additional quantity for another 105 linear feet.

After each section the FRP Gang Form units were used, they were removed and then placed into their respective next position of use. Each FRP Gang Form Section was 15 feet long. A total of seven Gang Form Sections were used, allowing the contractor to form and pour 105 linear feet of Counterweight Beam at one time.

By thru-bolting and setting the Heavy Duty Jacking Brackets at the top of the existing concrete wall below, as opposed to erecting temporary falsework equipment from grade up to the underside of the Ring Beam, considerable costs were saved by the contractor by using SCI's system.

All lifting, lowering, lateral movement and other handling of the FRP Gang Form Units was done by crane due to their size and weight. Workers continually reused the FRP Formwork & Falsework System as the concrete construction work for the Counterweight Beam progressed around the Stadium.

Structural Contours, Inc., also engineered and supplied most of the other miscellaneous concrete accessories, formwork and falsework systems for the flat concrete slabs and concrete drop beams. SCI also furnished the required temporary re-shores (supports), access scaffolding, concrete form ties, and other related equipment that was necessary for the project.

The cement from the original catwalks were now gone, although the steel beds of these walkways remained. From these original footpaths, fans had seen the Mezzanine (now Loge) and Field Level stands beneath them. Fans sitting under the newly remodeled stands would now see that white acoustic ceilings covered the area where the pathways were in order to aid the loudspeaker sound system. Pigeons now also lost many former roosting areas.

Unistress Corporation, located in Pittsfield, Massachusetts, supplied precast concrete for the renovation, such as "stringers" used for the new seating construction in the Upper Deck of the renovation, as well as Yankee Stadium's trademark frieze.

While the visitors' locker room offered just the basics, the Yankees locker room offered spike-proof purple carpet and a sauna bath for the players. Each four-foot-deep by four-foot-wide red, white, and blue cubicle came with a mirror, a recessed ceiling light, and an electrical outlet. Players could play bumper pool in their paneled lounge. The Press Level's team offices already had a blue rug and Yankee pinstriped blue on a gray background.

The dugouts would be air-conditioned for the comfort of the players. This was tricky, as they couldn't have a draft hitting the hot, perspiring players. Engineers such as Mariano Molina devised a laminar type of flow system similar to that used in hospital operating rooms, which would provide comfortable radiant cooling and even air distribution at slow-discharge velocity.

The Clubhouse Level contained a batting cage and gym for the players. One flight below, at Ground Level, the Stadium Club, a two-tiered private eating and drinking facility, would serve up to 500 patrons. A nearby cafeteria could feed 300 hungry souls. [9]

Most of the work necessary to accomplish the remodeling entailed completion of interior items, such as concession stands, clubhouses, and offices. The Sherwin Contracting Company, 150-08, Roosevelt Avenue, Queens, served as general contractors for the Canteen Corporation, the concessionaire at Yankee Stadium. Canteen's 70 selling spaces, hawker stations, souvenir stands, Stadium cafeteria, and Yankee dining room covered 3 1/5 miles of floor area. Sherwin completed the multi-million dollar construction of these areas in three months, finishing shortly before Opening Day. [10]

Concessions and ticket costs

Food at Yankee Stadium would cost more than at Shea. Dave Anderson of *The New York Times* authored an article in the May 9 edition in which he compared prices at the two stadiums. "As for the concession prices, that's simply a matter of spiraling costs. What was to have been a $2 million operation blossomed into a $5 million operation." [11]

The comparison of the two teams broke down like this:

Shea Stadium	Item	Yankee Stadium
$1.00	Hero Sandwich	$1.35
.75	Ham Sandwich	1.35
.65	Egg Salad Sandwich	1.20
.55	Hot Dog	.65
.70	Beer	.80
.35	Soda	.45
.38	Ice Cream	.50
.25	Cake	.40

.35	Peanuts	.40
.25	Potato Chips	.40
.35	Cracker Jacks	.45
.25	Coffee	.35
.25	Popcorn	.40
1.00	Yearbook	2.00
1.25	Pennant	1.35
2.50	Cap	3.25
2.50	Helmet	2.70
4.00	Autographed Ball	4.90

Diamond Club (Shea)		Stadium Club (Yankee)
$3.00	Shrimp Cocktail	3.85
.85	Soup de Jour	1.50
7.50	Roast Beef Au Jus	7.50
8.75	Sirloin Steak	11.00
.85	Baked Potato	1.25
1.35	Cheese Cake	1.85
.90	Ice Cream	1.25
.60	Coffee	.50 [12]

While the Mets would have numerous days of fan freebies, the only one the Yankees would have is Jacket Day. The Yankees also cut back on giveaway promotions. Gabe Paul explained, "We're trying to sell baseball, not giveaways." Paul related, "We cancelled Bat Day because we didn't want the kids banging the bats on the cement in a new ball park. We kept Jacket Day because they're soft goods. Jackets won't create any damage like bats will. But, basically, we're trying to sell baseball."

Ticket prices at Shea also cost less. "The Mets are working on a financial base set a long time ago," continued Paul. "And our occupancy provided them with a tremendous amount of income." He did not mention the income the Yankees gained by paying only $1 rent per year at Shea. The Yankees asserted that the Mets earned $2 million for the two years the Yankees played in Queens. Most of the revenue came from concessions and parking. [13]

For his part, Mets vice president Jim Thomson said, "But let's go back before then. Our prices were lower then, too. We've simply asked the Stevens (concession) people to keep the prices down. We work on volume. I think the fans appreciate that." [14]

Tickets for the season went on sale at the Stadium on March 2. Drew Schinelli, a seventh grade student at Mark Twain Middle School in Yonkers, skipped school in order to be the first person on line to buy an Opening Day ticket. He awoke at 5:30 a.m., then rode the bus and subway with three friends to the ballpark. They each purchased box seats for $5.50. Ticket booths, located at the Hall of Fame Plaza on East 157th Street, opened from 9 a.m. to 5 p.m. Schinelli had also attended the last game of the 1973 season. [15] Field Level and Main Level season tickets sold for $325.00.

Color-coded tickets matched the area of the Stadium where spectator seats were located. For instance, white and yellow tickets reflected Main Box seating, white and red ducats meant Upper Reserved viewing, and white and green indicated Loge Box. Besides obtaining tickets at the Stadium, fans could also purchase tickets thru Ticketron. This company provided electronic box offices in high-traffic areas, such as department stores and banks, to sell tickets to customers for various entertainment events.

Administrative offices were consolidated and expanded on the Mezzanine Level behind home plate. This was done by removing 21 sections of Mezzanine seats and replacing them with a concrete-filled metal deck. The front of this floor was secured by a hollow steel tube from Upper Deck trusses above. Each private office overlooked the baseball diamond. The Yankees' offices prior to the facelift were located on the exterior first base side of the Stadium. Before the renovation, players entered and exited the ball park from here.

Mansfield Contracting Corp., 41-41 150th Street, Flushing, acted as the prime electrical contractor for the undertaking. Their tasks included installing 885 1500-watt Sylvania Metalarc floodlights used to light the playing field. Along with a revolutionary computer aiming program designed by the Crouse-Hinds Company, the three tiers of lights produced uniform light levels on the field. Each light provided 142,500 lumens of light, equal to 450 40-watt incandescent lamps. This culminated in efficient, low glare, with no shadows. Photographers would be able to use daylight color film to photograph evening events. Mansfield also furnished and installed all electrical power, lighting, alarm, and sound systems. This part of the renovation cost the city $2,849,000. [16]

Wachtel, Duklauer, & Fein, Inc., served as the plumbing contractor for the renovation. It provided all of the plumbing systems, such as storm and sanitary drainage, hot and cold water, fire standpiping, and other necessary plumbing essentials. This contract amounted to $2,520,000. [17]

The Yankees had planned to create a Yankees Hall of Fame in the new Stadium on the ground floor. This plan was abandoned due to budget constraints. A souvenir shop arose instead. It seemed a shame that when so much money was being spent, that a little more wouldn't be designated to honor the unrivaled history of the team by creating such a worthwhile exhibit.

Ben Strauss Industries of Manhattan, painted the interior and sandblasted the exterior of the Stadium. The day before Opening Day, Billy Martin asked where the painters were. None of the dugout handrails had been painted. Victor Strauss had his workers paint them yellow, as specified by the rules of baseball. This was so the ballplayers wouldn't run into them when chasing foul balls. Since George Steinbrenner didn't like the color red on walls, only fire code regulation items and signs, as well as a pinkish-red outside the ladies rooms in the corridors received such treatment. [18]

The medallions that graced the top of the Yankee Stadium gates, featuring the eagle, catcher, and field were never replaced after they were taken down during the remodeling. Victor Strauss had his artists re-create the art pieces and presented two color fiberglass copies to George Steinbrenner in the late 1990s on one of his birthdays on July 4. These reproductions hung on the exterior wall at the entrance of the remodeled Yankee Stadium offices. [19]

The Amsterdam Paint Company in the Bronx, which had opened in 1927, supplied the paint for the renovation. Richard Fisher represented Praeger, Kavanagh, Waterbury, with regard to paint coatings. The main features of the Stadium to receive such coverings were stippled concrete for the archways and a glossy exterior, which would be more difficult for the paint to adhere to. The specialized exterior finish paint was a high-build coating for waterproofing the exterior of the Stadium. The shade of this paint was called Sequoia Dust. It was a modification of swimming pool paint. The reason was that the cold New York winters would allow moisture to seep behind an ordinary paint, thus causing the paint to peel. The standard film thickness used eliminated pinhole problems which would have been caused by the weather. Many other areas of the exterior received paints known as DT44, M499, and M500. These paint designations were found on the renovation blueprints.

Another specialized coating had been used for bumpers on the outfield wall. Blue paint faded in ultraviolet light, so by using waterproof elastometric coating, this issue was prevented. The elastometric coating stretched and moved with the building. It also joined hairline cracks and small voids which normally occur during expansion and contraction. [20]

The Norman Mechanical Company functioned as the heating, ventilating, air conditioning, and fire sprinkler systems purveyor on the job. It was not an easy task, as New York Yankee ingenuity had to be used to fit pipes and ductwork around existing structures. Their cost amounted to $2,431,000. [21]

The original field was excavated from eight to ten feet deep during the renovation. Excavated materials that came from the Basement Level were stored on the playing field. Most of this earth came from the footing excavation for the new row of columns at the Mezzanine Level. The final field level was five feet lower than the original Stadium field depth. Crews planted the natural merion bluegrass field in the fall of 1975. [22]

Towards the end of the renovation, Yankees assistant General Manager Cedric Tallis and team chief legal counsel Joe Garagiola, Jr. went to the Stadium to check its progress when the facelifting was nearing completion. They noticed the left field foul pole was installed correctly, with the three-foot netting facing fair territory. Workers, however, had faced the netting on the right field foul pole towards foul territory. The two worried executives weren't sure the improperly placed right field pole would be corrected in time for Opening Day, nor would the concession stands all be done on time. After reporting this to Yankees president Gabe Paul, Paul assured them both problems would be solved before Opening Day. They were. [23]

The trademark frieze returns

The most striking feature of the ballpark was the scoreboard, ringed by the white precast synthetic Gypsum Reinforced Concrete (GFRC) trademark Yankee Stadium frieze above. Michael Burke wanted to retain the flavor of the pre-renovated Stadium. In his 1984 autobiography, *Outrageous Good Fortune*, he related how he insisted the frieze be constructed around the grandstand, as had been done when the arena had been originally built. The architects said this was impossible, since the new structure could not support it as the girders of the past had done. Burke finally relented and said, "Then take it down and mount it around the perimeter wall behind the bleachers. We've got to preserve that characteristic somehow. Come back and tell me you can do that." They did. Each section of precast concrete frieze weighed 8,000 to 9,000 pounds and had to be bolted to a steel frame. [24]

In a television interview some years later, George Steinbrenner said that screen idol Cary Grant once visited Steinbrenner during the renovation, and asked if there could be some way to incorporate the famous trademark frieze into the new Stadium. That appears to be a nice, but untrue story. On April 14, 2009, *The New York Times* published an article titled, "A Distinctive Façade Is Recreated at New Yankee Stadium," by columnist Richard Sandomir. Marty Appel, who was the Yankees assistant public relations director in the early 1970s, said, "the design was in place by the time George bought the team." [25]

Besides being the famous Yankee Stadium symbol, the frieze acted as a counterweight. Renovators added several rows of cement to the bleachers. The ring at the top of the bleachers was 1,600 cubic feet of poured cement that sat on the old Stadium wall. This prevented the bleachers from tipping over. Architect Robert C.Y. Young noted that Barbara Paley, wife of CBS founder and chairman William S. Paley, was very nostalgic about the famous Yankee Stadium frieze that encircled the Stadium grandstand. She was very happy when the frieze above the center field scoreboard matched the exact size and dimensions as the original copper frieze which was removed for the renovation.

The new $2.5 million 560-foot scoreboard was located in the outfield, rear of the bleacher seats. Designed by Conrac Corporation, it came in seven sections. Four panels would be used for advertising, and three for game information, instant replays, animation, and messages. It would be the most up-to-date scoreboard in the major leagues, and house the first instant-replay display in baseball. The scoreboard would stand at 24 feet tall, except for the center Telscreen, which had a height of 40 feet. Over 100 tons of A-36 structural steel would be used in the scoreboard.

The steel frame supporting the scoreboard measured 560 feet by 45 feet. The front of the scoreboard consisted of fabricated extruded aluminum. Seiko provided the official time. The outfield walls now stood at seven feet tall in left field, and ten feet high in right field. [26] Conrac was currently installing five Telscreens in Montreal, Canada, for the 1976 Summer Olympic Games. Conrac's principal office was located at 330 Madison Avenue in Manhattan.

Klepper Marshall King Associates (KMK) of Chappaqua, Westchester, New York, served as the acoustic consulting firm for the sound system during the renovation. Their primary focus was to work on the sound amplification in the Stadium. This plan consisted of a main loudspeaker system, with the principal coverage in a vertical group of 16 low-frequency speakers directly in line with home plate. Approximately 12 high-frequency sectional horns were placed above the new scoreboard. Dave Klepper had the idea of building the tall column of high-and low-frequency horns. An arrangement of delayed sound loudspeakers around the soffits (ceiling) of the Grandstand, lobby, and concession areas of the ballpark to the home plate area of the Stadium completed the scheme. The distance from the loudspeakers in the Bleachers [to the lobby] was perhaps 750 to 800 feet, whereas a typical theater measured only approximately 150 feet and was enclosed.

Eventide Inc., located in Little Ferry, New Jersey, custom made a big delay unit for the job. Electro-Voice (E-V), located in Burnsville, Minnesota, supplied the loudspeakers for the project. Jim Long of E-V and Larry King of KMK collaborated closely on the project. The designers built a model to replicate how sound would reflect in the park.

The sound system used about 100 decibels of volume. To aid the system, white perforated metal ceiling panels covered the Grandstand ceiling. These sheets, located in the Mezzanine and Grandstand, enclosed one or two inches of mylar glass fiber to help with sound absorption from the fans and loudspeakers. KMK requested that the seating in the Stadium be porous so as to maximize this effect. Supplemental speakers over the Main and Mezzanine decks, lobbies, concourses, and press area completed the sound system. Bob Sheppard, the Yankees' legendary public address announcer, spent weeks testing the system. [27]

American Seating of Grand Rapids, Michigan, supplied the 54,028 royal blue plastic grandstand seats for the facelift. The Stadium chair, model #406, measured 21 by 22 inches. These one-piece double-walled Dexlon® plastic seats replaced the 18- and 19-inch wooden seats built in the original arena.

These chairs measured 30 inches from top to bottom, 15 3/8 inches from the back of the seat to the front of the arm rest, and 21½ inches from the rear of the chair to the bottom of the seat when it was in use. When a spectator sat down, the seat itself was about 17¼ inches from the floor. The company based these new seats on the patterns of the originals installed in 1923. In all, the remodeled home lost some 10,000 seats. This contract let for $1,766,824.

A total of 2,398 plastic molded, individualized bench seating in the bleachers replaced the similar seats removed from the demolition phase. Another 7,500 bleacher seats could be used for baseball games and other events. [28]

Aside from the scoreboard area and seating, another major change was the cantilevered, roofless Upper Deck. Workers accomplished this feat by removing 36 H-columns from the inside edge of the Stadium. These posts held up the Mezzanine and Upper Decks, as well as the roof. These were replaced with 106 20-inch A-36 structural steel columns placed behind the seating area. These new pillars combined with the cable-counterweight design to sustain the steel trusses that bore the weight of the stands and new roof canopy. This part of the modernization used most of the 1,600 tons of reinforced steel manufactured for the project.

These columns worked like a fulcrum. The grandstand was tilted backwards by two-inch pre-stressed galvanized steel tie-back cables attached to every column. These 106 cables were secured to a concrete counterbalance beam, which was mounted at the upper rim of the Stadium's outside wall. Karl Koch Company installed the precast concrete "stringers." These ten rows of added seating in the rear of the Stadium served as a counterbalance to the Upper Deck, which hung up in the air, much like the towers of a bridge support. The new seats began at Row K of the Upper Reserved seats. The new configuration didn't fit seamlessly, as fans had to watch their step on that row, which rose 1½ inches higher than the other rows, lest they might trip.

ASARCO Incorporated, 120 Broadway, New York City, applied a zinc coating to the steel used to reinforce the concrete in the upper level of the Yankee Stadium renovation by galvanizing the mesh, as well as steel rebar under the surface of the decking, and near the surface of the seats. The shims that kept the 40 foot "L" shaped seating in line received this same protection. This zinc layer prevented the steel from corroding from rain and snow. Moisture from weather would have otherwise seeped through the concrete, which would have then cracked and fragmented, thus weakening the structure.

The Upper Deck Reserve held 21 rows, A thru X. However, there were no rows I, O, and Q. Many theatres are the same way. The Upper Box sat rows A thru F. There were two rows of seats per letter, totaling 12 rows. The entire Upper Deck totaled 33 rows, with an aisle in the middle. The lower two-thirds of the Upper Deck remained original. In all, 41 percent of the ballpark's seating (23,607 seats) was located in the Upper Deck.

Row C of the Upper Box seats was where the aisle was located in the original Stadium. After the renovation, this row had a rail in front of it. Normally, if you sat down and kicked, your foot would hit the seat in front of you. In Row C, your foot would now hit the head of the person in front of you. [29]

Praeger Kavanagh Waterbury, a Division of Madigan-Prager, Inc., 200 Park Avenue South, New York, NY 10017, was listed as the Engineers-Architects. The 173 pages that made up the set of prints were dated October 1, 1973. The Department of Public Works Economic Development Administration designated this project as Capital Budget Number ES 98. The blueprints carried the title, "Modernization of Yankee Stadium." The Exterior Elevations & Cross Sections drawings represented a scale of 1/32=1'0". This page, number 40 of 173, portrayed the outside exterior, cross section of home plate looking south, and escalator towers.

Old vs. new dimensions

Below are interesting comparisons of Yankee Stadium.

Height of Yankee Stadium (Numbers are written as shown on the blueprints).

1976		1923	
Top Row Elevation of Grandstand	131' 5"	Roof High Point	127.5'
Top of Parapet Elevation	104' 9½"	Roof Low Point	122.5'
Upper Level Elevation	86' 9½"	Upper Deck	112.25'
Mechanical Level Elevation	74' 0"	Upper Deck Concourse	74.0'
Mezzanine Level Elevation	64' 0"	Mezzanine Deck	64.0'
Club Level Elevation	52' 6"		
Main Level Elevation	41' 0"	Main Deck	41'.0"
Ground Level Elevation	24' 6"		
Basement Level Elevation	19' 0"		

Plans on the 1973 blueprints called for the exterior concrete to receive a "pebble dash" texture. The vast majority of the concrete and masonry would be painted M499, which looked to be a grayish color. Most of the metal siding, fascias, panels, and soffits would be color DT44. The loudspeaker would also be the color M499. The majority of trim was to be colors M499 or DT44. These colors appeared to be off-white.

Louvers in metal siding were to be of a baked enamel to match the color of its adjacent siding. Doors were to be painted DT44 when contiguous with the siding on panels. When contiguous with concrete, plans called for the paint to be M499. Side panels, soffits, and metal wall rails on the escalators would be painted DT44. [30]

Yankee Stadium Field Dimensions (Feet from home plate):

Year	LF Line	LCF	Deepest LCF	CF	Deepest RCF	RCF	RF Line
1973	301	402	457	461	407	344	296
1976	312	387	430	417	385	353	310 [31]

Along with the "new" ballpark, the Yankees named Toyota as the Official Car of the New York Yankees. A pinstriped Toyota Celica would be used to bring in relief pitchers from the bullpen. The Toyota Celica received Motor Trend's Import Car of the Year award for 1976.

Through the 50 seasons of the original Yankee Stadium's existence, the Bronx Bombers won 27 American League pennants and 20 World Series titles before 64,788,405 paying patrons. This attendance figure only refers to regular season game attendees. This doesn't count the customers who had witnessed the World Series, football games, religious rallies, 29 boxing matches, or any other number of special events held in this hallowed edifice.

Mayor Beame dedicated the "new" Yankee Stadium when he addressed a few hundred invited guests on April 13. Everyone received a color 7"x9", eight-page Dedication program of the sparkling ball park. During the invocation, the Reverend William G. Kalaidjian of the Bedford Park Congregational Church in the Bronx added a prayer that the team would win the pennant. The Xavier High School Color Guard, located on West 16th Street in New York City, provided the Raising of the Colors. The Cardinal Hayes High School Band, situated on the Grand Concourse, near Yankee Stadium, supplied the music. Lucy Monroe sang the National Anthem. The Mayor and Robert Abrams tried on Yankees shirts for the occasion.

His Honor's enthusiastic official remarks read as follows: "The opening of the new Yankee Stadium is a great day in the life of New York City, a day all New Yorkers can be proud of and share together in knowing we have a sports complex which is one of the most modern and magnificent in the world. This is a day we can all extend a welcome to those who will not only use this facility, but to those who will come to see the finest professional teams playing in the Stadium."

"New Yorkers are also steeped in tradition. It is in this vein that we are also proud to have the Yankees–one of the finest baseball teams in the world–playing in the New Stadium–home of champions."

"However, the Stadium will not only be used for America's favorite pastime. It will also be used for football competition, soccer games and other sports and entertainment events. With the support of its teams and fans, by the dedication of the architects, builders and the City departments, the new stadium should revitalize sports and business for the City." [32]

Besides the Mayor, Herbert J. Simins, P.E., Commissioner, Department of Public Works; John T. Carroll, P.E., Administrator, M.S.A. Presiding; and Robert Abrams, President, Borough of the Bronx, all spoke to the audience.

Mayor Beame took an at-bat at home plate, with Municipal Services Administrator, John T. Carroll pitching. Robert Abrams umpired. A construction worker yelled, "Stick it in his ear!" The Mayor became the first batter to be pictured on the new scoreboard. And, he did leave the batter's box with both ears intact. His Honor unveiled a plaque dedicated to the renovation of the Stadium.

Michael Burke mumbled, "Beame is talking very enthusiastically for a man who abstained when the Stadium was up for votes in the Board of Estimate." The cost had now been estimated between $70 million and $100 million. Beame said of the renovation, "It is worth the money. It's here to stay and it will be a tremendous attraction. I'm rooting for a subway series." Some city government employees believed the cost could escalate to another $150 million over the next 31 years due to tax exemptions, interest, and the cost of parking facilities.

Burke, the main force behind the remodeling, said, "I'm immensely proud and thrilled by it. A lot of hard work went into it, a lot of dedication and hard hours. This justifies every ounce of effort." In an April 15 article in the *New York Post*, Burke recalled how the motivation for the refurbishment of Yankee Stadium came to him about 1967. "As one sat in Yankee Stadium and had a piece of concrete fall on one's head, one realized the painting of Yankee Stadium was merely cosmetic. We could not stay there indefinitely under those conditions."

Realizing the Stadium's age, lack of parking, and adverse neighborhood atmosphere, plus the need for access roads to the Stadium, Burke contacted city planners, but reached a dead end. Burke then related, "One day John Lindsay was at a game and I asked him up to my office for a drink. He said, 'I know we have to do something to help you.' I said, 'Fine, what are you doing Monday?'" [33]

The two leaders talked about the situation and soon realized a new stadium was unaffordable. M. Donald Grant, President of the New York Mets, vehemently opposed sharing Shea Stadium with the Yankees. The New York Giants football team wanted the Yankees to join them in New Jersey. Burke told Mayor Lindsay, "my preference is for staying in the city. I thought the Yankees leaving as well as the Giants would be a devastating blow for the city."

As Burke recalled, "Lindsay not only wanted to help the Yankees, he felt a refurbished Yankee Stadium would be an act of faith in the city." Renovating the Stadium was the only way to solve the problem. A virtual war among the politicians occurred, but the goal was somehow accomplished. A thankful Michael Burke said, "I'm immensely proud of the Stadium. The ten years I spent with the Yankees were the happiest ten years of my life. No one can ever take that from me. It has been a long ten years. One doesn't mind working that hard when one sees it all coming to a kind of fruition with this new club, with Billy Martin as manager and a new Yankee Stadium."

George Steinbrenner chimed in, "We're doing great right now and the better we do the better the city will do. I think we're going to really draw. We're getting a good ticket demand already for games with Boston and Baltimore in July." Tickets were already sold out for tomorrow's inaugural game. [34]

Across the street at the Jerome Cafeteria, at 161st Street and River Avenue, cafeteria manager Frank Bludniker looked forward to the baseball season. The establishment sported new floor tiles, and the burned-out bulbs spelling the name of the eatery were being replaced. Mr. Bludniker optimistically said, "The neighborhood has to get better. We'll have more people. We already have more cops."

One elderly woman also cheerfully expressed her joy at the new dawning of the sparkling colossus. "For me, the new Stadium is a special pleasure. My grandson, an architect in Syracuse, will be here for the opening game."[35]

Opening Day - Play Ball!

Thursday, April 15, marked the return of Yankee Stadium's Opening Day. The team had been on the road since April 8. They played two games in Milwaukee and another pair in Baltimore. Today they would play the Minnesota Twins. The Yankees estimated the renovation to be 98 percent complete. The major unfinished areas were some concession areas inside the Stadium, the outside pedestrian foot bridge, and highway improvements.

Workmen were hammering blue rubber padding on the inside of the Yankee dugout. The roofs were built too low. Excited Yankees jumping up and down during a rally would be injured when they'd hit their heads on the roof, if not aided by this protection.

Electricians were still installing lighting, the pitcher's mound was too low, and the scoreboard clock read 14 minutes late. The Telscreen portion of the scoreboard didn't work, thanks to technical difficulties. Batting orders and out-of-town baseball scores had not been displayed. Some confusion arose because some of the players' uniform numbers did not always match what was on the scoreboard. Perhaps the only person who was happy about the scoreboard was Oscar Gamble. It said he was batting .999. The Yankees' sauna also did not cooperate. And Billy Martin's manager's office lacked carpet.

As Billy pointed out, "It's amazing how the carpet stops right here." It covered the clubhouse, but ended in front of Billy's door. He said of his white cement block walls and bare cement floor, "You think they're trying to tell me something?" Also, his shower head was broken. Aside from that, the Bronx skipper proudly declared, "It's the sharpest park in the league, without a doubt. It's even prettier than those new parks. I just hope it has the same number of wins it used to have, like about 104." [36]

The Yankees expected a sellout crowd. The grounds crew had worked into the early morning hours and started working on the field again at 7 a.m. Surveyors measured the mound to make certain it was the regulation ten inches high. After measuring it, Umpire John Stevens said it was still too low. The pitchers certainly noticed it. The infield itself was wavy and sloped towards the outfield. Observed the one and only Yogi Berra, "They must have graded this field in a rowboat." [37]

Billy Martin said of the Stadium, "It's great. I think the thing I miss most is the green lattice work that hung down from the Stadium." "Me, too," agreed Yogi Berra, "but you see they put it out in center field and painted it white. It still is a lot like the old Stadium." Someone supposedly also heard Yogi say, "It's changed a lot. It's still old, but it's more modern." [38]

With the outfield fences closer to the plate, Yankees left fielder Roy White felt odd. "I didn't know where I was at. I can't gauge the distance out there yet." Others also felt the differences. "I got lost coming into our clubhouse," noted coach Elston Howard. Yet the team was very happy to be home. Only eight of the players from 1973 were on the current team roster. [39]

Thurman Munson said, "I liked the old park. I liked the tradition and the memories. But I'm sure we'll get accustomed to the new park. It's beautiful." Infielder Fred Stanley exclaimed, "It sure is a nice park. The old Yankee Stadium seemed dark. This is bright." Ace relief pitcher Sparky Lyle observed, "They've got a poker table in the lounge of our clubhouse, but we're not allowed to play cards." [40]

The Commerce Comet, Mickey Mantle, remarked, "There was a great, dark mystery about the old Stadium when I first came here from Oklahoma. I still get goose pimples just walking inside it, but now I think this is about the prettiest ballpark I ever saw." He added, "It really hasn't changed that much. They've got hairdryers and mirrors and lights in each locker stall, and the façade is gone, and the fences are in a little. But it isn't that much different." [41]

The Yankee Clipper, Joe DiMaggio, said, "I used to enjoy seeing the el (train), and that's blocked out now. People can't see from the roof (from their apartments). We used to have more people sitting up there than in the bleachers some days. The crowd is different, too. More young people. I wonder if it seems that way because I'm older. I know I'm glad I came. I wanted to see this. It still has the charm of the old Stadium. It hasn't lost it completely. They reduced the size of the field, but they haven't taken away its shape." [42]

Sitting behind the Yankees dugout, New York Governor, Hugh Carey, appeared at the game with 10 of his 12 children. Carey stated, "It's a rebirth of the Yankees, in a sense. You look out and see the old and the new of New York together." Across the aisle from him sat New Jersey Governor, Brendan Byrne. Byrne quipped, "No, I'm not here trying to steal the team. I've been coming to opening day here for 15 years. He brought his wife and three children to the game. Byrne asked Mrs. Lou Gehrig, who sat in front of him, "Have you seen our new stadium? Lou Gehrig would have been proud to play there." [43]

From the visiting team's point of view, Minnesota Twins manager Gene Mauch said, "Years ago you were astounded by the tradition and immensity of Yankee Stadium. Now it's astounding in its beauty. It's right there with Dodger Stadium as the most beautiful park in baseball." [44]

Mauch's reserve designated hitter for this game, Steve Braun, grew up in New Jersey. After obtaining his driver's license some years earlier, he drove to the Stadium to see what it looked like, even though the team was on the road. "Today, comparing the old and new creations," he thoughtfully uttered, "My first impression was that it wasn't the same. Then I saw the similarities. The shape of the playing field, shorter than the old one, but consistent to it with the deep left-center. The structure itself with three decks. It's funny. The more I sat there and looked, the more it looked like Yankee Stadium." Since the shape of the park was really the same as the pre-renovated Stadium, Yankees fans also felt at home. [45]

Fans began lining up at thc gates at 10:00 a.m. The Yankees were worried, as Stadium ticket takers were on strike until ten minutes before the gates opened. Management gave in to demands in order to avoid the impending disaster. The gates opened a half-hour late, at 12:30. The 250 ushers would be very busy escorting the throngs of people to their seats, as would the 286 vendors who would hawk hot dogs, beer, soda, and other gastronomic baseball fare.

As for fans' views of the new Babe's Place, Frank Sacco of the Bronx noted, "There's one word to describe it, and that is 'awesome'." He felt that without the metal columns, the new Stadium looked "a hell of a lot bigger" than the old one. Along with many other fans in the upper reaches of the park, Sacco felt the aisles to be much narrower, and therefore, "it's much harder to climb to get up here." Sacco's 16-year-old son called the place "fantastic." [46]

Kim Porter, from Throgs Neck, sat in the Bleachers. He liked "having a seat of my own" but cited the lack of leg room for the spectators. Many fans agreed, including Rosemary Weigel, a resident of Whitestone. "I think the Stadium's beautiful, although I wish we had more leg space. But it's a wonderful view without the poles." Bleacher fans had few, if any, vendors to hawk food. Some concessions at the Stadium ran out of hot dogs. [47]

Carol McAlister of Manhattan called the new showplace "enthralling." "A sure winner," said Paul Raisides of Fairfield, Connecticut. "A grand slam hit" was how Bud Wormstitch of Wayne, New Jersey, described the newly decorated home. Ron Dvorkin of the Bronx gave it "four stars." Overall, fans thought the new Stadium looked great, but was not worth the $100 million or so price tag. Tate Preston, of Mountain Lakes, New Jersey, didn't mind forking over $2.25 to park in one of the new parking garages. He felt his car would be reasonably safe. Not everyone was on the bandwagon. [48]

Protestors also arrived

Protestors from the local area met fans across from Macombs Dam Park, as they objected to the high cost of the remodeling of the ballpark, while not much funding had been spent on the environs for residents of the area. The Reverend Patrick Ahern, Terence Cardinal Cooke's vicar in the Bronx, was one of ten speakers at the rally. He lamented the escalating costs of the renovation. "That's an awful lot of money," he said. "If they gave us a hundred million for the neighborhood, they'd see what we'd do with it." [49]

A group called Sports For The People organized the gathering. They supported a bill that Councilman Louis Almedo of Brooklyn was going to present to the City Council, which called for a 5 percent tax on Yankees earnings to be paid to the neighborhood. This money would be used for improvements in the area.

In early December of 1975, the group said they might protest Opening Day unless the city came up with $2 million to revamp Macombs Dam Field. An earlier meeting by the Committee to Save Macombs Dam Park called for upgrading the park with an eight-lane, all-weather track, and a football field with artificial surface, double-deck grandstand to seat at least 5,000 people, and light towers that would permit 24-hour use of the park. Estimated funding would run between $1.8 million and $2.4 million. [50]

The park contained a football field, running track, and two baseball fields, but dangerous conditions due to the park's decline prevented many track and field events from taking place there. Even the water fountains were broken. Lawyers for the group worked on a taxpayers lawsuit to stop completion of Yankee Stadium's renovation on the grounds that the city broke its promise to rehabilitate the surrounding area. For all intents and purposes, the suit went nowhere. Now they were back in full force.

As Cary Goodman related to the author in an interview in 2011, "Actually, we won that fight because we scheduled a mass jog-in for the day the Stadium was scheduled to open in 1976, which was tax day, April 15. And, we had something in the order of 3,000 to 4,000 people march to Macombs Dam Park and jog around the running track, and then spread across the whole park."

"Once they did that, we did what we called, 'activist exercises,' which meant that we were touching our toes to the four-count of 'tax the Yanks and the banks, save our parks and school.' And we were on the Walter Cronkite show that night. It was the topic of a whole series of articles and coverages for the Opening Day ceremonies."

"The state legislature actually wrote in some special language to their budget. I guess it's called 'budget modification,' in which they gave money for Macombs Dam Field rehabilitation. They also recognized the importance of what we were saying, and linking it to the Hostos Community College, which is just up the road from Yankee Stadium. It was previously scheduled to be closed. They agreed to keep it open."

"And the same with Lincoln Hospital, which is sort of the flagship of the New York City hospitals system in the Bronx. Lincoln was scheduled to be severely cut. And they reversed the scheduled cuts at Lincoln Hospital. So, we actually had an extremely salutary effect on the situation, and we all left on April 15 feeling as though we'd accomplished a great deal. So, it's a very important part of the Yankees' rebirth and the Yankees sort of understanding of the importance of working with the community."

"That brings us back to the question of the hospital and community college there. They were on the cutting block. We made the argument that it would be imprudent to have $150 million or $100 million of public moneys dedicated to refurbishing a ballpark where only 11 people would play at a time, and at the same time cutting funding for a hospital and community college."

"I think everybody was shocked when it went from $24 million as the first initial number, then, I think it almost tripled the next time there was any public discussion of the figures. I think that was the real jolt to the people. Then we expected there was going to be a roller coaster ride from there."

"And, not a thing got done to help the area around Yankee Stadium. The way I got involved was that a jogger in the park by the name of Myles Jackson heard of Sports For The People through the press. He called me up and asked, 'What are you going to do to help us at Yankee Stadium?' We were shocked that anyone felt it was our role to get involved because we were a small…more like a book club. People who would read books on sports and discuss issues. That was the defining effort for us."

"The Bronx was a national symbol of urban despair and decay, and I think our role was to say that by banding together and by having a principal position that everyone can understand - for example - you don't give a private company a huge amount of money while you're slicing into public institutions. You could turn that despair around. You can combat the decay that was going on. It took a while, but it's undeniable now that that area is certainly recovering, and has made a turnaround."

"I think that's the message that came out of that whole process. That people need to stick together and have a belief system or value system that sharply identifies what the problems are, and how to solve them."

"For that purpose, Sports For The People was really great because it reached into communities that never really thought about political protests, or never really paid too much attention to the idea that sports had a public and political component to it. And to that extent, it was a really, really successful effort."

"That became sort of the lynchpin for our political argument to the city, and at that time they had something called the Emergency Financial Control Board, which was where New York State took over responsibility for New York City's budget, since it was close to delinquent, and the governor appointed a panel of important and patrician people to make sure that not too much money was spent, and the city sort of rebalanced the budget."

"And, so that Emergency Financial Control Board was really the executor of the city's financial plan during that period of time. I think it may have been from 1975-1978. We felt these guys were missing the music when they were ready to plunk all of this money into the Stadium and not the most vital neighborhood institutions in that community."

"I don't know if you know what happened to Sports For The People, but in the next years it became sort of a national sports advocacy organization. We set up a coalition with the National Football League Players Association to defend high school athletes from being ripped off by colleges who came to recruit them. And then we also participated as a major element in a campaign to get equal sports for females and seniors. In fact, we were the founders of the Senior Olympics."

“So, with the Yankee Stadium protests and our efforts there, it became the starting point for us to really become a major voice in sports reform and athletic advocacy. If you go back and look back at the press of 1980 and 1981, Sports For The People and Center For Athletes Rights and Education are going to pop up any time you punch in anything having to do with advocacy or political protests."

“We were at the NCAA with legislation being introduced by college presidents, and I was on the Today Show with a lot of troubleshooting and advocacy work, all of which stemmed from the Yankee Stadium effort." It was ironic that Sports For The People began its humble origins in the shadow of the great monolith that would spawn a new age of Yankee resurgence. [51]

The magic never left the stadium

The newest dynasty of baseball's most successful troupe started working out at 11:20 a.m. The 1:30 p.m. ceremonies would feature all of the living members of the 1923 Yankees as well as other Yankees and football heroes. Magic names such as Joe DiMaggio, Mickey Mantle, Whitey Ford, Don Larsen, Yogi Berra, Mel Allen, and Yankees clubhouse man, Michael “Pete” Sheehy were some of the legends to appear. This was Sheehy’s 50th year of such service to the club. He had replaced Fred Logan in 1927. Naturally, Mrs. Babe Ruth and Mrs. Lou Gehrig attended this historic day.

Famous New Yorkers such as Toots Shor and former Postmaster General James Farley graced the field, as did boxing great Joe Louis. Football stars included Frank Gifford, Kyle Rote, Johnny Lujack, Glenn Davis, Doc Blanchard, former New York Jets coach Weeb Ewbank, as well as Phil Iselin, the team’s current owner. Said Iselin, “It’s fabulous. It’s a great boost for the city. The city needs new things.” [52] Former Mayor Lindsay did not accept an invitation to appear at Opening Day, as he was on the West Coast. He’d be gone on business for several weeks, as he was now working for a law firm. Current Mayor Beame also missed the historic event.

Eighty-five-year-old Bob Shawkey, the first Yankee ever to pitch in this sacred cathedral, would be on the pitcher’s mound in a sports jacket and tie, to throw out the first ball before today’s 52,613 paying fans. He came in from Syracuse, New York, and was one of six members of the 1923 team to appear at the game. The ball he pitched was the original Opening Day baseball he used on April 18, 1923, when the grand ballpark first opened. The National Baseball

Hall of Fame lent the prize ball for the occasion. The other members of the 1923 Yankees joining Shawkey for the festivities were Whitey Witt, Oscar Roettger, Waite Hoyt, Hinkey Haines, and Joe Dugan.

The 45-minute festivities included introducing former Yankees and celebrities associated with Yankee Stadium, as well as the scoreboard displaying great historical events that occurred at the ballpark. The special guests of the day were Mrs. Ruth, Mrs. Gehrig, former Postmaster General James Farley, Pete Sheehy, restaurant legend Toots Shor, and former Yankees announcer Mel Allen. The 88-year-old Farley had attended his first Yankee game in 1904, and was a lifelong fan. When asked how he liked the new place, Farley said, "I was here the day it opened. I was here, and so were Al Smith and Jimmy Walker. ...I've been here for every opening day since then, too. How do I like it? It's new, it's all new." [53] The entourage assembled near second base.

Mrs. Ruth proudly exclaimed, "I think the Stadium is beautiful. The Babe would have loved it." [54] *New York Times* sportswriter John Drebinger, who covered the first game in 1923, echoed her sentiments, saying, "The Babe would have liked this place. He loved beauty parlors," referring to the Yankees players having hair dryers and mirrors. [55] Billy Martin proudly proclaimed, "Yankee Stadium is beautiful. It's great to be back. We had to break the stadium in right." [56] Sparky Lyle said, "I couldn't wait to get back here. I loved playing here. Even though the Stadium has been redone, it still has the charisma the old Stadium had. I didn't know if I was going to be here for the return, but I'm glad I was. The opening day was one of the best opening days I've seen for a while." [57] "It sure is a nice park," noted infielder Fred Stanley. "The old Yankee Stadium seemed dark; this is bright." [58]

The New York Times reported 54,028 worshippers attending the game. This was the largest crowd for a Yankees home opener since April 19, 1946, when 54,826 fans came out to the park. The temperature, in the 70s, provided a beautiful day for a game. Three music bands were on the field to add to the festivities. They were from Lafayette College, Brooklyn College, and Greenwich High School. Bobby Richardson recited a prayer after the activities ended. Then, as usual, Metropolitan Opera great Robert Merrill led the audience in singing the "Star Spangled Banner." His voice had to be at its peak, as he had over 100 instruments to help him.

Southpaw Rudy May started this historic 2:00 p.m. game for the Yankees. His first four pitches to second baseman Jerry Terrell were balls. The next batter, right fielder Dan Ford, smacked a home run over the 430-foot sign in left center field. In the old Stadium, this would have been a long out in "Death Valley." But the shortened fences made a difference. Billy Martin replaced May with Dick Tidrow in the third inning, as the Twins were leading 3-0. Right hander Dave Goltz started for Minnesota.

The first Yankees run came in the third inning. Shortstop Jim Mason doubled to right. He reached third base on a Mickey Rivers single to right field and scored on a Roy White force out. The Yankees scored another four runs in the fourth inning to gain a 5-4 lead. Twins manager Mauch brought in lefty Vic Albury to replace Goltz.

Two newly acquired outfielders, Oscar Gamble in right and Mickey Rivers in center, got three hits to knock in two runs apiece. Second baseman Willie Randolph, also in his initial year in pinstripes, got two safeties. With a six-run eighth inning, Dick Tidrow easily won the game, and Albury took the loss. Lefty relief ace Sparky Lyle earned a save by pitching the last 1 2/3 innings for the home team. The Yankees trounced the Twins, 11-4. They hit no home runs, but with 14 hits, the Bronx Bombers lived up to their name in the renovated ballpark's debut.

Two days later, Thurman Munson hit the first Yankees home run off Jim Hughes at the new Yankee Stadium. This was only hours after being named the Yankees' captain. No other Yankee had held that hallowed title since Lou Gehrig. Gamble and Rivers also homered, and Ed Figueroa pitched the Yankees to a 10-0 victory over the Twins.

More questions about renovation expenditures

The New York Times published an article on April 15 titled, "STADIUM'S COSTS NOW SEEN AS LOSS." As the subheading explained, "New York Officials Concede Outlay on Yankees' Home May Be $100 Million." A Bronx grand jury was now studying the politics involved in the remodeling. Fear arose that costs might be five times as high as the original $24 million estimate. [59]

Economic Development Administration (E.D.A.) counsel Henry Gavan called the renovation "a damn bargain." Shortly after the city agreed to modernize Yankee Stadium, the E.D.A. published a multi-color brochure in support of the endeavor. The pamphlet read, "New York City has committed $24 million for the purchase and renovation of Yankee Stadium because this investment is certain to produce income for private business and, consequently, for the municipal treasury." The pamphlet also told of the reformation of the surrounding area, although this never happened.

In an interview at Madison Square Garden, which Mike Burke now led, Burke said, "It was certainly known from the start that the cost was going to be more than $24 million. When I went before the Board of Estimate, Garelik asked if I'd agree to a $30 million ceiling. I said "no." He asked if I'd agree to $35 million. I said "no.""

Burke explained that the Yankees earlier hired the engineering firm of Madigan-Praeger, Inc., to study the costs of a renovation if the Yankees did it themselves. The company came up with a $16 or $17 million estimate. Once the city took over, changes occurred in planning. In the interim, building costs rose drastically. At a September 7, 1973 strategy meeting with city officials in Deputy Mayor Edward Hamilton's office, the capital cost of the endeavor was shown to be "in excess of $80 million."

A month after that meeting, bureaucrats told the Board of Estimate the price tag would be $40 million to $50 million. Comptroller Abraham Beame felt it would run up to $53 million. By September of 1975, officials thought the cost would be roughly $57 million. Currently, the Department of Public Works believed the total would be between $91.4 million and $97.4 million. The uncertainty of the result of condemnation procedures to set the price of the pre-renovation Stadium and grounds reflected the $6 million difference.

The Yankees and Rice University fought over who owned the seats and fittings of the wooden seats which were taken from the Stadium in 1973 and replaced. This argument had to still be resolved as of April 1976. The city would foot the $9-15 million cost, no matter who won. Also during this time, the Department of Public Works assessed direct building expenses as the following:

Yankee Stadium	$53,873,741
New Parking Lot	$1.5 million (yet to be built)
Renovation of two old Parking Garages	$453,701
Parking Deck on the new Farmers Market Building in the Bronx Terminal Market	$1,089,558
Purchase of nearby plot of land in exchange for a parking area	$790,000
Subway Renovation	$1,168,362
Miscellaneous Costs	$817,602

These costs included two parking garages built on city property by Kinney Systems, Inc. Even though Kinney's was not a direct capital cost, the city could have purchased the two garages for $22,713,320. Rather than do that because of the economic crisis facing the city, the city chose to pay about $2 million a year in rent. The $91.4 million to $97.4 million estimate did not include the $16 million for the Major Deegan Expressway interchange. State and Federal money would take care of that.

Additionally, the total did not include the loss in tax exemption, as the city used to collect $570,000 annually in rent and taxes from the Yankees before they moved to Shea Stadium. There was also no true quote regarding administrative costs in endorsing and leading the renovation, legal costs, or minor financial spending before official approval of the revamping.

The Mets had exclusive rights to baseball games played there, so they chose not to share these privileges. Therefore, New York City assigned the Mets its own share for the Yankees' game concessions. This estimate came out to between $1 million to $1.5 million for the two seasons at Shea.

New York City dedicated part of the 32-acre, 65-year-old Bronx Terminal Market area for parking. The city had amended its 1972 lease with the Arol Development Corporation in 1973 in order to take back the site. The city found a different tract for Arol, which was now relieved of building new structures and repairs. This would cost the city an extra estimated $10 million. Aside from this and the work to be done on the Major Deegan, the cost to the city was estimated to be over $100 million. This did not include debt service.

Based on a conservative average interest rate of 7.5 percent on $75 million in expenses, New York City would shell out $5.62 million in annual interest connected to the refurbishment. Rents and commissions collected by the city would lower this somewhat. A Department of Public Works spokesman declared, "We're paying off the Stadium 100 percent."

In *The New York Times* article of April 15, Mr. Gavan, however, stated that the E.D.A's last estimate of annual income from Stadium admissions and concessions amounted to $2.25-$2.5 million, or less than half of the estimated yearly interest. Gavan also claimed nearly a million cars yearly would have to park in Stadium lots to break even with the city's annual payments to Kinney parking. He doubted that this would occur.

The good news was that Gavan and others thought unforeseen earnings could be immeasurable. For instance, in the coming years, should the Yankees play in the World Series, that would invariably add to the city's and local community's coffers from fans purchasing food, souvenirs, tickets to games, parking, etc. It most certainly lifted up the morale of the area to have a newly modernized stadium, rather than the Yankees fleeing the area as the Giants and Dodgers had done. The newspaper column ended with the sentence, "But, they will never call it the House That Truth Built." [60]

To add to the treasury, the North American Soccer League's superstar, Pele, led the New York Cosmos in the Stadium's first post-renovated soccer game on May 2. The afternoon contest against the Chicago Sting was the first of 12 such contests the Cosmos would host at the famous landmark. The Cosmos had played the previous year at Randall's Island.

The agreement with the Cosmos stated that any game could be called off by the Yankees four hours before the kickoff. Also, the soccer team would earn no funds from parking or concessions despite the fact that one day of play at Yankee Stadium would cost the same as one season at Randall's Island. Any field damage would be repaired by the City of New York.

The Cosmos expected 20,000 spectators and were glad to see 28,436 instead. Although the home team lost, 2-1, hope turned to reality when Pele scored a goal for the Cosmos. The Babe Ruth of soccer also didn't disappoint the faithful, as he exhibited a number of his dazzling moves.

On May 11, former Yankees skipper Ralph Houk returned to his old stomping grounds as the manager of the Detroit Tigers. The gray Detroit uniform could never cover his love for the Yankees. He exclaimed, "Beautiful, just beautiful," when he visited the mammoth park from the visitors dugout. "This is the first time I've seen it." He wondered, "Where are the monuments? It looks strange without the poles in the stands. The façade is a good idea." [61]

Yankee Stadium was the scene of a confrontational crowd when the Reverend Sun Myung Moon held a rally at the ballpark on the evening on June 1. The 25,000 attendees fell far short of the predicted 54,000. Moon used a Korean interpreter to translate his words into English. He drew followers as well as cynics. Several thousand spectators booed and left the Stadium. Others threw firecrackers, decorations, and programs in protest. A number of parents shouted, "Moon, go home!" Even the heavens rained before the program started. Over 400 demonstrators picketed his "God Bless America Festival" from outside the Stadium.

Baptists, Lutherans, and Evangelical Christians attended. Some protestors condemned Moon as a "fascist dictator, false Christian, and deluder of American youth." Many people in the United States felt he was brainwashing young people, who were called "Moonies." He spoke a little over an hour during the three-hour event. Musical and dance groups entertained the rest of the time. Over half of the crowd departed the stands before the assembly concluded. Moon had been much better received at Madison Square Garden two years earlier. [62]

Attendance on the rise

Statistics showed that the Yankees would probably outdraw the Mets for the first time since 1963. If they were to stay in the pennant race, they might exceed the two million attendance mark for the first time since 1950. By June 8, the Yankees had played before an average of 26,792 fans, while the Mets averaged 18,437. The Yankees were now 190,000 fans ahead of last year. The biggest reasons were the "new" Yankee Stadium and their winning ways on the field.

The fiery leadership of manager Billy Martin was backed up by such stars as speedster Mickey Rivers, who normally led off the batting order. Mick "The Quick" very often followed getting on first base by stealing second base. Solid hitting by such stars as Thurman Munson, Chris Chambliss, and Graig Nettles led the offense. Nettles also led the defense with his golden glove at third base. Pitchers Ed Figueroa, Dock Ellis, Doyle Alexander, and Grant Jackson provided winning pitching for the team. The rest of the team would fill in very ably where needed.

Interestingly, fans at the "old" Yankee Stadium appeared to be better behaved than those in the current ballpark. Danny Colletti, who drove Yankees and relief pitchers in the official pinstriped Toyota Celica, noticed the fans throwing more trash at the car than in the past. This included empty beer cans. The rowdiness seemed to take hold when the team played at Shea Stadium. [63] Most likely the best deterrent to such disorderly conduct would be to have a greater, more visible police presence.

The Yankees played the Mets at the Stadium in the annual Mayor's Trophy game on June 15. The Bronx Bombers defeated their hometown rivals, 8-4. Overall, this was their eighth win, against six defeats in the series. The teams showcased injured players, the Yankees' Elliott Maddox and the Mets' Mike Vail. Maddox had injured his knee the previous June and had an operation. Vail had dislocated his right ankle while playing basketball in February. Neither was ready to play, as they still had to recuperate and hone their baseball skills. Maddox grounded out and walked twice. He scored a run, but took himself out of the game. Vail had a hit in three times at bat. He also made an error in right field, giving the Yankees two runs. Vail remained on the disabled list. The Yankees scored six unearned runs for the night.

The Yankees' first baseman, Carlos May, was the star of the game with four singles in four times at bat, as well as three RBI. Right fielder Oscar Gamble was also a hero, as he hit a run-scoring single and a two-run homer. The Mets brought up catcher Jay Kleven from Tidewater for the game. He singled home two runs, walked, singled again, and scored a run. Not a bad day, though he had to go back to Tidewater the next day. His major league career consisted of two games later in the month. He had to go back to Tidewater the next day. Yankees pitcher Catfish Hunter pinch-hit and grounded out. He received the loudest applause of the night. The game was played in front of 36,361 fans.

Historically, the first Mayor's Trophy Game took place in 1931, in order to raise money for Mayor Jimmy Walker's Unemployment Relief Fund. The Yankees played the New York Giants on Wednesday, September 9, before a crowd of 60,549 at Yankee Stadium. Lefty Gomez pitched the Bronx Bombers to a 7-3 victory over Freddie Fitzsimmons and relief pitcher Bill Walker.

The Brooklyn Dodgers also participated in two Mayor's Trophy games on September 24 at the Polo Grounds, in which the Bums lost both games of the doubleheader. The Giants beat them by a score of 3-1 in the first game. The Yankees defeated the Dodgers in the second game by a score of 5-1.

Currently, June 15 was a very significant day for the Yankees, as they acquired Ken Holtzman, Doyle Alexander, Grant Jackson, Elrod Hendricks, and Jimmy Freeman from the Baltimore Orioles. The Birds traded for Rudy May, Tippy Martinez, Dave Pagan, Scott McGregor, and Rick Dempsey. The Yanks also bought the rights to Oakland A's pitcher Vida Blue for $1.5 million, but Commissioner Bowie Kuhn nullified the deal, using the "best interests of baseball" clause. Kuhn also voided the sale of two other A's stars, outfielder, Joe Rudi, and relief pitcher, Rollie Fingers, to the Boston Red Sox for $1 million each, mainly because of the ongoing animosity between Kuhn and Charlie Finley.

On June 21, the Yankees ended their ten-year program with Consolidated Edison to allow 3,000 to 5,000 underprivileged children free admission to 25 baseball games a season. The Yankees asked Con Ed to have one chaperone for every eight kids. The group sat in the Upper

Deck left field stands. The team cited "crowd behavior" as the reason for discontinuing the program. Recent incidents of fighting in the stands and rest rooms, as well as violent gangs threatening unarmed stadium security guards, led to the decision. These skirmishes had occurred at quite a few games during the year. The Yankees and Con Edison would try to achieve "better security and crowd control." [64]

This could not always be achieved. In part, Dick Young of the *New York Daily News* commented in his column on June 27, "It's so easy to make a villain of the New York Yankees, and so unfair: These aren't angelic little kids we're talking about. These are marauding bands of hoodlums who terrorize the good kids, rob them, beat them, hold pointed knives to their throats. These are little monsters, not little angels." [65]

Also, numerous escorts left their charges and enjoyed the game from the lower stands. Most of these youths were age 15 or younger. Con Edison won a temporary injunction for at least the next few games to let the kids see the games.

The Yankees did continue to support other such groups as Yankee Juniors, which was associated with the Boy Scouts. They and other such groups continued to attend free games, as they caused no problems. Con Ed felt the Yankees' current hold on first place in their division led to this decision. One constant concern by the club was that it had to fight the image of a crime-ridden area. Another was the safety of its fans.

Area residents heard good news on July 6, when the ball club announced it would spend $35,000 to improve baseball fields and paddleball courts at Macombs Dam Park. The team called this the first phase in spending Yankees income to upgrading the surrounding area. Spokesman Marty Appel said the team wanted to "return some of the support" to the fans, who had greatly increased attendance at the Stadium. Work would begin shortly and take about six weeks to complete.

More positive results for the Bronx came the next week when Thurman Munson, Chris Chambliss, Sparky Lyle, Willie Randolph, and Mickey Rivers represented the Yankees at the July 13 All-Star game at Veterans Stadium in Philadelphia. Only Randolph and Lyle didn't play. The N.L. walloped the A.L. by a score of 7-1. Meanwhile, by the end of July, the Yankees were in first place by 10½ games. Besides a sparkling new ballpark, the team had gelled their talents throughout the season.

The magic of Old Timers' Day, one of the biggest events of the year at Yankee Stadium, took place on Saturday, August 7. This 30th annual reunion showed off the team's radiant home in all its splendor. Mickey Mantle, Joe DiMaggio, and Whitey Ford all agreed that they never thought the Yankees would have a pennant-contending team again so early. They credited Billy Martin's managing. Elston Howard also hit the nail on the head when he said, "George Steinbrenner is spending dough, and that's what you have to do these days to win. He'll ask what you want and then go out and get it." [66]

The program began at 1:15. The Old Timers played two innings of baseball, with this year's theme pitting opposing players who had great moments vs. Yankees who had great careers in Yankee Stadium. Names that brought great memories of the day included Mrs. Ruth and Mrs. Gehrig, Sandy Amoros, Ralph Branca, Joe Collins, Dick Howser, Harmon Killebrew, Hector Lopez, Willie Mays, Gil McDougald, Vic Raschi, Pee Wee Reese, Allie Reynolds, Phil Rizzuto, Bill Skowron, Warren Spahn, Bob Turley, Lloyd Waner, and Maury Wills. Naturally, Robert Merrill sang the National Anthem, and Mel Allen served as announcer for the game. Frank Messer acted as Master of Ceremonies. The game ended in a 3-3 tie. Joe DiMaggio sat it out. Afterwards, the current Yankees played the Baltimore Orioles, but the Birds won, 7-4.

Locals react to the new ballpark

The New York Times ran a story called, "A Rebuilt Stadium Little Aid in Bronx," on August 10. Author Michael Katz interviewed several local Bronx residents to see what effect the modernization of Yankee Stadium had on the neighborhood. Most thought it had not helped.

Vance Warren, who ran the Discount TV and Audio Center on East 161st Street, said, "There's been no increase in business, but a big increase in crime." He continued, "People don't come here to shop. They come here to see a ball game. I didn't go to Ebbets Field to shop in the old days. I went to see the Dodgers." A 44th Precinct police sergeant noted, "There's more people around at games, and where there are more people, there are more muggers." On River Avenue, only two of 50 bowling lanes were being used at Stadium Lanes. Al Weiskopf lamented, "What has the new Yankee Stadium done for my business? It's destroyed us."

Residents and business owners agreed that more money should be spent on the neighborhood, and not just the ballpark. Myles Jackson, of Gerard Avenue, was chairman of the Macombs Field Program. His inspiration would be to convert Macombs Dam Park from an inadequately kept park into a viable 24-hour-a-day, well-kept athletic complex, featuring a quarter-mile track and artificial grass football field. As he stated, "It's the kind of project that could show how the inner cities of this country could be saved, and it could be built for $3 million. Had they incorporated that idea into the financing for the new stadium, it would have cost next to nothing compared with the $100 million."

The businesses profiting the most were eateries and souvenir shops. Tommy Deplas of Dina's Coffee Shop said he brought in $100 more a day when the Yankees were in town. Bernie Harris, president of the Stadium Area Merchants, Civic and Professionals Association Inc., owned the Graded A Beef Company butcher shop on Gerard Avenue. He believed the neighborhood could be saved. "I have great faith in the area. In fact, I just purchased this building." [67]

Pranay Gupte authored a story in *The New York Times* on August 21, titled "Residents near Yankee Stadium Say City Reneged on Renovation Promise." Residents were angry that while the city spent over $100 million on Yankee Stadium, very little went to the surrounding area. State Assemblyman Jose E. Serrano, who represented the locality, said, "We are a languishing neighborhood. We are languishing in the shadows of Yankee Stadium." The Grand Concourse was once fashionable. While some areas still had good business, the South Bronx had the highest crime rate in New York City. The $2 million or $3 million promised by the city, but never delivered, left bitterness in its wake. [68]

Purchasing and leveling derelict buildings, and improving street lighting helped sell the Stadium facelift. Inhabitants said that not only muggings and burglaries had risen since the Stadium reopened, but visiting fans had a negative effect as well. Francisco Lugovina, chairman of Community Board 1, which oversaw the area, bemoaned, "Look around you. What do you see?" He pointed at overflowing trash cans. "It's bad enough here without the fans. When they have events in the Stadium, not only do the trash cans overflow with garbage, so do the streets."

In 1975 the Parks Department planted sycamore and maple saplings along Gerard Avenue to spruce up the neighborhood. Even they were dying, which is what residents compared their neighborhood to. Danny Mercadante, who owned a discount store at 94 East 161st Street, said, "Especially after football games we get a rowdy crowd. We shudder to think what will happen after the Ali-Norton fight next month." [69]

Fans suffered, too. Tires of about 100 cars were slashed during an August football game between the New York Giants and New York Jets. A grand jury was also investigating the death of a fan who went to the game and was fatally shot by an off-duty policeman who was also a spectator.

Clinton Cox of the *New York Daily News* wrote a story in the newspaper's *Sunday News Magazine* of February 27, 1977, titled, "The Angry Neighbors of Yankee Stadium." Local residents greatly resented the home of the Yankees when many of them could not afford to see a game from the luxury boxes and VIP rooms their tax money helped to create. [70]

Macombs Dam Park, located next to the Stadium, had a water fountain that hadn't been working for two years. The city said it had no funds to improve the park. Budget cuts affected local senior citizen centers. Lincoln Hospital, several blocks away, didn't have enough doctors or medicine on hand to help everyone that came through its doors. Morrisania Hospital, another neighborhood hospital, closed its doors.

Police and sanitation services were reduced. Rent and crime rose as whites moved out and blacks and Hispanics moved into the area. With all of these problems, the South Bronx suffered a terrible image problem.

Macombs finally received some attention, such as new sod and cinders for a track, and the Parks Department cleaned up trash under the grandstands after Myles Jackson's group staged a publicity run to the Mayor's office at Gracie Mansion.

Jackson attested that he used the subways for the past three and a half years at all hours of the day and night with no problems. Yes, there were problems with muggings and other crimes, which affected all races. The elderly felt it most acutely. At meetings residents complained that at Yankees games the police could be found in groups of four and five on various street corners. It was a different story when there were no games. There were very few police to be found then.

Local merchants tried to make the area safer by starting the Stadium Patrol Association, but not much changed. Besides crime, many landlords didn't care about fixing their buildings. Plumbing problems, broken elevators, vandalism were some of the numerous troubles to be encountered. Service agencies weren't too keen to help people, either. There were now no major YMCAs to be found in the area.

One bright spot was the Neighborhood Association for Intercultural Affairs (NAICA). As its president, Evaldo Ruiz, pointed out, the all-volunteer organization had taken children on trips and given free lunches, organized tenants in numerous deteriorating buildings to administer the buildings and make repairs. NAICA had also gotten medical care for people who could not pay for it. People of varied racial groups belonged to NAICA. [71]

The Yankees knew of their lack of popularity in the neighborhood. George Steinbrenner pledged $5,000 to the New York Sports Association, if the group came up with $5,000. The money would be used for an architectural study for the sports facility Myles Jackson wanted.

In the summer of 1976, the Yankees announced Neighborhood Project No. 1. This was a $35,000 plan to repair baseball fields and paddleball courts. The courts would also have lighting installed. Steinbrenner said the $35,000 "is just a start, and within the next several months we will be revealing additional plans to help out in this city." The funny thing is that the lights, which were the most expensive part of Project No.1, lit up the Yankees' VIP parking lot.

Work was still proceeding on ramps that would allow Yankees fans to drive directly from the Major Deegan Expressway into Yankee Stadium parking areas without having to go through the local neighborhoods. An enclosed walkway from one parking area, as well as a large police presence, would ensure that customers would stay in "Yankeeland." This is what Myles Jackson referred to as "ghettophobia."

Clinton Cox ended his commentary by saying that not one penny was spent that would not benefit the New York Yankees. Myles Jackson said, the city's spending priorities had "nothing to do with the budget crisis. They have everything to do with the attitude of the city toward its youth." Cox said this attitude also had to do with the city's young adults, middle-aged, and elderly citizenry. [72]

Back on the baseball scene, history was made on September 19 when Jim "Catfish" Hunter pitched his 200th victory on the road against the Milwaukee Brewers. His 2-1 victory came against Jim Slaton, who gave up a two-run double to shortstop Jim Mason. The game only lasted 5½ innings due to rain. Thurman Munson helped the cause by picking Robin Yount off third base in the fourth inning. Sixto Lezcano followed with a fly to deep right that would have scored Yount. The Yankees' "magic number" was down to three to clinch the East Division title over the second-place Baltimore Orioles. Though they lost their next six games, the Bronx Bombers clinched the division on September 25 when they defeated the Detroit Tigers, 10-6, in the Motor City.

A different sort of contest was on the agenda on the night of September 28. A crowd of 30,298 boxing fans spent $2.4 million to see world heavyweight champion Muhammad Ali in his 20th title bout to defend his title against challenger Ken Norton. Attendees included former boxing greats Joe Louis and Jack Dempsey, who escorted his wife. The New York Rangers hockey team also witnessed the happening.

The 34-year-old, 221-pound Ali defeated the 31-year-old challenger by decision. The three judges gave Ali eight of the fifteen rounds in a unanimous decision. Norton and the crowd were in disbelief. The 217½- pound Norton cried, "I thought I won it. Ali knew I won it. The people knew I won it."

Ali said, "I knew I was ahead. I didn't think I needed to win the last round to win. My corner was keeping tabs." Neither boxer scored a knockdown on the cool night. Ali failed to get his predicted knockout within five rounds. Ali was guaranteed $6 million and Norton earned $1.1 million.

Yankee Stadium was a mess, as 2,000 off-duty police officers protested outside the Stadium, waved an American flag, and carried signs that said, "Beame, Take Your Chart and Sit on It." They denounced the Mayor for giving officers a heavier work schedule. The 500 officers on duty for the fight sympathized with their buddies. Traffic was a nightmare. Muhammad Ali was delayed in his limousine, and actor Telly Savalas in another. Groups of teenagers picked pockets. One man even had two $50 tickets for the fight stolen right out of his hand. It was a rough night. [73]

Baseball news was better than the boxing headlines as the Yankees ended their most successful season in 12 years on October 3. They were scheduled to play a double-header vs. the Cleveland Indians. But rain prevented play on this last day of the schedule. In 159 games, the Yankees had a record of 97-62. The team finished 10½ games ahead of Baltimore. Attendance for the year was 2,012,434, or an average of 25,314 per game. This was a whopping 724,386 more than in the previous year at Shea. This was their best record since 1964, and highest turnout since 1950.

Below is a list of Yankees regular season game attendance through the years:

Location	Total Attendance	Average Game Attendance
Hilltop Park (1903-1912)	3,451,542	3,115-6,549
Polo Grounds (1913-1922)	6,220,031	4,525-16,746
Yankee Stadium (1923-1973)	64,788,405	13,000- 21,000
Shea Stadium (1974-1975)	2,561,123	15,900
Total	77,021,101	

Thurman Munson ended the year with a .302 batting average and led the team with 105 RBI, and third baseman Graig Nettles led the American League with 32 round-trippers. He was the first Yankee to do so since Roger Maris hit 61 home runs in 1961. Roy White led the league with 104 runs scored. Ed Figueroa lost his last two pitching starts and just missed notching 20 wins. He would have been the first hurler from Puerto Rico to accomplish this feat. "Catfish" Hunter posted a 17-15 record for the year, his worst record in seven years.

George Steinbrenner was willing to make the Yankees champions again – and quickly. Rather than doing it the old-fashioned way of waiting for players to make it through the ranks of the farm system, he bought and traded for players he thought would bring immediate success to the Bronx. Gabe Paul had an eye for talent and George had the wallet. The Yankees had a "new" Stadium and now they had a new style to match.

The traditional Yankees concept of home run hitters was now left in the dust. Speed in the field and on the base paths was the new order of the day. Historically, the Yankees had great pitching. That didn't change now, as a team can't win pennants without strong moundsmen.

Billy Martin also had an eye for talent, and he had proven himself to be a great motivator in the clubhouse. He enjoyed hustling, aggressive baseball. As Steinbrenner himself had said, "I know this much about Billy Martin: As a manager, he has no peer." Billy signed a three-year contract in early September. Both he and "the Boss" were of the same ilk. They were both winners, and they frequently butted heads because of their explosive dispositions. It was a love/hate relationship. Fortunately for the fans, both loved baseball, both loved the Yankees, and both loved to win.

The 1976 Yankees earned $9-10 million from gate receipts during the regular season. Playoff and World Series games would raise that figure. Financially, the team would be in the black instead of the red for the first time since 1964. Besides trading for and buying talented major league players, the forceful Steinbrenner set about rebuilding the neglected farm system. He had Gabe Paul, who knew what was needed and the money to make the dream become a reality. His goal was to turn the Yankees into the Yankees.

The Yankees faced the Kansas City Royals in Royals Stadium on October 9, for their first American League Championship Series (ALCS). New York won the first game, 4-1, behind Catfish Hunter. He defeated Larry Gura. Paul Splittorff then evened the series the next day, as the Royals conquered Ed Figueroa by a score of 7-3.

Yankee Stadium provided the setting for Game 3, on October 12. The home team won, 5-3, as Dock Ellis triumphed over Andy Hassler. Sparky Lyle earned a save, and first baseman Chris Chambliss hit a home run. Game 4 at the Stadium went to Kansas City, as Doug Bird bested Catfish Hunter, 7-4, despite two home runs by Graig Nettles. Steve Mingori recorded the save for K.C.

The fifth game at the Bronx ballyard would decide who would go to the World Series. K.C.'s John Mayberry started things off early when he hit a two-run homer for the visitors in the first inning. However, after seven innings the Yankees led, 6-3. The Yankees' speedy Mickey Rivers had four hits, and Munson and Chambliss each rapped three hits in the game. The Royals tied the game on George Brett's three-run home run in the eighth inning. Raucous Bronx Bomber supporters showed their objection by throwing bottles and other trash onto the field. This delayed the game by five minutes, as the grounds crew cleaned up the debris.

In the bottom of the ninth, at 11:13 p.m., Chris Chambliss lifted Mark Littell's first pitch, a high fastball, over the right-center field fence to win the game and put the Yankees into the World Series. That was the easy part for him.

Many of the excited 56,821 fans streamed onto the field before he even touched second base. Where the shortstop played, Chambliss was bowled over by the mob. He had to zigzag and act like a football player to continue around the bases. Third base was gone before he got there. Since humanity had piled around home plate, he never did touch it. He had to come out two hours later with two policemen to escort him to touch the dirt where home plate had been--a fan had taken it as a souvenir. Now his home run was official. Dick Tidrow was the winning pitcher. The Yankees had just wrapped up their 30th pennant and were in the World Series for the first time since 1964. The dry spell was over.

Jimmy Esposito, the longtime Maintenance Superintendent at the Stadium, would make sure the grounds crew would have the field in shape for the World Series. He'd spent 15 years as a groundskeeper with the Dodgers at Ebbets Field, and another three in Los Angeles after the team moved. He came back to New York in 1960, becoming the chief groundskeeper at Yankee Stadium. [74]

The Yankees played the defending champion Cincinnati Reds, who were making their fifth post-season appearance in seven years. Sadly for the Yankees and their followers, the Big Red Machine steamrolled the Yankees in a four-game sweep. The first two games took place at Riverfront Stadium on October 16 and 17. The Reds won these by scores of 5-1 and 4-3. The teams played on October 19 and 21 (after a rainout) at Yankee Stadium. Sparky Anderson's men won the third game, 6-2, and overpowered the hapless American Leaguers, 7-2, in the fourth and final game. As was the case when the Series began, the next World Series game the Yankees won would be their 100th. Cincinnati Reds catcher Johnny Bench earned the Most Valuable Player (MVP) award in the World Series.

Still, it was an amazing year for the Yanks. On November 16, the Baseball Writers' Association of America voted Thurman Munson the American League's MVP for 1976. He received 18 of 24 first-place votes, with a total of 304 points. Kansas City's George Brett came in second with two first-place votes and 217 points. Munson was the first Yankee and first catcher to win the coveted award since Elston Howard did so in 1963.

Reggie Jackson enters the scene

George Steinbrenner gave Yankees fans an early Christmas present on November 29 when he signed Reggie Jackson to a five-year, $2.9 million contract. Although some teams offered a few hundred thousand dollars more, money wasn't the only thing on Reggie's mind. He thought he wanted to play for the Phillies or Dodgers. However, he didn't feel as though they wanted his services as much as the Yankees did. As he told *The New York Times*, "As well as I was treated by the front office in Baltimore, I didn't feel I had a home there. As well as I got along with the players in Oakland and even though I lived there, I never felt at home. But Steinbrenner made me feel at home." [75]

Billy Martin wanted Joe Rudi because he felt Rudi was a more complete player than Jackson. Thurman Munson told Steinbrenner, "Go get the big man," referring to Reggie. "He's the only guy in baseball who can carry a club for a month. And the hell with what you hear. He hustles every minute on the field." Munson was known for his great competitive spirit. And, George Steinbrenner was known to be a man who normally got what he wanted. He made his goal crystal clear. "We won a pennant, but I want a [World Series] ring."

The Yankees owner met with Jackson in and out of New York. He showed the star slugger around the city. They hit it off well. Also, Reggie wanted to establish a retirement home in Arizona for Negro League ballplayers. Steinbrenner sympathized with the idea. That seemed to help solidify the deal.

As Reggie said, "Other clubs offered more money, but I think certain things are a lot more meaningful than money." In addition, the slugger seemed to sense the historical sense of being a Yankee when he said, "It will be exciting playing in Yankee Stadium. I can't imagine what it will be like to put on the pinstripes. It will be exciting hitting home runs in Yankee Stadium as a Yankee." [76] No doubt he pictured many baseballs flying off his bat over the short fence in right field. The Yankees were also a World Series contender. Ten days earlier, the team had signed free agent lefty pitcher Don Gullett to a six-year contract worth a reported $2 million.

It looked like the New York Yankees' destiny was going in the direction George Steinbrenner envisioned. With his leadership, his will and willingness to spend money for talent, and a newly refurbished Yankee Stadium, the New York Yankees were about to embark on a new era.

Renovated Yankee Stadium, Opening Day, April 15, 1976. Fans and celebrities packed the newly remodeled Babe's Place. The Yankees defeated the Minnesota Twins by a convincing score of 11-4. Photo courtesy of the NATIONAL BASEBALL HALL OF FAME LIBRARY, COOPERSTOWN, N.Y.

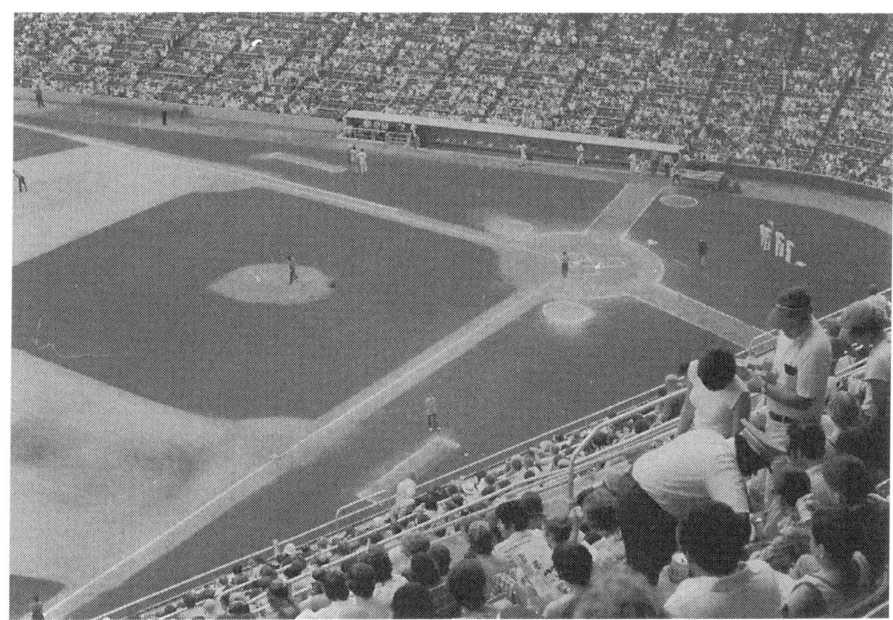

The view from the upper deck looking toward the Yankee dugout, July 24, 1976. This was the first game I attended in the newly remodeled Yankee Stadium. I felt at home!

The scoreboard and bullpens from the upper deck of left field. Monument Park is in the fenced-in area where the American flag is flying, July 24, 1976.

A vendor selling souvenirs on Ruppert Place, looking south towards home plate. It was now only open to pedestrian traffic, July 24, 1976.

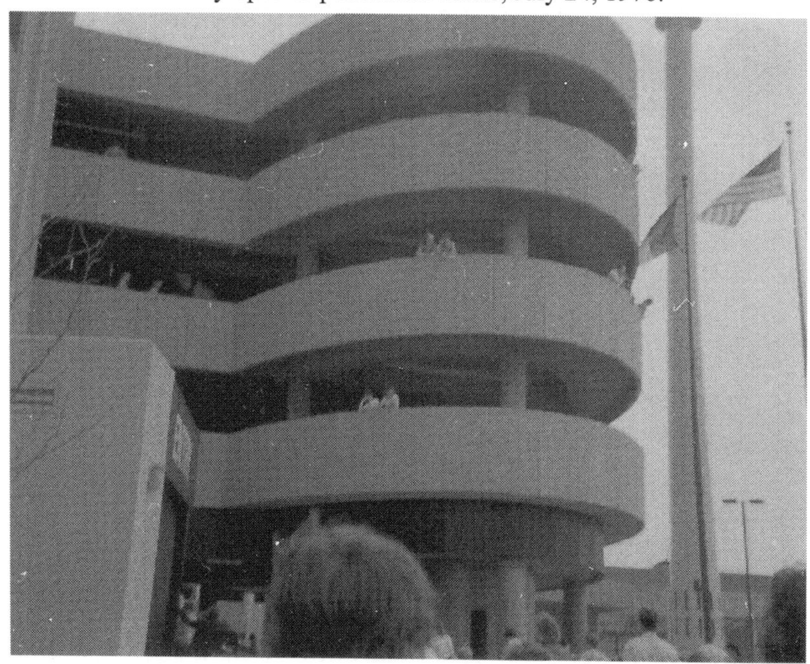

Looking up at the Gate 4 escalator tower and Babe Ruth's bat, July 24, 1976.

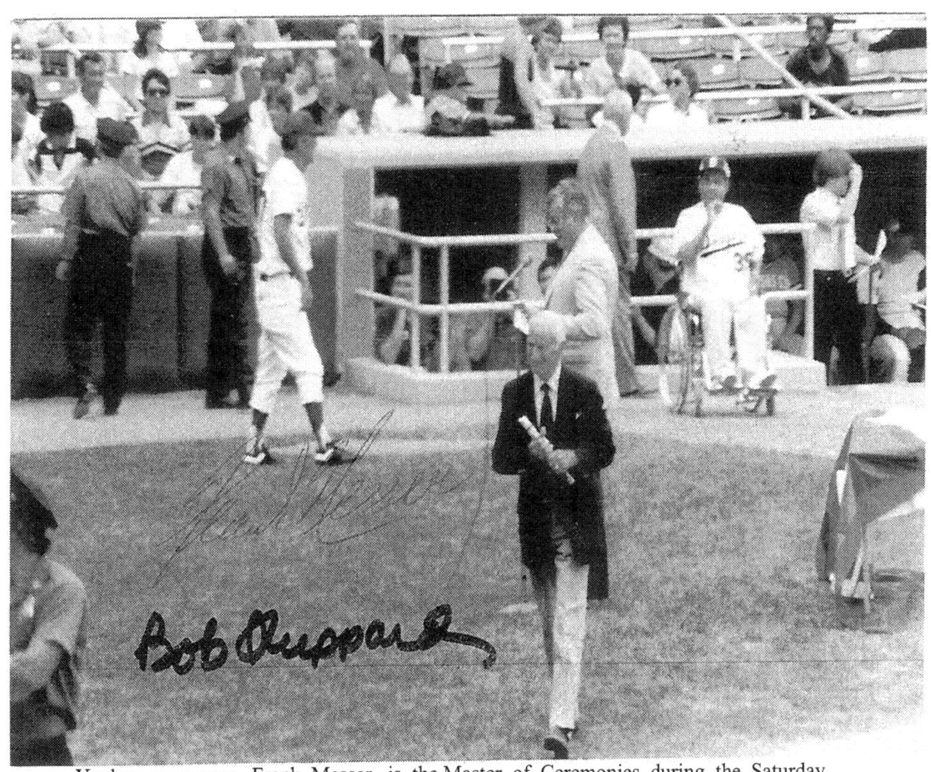

Yankee announcer, Frank Messer, is the Master of Ceremonies during the Saturday, August 22, 1981, Yankees Old Timers' Day game, which honored Don Larsen on the 25th anniversary of his pitching the only perfect game in World Series history. Dodgers catcher, Roy Campanella, is seated in the wheelchair in the background. Legendary Yankee Public Address announcer Bob Sheppard is in the foreground.

Another Yankee icon, clubhouse manager, Pete Sheehy (white T-shirt) above, stands in the Yankee dugout during a game, July 24, 1976.

The trademark Yankee frieze in the renovated stadium (above). The frieze that circled the stands before the 1970s modernization had been replaced by floodlights. This photo was taken from the left field stands on July 24, 1976.

The upper deck stands looking from left field towards home plate, July 24, 1976. Monument Park (below), featuring monuments honoring Lou Gehrig, Miller Huggins, and Babe Ruth. Toyota was the "Official car of the New York Yankees," and used to bring relief pitchers into the game, July 24, 1976.

The yellow ridge above the cracked stairs marks Row K, which represents the new portion of the post-renovated upper grandstand. Photo courtesy of Pete McNally.

Yankee catcher, Thurman Munson, swinging at a pitch, July 24, 1976.

Boston Red Sox catcher, Carlton Fisk, at bat. Thurman Munson is catching and Jim Evans is the umpire, July 24, 1976.

Mick "The Quick" Rivers at bat. The Yankees won the game, 4-1, July 24, 1976.

Yankee Stadium as seen from Macombs Dam Park, August 28, 1977.

Chapter Six

THE HEROES SPEAK I

(The 1970s Yankee Stadium Renovation)

Below is a general copy of the letter I sent to approximately 750 former baseball players, umpires, baseball executives, and sportscasters about 2005 and later. I wrote to Yankees and opponents that would have played in the Stadium in the World Series, All-Star Game, etc. The vast majority of replies were via the mail. Some were in person, e-mail, and even a few by telephone. Sometimes I wrote to the same person at least twice, as indicated by the different response dates.

I asked the Yankee Stadium renovation question of many people similar to the way as is shown below. In the 1970s and 1980s I also asked the question "How do you feel about the renovation of Yankee Stadium?" As well as "Do you approve of the renovation of Yankee Stadium?" That is why many respondents gave a "yes" or "no" answer. I felt it was historically important to publish those answers as well as the longer responses.

I also thought it was historically valuable to record who responded, even if the person just signed some photos or baseball cards. This would still show who responded to my letter in some way.

Dear Mr. __________,

I'm a big New York Yankees fan who is 52 years old. I grew up in West Hempstead, Long Island, New York, from 1956 thru 1977, and had the pleasure and honor of going to many New York Yankees games. I still love the "old" Yankee Stadium.

During the renovation of the Stadium from 1973 thru 1976 I visited the site 13 times and took about 230 photos with my Kodak Instamatic 100 camera. I've enclosed a couple of sample copies for you.

I'm still collecting information regarding the renovation, as I am writing a book about this event. I have never seen one written about the revamping of Yankee Stadium, and I have found some good solid facts about it. The reason I'm writing to you is twofold:

1. I would like to know your thoughts about the renovation of Yankee Stadium for inclusion in my book. Since you've had the pleasure and honor of playing at the Stadium, I would think you'd have a very interesting point of view that spectators such as myself would like to hear.

2. Do you know of anyone with specific "gee whiz" information, such as what happened to the dirt from the field and the concrete taken away from the Stadium? What happened to the seats, lights, and other artifacts? Or any other facts that you feel may be relevant or interesting.

Thank you for your time and kindness, Mr. _________. I look forward to hearing from you. God Bless You.

Respectfully,

Michael Wagner[1]

PERSON AND RESPONSE DATE	RESPONSE
Bernie Allen March 7, 2005	I am sorry. I don't have much information to share with you. I enjoyed playing at the Stadium.[2]
Sparky Anderson February 10, 2005	Sparky signed a photo of the renovation for me.[3]
Marty Appel Public Relations Director, 1973-1977 January 7, 2004	Marty recalls a lot of seats were destroyed during the last Yankees game from kids kicking them out of their anchors and trying to take them home. He spoke to me on the phone.[4]
Sal Bando February 20, 2005	It became a better hitters park & background to hit.[5]
Red Barber Legendary Announcer November 10, 1981	The tax payers should not have to pay over $100 million for it.[6]
March 18, 1986	No feeling.[7]
Larry Barnett Umpire January 15, 2008	Yankee Stadium is the true history of baseball. The great honor I had the first time I worked there was great. I will always remember that day. Larry Barnett, A.L. Umpire, 1969-99.[8]
William Bartholomay Atlanta Braves Owner June 4, 2008	Dear Michael: I enjoyed your recent letter as respects to Yankee Stadium. I have always thought of Yankee Stadium as a shrine rather than a ballpark. It is indeed unique and over the years I have attended other events there such as NFL Football games, College Football games and Heavyweight Boxing Championships, etc. I have also enjoyed the baseball experience many times.

I congratulate you on your interest in baseball and I am sure you will enjoy the "New Yankee Stadium," which promises to be a magnificent structure!
Regards, William C. Bartholomay[9]

Buzzie Bavasi
Brooklyn/L.A. Dodgers Executive
January 15, 2008

Dear Michael: Many thanks for your nice note. I am not too familiar with the renovation of Yankee Stadium. I do know that it is still a left hand hitters park. Keep in mind when my clubs met the Yankees in a World Series it was usually in the original field.

No, I know nothing about the dirt and cement from the stadium. I can tell you that when we left Ebbets Field after the last game we let the fans dig up the infield, take the bases and the seats. I am sure the Yankees did the same thing.
Regards, "Buzzie" Bavasi.[10]

Yogi Berra
March 21, 2005

I'm a bit sentimental about the old Stadium, lots of nice memories playing there. It's changed a lot-it's still old but it's more modern. I guess the big thing is the fences were brought in, and maybe you don't have almost 70,000 people at World Series games anymore.

The other thing is the clubhouse is pretty luxurious-and much more comfortable than when we played. The Stadium's changed but it's still a great place for baseball-it's still like a shrine.

Hope this helps, and best of luck with your project. (And if you find anyone with pieces of the old Stadium willing to loan or donate to the Yogi Berra Museum, please don't hesitate to contact me!)[11]

Ewell Blackwell
March 27, 1975

Good.[12]

John Blanchard

Interview at New York Yankees Fantasy Camp, Legends Field, Tampa, FL during a rained out day. Wednesday, November 15, 2006. I showed him some photos I took of the renovation.

J.B.: I like it. The work the City of New York had done…didn't they put the cab on that?

M.W.: So you like it better than the old Stadium?

J.B.: The renovation I don't like. I don't like the bringing in of the fence. I don't like that. The hitters do. The pitchers don't (laughs). The overall Yankee Stadium renovation…yeah, I like it. I thought it was well done. You can only do so much to an old ballpark. And, they did it. It's very good. It's still "The House That Ruth Built," and they didn't vary too much from it. Now…they're going to tear this beautiful place down, and I tell you there's going to be a lot of fans in New York that will feel badly about that.

M.W.: I'm hoping what they'll do is take debris from the Stadium and put it in the new one. I guess for good luck. So you could say that part of Yankee Stadium is here, I guess.

J.B.: Here's what I plan to do… I would like to have something from there… preferably a couple of seats.

M.W.: I'm sure they're going to sell them.

J.B.: They're going to sell them alright. I've heard numbers from $300 to $400, and they'll get their money for it. Good Lord, they have 60,000 of them.

M.W.: They still sell old seats from the Stadium when you played, on ebay and auction houses, and they usually sell for $1,000, $1,500, or so.

J.B.: I'll never get one, but I'd love to have one. The concrete…when the big (wrecking) ball hits the side of that building, little chips of concrete…my sons and grandsons said, "Grandpa, can you get a piece of the concrete? Then my older son said, "Geez, Dad, when you go back next time, like during an Old Timers' Day game, we can get out there early." They want little vials of dirt around home plate. I thought, "God, why didn't I think of that?"[13]

Milt Bolling
November 20, 2007

Have not seen the renovation personally; however, I liked the original. Sorry. I can't help you.[14]

Red Borom
November 5, 2007

Dear Michael: It was good to hear from you and to know of your book project of Yankee Stadium. I have no idea as to what happened to the seats, lights, concrete or dirt from the field. My only memory was of the unusual dimensions of the field. It was so oddly shaped, 296 feet down the right field line and 470 feet in left center, known as "death valley." Left field line I believe was 340 feet. I saw two broken bat home runs down the right field line.

I'm sure if you could contact some former Yankee players, they could give you more information about the stadium. Best of luck with your book. Sincerely, Red Borom[15]

Dick Bosman
December 17, 2007

Michael – I don't remember much about the renovation except we had to play at ratty Shea Stadium. I didn't pitch much there & that was OK with me! I did like the things they did although I loved to pitch in the 'old' Stadium. Thank you for your interest. Sincerely, Dick Bosman[16]

Jim Bouton
January 11, 2004

Yankee Breakfast. Live Oak Civic Center, Live Oak, Texas. Hosted by Larry Dluhy (L.D.) of Sports Collectibles of Houston, Sunday, January 11, 2004. Jim Bouton and Gary Bell were the guest stars at this morning event.

MW: Jim, I have a two-part question. Back when the Stadium was getting renovated in '73 to '75 I went about 13 times and took about 230 photos. I'm in the process of writing a book, and am having a hard time collecting information anywhere about it. There are no books on the renovation. How do you feel about the renovation of Yankee Stadium and any tips for me as a person who wants to write a book?

J.B.: I didn't like the renovation because it called for taking off the top part of the beautiful facade - it had this beautiful tan cement ... sort of like the Alamo. In place of it they inserted this modern looking cantilevered structure that clashed with the rest of the facade. Then those awful spiral elevators blocked the view of what remained of the lower facade. Inside, they removed the classic arched facade altogether and simply copied it against the wall in centerfield, which gave it a pasted on look.

The whole thing doesn't work architecturally or historically. But I'm an old fashioned guy. Baseball goes back generations. Lots of people chart their lives by the game ... they see the game as their religion - and the ballparks are their temples, their churches. They shouldn't be torn down and should only be renovated with care. And they should have to get permission from local Preservation Societies.

JB: How do you get the book written?

MW: Right.

JB: You have to write a very good outline and then show it to the agent.[17]

Bobby Bragan
January 10, 2008

Dear Michael: Thanks for your letter of recent date. Yankee Stadium is about to be rebuilt and I left a message with George Steinbrenner to make certain it has "FAIR POLES" instead of FOUL POLES. My brother, who owns the Jacksonville team in Southern League "AA" and the Ft. Worth Cats (Independent) are the only two teams in professional baseball with "FAIR POLES." Burlington Northern Santa Fe Railroad Co. spent $25,000 erecting the poles in Ft. Worth at La Grave Field.

I've been talking with John McHale, Jr., in the Commissioners Office about changing Baseball Rule 2 – to read "Fair Line and Fair Pole." However he tells me the rules committee meets so seldom he hasn't had the opportunity to do anything. This hasn't anything to do with Yankee Stadium as per your request.

People love Yankee Stadium – the players love Yankee Stadium

- the crowd, the playing field – the accessibility to get there – subway ride and get off at Yankee Stadium – no parking problems. And the fans are really true baseball fans – upper deck or box seats – they cheer and they boo! It was different at Ebbets Field – I played in both – and if you had a Dodger uniform on you would not be booed even if you made a critical error.

I played in Philadelphia too – and [they] booed louder than any crowd anywhere if you booted one in the late innings. Bob Uecker said his greatest thrill in Philadelphia was seeing one of the spectators fall from the second deck. He was still booing when he recovered from the fall. They try out stage shows in Philly before going to Broadway.

My greatest thrill as a player came in game 6 of the 1947 World Series 6th game – I was in bull pen and haven't been to bat during the first five games – Burt Shotten – who replaced Durocher for the season when Leo was suspended by A.B. Happy Chandler for allegedly leaving tickets to Memphis Engelberg a gambler – Leo was later vindicated –

Anyway Shotten called for me to come pinch hit for Ralph Branca – I doubled off Joe Page. My mother and father had come up from my house in Birmingham, Ala – and since I hadn't been to bat during the first five games – they were in the rest rooms when I got my double. HA HA HA.

Yankee Stadium – Wrigley Field – both were always manicured – no bad hops – as was Ebbets Field – I can't imagine any player not enjoying playing in these fields –

St. Louis when the Cards & Browns both played at Sportsman's Park was the worst to play on – for the ground keepers didn't have the time to get the grounds prepared –

Michael I hope I haven't drifted too far off the subject and if you wish further comment I'm at (he gave his phone number) in Ft Worth, Texas, where I own the Bobby Bragan Youth Foundation (BBYF). It has been the most satisfying experience of my life- Respectfully – Bobby Bragan

He also sent a signed card of himself and an unsigned card of President George W. Bush[18]

Ed Bressoud
November 6, 2007

Luck to you on your book. Playing there was a special experience – but I cannot contribute to the gee whiz.[19]

Lou Brissie
January 20, 2008

Michael: I prefer renovation to New Stadiums. We retain the history and traditions. Ruth or Foxx hit one there on that seat – Gionfriddo caught Joe D's drive there. The new stadium will go on as a tribute to government spending and concrete. Thanks for asking. Lou Brissie[20]

Bobby Brown Yankee Player & former American League President February 22, 2005	Michael: The old Yankee Stadium with 72,000+ fans on a big game day was hard to beat. The old field with its vastness was really treasured by me. To watch the visiting teams, especially the National League teams during the World Series, get up on the top step of the dugout and stare out into left, left-center, and center fields was priceless. The sight lines of the renovated Yankee Stadium are much improved over the old Stadium. Removing the pillars was a tremendous benefit to the fans. The seats are now wider, and the decreased seating capacity makes season ticket sales better. Yankee Stadium is still Yankee Stadium, but the old Stadium jammed to capacity was a sight to behold.[21]
Tommy Byrne October 25, 2004	Hi Mike – Good luck with your project – like university campuses – like hospitals – like all the major needs of our country – all must be upgraded, maintained, or fall. – Yankee Stadium is the park of baseball – Since it was cheaper to improve the facility @ its present location – one answer – move with the times. God Bless, Tommy Byrne. It has always been my 'home,' away from home. Good luck – may I "live" to read your expression. Tommy also signed a renovation photo for me.[22]
Joe Carrieri Yankee Batboy 1950s March 20, 2008	Hi – I am not happy about the move – Babe Ruth, Joe DiMaggio, Phil Rizzuto, Yogi Berra, Lou Gehrig, Mickey Mantle roamed the field of Yankee Stadium – It will not be the same – Joe Carrieri[23]
Paul Casanova January 29, 2008	Paul signed the two renovation photos for me.[24]

Ben Chapman March 25, 1985	I liked it the way it was.[25]
Horace Clarke February 8, 2005	Horace signed two renovation photos for me.[26]
Gil Coan November 14, 2007	The old stadium I played in was a monument to the great teams of the '20s & '30s. Your best bet for what happened to items eliminated from the old stadium would be Baseball Hall of Fame – Cooperstown, N.Y. Sincere Best Wishes, Gil Coan.[27]
Jerry Coleman December 2, 2004	The dimensions of the field have changed dramatically- 461 to CF to 405 now. The steel beams are gone for a better view-![28]
Earle Combs August 18, 1975	I suppose it was necessary.[29]
Jocko Conlan August 18, 1975	Yes.[30]
Bob Costas Sportscaster February 5, 2008	Michael – Please excuse my informality here. I can't help you with question 2 – But as for #1 – while I give the Yanks a lot of credit for maintaining the "feel" of the old Stadium with touches of the façade – and honoring history with Monument Park – something was lost when the original awesome dimensions – 461 to center (monuments & flag pole on field!) 457 – to Death Valley – etc. – went away – not to mention the low fences down the lines & to straightaway left and right, which allowed for circus catches as outfielders robbed batters of Hrs – and often tumbled into the stands! All The Best – Bob Costas[31]
Chuck Cottier November 6, 2007	Dear Mr. Wagner, The old Stadium was a great place to play, but there comes a time for newer and better Stadiums.

I do not have any "Gee Whiz" information for you. Best Wishes, Chuck Cottier[32]

Stanley Coveleski
September 20, 1975

No.[33]

Del Crandall
March 22, 2008

I'm sorry, Michael, I really don't have much to give you. I just know that playing in the House That Ruth Built was a big, big thrill. The revamped Stadium was just another Stadium. Del[34]

Robert Creamer
Author
April 18, 2008

Dear Mr. Wagner, I'm afraid I can't be much help to you. At various times I was both a writer and an editor at Sports Illustrated and in the 1970s at the time of the Yankee Stadium renovation I was not covering baseball and had no direct experience with the stadium. I don't recall any particular thoughts or feelings about the revamping of the old ballpark.

As for knowing anyone with specific "gee whiz" information about what happened to dirt, concrete and so on taken from the old Stadium, I have no idea at all. It seems to me that, fifteen or twenty years earlier, people were much more interested in artifacts from the departed Polo Grounds and Ebbets Field than they were in the Stadium in the mid-1970s.

There is one name I can give you in relation to the Stadium renovation, although I have no address and don't even know if she's alive. Her name is ________________ and she did publicity, I believe, for the firm (or one of the firms) doing the renovation. She was (is, I hope) an exceptionally intelligent person and would be a help to you, I believe, if you can locate her. Sincerely, Robert Creamer[35]

Frank Crosetti
October 4, 1976

I think it is great.[36]

Ray Culp
March 25, 2008

Ray signed a renovation photo for me.[37]

Bud Daley
February 22, 2005

I don't like the fences moved in, it takes away from the park.[38]

Don Denkinger
Umpire
January 26, 2008

Michael – I'm sorry but I only remember working home plate opening day of the reopening. It was very exciting! Thanks – Don Denkinger, Major League Umpire #11, 1969-1998[39]

Bobby Doerr
October 17, 2004

I did get to play in Yankee Stadium before it was renovated. It was a hard park to play in for a right hand hitter. First the shadows were bad in day baseball, then always big crowds in the center field bleachers were open with white shirts, then straight away center left field and left center was a long ways out. Don't know how DiMaggio had such great years there. He was the best I saw in my career.

Center field was lower than the infield playing field. I know when you sat in the third base dugout the center fielder was always lower than the infield. That's about all I can tell you.[40]

Al Downing

Interview at New York Yankees Fantasy Camp, Legends Field, Tampa, FL during a rained out day. Wednesday, November 15, 2006. I showed him some photos I took of the renovation.

A.D.: I think that in everything in life there comes a time…if this was your house, you would have to consider a renovation, and this is a house, so therefore you have to consider a renovation to make the customers comfortable when they're coming in. I mean, it's nice to say that it's a landmark. But by the same token, you've got to keep contemporary, because people want to come into newer things. They like newer edifices. So therefore, the Yankees deserve to have the finest facility there is, and it has to be a modern facility. The old one could never be modern because you have to keep retrofitting and things like that, so you might as well build a new one.

M.W.: I guess most of us have a hard time with the facade being taken away.

A.D.: The facade is just a part of the whole thing. It's the aura. So therefore its everything, it's not just the facade.

M.W.: So it's still Yankee Stadium – no matter what.

A.D.: It's still Yankee Stadium when you go in. The tradition of Yankee Stadium is there from the ground up. It's more than a facade. In your mind when you go there, the facade represents it.

M.W.: Well, you know it's Yankee Stadium anyway.

A.D.: Exactly.[41]

Joe Dugan
May 22, 1975

Good – it needs it.[42]

August 18, 1975

Yes.[43]

Bob Engel
Umpire
January 25, 2008

Dear Michael – Sorry, I can't help you. As you can see by the card I am wearing the N.L. patch you see on the card. This was before inter-league play began and although we belonged to the Major League Umpires Association, we were either A.L. umpires or N.L. umpires. Inter-league play did not happen until after my retirement. Therefore, in my 25 years as a National League umpire, I have never set foot in Yankee Stadium. Even more surprising is that after 3 World Series, 7 Championship Series, and 4 All Star games, the Yankees were never involved as a team. I had Joe Torre as a manager in St. Louis and Atlanta, and Yogi Berra as a coach in Houston, but just never made it to Yankee Stadium. Sincerely, Bob Engel, N.L. Umpire, 1965-1990.[44]

Cal Ermer
May 1, 2008

Dear Michael, I wish I could help you out. I would say the park is getting old and the new stadium will get more

money, and they have to get a lot. That way they have to get enough to pay their players. The many million dollars they are giving the players. It's a different world now and money is not the same. I hope you can read my writing.
I was in 64 years in playing and managing Minn. Twins. I love the game. Hope you can write a good book. Frank Sinatra, the great singer in the 40s sang, "There Used To Be A Ballpark." Try to get it. Good Luck, Cal Ermer.[45]

Carl Erskine
March 29, 2005

Hello Michael. I can't give you much on the stadium renovation – I suggest you contact the Yankee office & their sports information director – they must have what you're looking for –

I'll give you one true story which I used in my book, *"Tales From the Dodger Dugout:" Extra Innings* (Publisher: Sports Publishing 1-877-807-6034).

In 1949 we played the Yankees in my first World Series. We were a young Dodger team – many of us were seeing Yankee Stadium for the first time. The Yankee locker room was moved from the 3rd base side to the first base side – I believe the Yankees made a very deliberate move to shake up a young Dodger team.

As we entered the visitors locker room – still in place & not yet moved to the Yankee side were two lockers – uniforms & all of Babe Ruth & Lou Gehrig – Yes, we lost the series 4 games to one –[46]

Bob Feller
October 25, 2004

Bob surprised me with a phone call. He told me that we all like the old things. Baseball is built for merchandising. There's nothing wrong with that, but it's more apparent now than when he played. He also told me that he wrote three books and never made a nickel on any of them.[47]

Herman Franks January 14, 2008	Dear Michael, I have really [rarely?] thought about the renovation of Yankee Stadium. Best Wishes, Herman Franks.[48]

Oscar Gamble

Interview at New York Yankees Fantasy Camp, Legends Field, Tampa, FL during a rained out day. Wednesday, November 15, 2006. I showed him some photos I took of the renovation.

I like it better after the renovation because it was brought up to date. They kept a lot of the symbols and stuff. I think they were having a lot of trouble at that time with the foundation, so they had to redo the construction, and I think they did a good job. I played in it with the visitors team. In 1976 I had the chance to play in it when it was new when they did it over, and they did a nice job. And it's still going on today. If they wouldn't build another one now, it would last another 30 years.[49]

Joe Garagiola, Sr. February 21, 2005	Never played in Yankee Stadium. Joe G[50]
Joe Garagiola, Jr. January 7, 2004 Baseball Executive	Joe phoned me. We got along great. What a beautiful speaking voice! Joe didn't have much information about the renovation, but suggested I call Perry Green and Marty Appel. Joe was counsel to George Steinbrenner in the 1970s. Joe related a funny story when he and Cedric Tallis visited the Stadium shortly before the remodeling was completed. The left field foul pole was installed correctly. The right field pole, however, had been mounted with the three foot foul pole netting mistakenly facing foul territory. After explaining to the worker that since only one of the poles was facing the wrong way, he'd only have to fix one and not the other. This solved the problem. Mr. Tallis feared the concession stands would not be finished in time for opening day. Gabe Paul assured him they would be. They were.[51]

Billy Gardner January 8, 2008	Signed two photos of the renovation.[52]
Ned Garver January 14, 2008	Michael – I write about my feelings on Yankee Stadium in my book. Ned[53]
Charles Gehringer November 24, 1974	I imagine it will be real nice, however they will still have a severe parking situation.[54]
August 18, 1975	Yes.[55]
October 4, 1976	I have not seen it except on T.V. Looks like a nice park.[56]
Dick Gernert January 14, 2008	It was good for the fan because they removed a lot of the posts. It was also shorter for the hitters. Have no idea.(#2)[57]
Jake Gibbs January 18, 2008	Michael – I think they did a great job in its renovation of the Stadium. It probably was time to do something, but I enjoyed playing in the old Stadium – tradition, the good teams & players, the bullpen in RF. It was a great place to play. 2. Don't know.[58]
Rudolph W. Giuliani former Mayor of NYC December 22, 2004	Since he's a big Yankees fan, I sent him some photos of the renovation and thanked him for his leadership during the attacks of September 11, 2001. He responded: "Dear Mr. Wagner: Thank you for your recent letter. Your kind words and thoughtfulness are greatly appreciated. Sharing these photographs of the Yankee Stadium renovation is truly generous. Best wishes to you in all your future endeavors. Sincerely, Rudolph W. Giuliani[59]

Russ Goetz Umpire January 26, 2008	Mike – Very interesting your data of Yankee Stadium. As much as I would like to contribute to your input I do not have any that would be of use. I do know my 1st game in Yankee Stadium in 1968 was quite the thrill since all the stories I had been told over the years. I do know I had one of my big moments there when Billy Martin brought his Detroit Tigers in for a game Friday night. His team was delayed by rush hour traffic & sent his starting line-up ahead to try to make game time – however they were late. Eddie Brinkman was his SS. I called him out on strikes & he disagreed & swore at me when I ejected him. Martin came in from his 3rd base coaching box & I also ejected him. Then his pitching coach Art Fowler gestured from the dugout & he too got the HEAVE-HO – on one pitch I chewed 3 – Everyone was upset, game delay, which of course made all on edge. For now – do take care. Russ Goetz, Retired A.L. Umpire, 1968 thru 1983.[60]
Burleigh Grimes August 18, 1975	What I approve of don't count.[61]
Dick Groat October 22, 2004	I hated hitting at Yankee Stadium – Horrible background.[62]
Michael Grossbardt Official Photographer for the New York Yankees 1968-1979 February 18, 2009	I like the original Stadium more. It was more photogenic. The pre-renovated scoreboard looked more beautiful in photographs, and the pre-renovated Stadium had a nostalgic look and beauty to it. We spoke on the phone.[63]

Don Gutteridge January 11, 2008	I am not able to tell you much about Stadium. I played there before and after the renovation. I was always awed to play there. It is really an awesome place. I believe old seats were sold and some were reserved and used. Dressing rooms were upgraded too. Sorry I cannot help much. Don also sent a signed baseball card.[64]
Bill Haller Umpire February 19, 2005	Dear Michael, Thank you for this nice letter. I would contact the New York City Public Affairs Office or the New York City Sports Authority office to find out what happened to the seats, etc. from the old Stadium. I'm like you. I like the old palace!! Better than the new, but as we both know <u>Money, Money, Money.</u> [65]
Jack Harshman March 21, 2008	I really and truly, honestly cannot give you an expert opinion because I didn't see it. But, the old ballpark was one of the ones that obviously had a great many memories to it. The House That Ruth Built obviously was well, well respected and…I enjoyed going there. I never had much luck there. But, I liked going to the Stadium. But, like I said, I didn't do well there. Of course, I don't think many pitchers did because they were the class of the act then. During the late'50s they were the obvious team to beat. With the White Sox we had one real good chance that we let slip away. But, they just had the best team, that's all. The team with the best horses is going to win the most races. That's basically what it amounts to.
M.W.:	Especially back then with Mickey, Whitey, Yogi, and the rest of the gang.
J.H.:	Sure. Absolutely. They had an outstanding lineup. They

just had a helluva ball club. Great pitching, great defense. I mean, they had the whole thing.

M.W.: Do you have a favorite memory of your time at the Stadium?

J.H.: You know what? It was the only American League stadium that I did not in fact hit a home run in. When I was pitching that was the only stadium that I did not hit a home run in.

And that wasn't necessarily something that's my outstanding remembrance of it obviously, but it is something that is a little bit of an oddity. Because I did in fact hit home runs in eight different American League stadiums, because at the time I went to Chicago, the Philadelphia Athletics were still in Philadelphia. And, then when they moved to Kansas City, I hit home runs in those two parks, and so, that's what made up a total of eight. One was old Shibe Park, and then when they moved to Kansas City.

But, I don't remember a whole lot of things that were outstanding as far as me were personally concerned with that stadium, but I pitched pretty decently there. It just didn't work out very well with wins and losses.

M.W.: Especially when you faced those guys.

J.H.: Yeah! When I went to Cleveland in 1959, Joe Gordon was managing the Cleveland ball club at the time, and I started a ballgame there against the Yankees, and Bob Turley was pitching. He and I both pitched through the tenth inning, and it was a no score game. And, (laughs) they took him out and we had the bases loaded in the top half of the eleventh with nobody out, and Rocky Colavito was on second base, and I forget who it was who got a base hit to center field, and Rocky got thrown out from I guess about twenty feet short of home plate. Mantle came up with it and threw him out easily. So, we got the one run that was on third base, obviously, but then that was the one run that we got.

And then they scored. I think Mantle, as a matter of fact, hit a home run in the bottom half of the eleventh inning to win the ballgame for them off of me. But, that's the kind of luck I had. I just never did have a whole lot of good luck against them. That could be considered somewhat not good (laughs).

J.H.: I wish I could have given you more of what you're looking for, but like I said, I was there those eleven times times seven, as a player. I hope you get what you're looking for.

M.W.: Thank you for your time, Mr. Harshman. (another man who speaks beautifully).

J.H.: You're welcome. Bye, bye.[66]

Clint Hartung
January 8, 2008

Signed two photos of the renovation.[67]

Ernie Harwell
March 20, 2008

Dear Mr. Wagner – Can't help much re: Yankee Stadium. I liked old version much better. I broadcast football there, too & it was a terrible spot to work from – too far away from field.

The baseball was not greatest, but OK. B(obby) Richardson fouled back a line drive & hit me in ribs.

I did my 1st W.S. there 1963 – in second game. *One Flew Over Cuckoo's Nest* used my tape from NBC Radio Co.

Don't know about seats, lights etc.

Good luck on book. Ernie Harwell.[68]

Grady Hatton March 22, 2008	Michael, I loved to play in Yankee Stadium – sorry to see it go. I have no idea where they moved all the stuff from the field or stands. Grady Hatton P.S. – Thanks for pictures of Stadium.[69]
Solly Hemus January 8, 2008	Dear Michael – I played primarily in the National League. I enjoyed coaching with Cleveland at Yankee Stadium and my main thoughts when I was in the ball park was knowing that Lou Gehrig & Babe Ruth was responsible for all the after thoughts of the Stadium – there was a young lady (& great baseball fan that had Whitey Ford distribute her ashes on the playing field at her death. If you remind me I will be happy to get her name. She was from Houston. Best Wishes – Solly Hemus.[70]
Tommy Henrich September 16, 1981	I guess it had to be – To me, as regards to the problems of Baseball, it's a small matter. I have been more concerned in the past over O'Malley talking Stoneham into the two of them breaking up the greatest rivalry that Baseball ever knew – Mike – I'll bet no other Ball Player reveals his soul to you as I have – Good Luck[71]
Whitey Herzog February 19, 2005	Mike, Yankee Stadium is to baseball what Augusta National is to golf. My rookie year I'd get goose bumps when I got off the subway. Hopefully the Yankees will always play there. History is a wonderful thing.[72]
Jim Hickman February 22, 2005	I was there for a couple of games. It would be hard to make a judgment on the renovation. I was glad to have the opportunity to play there.[73]
Donald Honig Author	Dear Mr. Wagner: Thank you for your letter about Yankee Stadium. I am afraid, however, that there is little I can add

April 2, 2008	to your own knowledge of the renovation performed there in the 1970's. I was not a Yankees fan and so paid little attention to it. I do remember many Yankee fans being upset by it, their feeling being that something hallowed was being tampered with. And now the whole thing is to be taken down. Where will the ghosts go? I'm sorry I cannot be helpful to you. Best of luck with your project. Sincerely, Donald Honig[74]
Ralph Houk August 3, 2003	Yankee Breakfast hosted by sports promoter Larry Dluhy of Sports Collectibles of Houston, Texas. This event took place at the Live Oak Civic Center, Live Oak, Texas. Guests consisted of Ralph Houk, Bob Cerv, Bill Skowron, and Bob Turley. "I like, I like all the old parks. All the old parks. The smell of beer, popcorn, and all that."[75]
Elston Howard August 18, 1975	Yes.[76]
Frank Howard January 8, 2008	He sent a signed 2007 Allen & Ginter's baseball card.[77]
Waite Hoyt September 17, 1974	Guess it will be wonderful except as I understand it, still no parking space.[78]
Billy Hunter March 27, 1975	I'll be glad when they move back. I don't like Shea Stadium.[79]
Larry Jansen January 8, 2008	I was a New York Giant not a Yankee. He also sent a signed business card.[80]

Tommy John

Interview at New York Yankees Fantasy Camp, Legends Field, Tampa, FL during a rained out day. Wednesday, November 15, 2006. I showed him some photos I took of the renovation.

Personally, I like old Yankee Stadium. As part of the deal, I think uniqueness is part of baseball. And now, what they're trying to do is bring back old style ballparks with modern technology. So, they're making all these walls at angles, like Ebbets Field on the wall and the angle there in right field. That's the way it was because they tried to fit a ballpark in a small area. With Yankee Stadium, they just kept moving left field and the fences in so much that now Yankee Stadium really doesn't favor…it still favors left handed hitting, but right handed hitting is not that tough to get balls out of the ballpark now. It used to be…I know that in my first year with the Yankees in the old ballpark… after they fixed it but before they moved the fences in, where you had to hit a ball in the bullpen for a home run, I pitched a game against the Brewers, and Gorman Thomas had to hit 1,800 feet of fly balls. And, Mickey Rivers had black on him because he was scraping the wall on every catch, because he (Thomas) was hitting the ball to left center field at 445 feet or whatever it was then. And, he was out, he was out, he was out. Finally on the fourth time, Gorman Thomas threw his helmet and said, "I CAN'T TAKE IT…I CAN'T TAKE IT ANYMORE…I CAN'T TAKE IT ANYMORE!!!" And, he just said, "This ballpark's just too big for me!"

And, when we came in with the Dodgers in '77 and '78, our right handed hitters saw the ballpark. We took batting practice there and the right handed hitters were whipped. So the Yankees had a leg up on everything because you knew right handed hitters…you either pulled the ball right down the line, or you'd better be line-drive hitters. So, I personally, I like the old ballpark, with the uniqueness. And I hope they never tear Fenway Park down because it's the same way.[81]

Eddie Joost February 19, 2008	Played in that great Stadium for 8 yrs – Phila. As, Red Sox.[82]
Arndt Jorgens September 8, 1975	It needed the renovation – too many posts in the old park.[83]

Eddie Kasko
March 21, 2008

Michael, Although the renovation took place after my tenure, it was very much needed. Biggest additions, more of a standardized outfield, and dugouts. Outfield fences were more like other present day parks – <u>not</u> like the old Polo Grounds or Ebbets Field. Dugouts were the worse places to see the game.

I have no idea what happened to all the artifacts, lights, seats, etc. Wouldn't the Yankee office know about that?

All the people with "gee whiz" information that I knew have passed away. Regards, Eddie Kasko[84]

Russ Kemmerer
January 10, 2008

Dear Michael, In response to your letter regarding the questions about the renovation at Yankee Stadium I can only say that my career in the major leagues was from 1953 until 1964, so although I was aware of the changes in the stadium I only saw them on TV and what may have been in the newspapers. In some manner similar to you the old stadium was the one I played in and loved as a kid growing up in Pittsburgh and listening to the World Series that always seemed to pit the Yankees against a National League foe. So I can not render much help to you in this regard nor the question regarding the artifacts.

In 2001 I wrote a book about my career, mostly about the four teams I played with, Boston, Washington, Chicago White Sox and Houston, and the men I played with and against. Ted Williams, "*Hey Kid Just Get It Over The Plate*," I thought that one paragraph from the book might help you to understand what a young 19 year old rookie coming into Yankee Stadium for the first time felt.

My rookie season was by far the most exciting year of my life. Thc only major league baseball park I had ever been in was Forbes Field in Pittsburgh. I had seen pictures of the

other parks. Yankee Stadium was at the top of my list. I could hardly wait to see "The House That Ruth Built." I was almost breathless as I walked from the visitor's locker room through the tunnel that led to the playing field. I stood on the top step of the visitors dugout and looked out over the most noted baseball field in the history of the game. I could almost feel the ghosts of the former heroes drifting out to their positions and waiting for the cry of "Play Ball!" to echo throughout the stadium. More than the ghosts of Ruth and Gehrig were in the stadium that day. It was Old Timer's Day and many of the Hall of Fame players of the past were there to be honored for their contribution to the game. I was on the same playing field with and talking with George Sisler, Bill Terry, Frankie Frisch, Mel Clark, Gabby Hartnett, Charles Gehringer, Pie Traynor, Lefty Grove, Joe Cronin, Carl Hubbell, Joe DiMaggio, Paul Waner, Jimmy Foxx, Rogers Hornsby, Bump Hadley, and Hank Greenberg. It was truly my "Field of Dreams" experience. I cherish the baseball they signed for me. It was a day I will remember my whole life. That's the best I can do for you. Sincerely yours,
Russ Kemmerer[85]

John Kibler
Umpire
February 19, 2005

Michael, I only got to work at Yankee Stadium during World Series, Yanks & Dodgers 1978. However I lived in Upstate N.Y. as a youngster, and saw my first big league game in Yankee Stadium long time ago. Ha.[86]

Ralph Kiner
March 18, 2005

Dear Michael, They did a good job on the renovation although I would have preferred they left it as it was just for comparison.[87]

Ed Koch
former Mayor of NYC
July 19, 2007

I'm not a baseball devotee and have no helpful insights into the renovation of Yankee Stadium. Good luck on your forthcoming book. All the best. Ed Koch[88]

Mark Koenig August 3, 1974	I hope they are able to fill it with fans.[89]
October 20, 1975	Yes.[90]
September 24, 1981	Ridiculous[91]
Jerry Koosman February 24, 2005	I played in both parks and like the new one. I don't know what happened to that stuff but remember sharing Shea Stadium with the Yankees – our field took a beating those days & a lot of errors were committed by our fielders because of the habits the Yankees left there![92]
Bob Kuzava January 8, 2008	Thanks for your nice letter. I can't be much help because I haven't been back since 1954. It was great pitching in the Stadium. Yours in baseball, Bob Kuzava[93]
Vern Law October 26, 2004	During the period of renovation – I was coaching here at Brigham Young University. But it was a thrill for me to play and pitch in the 1960 World Series. I thought it was an awesome experience because of the history of the Yankees that the world was aware of. The '60 Yankees were a great team with a wonderful history of success, but I think sometimes just because they're the Yankees some take it for granted that that assures them of a Championship. Although we were 25 nobodies on the field with them, we pulled it off. The way the field was situated when we played there it was hard to pick up the ball as a hitter because of the fans sitting in center field. You really had to concentrate on the ball and try to pick it up early. My 1st time hitting I didn't even see the 1st pitch, but after a couple of pitches was able to do so. Personally I didn't think they'd ever revamp the stadium because of the history of the park.[94]

Walter "Buck" Leonard
December 7, 1975

Yes.[95]

Fred Lindstrom
September 3, 1976

Marvelous. George Steinbrenner and the city of N.Y. are to be highly complimented for a tremendous job.[96]

Phil Linz
January 12, 2008

Sent a signed business card and signed two photos of the renovation.[97]

Ed Lopat
August 3, 1974

Yes.[98]

Hector Lopez
February 19, 2005

I do not know too much about the renovation. The time of that I spent all those years in Panama, where I was born. One thing I can tell you about the old Yankee Stadium. It was a very big ball park and full of history.[99]

Hector Lopez

Interview at New York Yankees Fantasy Camp, Legends Field, Tampa, FL during a rained out day. Wednesday, November 15, 2006. I showed him some photos I took of the renovation.

H.L.: That's it! That's Yankee Stadium!

M.W.: Do you like the renovation of Yankee Stadium?

H.L.: Oh, yeah. I have no problem.[100]

Lee MacPhail
Yankee Executive
February 8, 2005

I was with the Yankees in NY from 1949 to 1958, and from 1967 to 1974. I think Yankee Stadium is great. I think all changes were made to make it as convenient and enjoyable for fans as possible, but still keeping it good for the team on the field.[101]

Max Mantle, Sr.
(Mickey's Cousin)
March 22, 2008

Max was kind enough to phone me in response to my letter. He said Mickey didn't like the renovation because they moved the fences in. Mickey didn't talk about it much. Max didn't like it either because it made home run hitters out of singles hitters.

I said that I liked baseball better when Mickey played because the players played for the love of the game, and that today's players are grossly overpaid. Max said that he and Mickey talked about that in the 1990s. Max asked Mickey what he'd be making as a ballplayer in the 1990s instead of when he played. Mickey said, "Well, I'd go up to George, put my arm around him, and say, 'Hi, partner.'"

I asked Max how the Mantles are doing, and he said, "Fine." Max mentioned that he'd never been to Yankee Stadium, although he had opportunities. Also, when he got married, that he threw out all of his baseball cards. I told him that my Mom threw mine out. We laughed (I cried inside!). Max said he wished he'd saved everything.

I asked Max if I could be on the lookout for anything he might be looking for. He said, "No, but I'm still a big Yankee fan." I asked Max if he'd ever heard of the internet site, "Baseball-Fever." I told him it's a wonderful site that has everything you can think of about baseball. No, he hadn't.

Max does, however, have the same warm, friendly Midwest drawl as Mickey. Although I've never had the pleasure of meeting Max, I felt as though I were talking to an old friend.[102]

Marty Marion
March 10, 2005

Yankee Stadium was a great place to play a baseball game, other than that I draw a blank. Best Wishes, Marty Marion.[103]

Roger Maris November 14, 1978	It's OK.[104]
Morrie Martin January 18, 2008	Morrie signed a renovation photo for me.[105]
Charlie Maxwell January 8, 2008	Charlie sent a signed index card.[106]
Joe McCarthy January 23, 1974	No comment.[107]
January 18, 1975	I suppose it had to be done.[108]
August 18, 1975	Would have to see it first.[109]
August 9, 1976	Can't say, as I have never been in it.[110]
Lindy McDaniel August 18, 1975	I had absolutely no voice in the matter, but I doubt if I would have voted for the bonds.[111]
March 17, 2005	Dear Michael, I was traded from the New York Yankees before the renovation took place. I was more concerned about the renovation of the Yankee players in which only six remained in 1974 from the year before. Lindy McDaniel. P.S. – I do have the old Yankee "bullpen" fence in my possession.[112]
Danny McDevitt March 17, 2008	Danny sent me a signed four page Limited Edition about the last game the Brooklyn Dodgers played at Ebbets Field on September 24, 1957. (Danny pitched and won that game for the Bums.)[113]

Gil McDougald
June 30, 1974

It might not look like the Yankee Stadium of the past but it was necessary to be remodeled.[114]

October 25, 2004

Dear Michael, Jim Thompson was the NY Yankee Superintendent at this time & responsible for the new construction. If you call the Yankees might know about his address if still alive.

I told Jim when he invited me over one day to see the new ballpark that it looks like a Little League field in comparison to when we played there.

I know baseball seats were sold off at the Stadium, but I don't know about anything else. Sincerely, Gil[115]

Charlie Mead
January 12, 2008

Dear Mr. Wagner, Thank you for your letter, but I'm afraid that I must disappoint you because I never played in Yankee Stadium. However, I did play at the Polo Grounds when I was with the New York Giants in 1943, 1944 and 1945. Never the less I wish you the best of luck with your forth-coming book about Yankee Stadium.
Sincerely, Charlie Mead.[116]

George Medich
March 28, 2005

Mr. Wagner: Thank you for your letter regarding the old Yankee Stadium. First my apologies for being so tardy in replying, retirement does that to people.

I want to preface my response by saying that the years having given me quite a different perspective of playing Major League Baseball. Particularly with the Yankees. While I was playing, I was so consumed with performance that I never was able to put into perspective where I was or exactly what I was doing. The fact that I was privileged to be doing what I was doing was always greatly over-shadowed by what I was doing (sounds like Yogi).

I was with the Yankees in 1973, the last year in the old stadium. I got to pitch the next to last game there and threw a shutout against Detroit. After the game Ralph Houk called me into his office and told me he wasn't coming back: his words "I can't stand that sob." Guess who. Right after that I left for Pittsburgh to continue medical school. I don't recall when I found out that remodeling was going to happen there in 74 and I figured I'd be back there in 1976 with all the other guys, Thurman, Lou, Dobber, Graig, Elliot Maddox.

That winter I got traded to Pittsburgh. It slowly began to creep into my consciousness what an honor it had been to play for the Yankees in the old stadium. The air and heir of history was so thick there we couldn't see it: like being in a smokey room. I remember driving up to the stadium on a day when I saw my name on the big marquis outside the stadium. In my deepest thoughts I realized a dream a lot of boys have: I was in the Bigs. Not only in the Bigs, but with the Yankees.

Another thing, the first old timers day, I come into the clubhouse and there is someone in my locker. [I didn't know the old timers used the players lockers] as I approached my locker Mickey Mantle turned and said "Excuse me, am I in your way?" I almost said "Who me?" After all he had this locker long before I did. I almost asked Pete, the clubhouse man, if I could dress someplace else. [we're not worthy!] He was just a regular guy, like Whitey, who was my pitching coach, Yogi, Elston Howard, Joe Pep, Dick Stuart, Tony Kubek. Joe D was not a regular guy.

Thanks for letting me expound. I am by far the luckiest and most grateful man on earth to be allowed to do what I have done in my life: played golf at TPC Sawgrass, football at Notre Dame's field, the Orange Bowl, LA Coliseum, Nike Stadium, Annapolis, Pitt Stadium, Nittany Stadium: the greatest is that I was allowed to become a Yankee: to be part of the royalty of the game. To have that hallowed ground as my home for awhile. Like I heard before, "You don't know what you have until it's gone." (Willie Nelson?)[117]

Sam Mele
March 24, 2008

Sam signed a renovation photo for me.[118]

Charles Metro
April 7, 2008

My thoughts about Yankee Stadium – I hit my first 3 bagger there to win the game.[119]

Johnny Mize
September 2, 1975

yes[120]

Mickey Morabito
Yankees Public Relations
May 26, 2005

Mickey phoned me, which was a nice surprise. He recalls it was a hassle to work at Shea Stadium for two years. He never went to Yankee Stadium due to the construction, but did go after it was completed. Marty Appel was Mickey's boss. Mickey had no anecdotes, but suggested I try *The New York Times* Archives for information.[121]

Gerry Moses
April 15, 2005

The old Yankee Stadium had great history. [By] The fact that the clubhouse manager still had many of the great players memorabilia. In those days players used a large thigh bone used to rub against the sweet spot on the bat to keep it from splinting. Babe Ruth's Bone was still in the Club House. The new Yankee Stadium will have its own history in time.

The only thing I remember about the chairs was that I was supposed to get one & didn't.

Tidbit – Duke Sims & I flipped to see who would get to catch the last game played in the old Stadium. He won & caught.[122]

Don Mossi
February 1, 2008

Don't have any info for you. Liked the old Stadium, but a lot of repairs were needed. Hate to see all the old ballparks destroyed.[123]

Bill Nicholson
March 3, 1975

Yankee Stadium was a great ball park, but it definitely needed modernizing. I think it will be great when they finish the job on it.[124]

Irv Noren
March 27, 1975

a lot of money but it's good[125].

Billy O'Dell
August 7, 2008

Billy signed a photo of the renovation.[126]

Bob Oldis
January 28, 2008

I Love going to Yankee Stadium to see the monuments of the great Yankees, to see their renovation of old Yankee Stadium. I didn't like it, but things got to move on and update everything. Good Luck, Bob Oldis[127]

Peter O'Malley
January 24, 2008
Dodgers Executive

Dear Mr. Wagner: Many thanks for your letter to Peter O'Malley regarding the photographs that you shot of Yankee Stadium's renovation, which you are now making into a book.

Mr. O'Malley currently is recovering from surgery. He said that he does not have any specific recollections to share with you for the book, but he sincerely appreciates the invitation to participate. We wish you the best with the book project! Warmest regards, Brent Shyer, Vice President Special Projects.[128]

Jim Pagliaroni
January 30, 2008

MICHAEL – I finished my career in 1970 – did not play in renovated stadium –but loved renovated stadium.[129]

Camilo Pasqual
April 2, 2008

Dear Wagner, I will like to help you but you should contact the Yankees ground keeper. Good Luck. Camilo Pasqual[130]

Marty Pattin
February 1, 2008

Dear Michael, I had the opportunity to pitch in Yankee Stadium before renovation. Left field & centerfield were spacious and right field was a nightmare for a pitcher. The short right field fence was an easy hr. shot for all left handed hitters. After the renovation of the stadium the fences even out in distance except for c.f.

Before I retired a good friend of mine gave me an old Yankee Stadium seat which I still have. Hope this answers your questions. My thanks and Best Wishes. Marty Pattin #33[131]

Roger Peckinpaugh
August 18, 1975

Silly Question.[132]

Jim Perry
March 6, 2008

I played in last game at old Yankee Stadium that Ruth built. J.P.[133]

Johnny Pesky
February 19, 2005

Michael, I still liked the "old Yankee Stadium" However, the new one is a beauty!!

Am sure you could get more info from the Yankee P.R. people.

I am a Red Sox, however I like the Yankees too. Especially Joe Torre.[134]

Fritz Peterson
January 31, 2005

Mike, I felt honored to be the starting pitcher for the last game played in the house that Ruth built. The new place is fine but it isn't the real thing (nor could ever be nor was ever meant to be).

Even though my scouts promised I'd be in a series if I signed with the Yankees, I never was. However, playing for the "real" New York Yankees was worth more than being in any series could be.

Baseball has changed, the world has changed, but the Yankees will always be the Yankees and it was an honor to be the smallest part of a big tradition!
P.S. – Good luck on your book.[135]

Dave Phillips
Umpire
March 3, 2005

Dear Mike: I worked last game in N.Y. Yankee Stadium – (Sunday) Det. Tigers…Remember going to airport & watching fans carrying seats and anything they could remove from Stadium & at that time was absolutely amazed – because people did not save anything like that in those days.

During game – you could hear people sawing and hammering in the stands as they were trying to remove anything they could remove.[136]

Mario Picone
March 5, 2008

Signed two renovation photos.[137]

Joe Pignatano
January 19, 2008

Wish I could have gotten one of those seats now…
I think the Yankees need a new park.[138]

Duane Pillette
January 11, 2008

I'm very sorry that I cannot give you my feelings about the new stadium. I have only seen it when I watch a Yankee game.

But you're in luck – I received a letter from an ex – Yankee & Mets bat-boy (enclosed). His name & address are on the letter he sent me. If you contact him he can speak for me – because once you put on that Yankee uniform – whether it be a bat-boy or a jock, we all feel the same about the house that Ruth built. Good Luck – Sincerely, Duane Pillette.
P.S. – I clipped the bottom of the second page to answer his questions.[139]

George Pipgras
May 27, 1975

Great.[140]

Herb Plews
March 17, 2008

Dear Michael – Hope you have good luck with your book. Should be interesting. As a kid I always remember listening to Yankee World Series on the radio – thinking some day I hope to play there. What I did imagine did happen. Seeing the Stadium for the first time was very emotional. Having been in the Yankee farm system I knew many of the players. Playing the Yankees brought out the best in most teams. It was always very special.

I have no idea, Michael, what ever happened to so much of the replaced artifacts.

On the reverse of the renovation photos, Herb wrote, "To Michael, With Fondest Memories, Herb Plews"[141]

Frank Quilici
February 13, 2008

Minnesota Twins. Hi Michael, I'm sorry for the delay. Billy Martin took me under Yankee Stadium in 1969. It was close to our locker room. We went up some steps and walked into a small room that had a pot belly stove in it. There was a bench to sit on, which we did. He said you know where you are & he smiled. I said no! He said this is the original locker room where Babe Ruth and Lou Gehrig and their Yankee teammates dressed. Joe DiMaggio was Billy's first roommate when Casey brought him up from Oakland and took him there. Good Luck. Frank Quilici[142]

Rich Reese
March 17, 2008

Michael, Can't help you with question #2. I grew up on a farm in Ohio town of 1800 people. In 1964 at the end of the year I was recalled to the Twins From "Class B" ball. I met the team in NY. My 1st big league game was in Yankee Stadium. It sent chills down my spine when I walked on the field for the 1st time. I will never forget it. Rich Reese[143]

Rick Reichardt January 26, 2008	Mike – Can't be of much help – no recollection – my last year was '73 – I do know Yankee Stadium was not kind to me from a home run perspective – zero in ten years. I do know, in the old days – relief pitchers would slip out and have a beer at a bar right outside the stadium – 'how bout that!' as Mel Allen used to say. Good Luck, Rick Reichardt.[144]
Merv Rettenmund January 25, 2008	Once they removed the façade they ruined the looks of the stadium. But by removing the façade they have no shadows during day games, on the field. It use to be a real deal to see late in the afternoon. Check the old World Series tapes. The shade is bad, the façade beautiful. Merv Rettenmund[145]
Allie Reynolds August 3, 1974	It had to come, we're in a new era.[146]
August 18, 1975	Progress helps & hurts, it will not be the same, but it will be a magnificent place to play – much better for the fan.[147]
Dusty Rhodes January 14, 2008	Dear Michael, I played in the Polo Grounds. You can call me if you like. Dusty Rhodes. Dusty was kind enough to give me his phone number, so I called him.[148]

January 18, 2008 (phone call)

D.R.: Hello.

M.W.: Hi, Mr. Rhodes. This is Mike Wagner, I'm the gentleman who's writing a book about the renovation of Yankee Stadium. I want to thank you for writing back to me and letting me call you up. I do want to apologize on one thing. I know you didn't play in Yankee Stadium, but I thought maybe you played in the Mayor's Trophy game or something like that.

D.R.: I played in a couple of exhibition games.

M.W.: Would you tell me how you felt about the renovation of the Stadium?

D.R.: You see, I was across the river there, with the Polo Grounds. That had nothing to do with Yankee Stadium.

M.W.: Right. I understand that. But, I'm sure you visited the Stadium many a time.

D.R.: Oh yeah, we played a couple of exhibition games there.

M.W.: So, you as a former Major Leaguer, were you in favor of the renovation or were you against it?

D.R.: Yeah, I'd like to see them build a new one. Yankee Stadium's been there a long time.

M.W.: Oh, I know, I know. I took about 230 photos of the renovation when I was there, because I went to school in Brooklyn at New York City Community College.

D.R.: Well, I went to Alabama.

M.W.: Right. I understand that. I know you were born in Mathews.

D.R.: Yeah.

M.W.: Do you have any other comment you'd like to make, Mr. Rhodes?

D.R.: No…not really…because the Yankees…DiMaggio was my favorite. I was at the Old Timers' game, and went up to get some tickets, and Joe was there, and I told him, "You know, I don't even know how to get down to Yankee Stadium." He took me down to the Clubhouse.

M.W.: Oh, that was nice of him!

D.R.: He was a gentleman.

M.W.: I'm just curious. I guess you didn't want to go to San Francisco. I guess you wanted the Polo Grounds and Ebbets Field to remain…

D.R.: Rigney and I didn't get along too well. You see, I was Leo's (Durocher's) boy, and the last time that I…it was '59…we were playing in San Francisco…I didn't go in '58 – I played in the Coast League…I pinch hit, I think it was twice, and I got base hits, so we won the ballgame. And the last base hit I got was against Elroy Face in Seals Stadium with the bases loaded, and we won that ballgame. So, we were ahead by six games and we wind up losing by two.

M.W.: Oh, no! That hurts! I read that you said that after Leo left the Giants, that baseball wasn't fun anymore.

D.R: It's a funny thing. When you get to the top, it really ain't fun no more.

M.W.: Really?!

D.R.: It really ain't. You tried, and tried, and tried, and then when you get there, it really ain't fun.

M.W.: Wow! Well, what was the most amazing thing you saw? Was it Willie Mays' catch off Vic Wertz in the 1954 World Series?

D.R.: Oh, that was a routine catch. Hell, you should have seen some of the catches he made. Willie's the greatest player who ever lived, I guess.

M.W.: I know he was a helluva fielder, and all-around ball player, period.

D.R.: Yeah, he was the best. And, Monte Irvin's a gentleman. Hank Thompson was my buddy. We had a good ball club. There were three cliques, and I was in all three cliques. There was the Spanish, the colored, and the white. I was in all three of them.

M.W.: That's great. Obviously, you get along well with people.

D.R.: I get along well with everybody because it used to be a lot of fun…a lot of jokes.

M.W.: Wow! It's great to have fun. Sadly, nowadays everything's money. You guys played for the love of the game.

D.R.: Years ago I didn't even know anything about marijuana. We drank a lot. That was it. Marijuana or dope…I never heard of it. And, I imagine if they did it, we would have said something more than likely.

M.W.: And, now with steroids, you wonder if any of these home run records are any good.

D.R.: I don't know. They're going to wind up killing themselves.

M.W.: Well, I hope not.

D.R.: Well, you know that Lozano, or whatever his name is that played with Oakland…

M.W.: Uh huh.

D.R.: Well remember, he died of steroids. It's a damn shame.

M.W.: I know it really is. I'm really curious…a lot of people didn't get along with Leo. How come you love Leo so much?

D.R.: Well, I'll tell you. I like the guy who goes out and plays the damn game. You know what I mean, to win. They don't do it today. They all started hitting the ball to right field with a man on second to try to get a base hit. You know that's right.

M.W.: Yes, it is.

D.R.: We tried to win. We played together.

M.W.: That's how it should be.

D.R.: That's the way it should be.

M.W.: I liked Leo because he'd get into these arguments with everybody. I guess he's very colorful.

D.R.: Oh yeah, he was. And if you would hustle 100 percent, goddamn, you can play for him.

M.W.: I believe it. I was in the Air Force, and I was a gate guard at Randolph Air Force Base, here in Texas, and I met a cousin of Leo's. And, he did meet Leo when Leo was a manager in Houston.

D.R.: Yeah, he went to Houston from Chicago. Yeah, Houston was a nice place, wasn't it?

M.W.: He was there for a while, him and Yogi.

D.R.: He had Yogi as his coach?

M.W.: No, I don't think he did. I went to spring training in the '90s, when Yogi was with Houston. That was after Leo. But I know Houston had Yogi for a while, and it was funny to see him in a Houston outfit instead of the Yankees pinstripes.

D.R.: Leo was tough. I mean, he was tough.

M.W.: I know. There were times in Winter Haven when we met Ted Williams…

D.R.: Yeah, Ted, he's the guy. He was an ex-pitcher. You couldn't get around him too much…

M.W.: He was great. He was very nice to all of us autograph collectors, and when he spoke, we just shut up because that was the God of baseball talking.

D.R.: He was the greatest.

M.W.: Yeah, and the thing I liked about Ted is that when we were around him, he seemed to have…he was a very confident man, but he wasn't cocky, he was very nice to us.

D.R.: Well, Johnny Podres just died, didn't he?

M.W.: Johnny died a couple of days ago.

D.R.: Oh, God! What did he have, a heart attack?

M.W.: I'm not sure if it was a heart attack. I think he had an infection and some other things going on. And, I think it was his heart, also. He was in upstate New York.

D.R.: Yeah, I just got out of the hospital. I had an infected lung.

M.W.: Oh, I'm sorry. How are you doing now?

D.R.: And I had biotics. I was taking these biotics I was taking through the arm, so I don't take that no more. I'm feeling a little better.

M.W.: Well, there's nothing like good health. I'll tell you that.

D.R.: You better believe it. You can talk money all you want to, but you you've got to have your health.

M.W.: Look at Aristotle Onassis. He had all the money, but no health, after a while.

D.R.: Yeah, you're right, and I…it's kind of tough…these guys send me baseballs, and I've got to take it to the Post Office, and I just can't do it.

M.W.: I know, I know. How did you get the name, "Dusty?" I never heard that.

D.R.: All roads are dusty I guess, until you pave them.

M.W.: Oh! Okay, so it's a play on words.

D.R.: Yeah.

M.W.: Okay, Wow! Well, I do want to thank you very much, Mr. Rhodes.

D.R.: No, no. My name's "Dusty."

M.W.: Dusty. I want to thank you very much, Dusty.

D.R.: I talk to Willie (Mays) every once in a while and his wife is named Mae, Davey Williams and George Spencer, I talk to, and there's only a couple of guys now that I keep in touch with.

M.W.: Do you keep in touch with Bobby Thomson?

D.R.: No, no. But, the last time I've seen him was about ten years ago.

M.W.: Really? I met Bobby at the Yankees Old Timers' games in the '70s.

D.R.: He is a real gentleman.

M.W.: He is a gentleman, and I'm always going to remember that. He was always a nice gentleman.

D.R.: Yep.

M.W.: See, that's what I like about you guys who played back in the good old days…like I said at Spring Training in the '90s I went to the Yankees camp, and Ed Lopat was there. I was surprised to see Eddie there. Well, during *The Star Spangled Banner*, a couple of the current Yankees were talking while Ed was singing *The Star Spangled Banner*, and I'm thinking that's the difference with the old school and the new school.

D.R.: Eddie Lopat – he's still living, ain't he?

M.W.: No, Eddie died a number of years ago.

D.R.: Right, right. He couldn't break a pane of glass.

M.W.: I know he threw a lot of junk pitches at you guys. Eddie was great!

D.R.: There's a lot of great people around.

M.W.: There are. There are. And I'm very grateful for that.

D.R.: Alvin Dark just hit around .300, and he'd always get the man over to third, and if he tried just to get a base hit, I bet he'd have hit .350.

M.W.: Could be.

D.R.: All right. So, is there anything else you want to know?

M.W.: No. That's great, Dusty. I just want to thank you very much, Dusty. I hope you get well and you take care of yourself, okay?

D.R.: Thank you very much.

M.W.: God Bless You, Dusty. Take care.

D.R.: Bye.

M.W.: Bye. Bye.[149]

John Rice
Umpire
March 1, 2005: Mike – try a larger envelope I was retired in 1973. Try Marty Marty Springstead at the Commish Office. Marty was umpiring then & is now a Supervisor of Umps for the Commish, Working out of N.Y. Sorry.[150]

Bobby Richardson
November 23, 2004

Michael: Thanks for your letter & I had already retired & came back for the prayer of Dedication of the Renovated Stadium – [151]

Robin Roberts
October 25, 2004

Robin sent me a signed Baseball Hall of Fame Induction ticket from August 8, 1976.[152]

Ed Roebuck
January 9, 2008

Awesome tradition & unlike the regular stadium.
2. No.[153]

Phil Roof
February 22, 2008

Michael, I loved playing in Yankee Stadium. During renovation, I thought my career would be over before they would finish it. It was finished and I played thru 1977.

I have no clue what they did with the seats, dirt or anything else. Played 13 years in & out of Yankee Stadium, and coached for five years. (Phil also signed two renovation photos.)[154]

Al Rosen
January 16, 2008

Al telephoned and said that he was formerly President of the Yankees. Also, he played baseball for 10 years. He had no answers to my questions regarding dirt or concrete.[155]

Mrs. Babe Ruth
March 9, 1974

<u>Great</u>[156]

Al Salerno
Umpire
March 22, 2005

Dear Mike, This is the best I can do (he was kind enough to send me a signed B/W photo of him umpiring with Mickey Mantle on 1b). I don't have any other information. I worked the game Roger Maris hit his 61st HR, Sept 30 1961. I put some of the dirt near 3rd base in a bag lost through the years. I may have misplaced it. Sorry about that.[157]

Bob Savage
February 5, 2008

I would hope they would have the same playing field.
#2. No idea!! Bob Savage[158]

Carl Scheib
January 26, 2008

Its been a long time since I have been in a major league ball park. I am not against renovating a ball park as it is a good thing today. And of course in my days, many of the club houses needed a big up lift.

However I feel a little resentful at tearing down one of our old ball parks & moving to another location. However it may be necessary. We sit back and say what a beautiful park, it's a shame to tear it down.

I will say one thing about Yankee Stadium & guess it's my own personal feeling, but when you walked out on the field to play, a certain feeling came over you. A feeling of being in a great place, and a pride to be able to play in that park.

#2 question – no. Carl Scheib[159]

Chuck Schilling
March 27, 2008

In some ways I think it's a shame that a lot of the 'old' ballparks are, and have been replaced by modern new stadiums. But, that's progress.[160]

Joe Sewell
January 18, 1975

The Yankee Stadium of the 1930s was a monument to baseball, and all who played there was real proud they did. It was an inspiration every time you step on the field. As for the new Stadium, I cannot answer that as it has not been completed, and I haven't seen it as of now.[161]

August 18, 1975

It was in need of repair, so while repairing it they should make it more modern. I am for it.[162]

Bobby Shantz
March 27, 1975

I think it's great.[163]

October 23, 2004

Michael, I'm sorry I cannot help you because I have never seen Yankee Stadium since they made all these changes. I really don't know how they improved the stadium because I thought it was the most beautiful place I have ever seen and had the privilege of pitching there. Best four years of my life.[164]

Bob Shawkey
August 18, 1975

Yes.[165]

Frank (Spec) Shea
August 3, 1974

Yes, it will be more convenient and attendance will improve.[166]

Roland Sheldon
February 24, 2005

at 461' to dead center Y.S. was one of a kind. The renovation made Y.S. just an ordinary ballpark. They should have left it alone. If we kept the opposing hitter from pulling the ball and kept them in centerfield, the "Mick" would run them down.

One day Mickey hit a ball over the 461 area over the bleacher screen. White Sox centerfielder Gene Stephens ran back like he had a chance to catch it, then figured he'd have to play a carom. When it cleared the bleacher screen he shrugged his shoulders in disbelief.[167]

Bob Sheppard
Legendary Announcer
February 5, 2005

Dear Mr. Wagner, My memories of the Yankee Stadium renovation are not too clear.

This I do remember! The old PRESS BOX was an open air elongated booth hanging down from the loge level along the third base line. It took care of the print media, the radio (Allen & Barber, etc) and me.

No protection from all kinds of weather.

The new PRESS BOX is located behind home plate and is again located on the loge level.

But now I am enclosed in a glass booth with heat on cold

days and nights and – in the summer: AIR CONDITION. (Mrs. Sheppard claims that has prolonged my career.) Good luck with your project. God bless you![168]

Ernie Shore
August 18, 1975

Yes.[169]

Roy Sievers
February 22, 2005

Mike, The old Yankee Stadium was a great ball park. Tough to hit in because of the long left and right center fields. Tough to see in a double header because often the sun was slowly going down. Playing the outfield was tough looking into the stands with all the white shirts.

Played against some of the great players of my era there. Probably would be a tough place to play with the fans and sport writers.

Could not tell you what happened to the dirt from the field. I'm sure people brought the seats and what other artifacts they had left.

The old ball parks were great to play in. I'm just happy that I had a chance to play in them and against all the great players of my time – 1949-1966.[170]

Curt Simmons
January 11, 2008

Curt sent me a signed baseball card of himself.[171]

Harry Simpson
March 27, 1975

Think it will help the team and city.[172]

Bill Skowron
August 3, 2003

Yankee Breakfast hosted by sports promoter Larry Dluhy of Sports Collectibles of Houston, Texas. This event took place at the Live Oak Civic Center, Live Oak, Texas. Guests consisted of Ralph Houk, Bob Cerv, Bill Skowron, and Bob Turley.

"I like to hit in the new park. The other ballpark killed us. We couldn't wait to get on the road trips (Laughter). It was 461 feet to dead center. I mean, Ernie Banks and Ralph Kiner would not hit those damn amount of home runs that they had if it had been Yankee Stadium.

Down the lines it was 296. Down the left field line was 301. But how many pitchers pitch me inside and say "pull?" They say, "Hit the damn thing!" We used to hit the ball to the monuments and they'd laugh like hell (Laughter). Any other ballpark we played in at was a home run. Yankee Stadium was a tough park to hit in.

The greatest team I've ever played with was the '61 Yankees. We had a helluva ballclub.[173]

October 27, 2004

I don't know too much about the field. I know I would have liked to have hit in this (new) park.[174]

Duke Snider
June 27, 2007

He signed a Yankee Stadium renovation photo.[175]

Jerry Snyder
March 19, 2008

Dear Michael, I don't know much about the renovation, but I remember how close the stands were to the field. One time I made a throw from shortstop and it got by the first baseman and bounced into the stands and hit an old lady in the face. Bucky Harris, my manager, brought her down to the field the next day and introduced her to me. I was very embarrassed, but she was very gracious about it, and she was one of the oldest Yankee fans. Best Wishes, Jerry Snyder[176]

Russ Snyder
January 22, 2008

I hate to see these great landmarks of history taken down. There are only 2 parks left that I played in – Yankee Stadium & Fenway Park. Russ[177]

Marty Springstead
Umpire
February 19, 2005

Dear Michael: I'm in receipt of your letter of Feb. 16th. I think I can answer a few of your questions, but not many.

My thoughts about the renovation of the Stadium. I personally liked the original Stadium the best, with the Ledges, etc. I also know that the Stadium was cracking and falling apart underneath. So the renovation was necessary. I never had a different feeling of working with the old & the new, maybe except for the players. When I broke in the Yankees were Mantle, Maris, Ford, Richardson, Tresh, etc. The renovation was all done under the Mayor Lindsay term as Mayor of N.Y. – To find out where the dirt, cement, lights & seats went I have no idea. Today they sell the sod & seats as part of the past. In the 70's who knows. You are probably going to have to contact some one at the Stadium or Major League Baseball familiar with the change.

I wish I could help you more, but that's about it. Good luck in your project, as I'm sure many people will be interested in your findings.[178]

Jerry Staley
September 8, 1975

If it needed it – Yes.[179]

Dick Starr
January 31, 2008

MIKE: I am very sorry I cannot help you very much. My 1st time in the Stadium was thrilling to be there with the greats as DiMaggio and others. Also to be in the dugout when Babe Ruth was there. Also to win my 1st game and only one I started as a Yankee! Dick Starr[180]

Gene Stephens
February 12, 2008

The old Yankee Stadium was my favorite. God Bless, Michael. Gene Stephens[181]

Wes Stock
February 12, 2008

The stadium had so much history to it and the monuments in center field, but that's what happens in progress.[182]

George Strickland
January 10, 2008

MICHAEL – My last year going to Yankee Stadium – 1972- I don't know about the renovation of the Stadium – since we have a new stadium now – the game & times always change- the 50's were the best in the game – we can't go back home.[183]

Gay Talese
Author
March 21, 2008

Gay sent me a signed synopsis of his biography . He signed it "Very best to Michael Wagner, Gay Talese."

Gay also signed one of my renovation photos, "For Michael Wagner, Go Yankees!, Best, Gay Talese[184]

Ralph Terry
March 27, 1975

Looks good.[185]

Wayne Terwilliger
April 16, 2008

As long as they don't renovate the "old" P.A. announcer – He is one of my favorite people!!

I hate to see it renovated because I hit a home run off Whitey Ford in 1953 that scraped the back of the left field wall – and I want to remember that as it was!!!!!! Good Luck.[186]

Luis Tiant
February 4, 2008

Luis signed two photos of the renovation.[187]

Tom Tresh
March 15, 2008

Mike – The renovation of the Stadium was necessary for safety of the fans.

However, the fences were moved in which makes it a lot easier to hit home runs.- Tom Tresh[188]

Gus Triandos
January 15, 2008

Gus sent me two signed photos of the renovation.[189]

Virgil Trucks
January 12, 2008

Hi Mike, I'm sorry I cannot give you much information on the renovation of Yankee Stadium, as I finished playing in 1958.

I know this was the most memorable stadium ever played in. The club house guy for the Yankees is maybe able to help you. And good luck in your book.
Sincerely, Virgil Trucks (He gave me the name and address of the club house person).[190]

Bill Valentine
Umpire
February 18, 2005

Dear Michael; Yankee Stadium did need a renovation. I have been to the stadium one time since the renovation was completed and they did a very good job. You have to remember there are a lot of things in renovating a very old stadium that you just can not do. I know they moved the monuments, etc out of centerfield...probably was a good move but I did not remember anyone ever hitting one there while I was umpiring.

I have no idea what might have happened to items that they removed from the stadium. I am sure they offered some of the items on sale to fans and other interested people.

I umpired in a lot of leagues, including the American League during my 18 years as a professional baseball umpire...but there was no experience like walking up the steps of the dugout and onto the field in Yankee Stadium for the first time. For me it was the first time I had ever been in the stadium. Since the Yankees had been in so many World Series I knew what it looked like, but being there for the first time was something else.

Wish I could send you more information.[191]

Vito Valentinetti
February 20, 2008

I pitched at the old Yankee Stadium in 1958 – I think the obstructed views were part of baseball. The infield dirt was used at the Stadium after the renovation. The seats were sold to anyone willing to pay $125. each. The concrete was just disposed of. Vito also sent a signed index card.[192]

Ed Vargo Umpire March 8, 2005	I only worked W.S. in 1978 at Yankee Stadium. Don't know too much about the renovation. Thank you for asking.[193]
George Vecsey Sports Columnist April 20, 2008	Dear Michael Wagner: I wish I had something to contribute, but in those years I was a news reporter, and never got close to YS in transition. I'm sorry, good luck. George Vecsey.[194]
Mickey Vernon February 27, 2008	He sent me a signed 2006 Diamond Signatures baseball card.[195]
Gary Waslewski January 26, 2008	Michael, Unfortunately I wasn't in Yankee Stadium when the renovation started. My last year there was 1971 – the cement in the upper deck overhanging the Yankee bullpen must have been crumbling because some nuts/fans used to drop chunks into the bullpen area while we warmed up. Good luck with your book. G Was[196]
Bob Watson April 8, 2008	It was a pleasure and honor to play and bat 3rd, 4th and 5th. Also play 1st base for the NY Yankees. 2. Some of the seats were sold. As for the rest, I Don't Know! All the Best, Bob Watson, MLB/TEAM USA[197]
Ed Watt January 14, 2008	MICHAEL, I played in the American League from 1966-1973. I was with the Phillies in 1974 and the Cubs for 2 weeks in 1975. I have never been in "renovated" Yankee Stadium, so I have no feelings on the matter and know nothing of the "dirt, concrete, etc." from Old Yankee Stadium. Yankee Stadium holds a very significant place in Baseball History – and just walking into the Stadium the 1st time was a thrill.

Being from a small Mid-Western town I tired of New York quickly. I never tired of Yankee Stadium.
Sincerely, Ed Watt[198]

Steve Whitaker
May 14, 2008

Steve signed two renovation photos and sent me his business card.[199]

Roy White

Interview at New York Yankees Fantasy Camp, Legends Field, Tampa, FL during a rained out day. Wednesday, November 15, 2006. I showed him some photos I took of the renovation.

R.W.: I played in both Stadiums – the old one and the renovated one. I've seen the mockup of the new Stadium. There's a lot of history with the old Stadium and all that, which is great, but eventually some of these old things just have to go. They're not acceptable as far as playing in anymore. They're unsafe or you can't view the game as well as you can in some of the modern ballparks.

M.W.: So, you like the renovation they did in 1973-1975?

R.W.: It made it easier for me to play left field.

M.W.: Really!?

R.W.: It was a lot harder to play the old left field with 457 feet and a worse sun field and everything, so it was an easier park to play in the renovated stadium. The sight lines were a little better and you can pick up the ball a little better.[200]

Dave Wickersham
January 14, 2008

God Bless you & I hope your book is successful.[201]

Dick Williams
February 22, 2005

If Yankee Stadium had stayed the same it would be the best "old" stadium in the Major Leagues – better than Wrigley Field (Chicago) or Fenway Park (Boston). I played and managed at Yankee Stadium <u>old</u> and the <u>new</u> stadium and loved them both.

The Yankees should have any info on your second question.[202]

Stan Williams
February 19, 2005

I don't feel that many people feel that a "Renovation" is an overly exciting subject – However, anything connected to the N.Y.Y.'s &/or the Stadium usually, at least, gets someone's attention.

I first played in the "old" stadium, in 1960, as a member of the Nat'l League All-Stars. I remember the particular excitement of taking the mound in such a historic stadium. All the past glory, & tradition, just oozed from the place. It was a special feeling – not one I ever had in any other ballpark.

Being a traditionalist, I hated to see them renovate. I was quite surprised at how little the looks changed, though. I had the pleasure of playing in the 'old-park' (63'/64) & coaching several years in the 'New'-Park. Both are fine for me – [203]

Walt (No Neck) Williams
February 7, 2008

I really don't know. Just a pleasure to play there.[204]

Whitey Witt
August 3, 1974

I think its great for N.Y. There's only one N.Y.[205]

August 18, 1975

Yes.[206]

October 20, 1975

No.[207]

Bob Wolff
Sportscaster
January 16, 2008

Dear Michael, That's a big project you've undertaken. For more specific information I would suggest you contact the Yankees PR Department. You ask excellent questions, but I don't have those answers.

I do know that change is inevitable in sports. Teams change, styles change and so do ballparks. There's great tradition in the old structures, but some need repairs and owners today want more luxury suites and other revenue sources such as restaurants, gift shops and the like to add to their income.

The Yankees plan to retain the charm of Yankee Stadium in their new park which is good news. I televised or broadcast many games there and it was always a thrill to do so. Broadcasting Don Larsen's perfect World Series game there is one of my great memories in sports.

It was a pleasure to hear from you.
All best wishes, Bob Wolff[208]

Al Worthington
January 23, 2008

Michael, Sorry I cannot help you much. I visited Yankee Stadium after the finished work on the stadium. The reason I liked it was no more posts in the stadium & I was watching one of my college players pitch for the Yankees. He may know something (He gave me the player's address).
Sincerely, Al Worthington[209]

Ed Yost
January 15, 2008

He signed two photos of the renovation.[210]

Sal Yvars
January 14, 2008

I have no opinion on why a new Yankee Stadium is being built. The old Stadium seems to me should have remained.[211]

Gus Zernial
June 25, 1975

The Stadium needed to be made to standard size.[212]

Chapter Seven

THEY WERE THERE

The gentlemen in the following pages worked on the renovation of America's most historic baseball stadium. They were very kind in relating their stories with me. We, the fans of Yankee Stadium, are indebted to these kind and generous men for sharing their experiences.

Their knowledge has added greatly to the credibility of this work. And, their stories have ensured that their part of history in this undertaking shall not be lost to the ages.

Thank you, one and all, for giving your time and memories.

Robert C. Y. Young

November 15, 2003

Mr. Michael Wagner

Dear Mr. Wagner:

As I explained to you on the phone, I left all my references, books, reports and records behind me in the office when I retired in 2000. I thought I had retained copies of Yankee

Stadium Renovation Project at home, but alas, when I moved down to 'XXXXXX in 2001,

these were thrown out too. So as of now, I don't have any written records of this project, and can only recite from memory some of the pertinent facts.

When CBS bought the New York Yankees from the Ruppert family in the 60's, it stipulated that New York City would have to renovate the stadium facilities to "modern standards". The design contract for the renovation was logically awarded to the New York City architectural-engineering firm of Praeger Kavanagh Waterbury (PKW), which had just completed the project for the construction of the Shea Stadium in Flushing, NYC. John W. Waterbury, Partner of PKW, was the Architect-in-charge and Robert C. Y. Young, Associate, was the Project Manager and Structural Designer. John Waterbury should deservedly be credited as the "Father of Modern Stadium Design". When he and the firm of PKW designed the first post war (WW II) modern stadium, the Dodger Stadium in Los Angeles in the 1950's, he had formulated the guidelines for stadium designing, which are still being followed to this day. The more significant features of these guidelines are listed (not in order of importance) below:

1. Column-free stand structure so that every seat in the stand has unobstructed view of the playing field.

2. Use of sight-line study to ensure that every seat has a clear view of field activities.

3. Adaptation of ring-lighting concept for field illumination, in lieu of lighting towers, for more uniformly distributed intensity.

4. Wider seats and deeper seating aisles in consideration of spectator comfort.

5. Installation of back-mounted seats (without legs) to ease the cleaning of the seating areas.

These guidelines were followed during the renovation of the Yankee Stadium. Since the Stadium was an old structure of some fifty years, the fulfillment of these guidelines, while at the same time attempting to preserve the basic elements of the existing structure to the fullest extent, presented many challenging and innovative considerations.

The basic structural system of the old Stadium consisted of steel frames spaced about 25 feet (?) (I am not certain of this number) on centers, radial to the playing field behind the home plate and perpendicular to the first and third base lines. The front segment of each frame provided supports for three levels of seating decks: Upper, Mezzanine and Lower. The Upper Deck with a stepped concrete slab, was supported by a long-span, deep truss which in term was supplied by two main columns, as the part of the frame, at the front and back faces of the Upper Deck. The Mezzanine Deck, only about half as deep as the Upper Deck, also rested on a truss of lesser depth and span with front end framed into the front main column and rear end supported on another column forward of the main back column of the Upper Deck. On the other hand, the Lower Deck, also with a stepped concrete slab, was supported by additional, intermediate columns under the slab and was of conventional beam-and-column construction. The main front columns of the structural frames structure extended from the foundations through the Lower, Mezzanine and Upper Decks and gave supplies to the roof that spanned over the entire Upper Deck. The back segment of these structural frames had been designed, essentially, as part of a conventional beam-and-column building framing system. That portion of the Stadium structure, including the area below the Lower Deck, provided spaces for circulation ramps, offices, team maintenance facilities, vendor and concessionaire requirements, etc. The exterior of the Stadium was closed off by a heavy masonry wall independent of the steel framed structure.

At the outset of this project, Praeger Kavanagh Waterbury undertook a condition survey of the Stadium structure and facilities. The in-situ residual stresses in several main members of the steel framing were measured. In addition, several representative steel samples were taken and analyzed for the weldability of the steel members should it be necessary to add sections for strengthening. After the inspection, it was generally agreed that the steel structures, in general, could be preserved. On the other hand, the concrete seating deck slabs had severely deteriorated. Besides, the risers of the deck slabs did not conform to the sight-line requirements. It was thus decided that all the deck slabs were to be removed and that the steel structures thus exposed would be preserved to the extent practicable and strengthened by adding sections where necessary.

In order to upgrade the Stadium so as to achieve obstruction-free viewing, all the front main columns above the Lower Deck had to be removed. This drastic action would transform the main Upper Deck trusses from being a simple structure supported at both ends to a cantilevered one with support at the back only. The structural behavior of each member of the trusses had to be evaluated and reinforced where necessary. The more challenging task was to exploit a solution to provide adequate support at the back of the cantilevered truss so that it would not tip over. This was achieved by installing pull-back cable to the top of each truss at the support end. The cables were anchored into new reinforced-concrete perimeter beam on top of the exterior wall of the Stadium. This beam was in turn anchored into the existing masonry wall. The gravity weight of the heavy wall counterbalanced the pulling force from the cables and provided stability to the cantilevered trusses.

Another major structural change to the Stadium structure was the extension of Upper Deck to the back. This change achieved two purposes:

1. Adding more seats

2. Providing more stability to the Upper Deck structure by counterbalancing the cantilevered action in the front.

The added seating was an important consideration to the new Ball Club Owner because the seating capacity would have been significantly reduced with the introduction of wider seats and more aisle depths in the renovated Stadium.

The extension of the Upper Deck was achieved by attaching a pre-cast reinforced concrete c-shaped structural element to each of the upper chord member of the cantilevered steel truss. The joint at the extension point was studied and detailed to accommodate (a) the continuity of stress flow from the steel upper chord to the concrete extension member and (b) the interaction of the anchoring cable which was attached to this joint. With the elimination of the front columns and the extended Upper Deck area, it became impractical to install a roof over the entire Upper Deck. The elimination of a roof had, in actuality, a beneficial result: The cavernous effect in the old Upper Deck seating area had been removed, and it was now open to the sky and became a cheerier place to spend an afternoon at the ball park. The short upper anTIS of the pre-cast extension members also provided supports for a shallow roof which in turn provided a working platform for the installation of field lighting facilities around the Stadium.

One of the casualties as a result of the elimination of the front columns was the loss of the frieze panels that had adorned the front of the stand just under the Upper Deck roof eave. Mrs. Paley, whose husband was the Chairman of CBS, was nostalgic about these frieze panels and was pleased when new frieze panels of exactly the same design and dimension were replicated and installed along the back of the Bleacher Stand. A tradition of the Yankee Stadium had been preserved!

The seating slabs in all three spectator decks were replaced by L-shaped, pre-cast concrete elements with wide base as tread and shorter vertical as riser where the seats were actually anchored and supported. The risers had variable dimensions, greater in the back, to satisfy the sight-line considerations. Another major design consideration in this connection was the lowering of the playing field by several feet. The lowered elevation of the field truly offered every seat in the Stadium a viewing angle of activities at any location on the field. The lowering of the playing field also gave rise to the opportunity of adding a few more rows of box seats in front of the Stadium structure. These added seats, together with those in the expanded Upper Deck made up for the seat count loss because of new wider seats and deeper aisles. Thus, the spectator capacity of the Renovated Stadium remained about the same.

The back of the Stadium structure, the "building" part, housed the access ramps, circulation aisles, team facilities and spectator amenity requirements. The total space was limited by the confines of the existing structure. In order to create more room, it was decided that a new Mechanical Room would be moved out of the Stadium and constructed underground near the front entrance back of the Home Plate. Thus, it was possible to install all facilities demanded by the requirements of a new stadium. During renovation, the "building" part was completely gutted; structural members were repaired and/or strengthened as needed. One under-designed feature, however, still remained in the Renovated Stadium: this related to the access ramps. The ramps had been built around the perimeter of the Stadium structure and had slope, though in conformance with the code requirements of 50 years ago, but exceeding that specified in the modem code. With the space restriction there was no way to rebuild the ramps to satisfy the slope requirement. Thus the ramps were "grand fathered" under the old code and were approved by the City's regulatory agency. With this deficiency in mind, the spectator circulation before and after the game was studied. A computer simulation was made to determine the "emptying time" after a full-capacity game. As a result, it was decided that three circulation towers were added to facilitate the movement of the spectators. These towers were built outside of the original stadium confine: one behind the Home Plate and one each at the ends of the Left and Right Field stands.

Anyone standing on the playing field and looking at the Renovated Stadium would see the dramatic transformation of the Stadium Stands. However, from the surrounding streets, the exterior of the Stadium was basically preserved. The outside facades of the masonry walls were carefully restored and preserved. Some keen observer may also note another minor additive feature of the Renovated Stadium. At the insistence of Mike Burke, President of CBS, the chimney from the underground Mechanical Room was in the form of a baseball bat!

I hope the above notes that I have put forth from memory are useful to you. If you have any specific questions, I'll be happy to answer to my best effort. Good luck to your venture, and I'll be interested to read your final product.

With best regards,

Sincerely,

Robert C. Y. Young [1]

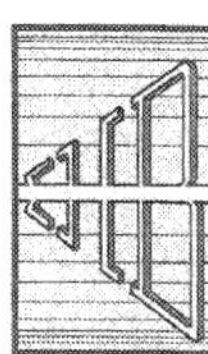

E.H. BRUNJES + ASSOCIATES, PC
ARCHITECTS-CONSULTANTS

Edwin H. Brunjes, R.A., President

33 Bourne Circle
Hamburg, NJ 07419-1284

Tel 973-827-5549
Fax 973-827-5493
E-Mail ehbrunjes@earthlink.net

Michael

Just a few suggestions for accuracy in your book;

- Both the parking garage and the pedestrian bridge were designed by me as Director of Design, Department of Public Works city of New York. The pedestrian bridge was constructed with public funds while the parking garage was constructed with private and public funds.

- The initial cost estimate for the stadium had to be less than the $25 million that it cost to build Shea Stadium, so by the flip of a coin the figure of $24 million was arrived at. At that time all concerned with the project knew that it would cost substantially more. The City Council as well as the Board of Estimate were aware of this as was the comptrollers office.

- The actual stadium renovation cost was $59 million with the cost of purchasing the land and stadium from both Rice University and the Knights of Columbus as well as the remainder of the environs adding another $51 million dollars bringing the total cost of the project to $110 million dollars.

I was wondering why someone from the west would be that interested in Yankee Stadium, now I know, you are a former New Yorker.

ED

Visit our web site www.ehbrunjesassociates.com

Previous | Next | Back to Messages Mark as Unread | Print

Delete | Reply ▾ | Forward | Spam | Move... ▾

Yankee Stadium Monday, January 12, 2009 12:48 PM

From:

To:

Cc:

M;

I'm Tim Crowley. Jerry Crowley was my father. Jerry and I were partners in real estate development and construction since his retirement from Walsh in 1982. You can obtain an '80's photo of Jerry from our web site www.TheCrowleyGroup.net and/or directly from Cynthia Montello, our web master who's' address is above and on the web site.

All that I can offer about Jerry Crowley and Yankee Stadium is this:

Jerry was the Construction Manager of the Building Group for Walsh Construction Company, a division of Guy F. Atkinson Company of California. Walsh was the general contractor at Yankee Stadium for the alteration project. The cost of the contract was always miss-reported and not as high as what people think. I don't recall the value however. The main purpose of the project was mainly to remove a number of unsightly columns that supported the roof. These columns obstructed the view of the field and were common in old stadiums as was Yankee Stadium in the '70's. The engineers designed a concrete cantilever support that was installed by Walsh up at the roof all around the stadium and the weight of the roof was then thrown back hence the columns were able to be removed and seats now had an unobstructed view of play. Seats were added naturally and the field elevations were raised as well.

Jerry always commented about all of the old seats that they threw out and how they would be worth good money today.

I forwarded your email to our sister Mary as she is a writer.

Feel free to send an email any time you wish with any questions you may have.

Let us know when the book is available so that we may be able to obtain a copy.

We thank

Tim Crowley-CEO
The Crowley Group
Greenwich CT - St Augustine FL

J. C. Crowley

Jerry Crowley spent his life in the building and construction industry and his legacy will live on in the magnificent structures he built. He will be missed and long remembered. 1925 - 2007

INTERVIEW WITH HARVEY LEVENE April 8, 2008

Harvey Levene was a security officer who protected Home Plate at Yankee Stadium during the last game before the renovation.

M.W.: What would you like to say about that last day at Yankee Stadium?

H.L.: When I was working there as a security guard, my boss told me to stand on home plate and make sure nobody takes it, because they were taking all of the other bases, and they were taking all of the seats out of the upper deck. This started around the eighth inning. I went down there and stood there. Some guy came up to home plate with a crowbar and offered me $20 if he could take home plate. I said, "No. I was told nobody could take it." He said, "Okay." And, he walked away, and that's about it.

When the grounds crew came out, they dug it up. It was about three or four inches into the ground. They dug it up and just took it away.

M.W.: How long were you a security guard at Yankee Stadium?

H.L.: I was up there before another outfit took over. I was up there about 20 years.

M.W.: Was this a private firm?

H.L.: Yes. It was Local #177, Special Guard and Officers Union. And we were contracted to Yankee Stadium. We did other work at Shea Stadium and Madison Square Garden.

M.W.: Do you know what happened to the debris from the renovation, such as dirt or cement?

H.L.: They probably kept the old grass and everything else. They put all new seats in because everybody was breaking them up, and around the eighth inning, they were banging away, and ripping up the seats in the upper deck. We, the security guards, took the seats away from them, and piled them up in the dugout so nobody would run out with them. One of the ballplayers came up to me. He wanted to take some memorabilia. We told him to go to the outfield and see what he could take from out there.[4]

VICTOR STRAUSS TELEPHONE INTERVIEW (notes) September 18, 2007

(Ben Strauss Industries)

Two plaques of the eagle, catcher, and field outside the Stadium were never replaced. Victor had his artists recreate them out of fiberglass. He gave them to George Steinbrenner for one of his birthdays.

With respect to the renovation, there was no thought to conservation or preservation.

Originally, the Yankees were going to create a Yankees Hall of Fame in the new Stadium on the ground floor. But this plan was abandoned due to budget constraints. Instead, a souvenir shop was built.

A lot of debris and dirt of the renovation was left under the stands.

Many contractors were not getting paid due to mounting expenses.

Yankee Stadium was supposed to have three or four expansion joints. This did not occur, again because of expenses. Cracks would later appear in the Stadium.

There was a movement to get more black workers due to affirmative action.

Victor's company painted the interior and sandblasted the exterior. Amsterdam Paint of the Bronx supplied the paint.

The day before Opening Day, Billy Martin asked where the painters were. None of the pipes near the dugout were painted yellow. Victor painted it.

George Steinbrenner didn't like the color red, so the pipes around the field were painted yellow.[5]

STEPHEN OFFERMAN TELEPHONE INTERVIEW (notes) September 20, 2007

Mr. Offerman worked for the Amsterdam Paint Company of the Bronx during the renovation of Yankee Stadium 1973-1976.

New York City approved of the specialized exterior finish paint, which was a high build coating for waterproofing the exterior of Yankee Stadium. The Stadium had three types of exterior concrete. Two were:

1. Stippled concrete for the archways.
2. A somewhat glossy exterior, which would have been difficult for the paint to adhere to.

This specialized exterior paint was a modification of swimming pool paint. The reason was that the cold New York winters would have allowed moisture to seep behind an ordinary paint, thus ending up with peeling paint.

The standard film thickness used for the Yankee Stadium paint eliminated pinhole problems, which would have been caused by the weather. The name of the color was Sequoia Dust.

Another specialized coating had been used for bumpers on the outfield wall. The blue paint faded from ultraviolet light. The waterproof elastrometric used in the new coating prevented such fading.

Richard Fisher represented Praeger Kavanagh Waterbury with regard to paint coatings.

Victor Beecher served as project manager for NAB-TERN.

As far as Mr. Offerman knows, the façade above center field in the renovated Yankee Stadium was made of all concrete.[6]

RALPH DREWES TELEPHONE INTERVIEW (notes) September 19, 2007

Ralph Drewes was Contractor Superintendent for NAB.

Dirt, cement, metal debris, etc. from Yankee Stadium was dumped in landfills in the NYC area or recycled. Usable earth backfill was used throughout the NYC area.

The façade at the top is a counterweight. Several rows were added to the bleachers. The ring at the top of the bleachers is poured cement that sits on top of the old Stadium wall. It prevented the bleachers from tipping over.

The façade against the scoreboard could be sheet metal, but Ralph is not sure.

Columns were removed from the mezzanine level. They used a Load Transfer to transfer the load. This was done by temporarily transferring the load held of one column at a time. Columns were cut out and sold for scrap.

NAB & TERN was a joint venture company. Each was responsible for certain work. TERN did most of the concrete and heavy work. NAB did most of the finish work, such as sheetrock. Victor Strauss was a sub-contractor to them for painting the Stadium.

NAB TERN received in the neighborhood of $30 million for the job. This included paving and creating sidewalks outside the Stadium.

With respect to infrastructure, improvements on the Major Deegan Expressway and the surrounding area was a huge project, as well. Another contractor built the parking lot next to Yankee Stadium.

Underneath the escalator near the giant Babe Ruth baseball bat is a boiler room for heat and hot water. It's about 25 feet down.

NAB is still in business. The NAB-TERN partnership lasted a number of years after the Yankee Stadium project, but eventually dissolved.

Karl Koch Erection worked on the project. Skanska, from Sweden, bought them out.

Colonial Sand and Stone supplied concrete. Several thousand yards of concrete went into Yankee Stadium. They went out of business.

The Yankees wrote a Change Order for the monuments of Miller Huggins, Babe Ruth, and Lou Gehrig to be housed in a warehouse during the renovation to prevent them from being stolen. This was the whole stone monument and plaque on the stone.[7]

TELEPHONE INTERVIEW WITH RALPH TEROWSKY (notes) April 13, 2009

Ralph Terowsky served as the Vice President of Tern Construction during the renovation.

According to Mr. Terowsky, the frieze above the outfield bleachers consisted of 20 panels that were each 20 feet long. They were made of precast concrete. He could not recall the name of the company that made the prominent Yankee trademark. Page A-44 of the renovation blueprints contained details of the frieze.

NAB-Tern built the outside concrete escalator towers.

Approximately 50,000 yards of concrete went into the Yankee Stadium renovation.

The counterweight alluded to by Ralph Drewes measured 1,500 to 1,600 feet long.[8]

MARIANO MOLINA August 20, 2008 (e-mail)

Mariano Molina is a principal of MDM Consulting Engineers, in New York City and Jersey City, New Jersey.

Michael:

Attached is some information regarding the Yankee Stadium project. The project was very dear to me for many reasons; one of which was the project and the other was that I really liked and respected several members of the design team, including Dick Fisher, who I speak of below. It was challenging from an engineering point of view because the project included diversified spaces with their own challenges:

The dugouts were air conditioned for the comfort of the players; however, the design could not result in draft to players that came from the field, hot and perspiring; we designed a laminar type of air flow similar to that used for operating rooms in hospitals to provide comfortable radiant cooling and even air distribution at slow discharge velocity.

The bat was a result of finding a place for the exhaust of the emergency generator diesel engine and the boiler flue. The location was dictated by practicality due to the proximity to the boiler room and the emergency generator room. The architects, John Waterbury, Richard Fisher from Iffland Kavanagh Waterbury (IKW) Architects and I, the mechanical engineer, project manager, and associates of Slocum and Fuller Consulting engineers, came up with the generic concept of the bat. It was later presented to the Yankee manager and to the City of New York, and the design was refined and implemented. There were issues. I remember that one of the junior architects assigned to manage the construction of the project got in trouble because she approved a shop drawing where the tip of the bat was not exactly as designed.

Incidentally, inside of the bat there is the chimney for the boilers and diesel engine exhaust pipe serving the emergency generator. I was the engineer who designed all the mechanical systems serving the Stadium, and I was also the Project Manager.

Richard “Dick” Fisher was a registered structural engineer and also a registered architect. John Waterbury was an excellent designer. Both of them died many years ago. Dick Fisher was instrumental in forming MDM Consulting Engineers because he gave me the first job we had as a company, a large project for the New York City Department of Sanitation (DSNY).

We have continued doing work for IKW and for the DSNY for the last 30 years. In 2008 we won an engineering design excellence award by the American Council of Engineering Companies of New York (ACEC) professional organization for one of our DSNY facilities.

The field lighting required ingenuity to prevent glare and shadow so that players could see and catch the ball. Also, the lighting needed good color rendering so that the uniforms would have accurate colors in TV.

All of the above is significant since the Stadium was designed more than 30 years ago, and there was not so much experience in the engineering profession for the design of open Stadiums.

I have a DVD that I will send to you about details of the design and some background information of MDM Engineers.

Please call if you need additional information.
Mariano

Below is the transcribed copy of the DVD, regarding Mr. Molina’s work at Yankee Stadium.

Announcer: When one thinks of Yankee Stadium, one word comes to mind…“power.” Mantle, Maris, DiMaggio, Gehrig, and the immortal Babe Ruth. That was also the name of the game to Mariano. That is to say, the generation of power.

Mariano: When I was the mechanical department head, and later on an associate of Slocum and Fuller, this was one of my most significant projects of the time. I remember with great enthusiasm, that I took this project. The fun related to all the great athletes, the fun that we…many of my colleagues had working on different phases of the Stadium. There are many aspects that were truly interesting.

Some places in the Stadium – press boxes, luxury boxes, and these areas, are being designed with flexibility for the occupants. To be either outdoors and enjoyed in an air conditioned environment, or to be indoors in a cubicle designed with all the comfort and commodities of a living room.

This is one of the three hot water generators that provide heating for the entire Stadium. Over there you can see one of the emergency generators that provide emergency power. You can see the boiler flue and the emergency generator exhaust piping, which leads into a tunnel. This tunnel extends to the famous baseball bat.

The baseball bat is not only a symbol of the great Yankee Stadium. It also includes the boiler chimney, the emergency generator exhaust that introduces ventilation air for some portions of the Stadium.

Announcer: Though the bat may not be the one players used to supply hitting power, it is batting a very healthy one-thousand, bringing comfort to everyone that works and plays in that great ballpark in the Bronx.[9]

TELEPHONE INTERVIEW WITH DICK MULLER #1 September 26, 2007

Cantilevers were used in Yankee Stadium so everyone could have a good view of the game.

Dick cut down old steel columns with an acetylene torch so cables could be put in where each column stood. This was done one column and cable at a time. Dick doesn't know if the columns were melted down or not.

Dick's job title was a "Connector." Two men acted as connectors for a raising gang, which usually consisted of six men. This included the crane and derrick operators, and the man who directs the crane operator from the ground. Connectors lined up the beams used in construction and secured the beam with two temporary bolts – one at each end. Jack Johnson worked with Dick.

Karl Koch Company was located in Carteret, NJ.

Joel Van Dommelin was the boss of the raising gang, and Dick's immediate boss.

Steve Koch was the engineer on the Yankee Stadium job. He's the nephew of Karl Koch III.

First the truss, concrete stairs, cable, and turnbuckles were installed, then the columns were taken out.

Vertical trusses were placed at every column. There were 118 columns. On top of the truss, Koch hung precut concrete steps to balance the cantilever like a seesaw. 3 ¾" wire cables attached at every stress point to turnbuckles that were about seven feet long in order to lift up cantilevers on the mezzanine.

Each truss was 40 feet long, 9 or 10 feet deep, by 12 feet wide. The first part of the process was to put in the truss. The truss was then strengthened with three or four more pieces of steel. Precast concrete piers were added with precast concrete steps and risers for all the seats. All that weight on top, and the cable and turnbuckle added weight to the top of Yankee Stadium. This also added 77 feet to the height of Yankee Stadium, as well as ten rows of more seating.

The lower end of the seesaw was supported by a column. The bottom half of the truss was supposed to come up ¼" or 3/8" according to the engineers and architects who designed the plan, but it went down ¼" instead. So Koch tightened the turnbuckles for a week, but the trusses never lifted up as planned, so they decided to live with it.

The iron workers didn't like the cantilever idea because they felt it wouldn't be strong enough to work.

Dick pre-cut all columns at the mezzanine every day. He worked on the job for 19 months. He also worked on the construction of Madison Square Garden in 1966, which was his very first job. He also worked at the World Trade Center and numerous office buildings in Manhattan.

When they installed the steel that support the light stanchions, it angles out as you go higher up. The angle didn't bother the workers. What did bother them was the psychological effect of having nothing under them. If they fell, they would die. Most people cannot survive a fall above 20 feet.

It was a treat to work on the Yankee Stadium renovation because it was so different. It wasn't the usual square building with corners. It was a challenge and people didn't truly know if what was put on paper would work in real life. Nobody died during the renovation as far as he knew, and injuries were minimal.

Dick's first trip to Yankee Stadium happened to be to Don Larsen's perfect game during the 1956 World Series. He was only 12. Towards the end of the game he couldn't see anything because the crowd, composed of so many men skipping work, stood up and blocked his view. Between that and nearly every man wearing a hat during that time period, he didn't have much of a chance.

Dick worked for Koch for 10 years.[10]

D.M.: The word "truss" is critical to this whole design. I can't remember how many we put in. If my memory serves me correctly, it's at every column point. So all around the entire structure, wherever there was a column, we put in one of these vertical trusses. And the truss ends at the top where the new concrete stringers start the additional seating rows. That's the best way I can describe how this new system took the load off the columns so the columns could be removed, and therefore, the mezzanine and upper deck would be cantilevered and hanging off with an unobstructed view.

The cables were – you've got to understand the words "tension" and "compression." They're opposites in physics and engineering. A cable can only be in tension, meaning it's pulled. And so, at these new concrete stringers, we attached these three inch cables to them. And, then the cables went outward to the outer ring of the building. And, they were connected to the building with a huge turnbuckle.

M.W.: I've seen them on wrestling.

D.M.: Yes, exactly! And, what it is, is two screws attached with…I don't know how to attach that thing in the middle.

M.W.: Eyebolts or something similar?

D.M.: It connects the two screws. And by turning the middle section of the turnbuckle, which is called a collar, you can tighten or loosen whatever this turnbuckle is connected to. So, therefore, when you tighten the turnbuckle, you're putting that cable in more and more tension, which then pulls down and out those concrete stringers, which then like a seesaw, lifts the cantilever inner sections -- the old existing sections, which used to be supported by the columns.

M.W.: Is this the same way a bridge is held up?

D.M.: Yes. Very, very much so. Think of the George Washington Bridge, with its two massive columns, or towers. Then you have cables on either side from both sides holding up all the roadway with more vertical cable. Think of those trusses as the fulcrum. In a seesaw, the middle of the seesaw is on what's called the fulcrum, which is a word that describes the middle of the seesaw. The seesaw tips up, down, and around.

So, the new vertical trusses that we put in…everything sat on top of them. This means the new concrete stringers and all the seating above that was on the outside, and the old existing cantilevered seat sections were on the inside. And, so, both of them had to balance like a seesaw around the trusses. The other way they stabilized that was with these cables. The cables pulled down on those concrete stringers out to the turnbuckles to the outside of the building, which you can't see, because the outside of the building covers it up. That's what balances the whole thing out.

If your seesaw was not of even length, you would have to have two guys on the short end to balance out the single guy on the long end.

M.W.: We've done that as kids.

D.M.: Exactly. And so, since the old remaining upper deck was 77 feet, how did you balance that? You couldn't just do it with 10 extra rows since there were many, many more rows on the inside. So, then we put those cables on the outside to pull down on the upper new section to lift the longer, older section when we took out the columns.

Let's talk about some other things. You used the word "frieze."

M.W.: It's, from what I understand, the proper term. Not "façade," although that's what most people call it.

D.M.: We always called it the "façade."

M.W.: That's what everyone calls it. I've heard the proper term is the "frieze," which is what I've been told by many people.

D.M.: Go back and research that again, and see if the word façade isn't the more commonly accepted name.

M.W.: I've written, "the frieze, more commonly called the "façade." I'm like you…I've always called it the "façade."

D.M.: I've never heard that word (frieze) before.

M.W.: I've been corrected by many folks, that it's a frieze, not a façade.

D.M.: I can tell you an anecdote now. I don't know if it's worthy of printing. I was thinking about it this morning. The company was downsizing. Karl Koch was our company. They also did all the steel on the World Trade Center, Giants Stadium in New Jersey later on, and a bunch of other projects. At a certain point they were downsizing, and my immediate boss, the guy that runs the "raising gang" -- that means to raise the steel...the raising gang has a "pusher." The pusher pushes the men and tells them where each beam goes. This was a crew of five or six guys, and I was one of the connectors.

At a certain point, because Koch was downsizing, we got a new pusher. And so they relegated my pusher, not to another supervisory position, but a worker's position. I got really mad. I said that was unfair and that my pusher was a good guy. So I went into the office and slammed my helmet down, and threw it across the room in front of all the bosses. I said, "You know where I live! Mail me my money!" At this point, my ex-boss, Joel Van Dommelin…he and I decided to go to the bar, under the el (elevated subway). Our boss put $20 in our hand and said, "Go drink this afternoon, and we'll talk later on when we carpool home. Joel and I went to the bar and drank beer for four hours, and got into the car – pretty well sloshed. We probably fell asleep on the trip home to Long Island.

In the meantime, two of the other guys in the raising gang decided to voice their objection in a different way. Their names were Jack Johnson and Bobby Green. What they did was, during the rest of the afternoon putting in trusses…they intentionally put them in backwards. I don't know how many they put in…probably four, five, or six. It was a substantial number. And so they intentionally didn't try to help out the new boss, the new pusher. His name was Ronnie Bourne, who by the way was an Indian, from, I believe, the St. Regis tribe reservation up near Montreal. Ronnie Bourne didn't know which way to put them in, and didn't realize there was a backwards way. He didn't think Jack and Bob would subvert him so much.

Anyway, it wasn't until the very end of the day that somebody noticed that all these trusses were in backwards. Well, to take them out and turn them around was a huge job. The next day, Joel had his job back as pusher and I went back to work, and everything turned out fine. And they found somewhere else for Ronnie to go and be a boss. In those days unions – especially the Iron Workers Union #40 in New York City was extremely powerful. But, today, it's a shell of its former self. In those days the union was so strong, since Jack Johnson and Bobby Green were good Local 40 members, they didn't fear reprisals from the company. But, they were union guys as opposed to company guys. So, they knew they could extract their price for having a boss replaced for no reason. And, so, we got our way.

Art Van Dommelin was Joel's father. Joel was the immediate boss…he was the pusher. Joel and I went to high school together in Freeport (NY). Ronnie Bourne was the guy they tried to make the new boss. It wasn't anything personal against Ronnie Bourne. It was that we didn't think that Joel should lose his job as the pusher. And, so I made a fuss and threw my helmet and the other guys went and screwed everything up.

Ronnie Bourne was a native Mohawk, as were many iron workers in those days. There were two reservations near Montreal. One was the St. Regis Reservation. The other is…this is a toughie. We used to call it…the

Indians called it Kahnawake. It sounded to us like "Kognawageh." All the Mohawk Indians come from one of those reservations.

M.W.: I understand the Indians are great at working at heights. I remember reading they work on a lot of bridges.

D.M.: Where that stems from was when the Canadian government decided to build a bunch of bridges across the St. Lawrence River back in the early part of the 20th century…these guys came from a really depressed reservation. And, they would do the work, and everyone just assumed they had superior balance skills. The truth is that there is no more higher level of machismo than in American Indians. If you think machismo is a word associated with that one, I can trump you with that one, because American Indians have an enormous sense of machismo. Looking death in the eye is simply a function of being an American Indian male. And so, a lot of that what you take for balance skills is simply wanting to look brave in front of you.

Ronnie Bourne has got to be from one of those two reservations. He's got to be…my goodness, how old would he be? He'd be pushing 80 right now. He didn't have any culpability in the story in terms of who did what. He was just there. The boss told him to go on the "raising gang," and we simply had our way of saying, "No, he shouldn't be the boss." It's kind of a cute story.

I remember exactly where I was, too. It was on the…if you think of home plate, it was toward the third base side of home plate. And I was putting in the vertical trusses right there.

Jack Johnson and I were connecting partners. Jack Johnson was one of those guys who put the trusses in backwards. He and I were walking on one of the walkways…I forget if it was one of the mezzanines, but it was somewhere on the first base side. We were on one of those walkways when that day came when Joe DiMaggio was out there on right field. Jack Johnson was a Local 40 connector. He looked down and he spotted Joe D. And he said, "I'm going down to get Joe DiMaggio's autograph!"

This guy was a huge Joe DiMaggio and Marilyn Monroe fan. And, when he spotted Joe D. just a couple of hundred feet away from him…it was all muddy and crappy. There was nothing out there. Just piles of dirt and mud from what the bulldozers pushed out there. When he spotted Joe D., he took off his hardhat, and dropped his belt…we had these belts we wore that carried wrenches and tool bags, etc. He said, "I don't care if they fire me, I'm getting Joe D.'s. autograph!" He went scooting all the way down the steps and went into right field to get Joe D.'s autograph. That was so much more important to him (laughs) than his job.

M.W.: The newspaper said Perry Green didn't mind because that would help with the morale of the workers.

D.M.: Iron workers think they're living because their buddies are watching them and seeing how fearless they can be. It's just a matter of status in the iron working community. It's all about portraying bravery.

If you have some time and would like to write about iron workers, I think a lot of people think, "Oh those Indians, blah, blah, blah…" You might want to…for a chapter, it's not directly pertinent to Yankee Stadium….but it's somehow associated with the idea that iron workers put this thing up in the 1920s and redid it in the '70s, and are certainly building the new Yankee Stadium. Iron working has a certain mystique about it, especially with the Mohawks, and the peoples' belief that they have superior balance skills and stuff like that.

I don't think people know this thing about the iron workers and the Indians…they certainly don't know that a large portion of iron workers were Newfoundlanders or descendents of men from Newfoundland. We always called them "Newfies." The Newfies were the last of the sailors that really could understand rigging, with things like masts, and booms. That directly related to the rigging that was necessary for what were called "guy derricks," which up until a short time ago, was the definitive way to erect a steel building – certainly in New York.

A guy derrick is nothing different with the way a sailing ship functions, with a mast and guys (cables) that spread out. Guys go to the top of the mast to keep the mast straight up and down. Then you have a boom, which goes up and down, again, with a series of cables and a motor that connects this whole thing together. The Newfies were a breed of guys that were used to bad weather and rigging, and using these guy derricks as a holdover from sailing ships. A large portion of iron workers in New York City, Local 40, were not only Mohawk Indians from Montreal, but also fellows from Newfoundland.

M.W.: I wouldn't do it (laughs).

D.M.: I did it for 10 years. I look back now and think I should have my head examined! I'm going to tell you a quick story. At this same time, the structural steel for the World Trade Center was being erected by Karl Koch. The World Trade Center was being put up. I didn't get to the Trade Center until the steel was finished. So, the first time I had an opportunity to get to the roof, I went up there with my apprentice. We had been doing some small renovations and stuff. We took the express elevator all the way up to the 107th floor, at which time it was about ten minutes to four. All the other trades were gone, so there wasn't anybody around. We just wanted to take a look around and use a ladder to get to the top.

They hadn't built the stairs yet, and they lowered the ladder. Mike, what I'm about to tell you, I swear to God is a true story. When you hear this, you're going to say, "This guy is either stupid or crazy!" I think both things apply when you hear what we did.

The sheet metal for the outside of that building hadn't reached that height yet. But what the sheet metal attached to were these clips that were probably, when they stood out from the steel, about an inch. They were a horizontal piece, if you can imagine a wide T, four or five inches wide. The sheet metal would attach to those clips. We stuck our heads out of the building to look outside. And all those Ts looked like they were all the way up to the top, the last 30 or so feet. So, I looked at Jackie Daley. His dad was one of the big shots in Koch. He married one of the Koch daughters.

"What do you say, Jack, do you want to go?" He said, "Sure, let's go." The two of us climbed from the 107th floor to the top of the tower. It was the south tower, I believe. We climbed up to the roof. We stood around there and thought we were going to find a ladder to lower down so we could climb down the ladder. There was no ladder on the roof. So, now we had to go back down the way we came up, which meant at a certain point we couldn't see our feet because of the nature of how it beveled up at the very top. We had to lower ourselves down on these clips and then feel with our feet for the next clip.

M.W.: Both of you must have just about died!

D.M.: It was not a happy thought, but we both made it. So, here we are. It was a combination of being brave or stupid, or a combination thereof. I told that story to…I was asked to…for a variety of reasons I was asked to give a speech at Columbia University about six months after 9/11. The Columbia University Graduate School of Architecture and Engineering had a three-day symposium, and they wanted to hear from somebody who actually worked on the World Trade Center. So, I told them some stories, including that one. When I described the details of the point of no return, where I described the stupidest thing I've ever done in my life, everybody howled. Then I realized, "Oh boy, this was really stupid!" And, so you realize that you somehow lived through some of these stupid moments. But, that was a great moment, and that's why I get a little sentimental whenever I think about 9/11.

Let's talk about the trusses. Go to *baseball-fever.com*. (Ballparks, Stadiums & Green Diamonds) Then go to (Yankee Stadium Renovation 1973-1975). There's a picture here from 9/19/74. The top left of the picture. If you look very carefully at the top center of the picture, right under the crane, you can see these things I've been describing as these trusses. From that point on, above that went the stringers. If you look in the middle picture, you can see the new section that rises above the old section. That's the whole critical part of how we eliminated all those columns we put in. You'll still see all the columns in all those pictures. The columns haven't been removed yet. I'll just have to sketch it out for you so you'll understand that the addition is what goes on top of those vertical trusses and all that new section.

You can see the old and new section in the upper deck in that middle top picture. It kind of blends in. You can see there's a different shade. If you look at those two pictures again, the top left picture is without those additional seats. The middle picture shows the additional seats. And those things are put on top of that vertical truss, which you can just see in the 9/19/74 photograph. There were vertical trusses every 20 or 30 feet all the way around. If you look at the right top picture, you can see those stringers, the bottom of which are attached to the top of the trusses.

I have something funny to tell you on Baseball Fever on your thread. You have a photo of Joe D. with a bat in his hand. There's a few things about that photo that I've got to tell you about. Very, very clearly, on the left center part of the photo, there's a fellow with a green shirt with dark blue sleeves and dark blue work pants. That's Jack Johnson. We had been up in one of those sections above Joe's right shoulder, and Jack came down, and climbed down the ladder to get to Joe D. It looks like he was a long way from Joe D., but he wasn't. So he was patiently waiting before that.

Also in that photo, at the very top, you see those things sticking up – those fingers? Those are the stringers. From that, there were steps by each one of them. From that, we put these "L" pre-cast concrete, which became the base for the seats. If you go to page two, there are some pictures that we have to talk about.

There's a picture of Joe D. leaning on a rail on the subway platform. Do you see the stringers up there? The bottom of those stringers look like they're sitting in no-man's land. The bottom of those stringers are attached to the top of the vertical trusses. The first thing we did was put the vertical trusses in. Then we attached a couple of extra pieces of steel to the mezzanine and the upper deck. The stringers were then put on top of the vertical trusses. You can see how that would balance off the overhang, or cantilever, from the upper deck and mezzanine.

The metal that looks like steps – that's the stringer. That's a pre-cast piece of concrete. From the top of the old grandstand was where the end of the new vertical truss was put, thereby connecting the stringer to the top of that. The sneaky part of Yankee Stadium is that all the seats that they lost, because there were no more seats behind where the new vertical truss was. All those seats were lost. To gain back those seats, they put the new grandstand seats way up high. But in the mezzanine, they lost all those seats because the vertical truss went into that seat area quite a bit.

M.W.: I know you had to get rid of the poles in order to cantilever the Stadium.

D.M.: The columns. The columns. Use the right terminology here. To get rid of the columns, we had to balance out the cantilever by adding seats to the top, and then hoisted to the cable. The top of the cable is attached to the bottom of the stringer, as well as the top of the vertical truss.

The bottom of the cable was actually a turnbuckle. The turnbuckle was enormous. We couldn't pick it up by hand. It was eight or nine feet long. The turnbuckle is an extension of the cable, and was located on the outside of the stadium near the top of the grandstand. The cable has to remain taut. There has to be a tension. The bottom of the turnbuckle was attached to the very outside of the building. The other end of the turnbuckle went to the cable, which went to the very top of the vertical truss, which was where the stringer sat.

M.W.: This sounds like the same way a bridge or tent is put up.

D.M.: If you think of a seesaw, where the middle of the seesaw is, that vertical truss that attaches to the bottom of the stringer. And, now you've got this huge 77-foot cantilever, which is an enormous cantilever that stretches out. We've eliminated the columns. You can see in the photo that there are columns on the left side and not the right side. Imagine how much work those columns did. Now, how the heck are you going to take that column out and balance it? With the use of the weight of the stringers and the new seats, and the cable and turnbuckle pulling down and lifting up the cantilever. Do you understand it better now?

M.W.: Yes, I do.

D.M.: If I remember correctly, Arrowhead Stadium, in Kansas City, is cantilevered. It was completed in 1972. It was a similar cantilevered and cable system. Cables have enormous tensile strength. They're made of really fine steel, and sewn together. John Roebling was the inventor of what they call "wire rope." He built the Brooklyn Bridge, and that was the first use of wire rope. They realized it has enormous, enormous strength with regard to tension.

We didn't think Yankee Stadium was very strong. We felt it wasn't as strong as it should have been. All the iron workers thought a 77-foot cantilever was way waaayyyy too much for the renovation. We made jokes about it the day we cut the columns out. Everything was done. We hadn't cut the columns down yet. All the tension and all the turnbuckles and all the cables were all tightened to specs, and all that downward pull from the outside was supposed to take all the weight off the columns, so that when we cut the columns – the overhang – the mezzanine and upper deck, were supposed to spring up a tiny bit, like a quarter inch. That would prove that the whole balance and truss system worked! All the theoretical balancing points and cables - all that weight - that it was a solid design that was going to work.

My job was to pre-cut the columns. So I went around every day with an acetylene torch and pre-cut all the columns. Pre-cut means you leave a little sticker. You cut the column about 95 percent through. So, I sat for days – I killed myself in the process – with lead paint and an acetylene torch. I cut these huge holes in the rivets and columns. I just left the stickers on the columns. Structurally, since everything was intact on the back, there was no compression on these columns any more.

Then came the day when I cut the first sticker. All the engineers were there. All the big shots were there with their measuring devices, like reverse micrometers so they could see how much the column went up. So, I cut the first sticker, and the column came down a quarter of an inch. It was supposed to go up a quarter of an inch. "Uh Oh!" Big time "Uh Oh!" So, we stood there while all the engineers and architects were checking out what to do, and at the end of the day they laid us off for a week. They were trying to figure out what was going on. Was this an acceptable mistake? As I recall, it was supposed to go up a little bit. It didn't. It went down a little bit. As far as the accuracy is concerned, you can have a fault of one-sixteenth of an inch or so, but not much more than that.

So they brought us back after a week. Their solution was to put extra tension on the turnbuckles. For weeks, we went around and manually tightened turnbuckle after turnbuckle. It was an awful job because the turnbuckles were galvanized. They weren't machinery smooth, and weren't made to be moved. Once you set them up, you had to tighten the daylights out of them.[11]

Doug Walker Interview May 24, 2007

D.W.: I had immigrated from Scotland. I was originally born in Scotland and I came over in 1962, and I worked for a construction company. I went to work right away. I was a union carpenter in Scotland, and I came over to New York and I got into the construction industry right away. And I worked with a company for about ten years, and then I switched over to this company called A.J. Pegno and Company from Whitestone, Queens, and they did quite a lot of work at the Stadium at that time. We actually did...did you see that big footbridge on the outside of the Stadium that goes across the railroad tracks?

M.W.: Is that the one that led to the Polo Grounds?

D.W.: No, it's not. The Polo Grounds was up a little further. The Polo Grounds was on the other side of the tracks. . . .A.J. Pegno was a construction contractor, yes. He was a general contractor, and they were out of Whitestone, Queens. College Point, I think, is where their office was. And, they did quite a bit of renovation there, Mike. We also did the River Avenue subway station, which is the subway station that takes you underneath Yankee Stadium. We also did all the renovation of the, I guess the Jerome Avenue line, if I remember correctly. The elevated subway that takes you right to Yankee Stadium, also. We did all the new stairways, risers, handrails...renovated the...it's called the River Avenue I think. That was the subway that was underneath the ground. We redid that whole station, too. And, at that time, I think restaurant bars were all being refurbished right diagonally across from the station at that time, too. I actually worked there three and a half to four years.

Like I said, there's a footbridge that was written up as one of the best architectural concrete jobs in New York City at that time. That was the footbridge that went from where the baseball bat is at Yankee Stadium...like a stairway that went up over the buildings, over the railroad track, down into where the market used to be. The food market used to be there. They made a large parking area so you can park on the other side of the tracks, walk over the footbridge...it was completely enclosed in plexiglass. It was quite a job. It took, I think, a year and a half to complete that alone. And, we were involved with some of the parking garages, and we did some of the work in the dugouts.

You know, Mike, my son-in-law, Greg, is such die-hard Yankee fan, I was telling him when he started dating my daughter when they were first in college, I said, "Greg, when they renovated Yankee Stadium, they were throwing the seats out by the thousands." You could have gotten them for nothing, Mike, and to buy two on ebay right now, it's over $1,000.

M.W.: It is. I went to the last game before the renovation, and we kicked some seats out. But the police made us give them back. They made us leave them there. I bought two of them at the Stadium later on.

D.W.: No kidding. I was there when the demolition was going on, as far as removing the seats. In fact, there was a bit of union trouble there at first, because there was an out of town union contractor that came in. They came in with a bunch of guys, and we had to picket the job a little bit. They tried to come into New York and get away without being union, do you know what I mean?

M.W.: Uh huh.

D.W.: The shop stewards are all over the place. There are shop stewards for the iron workers, the carpenters, the electricians. So the workers kind of put a stop on the guy a little bit. Actually, what they did was just make him union for that job. Even the ones in charge of renovating the seats and installing the new ones. They did a heck of a nice job, actually when they got it going. But I was telling Greg, I said, "Greg, I could have gotten them (seats) by the thousands for nothing. They were throwing them away."

M.W.: I've been dying to know this – maybe you know. All the dirt and debris and metal scrap and concrete scrap from Yankee Stadium, where was that dumped? I'd love to know that.

D.W.: Well, what they did, Mike, they dug about eight feet deeper. They came in and they dug it all out to give more seats on the angle. The original stadium led through the playing field. That was all dug out. Then they came in and filled in maybe half the dirt again, so they could add more seats around the perimeter. I don't know, but I think it was dumped in the Bronx someplace, but where, I don't know, because there were trucks coming out every second. I don't know if it was dumped in Freedomland, because…that became a big apartment complex (Co-op City). Maybe it was dumped there. I don't know. That was undergoing construction at the time, too.

I worked at the Trade Center, too, you know. We did the big powerhouse for Con Edison down there. It was adjacent to the Twin Towers. You know, that's about right. The shop steward that I had from the union came from the Twin Towers. His name was Bobby Brandt, and I'll never forget he had come…I think he was a shop steward down there on that job, or part of it, and he came up to work with me at Yankee Stadium. Yeah, that would be about right. It (dirt) could have been shipped there on the West Side Highway.

M.W.: So, you're a master woodworker.

D.W.: I was a union carpenter, and I was a general foreman on the job that we did at Yankee Stadium. It was a very interesting job for me, because I had never worked on a stadium in my life. And to see part of it, I was there when the ironworkers were doing what I call the post expansion work – putting up the upper tiers work – when these post expansion wires go into the ground…it was a grand and interesting job for myself in that time.

M.W.: Let me ask you something while I'm thinking of it. I know Yankee Stadium is cantilevered. What's a simple definition of "cantilevered?"

D.W.: Cantilevered is post tension. All the cantilever is tied down with these rods that go down into a base of concrete all the way down into the ground. It's inside the structure itself, and that's the reason it's called "post tension." That's what holds it and keeps it from falling down.

M.W.: So, I guess it's like a bridge.

D.W.: It's like a bridge, but it just suspends from the back. It hangs from one end, similar to a bridge, but it doesn't go all the way across. It just hangs out.

M.W.: Did you see any of the Yankee Stadium façade when you were working there?

D.W.: Yes, we did.

M.W.: It was copper, wasn't it?

D.W.: It was copper. It was green but it was copper. Copper turns that way when it's old.

M.W.: Some guys have said it was not copper, just tin.

D.W.: Now, the original was copper…I don't know…they took part of the façade down, the old one. They tried to keep as much of it as they could in the front, but it did change, as you know.

M.W.: The façade they have now in centerfield, I heard that's made out of concrete.

D.W.: It could be precast and just hung up there on the structure.

M.W.: Precast concrete, cement, or what?

D.W.: Precast concrete, hung up. There's girders that go across, and it's bolted onto that. It's like what they use in a lot of high rise buildings. It's like the perimeter of the building. It looks like it's concrete, which it is, and it's all bolted. They swing it up on a crane and the guys bolt it to the existing steel. That's probably what it is, precast. I'll try to find out, Mike, where that stuff was dumped.

M.W.: Also, what happened to the lights, the seats, or anything else.

D.W.: I know that most of the seats were thrown in dumpsters. Where they went, I have no idea. They were put in dumpsters by the thousands. Some of them were banged up by the time they were put into the dumpsters. It was hurry up, get them in, get them out, you know how it is. You know how New York is. . . . I remember, the restaurant in there, when my shop steward left me…this fellow was, I guess up in the union, he ran over to work for the company that worked in the restaurant inside the Stadium itself. And, he said there was so much stuff thrown out of there, it was unbelievable! A lot of people do take a lot of it, but most of it does get dumped. You just don't have time to sort it out.

M.W.: I'll bet they also threw out a lot of blueprints and documents.

D.W.: Oh, I'm sure everything went out. In fact, those were all wrought iron seats. They had a wooden back, if I remember correctly. The originals were wrought iron with a little wooden…like a one inch by six inch on the back, and then the seat was wood, if I remember correctly.

M.W.: I have a set here. What happened was that I left it in a neighbor's yard because we moved and I didn't have anywhere to put it, and the rain ruined it, so part of it's rotted.[12] Is there anything I can do for you, Doug?

D.W.: No, nothing, Mike. If I can get back to you and find out any more information for you, it would be my pleasure.

M.W.: Thank you, Doug., and have a wonderful Memorial Day weekend.

D.W.: Yes, you too, Mike, and good luck with your book.

INTERVIEW WITH JERRY MARSHALL August 22, 2008

Jerry was one of the owners of Klepper, Marshall, King Associates, Chappaqua, New York. They installed the new sound system during the Yankee Stadium renovation.

J.M.: It was an important project for us at the time. I think the engineering firm was Madigan-Prager, if I remember correctly.

M.W.: It was.

J.M.: I'll be as helpful as possible. . . .We were the acoustic consulting firm for the renovation back in the early or mid-'70s. And, primarily, for acoustics at Yankee Stadium, that was to do sound amplification systems. The main sound amplification system consisted of a large tower column of loudspeakers at the far end of the Stadium, directly in line with home plate. That would be home plate in line with second base. But, there were also a lot of distributed loudspeakers in the Stadium. Any that didn't have a line of sight to the main central column of loudspeakers was covered with distributed cone loudspeakers that were in the soffits, or the boxes, or whatever. I know we have the drawings of the original column, large tower of columns of loudspeakers, which were high frequency horns and low frequency boxes.

The firm at that time consisted of David Klepper, Larry King, and myself, Jerry Marshall. We consisted of only the three principles of Klepper, Marshall, and King. I'd be happy to tell you about any questions that may come to mind, but that's essential.

M.W.: From what I was reading, your company got the job because a Bogen dealer was awarded the job, but they didn't have the right equipment.

J.M.: No, we got the job because we did work with this firm before. We had a reputation in sound application systems. Any bidding that was done was after the loudspeaker system was designed, and went out to bid. Actually, if I remember right, Executone was the firm that tried very hard with the city to get the project, but I can't tell you too much more about that. But ultimately, the main loudspeaker manufacturer was Electro-Voice, as well as I remember. I'm pretty sure that's accurate. I know the central tower loudspeakers were made by Electro-Voice.

M.W.: Do you remember how much the bid was?

J.M.: I really don't. I'll look around for material in the office, but I don't think we have much anymore. I do architectural acoustics. I did the drafting of the sound system, but David and Larry were the principal sound system designers here.[13]

LARRY KING INTERVIEW August 30, 2008

Larry King worked at the firm of Klepper, Marshall, King Associates in North White Plains, NY, during the time the company installed the sound system in Yankee Stadium during the renovation of 1973-1976.

L.K.: I've been trying to remember the names of the architect and the various folks we worked with in the design phase, and honestly I can't remember.

M.W.: Was it Mr. Waterbury or Fisher?

L.K.: Mr. Waterbury was the principal now that you mention his name. He was a wonderful chap. I was only…let's see…in 1976 I was 35 years old at the time. I'm going to ramble around here.

M.W.: Go ahead, ramble.

L.K.: Interestingly enough, I met Jim Long through this project. We had a telephone business relationship, initially, regarding the project. This was because Electro-Voice (E-V) had just recently introduced what they called their "white" horns, which were constant directivity devices. They were a major improvement over what had been the typical multi-cell horn. They were made of white fiberglass.

I'm sure if you talk to Jim, you'll get the name of the designers who were behind developing the horn's directivity patterns. There's one particular designer at E-V who was involved in the design of those high frequency horns.

It was David Klepper's idea to build a very tall column of low frequency and high frequency devices. It was just a two-way loudspeaker system of lows and highs divided with electronic crossovers. I think at one point, initially, we decided to use either the JBL, Altec, or RCA radial horns that had been used for 35 or 45 years, mainly for motion picture sound systems, and occasionally for sound reinforcement.

About that time, when the Yankee Stadium job was specified and bid, E-V introduced its new horns, so Jim was eager to use it in this project. Eventually, we decided it was a good thing to do. We ended up with a combination of the E-V horns and their most appropriate compression driver.

The horns were arrayed in a vertical column. I think there were 12 low frequency Altec horns. The total number of high frequency horns in the array, I don't recall. There was an E-V promo sheet on this design. Also, Jerry Marshall kept a lot of archival material. The low frequency drivers were probably in Altec boxes, but I'm not sure.

M.W.: I know it was over 30 years ago. Do you know how much the contract was?

L.K.: Oh God, I don't know. I'm guessing it may have been in the $100,000 to $150,000 range. It was a lot for that time. It may have been a lot more. The system used distributed loudspeakers to cover the, what I call "under balcony" or "under Bleacher" seats around the whole horseshoe shape of the Stadium. They were electronically delayed. The sound from the center cluster, which I talked about earlier, was synchronized with the delayed sound loudspeakers. I don't know if you knew that or not.

M.W.: No, I didn't. One thing I read is that Bob Sheppard, the Yankees' legendary announcer, was testing the system for a couple of weeks.

L.K.: That's right. He was involved. We also had distributed loudspeakers – not just for the seated patrons in the Grandstand under the great big overhang, but also for the lobby areas, the concession areas all around the Stadium. The lobby areas and seating areas were acoustically coupled. There were no doors in the vomitory areas or circulation areas. Sound from the lobby could bleed into the seating areas. So, we had to delay those loudspeakers as well to prevent artificial echoes. Because of the differences involved, the delays weren't quite the same. The design fed the delay signals to the distributed lobby lounge speakers one zone later so we didn't have to double up on the delay units. There was a single multi-tap delay unit that was custom made by Eventide, Inc.

The Lexicon Delta-T delay was also one of the first to be used in a sound reinforcement system. It was employed in a portable sound system that KMK designed, and that toured with the Metropolitan Opera and New York Philharmonic to the city parks. If you lived in New York in the 1970s and 1980s, I'm sure you knew of the summertime park concerts that were free for the public, and they drew huge crowds.

Particularly after the new sound systems that we designed. It could play a lot louder and cover a much larger area than the previous sound system. Because of that, more and more people started coming. It turned into a big, big deal. The Yankee Stadium project and Parks Concert project were related in that they were using line array configurations of very highly efficient horn loudspeakers to reduce the vertical dispersion angle of the loudspeaker system so that it could distribute sound over a long distance.

With the Yankee Stadium project, the distance from the loudspeaker system to the most distant seats behind home plate at the upper reaches of the Grandstand, was in the range of 750 to 800 feet. It doesn't sound like a lot, but it was a lot. In a 2,500-seat theater the distance from the performer to the last row of balcony seats can be in the order of 150 feet.

The sound system produced 95 to 100 decibels at the distance of 800 feet, in order to overcome all but the greatest levels of crowd noise. We knew we couldn't totally override the peak crowd noise levels. Delivering another 10 decibels was just not practical with the money or the components we had at the time. Today, achieving this output level would be no problem because of the greatly improved quality of the sound system transducers and amplifiers. Anyway, we did that, and it was very cleanly designed and installed. Casey Systems, in New York, was the contractor who did the work.

M.W.: Do you know how long it took for Klepper, Marshall, King to install the sound system in Yankee Stadium during the renovation?

L.K.: The entire stadium was being renovated and expanded, so a lot of things were happening at the same time. Probably on the order of two years. From the beginning of the design through construction, make that one or two more years. We started maybe '73 or as late as early '74.

We built an acoustical model because we were concerned about echoes developing off certain surfaces, primarily the Grandstand's façade – not the seating areas. So, we built a small model and lined suspected echo-producing surfaces with light-reflective mylar foil. Then we used a light source to simulate the loudspeaker system, and we directed the light source toward these surfaces in a dark room so we could see where the reflections occurred on the playing field and seating area. As a result of that study, sound absorbing material was applied to these echo-producing surfaces.

In addition, the ceilings over the covered areas, where the Mezzanine and Upper Grandstand are located, were acoustically treated with a perforated metal panel system, on top of which was placed one or two-inch-thick glass fiber batts weather-protected in mylar bags.

M.W.: Is that why they put the ceiling panels in, because of the sound system?

L.K.: Yes. We wanted to control crowd noise and also reduce the amount of echo coming back from the distributor delayed loudspeakers. Of course, there was a Press Box and Sound System Control position, behind home plate.

The electronic organ was a major function of this facility. We wanted the center cluster to reproduce the sound of the organ in a realistic and loud enough way. It was very effective, at least initially. Over the years the sound system was upgraded and modified. We had nothing to do with any of those later changes. All of these changes were made to improve it as much as possible, as new and better equipment became available after the Stadium opened. I do remember that we told them that any kind of singing from home plate, such as the National Anthem, would be difficult for the singers because they would be hearing themselves with an almost one second delay. With the cluster at 450 to 500 feet away, the delayed arrival of amplified sound could cause an artificial echo that could shock and confuse the person singing.

When you factor in the speed of sound, which is roughly 1,100 feet per second, if you divide 1,100 into 500, you get roughly 5/10th of a second. If they'd never been in that situation before, they would have to sing a few bars before they could adjust to the amplified sound's long delay.

In another stadium later on, with a similar system, the Milwaukee County Stadium, where the Milwaukee Brewers used to play, we designed a foldback system – Yankee Stadium may have had it as well. I don't remember right now. The foldback system provided undelayed sound energy to the singer, including any accompaniment. This system could override the delay the singer could hear. Any rock and roll group has these. A typical name is "stage monitor systems."

The sound operator had to be able to control the main system, which was used mainly to amplify the announcer's voice and the organ, and maybe an occasional visiting band. Yankee Stadium also had an outfield mixer that we would employ when a band would play out there. Bands would play in the outfield by the main loudspeaker cluster so they wouldn't be confused by its delayed sound when they were to perform at home plate.

The outfield mixer fed the main console so the sound operator could mix and balance those remote bands. The direct sound of the outfield bands were all but inaudible at the main mixing position because of the distance involved. But, once it was picked up and amplified by the cluster, you could then hear it throughout the Stadium.

The problems would come when they would try to synchronize the bands playing with somebody singing at home plate. That just couldn't be done, so the National Anthem had to be done virtually a cappella (singing without instrumental accompaniment) or with the organ. They would have sung directly into the microphone without delay because the center cluster sound would arrive at home plate with that 0.5 second delay. If you were close to the person singing, if you were right at home plate, and the singer was loud enough, then you would have definitely heard an echo.

We solved that problem by using distributed loudspeakers that were delayed to cover seating behind home plate. We did that for Milwaukee County Stadium.

Something tells me that there was a trade magazine article about the Yankee Stadium project, perhaps written by whoever the contractor was who worked on the system. That would have been published most likely in 1976 or 1977. Jim Long of Electro-Voice would probably know.

M.W.: Let me ask you this one. The famous frieze, or façade that's over the Yankee Stadium scoreboard in center field…I've heard it's made of concrete, pre-cast cement, fiberglass, or even plastic. Do you have any knowledge as to what it was made from?

L.K.: They reproduced those…I think they were a combination of glass fiber reinforced gypsum (GFRG).

M.W.: I've read different things, and I don't know what to write.

L.K.: That's a good point. I don't really know. It may have been in precast concrete. It's more likely it was that because that was very sturdy and could stand up over a number of years.

Another thing about the renovation…we tried to have the seating as porous as possible. The sound absorption of the clothing and bodies of patrons would be maximized, so the seats, I believe, had opened areas between solid slats on the backs and bottoms.

L.K.: I would think there would be a demand for it. You'd better get in touch with your potential publishers right away. The new Stadium's opening up next year.

M.W.: I know. That's why I want to wrap it up, also. There's a wonderful site called baseball-fever.com. It has everything baseball on it. I have a thread with my Yankee Stadium Renovation book on it. So far there's been about 70,000 hits on it, so I know the demand is out there.

L.K.: Wow! You said earlier in our conversation, Mike, that you had a Kodak Instamatic camera and took 200 photos. Is that because you were interested in baseball? Is that correct?

M.W.: I went to New York City Community College on Jay Street in Brooklyn. I went 13 times and took 230 photos. I've always loved Yankee Stadium.

L.K.: I know where that is. You went just to take photographs?

M.W.: Right. During progress of the renovation. I had no idea I was going to write a book.

L.K.: You actually went during the 1970's renovation to take photographs.

M.W.: Yes.

L.K.: It's amazing. Amazing. Jim Long and I have become very close friends because of this supplying of main loudspeakers for Yankee Stadium. By the way, the distributed loudspeakers were also Electro-Voice. They were a reentrant horn. These horns are a version of a folded horn, and they were designed to reproduce roughly 200 Hz up to 8,000Hz, or so. They weren't fabulous loudspeakers, but they were relatively inexpensive and very efficient at producing sound. They were surface mounted. But, most people didn't see them because they were up there flush with the soffits. They worked really well.

Looking back on it, I wish we had been more involved in the operation of the sound system once the Yankees started using the Stadium. But, you know, the way construction goes, at least back then, once you did your job as a designer and you checked out the system technically to see that it worked according to the design, then it was turned over to the users, and they do the best with it that they can.

We did have interaction with the Yankees during design. There was a Press Room that we produced acoustic design for. Jerry Marshall did most of that work. It was where the press would interview ballplayers. That was in the suite of rooms that was in the administration section of the Stadium. There were audio and video tie-lines between the main sound control panel and Pressroom. There were provisions for TV and audio radio feeds.

Mr. Waterbury, of course, was in charge of the entire project. He and his team of architects and engineers…the engineers were all independent consultants who worked for the architect, just like we did. It was a very good experience for us because we had just started our own business in 1972.

Jerry, David, and I were part of the New York City office of Bolt, Beranek, and Newman (BBN). BBN was the principal acoustic consulting firm on the east coast in the 1960s. They were the consulting firm that gave the world Philharmonic Hall at Lincoln Center. It was rebuilt in the mid '70s, about the time Yankee Stadium re-opened. Lincoln Center has a wonderful archives department, and they have loads of material about the design and construction history of the entire campus.

Incidentally, next spring (May 19th, 2009), is the 50th Anniversary of the construction ground breaking for Lincoln Center. The design work was done in roughly 1955 on, and Philharmonic Hall was the first building in the complex to open, in 1962. The next theater was the New York State Theater, across the plaza, then the Metropolitan Opera, which opened in 1965. Between 1966 and 1969, the Beaumont, the Performing Arts Library at Lincoln Center, and the Juilliard opened.

With the firm I'm working for now (Jaffe Holden, of Norwalk, CT), I'm working on the renovation of Alice Tully Hall, and a new addition to the Juilliard School. It's been a great project to be involved in.[14]

- - - - - - - - - - - -

Suzanne Koch Fabrizio first contacted me on May 16, 2013. Her father, Steven Koch, worked on the Yankee Stadium renovation for Walsh Construction. The following pages contain memories and photos from both of these fine people.

Memories from Yankee Stadium by Suzanne Koch Fabrizio   June 8, 2013

It was the 1970's, and I was a young girl, growing up in Bayside, Queens. I came from a family of four; just one older sister, Kim, and our parents, Steve and Jean Koch. My dad worked for Walsh Construction Company. As a matter of fact, my dad worked for Walsh for about 40 years, so it was a part of my life too.

I will never forget when Walsh Construction got the job to reconstruct Yankee Stadium. My dad was going to be part of that. I told my friends that my dad was building Yankee Stadium. And how cool I thought I was!

I was young, only 9 when the project was completed and by that time, Dad was the project manager of the job. Needless to say, he had some authority at the job site, and fortunately for me, he took advantage of many opportunities to bring me to work with him and experience history in the making. I've always been a daddy's girl, so more often than not, it was just the two of us heading to the Bronx together.

Being at work with my dad was more exciting than I can say. Frankly, it didn't matter to me if I had to hang out in the trailer that they used as an office. But, fortunately for me, my dad showed me the ins and outs of Yankee Stadium during the different construction phases and I will never forget it. I can clearly remember walking through the stadium while under construction, wearing a hard hat, for obvious reasons. One day we were walking up these huge concrete zigzagging ramps that he explained would eventually be filled with Yankee fans as they entered and exited the stadium for a game. And there I was, just me and my dad.

My memories are plenty, and it's difficult to put them on paper. Like the time my dad brought me down to see the Yankee's locker room, and I can literally hear my dad's voice in my head saying, "hey guys, I've got my daughter with me today, is it okay if I let her take a peek at the locker room?", and there I was, standing in the Yankees locker room, with it's purple sort of colored carpet…thinking "wow, it's purple!"

Another time, my dad brought me to George Steinbrenner's office. We got there and I was privileged to sit in Mr. Steinbrenner's chair, which was just delivered! It was a huge brown leather baseball mitt that swiveled! I knew how lucky I was at the time, and couldn't wait to tell my friends. That same day, in that same office, I was introduced to Joe Garagiola, Jr. And it wasn't a dream.

There was one time that my sister joined my dad and I on one of our outings to Yankee Stadium. While we were there, we got to watch a television commercial being taped for Mr. Pibb soda. In the commercial was Billy Jean King and her brother, whose name I don't remember, but he was a professional baseball player. The commercial was being filmed on the partially finished field at home plate, and I can remember thinking it was odd that they were filming at Yankee Stadium, and the guy wasn't even a Yankee. We sat in awe of this commercial being taped right in front of our very eyes…one take after another.

So, my grandmother, who was my mom's mom, loved baseball. She was really a Mets fan, but baseball was her favorite sport. One time, Dad took the whole family, including Grandma to the stadium. At that time, the field was just about finished, and we spent hours checking it out…from the brand spanking new blue seats…to the dugouts…to the area where there was a monument with Babe Ruth's picture etched into it….to the pitcher's mound, where my grandma got to throw a ball! It was truly a day to remember! One that without a doubt ended with dinner at Stella Dora's restaurant!

I got to see and do things inside Yankee Stadium that most people didn't. I am bound and determined to find my favorite photo, of me and my dad sitting atop the stadium where the flags were mounted, with NYC behind us. I felt like I was on top of the world.

My story ends on opening day April 15, 1976. A date that I will never forget. My dad was the project manager of the newly rebuilt Yankee Stadium, and like celebrities, my dad, mom, sister and I were escorted into the stadium that day, to be there for the opening day game. It was fantastic and I couldn't have been more proud to be my daddy's little girl.

Steve Koch Telephone Interview #1 June 30, 2013

Steve Koch worked for the Walsh Construction Company as Project Engineer during the demolition phase of the renovation of Yankee Stadium. By 1975 he became the Project Manager of this endeavor. Steve was the last person working at the site for Walsh Construction until well past the April 1976 opening of Yankee Stadium. Steve said the renovation of Yankee Stadium was completed sometime in June of 1976. The page numbers Steve is referring to are in the hard cover book, "Babe's Place: The Lives of Yankee Stadium," first published in 2012.

M.W.: What did you think of "Babe's Place?"

S.K.: I enjoyed looking through it. I haven't read it from cover to cover. I looked through the parts that I remembered best, and I was waiting to talk to you, so I really haven't read it cover to cover. I was waiting to talk to you. You did a good job.

M.W.: Thank you very much. I know you would know what's going on. What would you like to talk about as far as your memories of the Yankee Stadium renovation?

S.K.: Well, you asked me in one of your e-mails some of the accuracies of what you had put in the book. If you don't mind, I'll make a couple of comments, as I think there are a few inaccuracies. But as you well know between you and me, there are some that no one else would probably know.

M.W.: Please do, please do.

S.K.: Maybe inaccuracies is an unfair word. But, for example, the first thing I noticed was on page 110. You list the bidders. And, later on in the book you mention some prime contractors that weren't in that first list. Does this mean anything to anybody? Obviously not. Just as an example, on page 110, you miss the second largest contract, which is called "Koch." And you do mention that on page 251. And again, does that mean anything? No, but it's to your benefit if you want to list everything and have accuracy, I just thought I'd tell you that. Plus, there were a couple of other prime contractors, such as American Seating.

M.W.: I do have them in the book, American Seating.

S.K.: Yes. My point is that in the front of the book when you list the number of bidders and who they were, you don't mention those prime contracts, although later on in the book you pick them up. It's a question of the front doesn't tie with the back. I can be a pain in the neck with details. It's no big deal.

M.W.: I got that information from Jay Schwall. What I did with Jay is that I typed up everything from his interview. I then mailed it to him for corrections so that he could then delete what he wants, add what he wants, or leave in what he wants. I'm going to do the same with you, Steve.

S.K.: Jay was there early on, and I remember Jay very well. Probably with some of these other contracts he wasn't really familiar with, because by that time he was gone. But, he should have known about Karl Koch. I'm surprised he missed that one because Karl Koch moved in before Jay Schwall completed his job. Some of what Jay Schwall was demolishing had to marry what Karl Koch was adding on. Anyway, it's of no big consequence.

M.W.: Did Karl Koch get the contract based on price only, reputation also, or something else?

S.K.: I believe they all got it on just price. Being a city job, a public job, it had to be publicly bid. Now, there may have been - and I don't remember this for a fact - there may have been some prequalification requirements, minimum requirements, so that just any Tom, Dick, or Harry couldn't bid. But, once you were qualified as a bidder, the low bid got the job.

M.W.: Did Karl Koch manufacture its own steel or did they get steel from a different company for the Yankee Stadium renovation?

S.K.: Karl Koch is an erector, and a fabricator. When I say a fabricator, they don't make the steel. Bethlehem Steel, U.S. Steel, or a foreign company - I don't recall - makes the steel. I think frankly that they used Bethlehem Steel, but that's a guess. It's been 40 years.

M.W.: I know you're going through the files to refresh your memory and get information. Were you able to pin down the date that the renovation was 100 percent done?

S.K.: No. I have nothing that really tells me that. And to define 100 percent done can be defined in several different ways. They opened up when they were supposed to open up. Was everything done that was supposed to be done? No. But people didn't know that. There were still some concession stands and some interior work that had to be completed 100 percent. I honestly don't remember - I'm thinking out loud now - whether the new Stadium Club opened up on Opening Day. I think it did, but I'm not sure. I hung around until probably June. I got called back some years later, too, when they had problems with cracking at the expansion joints. There was an issue with a falling beam some years later (1998) that fortunately didn't hurt anybody. So, I've been back to the Stadium long after the renovation that had to do with the construction or the warranties, or whatever.

M.W.: Do you know if Unistress Corp. of Pittsfield, Massachusetts, made the frieze (façade) that ringed the outfield wall of Yankee Stadium?

S.K.: I don't have anything in my files to confirm that. Did you ever speak to Ted Cohen? He was the NAB on-site General Superintendent. I don't even know if Ted is still alive. Ted was a little older than me, so he can still be around. Ted and Ralph Drewes sort of worked as a team, although Ted worked over Ralph. Ralph was the field guy - he was like the head superintendent in the field. But, Ted Cohen was what I would call the on-site Project Manager for the General Contractor, which was NAB Tern Berley, which is another detail, but not a big issue. They were generally referred to as NAB-Tern, but it was truly a joint venture of three companies, with the third one being Berley Industries. I believe they were just a financial partner. There actually was a fellow named Noah Berley, who would actually show up once in a while. So, it was the Simpson people from NAB, Ralph Terowsky from TERN, and Noah Berley from Berley.

Ted Cohen ran the show. He was on-site. There was somebody that NAB called their Project Manager, who was frankly a paper shuffler back in the home office. He put in the monthly pay requests, change order work, and things like that. But, Ted Cohen was the chief guy on site. He and Ralph worked as a team. But,

Ralph was the down and dirty guy with the concrete and the form work. When it got to the finishing stages and all...I don't even remember if Ralph actually stayed around to the bitter end. I'm not sure he did. I think he moved on once the heavy physical work was done.

M.W.: In the construction industry, or if you just want to speak for yourself, when you worked at Yankee Stadium, was the feeling, "Wow! Yankee Stadium!" Was there a feeling that this was a special job or was it just a regular construction job?

S.K.: It definitely seemed like a special job to me. I was excited to go there. I had just turned 33 years old. I was making a move up in my company, and it was a prestigious job. Especially to be acting in a no risk position representing the city as the construction manager, which brings up the subject - we didn't have to bid the job. We negotiated what they call a Professional Services Contract. When I say "we," I'm talking about Walsh Construction Company. There's a gentleman that signed the contract from Walsh. You had to be a professional engineer or architect in order to get the award. And he's a professional engineer. His name is Gerard Carty. The reason I bring that up is that he's a bit of an historian himself. He's still quite active, and you may want to contact him.

Candidly, once the contract was signed during the design phase, he really had nothing to do with the job. He was our chief engineer for the company, and chief estimator. Once the contract was negotiated and Gerard Carty signed it, he really had no involvement in the job whatsoever. However, like I say, he's sort of an historian himself. There's a national trade association headquartered in New Jersey called "The Moles." Moles is a 75-year old society of heavy and underground construction people. It really started with the tunnel building in the 1930s when they built the Queens Midtown Tunnel, which was Walsh Construction's first major job in New York.

Anyway, Gerard (Gerry) heads up The Moles. He's retired now. He's in his 70s or may be 80 already, but he's the Executive Director of The Moles and quite a guy that keeps his finger on everything, such as who passed away, what famous job was completed, or what contractor worked on a famous job, etc. You might want to contact him. He may have some insight you can use, although, as I've said, Gerry really didn't get involved in the construction. But, he's a pretty interesting fellow. The Moles is a prestigious, real tight-knit organization.

S.K.: Alright, moving on. But, mentioning Gerry - and this may sound cruel of me. I saw the letter from Tim Crowley. I worked with Jerry Crowley from the day I started at Walsh Construction, and I knew his son, Timmy, and the rest of his family. In all due respect, for your information, Jerry Crowley had absolutely nothing to do with Yankee Stadium. Absolutely nothing. And, if you read Tim's letter to you which is in your book in the back, he doesn't say Jerry had anything to do with Yankee Stadium. All he says is that his father was a Construction Manager for Walsh Construction. That's true. But we had more than one Construction Manager, and each Construction Manager was assigned responsibility for two or three construction projects, and Yankee Stadium was not one of Jerry's projects (laughs). Like I said, I was good friends with Jerry. Jerry obviously passed away, but it's just a little misleading, and do I care or does anyone else care? No. And if it makes Tim feel good, then that's fine. Jerry had zero to do with Yankee Stadium.

His counterpart, a gentleman named Frank Gleason, who passed away at an early age, maybe less than five years after the renovation was completed - he was the guy that was the Construction Manager in overseeing Yankee Stadium. All of this is almost trivia to people who weren't involved.

I could talk a long time about Jerry Crowley because not only was Jerry Crowley not involved, but Jerry Crowley quit Walsh, took a couple of the younger guys from Walsh, and started his own company called TBX Construction, which is still very active in New York City. But, he only stayed there a couple of years before his partners bought him out, and that's when he started to do I don't know what - land development or something with his son (Tim). Jerry left Walsh Construction around the late 1970s or about 1980. I'm not sure exactly when. But, I started working with Jerry from the day I started working at Walsh, which was October of 1965, right on through. And I did keep in touch with Jerry a little bit after he left Walsh. After I read Tim's correspondence, I had to kind of smile and think that Timmy meant well and didn't mean any harm. He doesn't say his father was involved. He said Walsh was the manager and his father was a manager, but that doesn't mean the two connect. I don't know if it's a mistake or misunderstanding. Timmy was very young at the time, so I don't know if it meant anything at the time. So, where was I (laughs)?

M.W.: What are your favorite memories or stories of the Yankee Stadium project?

S.K.: I'll give you a couple of those. First, let me give you a couple of statistics you may want to use. On page 262, you mention Slocum and Fuller doing the blueprints. That's definitely not correct. You make it sound like Slocum and Fuller was the reproduction company that ran off the blueprints. At least that's the way I read it.

M.W.: I thought they were.

S.K.: No. Slocum and Fuller is an engineering firm. I believe they were the mechanical engineers. They are no longer in business. I tried to look them up on the internet. They are now liquidated. But they were definitely not…it's irrelevant now… But anyone that knew them, it was a little bit of an insult to call them the blueprint guys. That's like saying you went to Kwik Kopy or something similar. But, that's not what Slocum and Fuller was. That's for sure. Accuracy wise, on page 254 - again, it's me reading - I hate to sound so critical.

M.W.: No, that's fine.

S.K.: Somewhere on page 254, you talk about the ground level being above the clubhouse level. That's just backwards. It's the other way around. On the bottom of page 254, you say the "clubhouse level contained a batting cage and gym for the players." Frankly, I don't remember that. I think that was the basement. "One flight up at ground level, the Stadium Club…," the ground level is not one flight up from the clubhouse level. It's the other way around.

Foul pole netting, page 259. Oh, I have a story to tell you that I know you'll like. And, page 261. The unfortunate part is that I can't tell you the…I need to check, but I can't tell you what they are doing today, but I know what we did that day. Page 261, number of columns. What the heck was I trying to say? It says the columns "were replaced with 106 20-inch A-36 structural steel columns placed behind the seating area." I don't know why I wrote myself a note on that. That may be right. I don't know if that's right or wrong. I thought there were more than that, but I could be wrong. I just don't remember. I wish I had a set of old blueprints.

M.W.: If I recall correctly, I think I got that from a Dick Young column for the *New York Daily News.*

S.K.: I wouldn't put much stock in that!

M.W.: Uh, oh!

S.K.: No offense to Dick Young, but news reporters write what they want to write and no one really ever questions it. Dick Young once wrote an article that just about got me fired about me being the Chief Engineer for Walsh Construction Company. I wasn't even a college graduate, and my boss just about had a heart attack! He said, "Did you tell him you were the Chief Engineer?!" I said, "No, of course not!" (laughter).

M.W.: Look at page 261.

S.K.: "These columns worked like a fulcrum." Is that what you're talking about?

M.W.: Right. "These 106 cables were secured…"

S.K.: I don't remember if there were 106 cables. Frankly, I think it was more. I vaguely remember the column numberings…Column 1 was in extreme right field to I want to say Column 137 in extreme left field. But, Michael, honestly, I could be wrong on that. This was a long time ago. For some reason, 137 comes into my head. One hundred and six does not come into my head.

M.W.: I'll bet you're right. Some things you just remember. Oh, by the way, who did make the blueprints for the Stadium if Slocum and Fuller did not?

S.K.: When you said "made them," are you talking about reproducing them?

M.W.: In construction, when you have blueprints made, someone makes them.

S.K.: It's just a reproduction outfit, and I don't remember who the heck we used.

Praeger Kavanagh Waterbury initiated the blueprints. They are the ones that created the blueprints. They had the tracings. They had the originals. But, then, all they do is send out the tracings, known as sepias, to a blueprint company, who runs off numerous sets. Honestly, that company that reproduces the blueprints is never mentioned or considered an integral part of the job. They have no responsibility for creating the print. All they do is make copies. So, it's not really something you see mentioned when talking about a job. The prints usually means who designed the building.

M.W.: So, should I delete the Slocum and Fuller paragraph?

S.K.: I think you should. It's not true, and Praeger Kavanagh Waterbury created and designed the blueprints. As I'm saying this, because it was a city job, and went through the Office of Design and Construction for the city, they may have taken credit for the blueprints to be honest with you. My point is that whoever reproduced them is really irrelevant and not meaningful to anything.

M.W.: Again, I don't know. I'm not in construction.

S.K.: I'm looking at something here. Ray Devine was the registered architect for the Bureau of Design for the city, and I think they had their name on the blueprints as well. But, as for participating in the design, but nowhere on the blueprints do you find the name of the name of the printing firm that reproduces them.

Speaking of the city, I'm holding a book in my hand which I will copy pages of and send to you, if you don't have it. It's called the *Municipal Engineer's Journal.* This is the second quarterly issue from 1974 that contains quite a writeup of the design and whole concept of the renovation of Yankee Stadium. It would be very helpful to you. In fact, it gives you a clear picture of the whole idea of removing the columns that used to block your view using the tie-back cables to support the upper deck, enabling the removal of those obstructing columns.

I don't mean to get too technical, but what we actually did was before we removed the column that was obstructing peoples' view, we added a new row of columns towards the back. That new row of columns actually wiped out about 10 rows of seats. It wasn't all the way back. It was about 3/4 of the way up the row of seats.

That's why they added more seats on the upper deck - to offset some of the ones we had lost. But, this book and the sketches in the book explain it very nicely, and rather than me dictating it to you and you having to interpret it, I think if I Xerox a few pages of this book and the whole article of the Stadium and send it to you, it will be very helpful. It even gives a cross section of the new Stadium and how it improved the sight lines, where the seating was added, and where the field was lowered - it was lowered about five feet, give or take. I got this book from Mike Aquino, who was a member of the Municipal Engineers.

M.W.: I have a copy of *The Constructioneer* from Jay Schwall. He sent me a copy of an article of the renovation. That's where I got the information of some of the equipment used in the renovation.

S.K.: I don't have that book, but this is a good one, and it's accurate. That's for sure. Stories, stories, Oh My God, where do I start with stories?!

Since you mentioned foul pole…the day they were setting the foul poles, this fellow, Ted Cohen came to me…he was the head guy for the general contractor. He came to me and said, "What do you want me to do with the foul pole?" I said, "What do you mean what do I want you to do with the foul pole?" (laughs) He said, "The edge of the foul pole is supposed to be dead accurate on the vertical line that would designate the foul line, whether the ball goes to one side or to the other. We have these surveyors out there with their instruments, and they have to make sure it's accurate. The foul pole is tapered, so what do we do?"

If you can picture this, the foul pole, as I recall, the section - let's say at the bottom, the first 20 feet of height was cylindrical, and it was quite a large diameter. Then it changed. It was on like a pedestal. It went from - and I'm just using numbers - it went from let's say 20 inches in diameter, then eventually tapered all the way to the top to, I don't know, maybe 100 feet tall, or whatever it was. It tapers down to say 12 inches. If you can visualize this, you obviously have to set the pole so that it doesn't look crooked and that it's leaning over. So, if you set it plum using, let's say, the center line, it looks good, and part of the pole is going to be in foul territory - to the right of center. I'm saying to the right of center because I'm visualizing my mind the pole in right field. What they're supposed to do is put the tangent of the pole vertical along the foul line. But, in order to put the tangent vertical, you'd have to tilt the pole because it's tapered. That would look stupid. Anyway, we ended up putting up, as best as I recall, the cylindrical part and the base, where it starts - the tangent - right on the theoretical foul line. Then the center of the pole is plum. So what really happens at the top of the pole, there's some distance to the right of the pole (and I keep saying to the right, because I keep visualizing right field), there is some distance, namely the distance is the difference of the - half of the distance of the change of the diameter of the pole - let's say the pole is 20 inches at the bottom and 12 inches at the top...that means it lost 8 inches. It really lost 4 inches on each side.

If those dimensions are correct, and I don't remember if they're correct, that means there's a 4-inch area to the right side of the foul line, that if the ball went to the right side, it would be called foul. But, technically, it would still be in fair territory because the pole is now tapered and well inside of fair territory. To this day, I don't know if the league ever corrected that or told architects that foul poles cannot be tapered, they have to be cylindrical all the way up. I don't know the answer. But, it always amazed me that...geez, what a question. If a ball ever grazes past the very top of the pole on the right side, it will be called a "foul," but it really was a home run. I guess the odds of that happening are slim, but the construction men are standing around scratching their heads and saying, "What do we do now?" (laughs)

M.W.: Let me ask you this one...were the foul poles used in the renovated Yankee Stadium the ones used in the original Yankee Stadium or were they new foul poles?

S.K.: Oh, no, no. They were new foul poles.

M.W.: Do you know what happened to the old ones, because Jay Schwall said the old ones were never for sale.

S.K.: No, I have no idea what happened to the old ones.

M.W.: So, they were brand new ones.

S.K.: As best as I remember. I don't recall them being old foul poles.

M.W.: Do you have any stories about the façade, or frieze? I understand they were blow torched and axed in order to destroy them.

S.K.: Frankly, I did not start on October 1, 1973, the day the demolition actually started. I started about 5 weeks later. But I didn't get there the very first day. When I got there, the demolition was well under way. I cannot tell you what happened to the frieze. No one at the time paid a lot of attention to whether it was something worth saving, a piece of memorabilia, or whatever.

M.W.: Do you have any stories about the new frieze that was put up?

S.K.: You know, I don't. It was sort of something not…

M.W.: I know back then very few people cared about memorabilia.

S.K.: You're right. And the frieze was something that was fabricated out of synthetic concrete, lightweight concrete…really, it was called "GFRC." It stands for "Gypsum Reinforced Concrete." It's really made with more of a mixture of plaster than concrete. It's because of the weight. While it was pretty, it was kind of used to screen the elevated subway line. I do have some pictures, which I'm sure you have. One of them is from *The New York Times* or *New York Daily News*. I have it here in front of me. I'm not sure where it's from. But, it's a picture of Jay Schwall's cranes working in the Stadium removing the frieze.

M.W.: Jay Schwall sent me those photos.

S.K.: I figured he did. I have a copy of a newspaper article, Thursday, August 29th, 1974, from *The New York Times*, and it's got a nice picture of Richard Muller, the iron worker you talked about. It's a nice writeup, but it's got a nice picture of Richard Muller when he was about 30 years old, with his long hair.

M.W.: I think I did see it. Dick was wonderful with information.

S.K.: He's a nice fellow. I remember him well. He was one of the iron workers that I can talk to. What I mean by that is that some of the iron workers can be pretty rough and don't take kindly to young supervisors telling them what to do or not to do.

M.W.: He speaks beautifully, and he's a great historian. He knows his stuff. He worked on the World Trade Center, as you may have seen in the book.

S.K.: Well, I knew Koch from the World Trade Center. Walsh Construction actually bid on the World Trade Center, unsuccessfully. So, I knew Koch. Speaking of Koch, there's kind of a little human interest story. By coincidence, the young engineer who was representing Karl Koch on the job...his name was exactly the same as mine. He was close to my age, maybe about three years younger. He came into our construction trailer on his first day on the job. When I say ours, I say we had a major complex, where we had meetings. It had the sign on it, "Construction Managers, Walsh Construction," etc. But it was the central meeting place. So he comes in the trailer one day. I guess it was his first day on the job. He introduced himself. I said, "Hi, I'm Steve Koch. What's your name?" I didn't know who he was. He thought I was being a smart ass. He said, "Oh, very funny!" I said, "What do you mean?" He said, "Steve Koch. I'm Steve Koch." I said, "Well, yeah, so am I." (laughs) It was just a coincidence, but we actually became quite friendly and I would see him later at these Moles dinners. I would suspect he's retired now because he's not that far behind me in age. I'm going to be 73 in October.

By the way, I'm holding in my hand...I saw in the book that you talked about the price of food and stuff in the Stadium Club as compared to Shea Stadium...I happen to have a piece of memorabilia...a menu from the old Stadium Club, not the new one, that I got out of the Stadium Club before they wrecked it. The interesting part of it is the price of the food they were serving. It also has a teriffic overhead photo of Yankee Stadium on the cover.

M.W.: Is it a foldout?

S.K.: Yes, it is.

M.W.: I used to have that. It got lost somewhere along the line in one of our moves. You know how things get lost when you move. I loved that color photo!

S.K.: In fact, it must have been taken, I would guess at a World Series day. There wasn't any empty seat to be found.

M.W: It could have even been an Old Timers' Day game. Those are my favorite games.

S.K.: It could have been. I think this was taken…I only say this because I took a picture like this myself from this location...if you were able to get up on the roof from the Courthouse the next block up across from the Stadium, you had a perfect view of the Stadium. I suspect this is where it was taken from because it's a heck of a shot. It's got the whole Stadium and the Harlem River in the background with the bridge going across it where the Polo Grounds were.

Anyway, I have a lot of photos and junk that wouldn't mean much to you. It means more to me than anyone else. I'm holding one here with Ted Cohen in it. Do you have a foldover from the dedication of the renovated Stadium from April 13th?

M.W.: I bought one on ebay some years ago.

S.K.: Oh, well. I could have sold you a few (we laughed). I would have given you one.

M.W.: What was the hardest part and what was the easiest part of renovating Yankee Stadium?

S.K.: Well, good question. I think the hardest part was to correct the mistakes or oversights in the design. Let me give you some good stories. The removal of the columns that obstructed everybody's view seemed to be one of the key elements of the renovation - and it was. But, oddly enough, despite all the engineering talent that came up with a suggested method to remove the columns, in the end, it took the iron workers with a practical approach to solve the problem. That's probably where I got friendly with Richard Muller. And, if I can bore you with this story…

M.W.: Bore me, bore me!!!

S.K.: Well, I found it fascinating, that despite the fact that I was quite successful with

Walsh Construction, I didn't even graduate college. I didn't have an engineering degree. I did go to school at night for a few years for Construction Management, and took Construction Engineering courses and all, but I never completed the number of credits, and was not interested in becoming a professional engineer. I was more of a construction guy.

But, Praeger Kavanagh Waterbury had on their drawings a proposed or suggested method of tensioning these tieback cables enough to allow removal of the old columns. To try to simplify it, their theory was that if you tightened up the cables enough, you would really lift the ends of the upper deck, thus lifting the load of the weight off of the old columns. Then you could just cut them away with a blow torch and take them away. They even went to the effort of designing the - I guess the tension was measured by some sort of gauge - something to measure the foot pounds as you tension the cable. Anyway, they had this as a suggested method.

In addition to that, they required the contractor of record, who was called Koch Erecting, to hire his own professional engineer to basically launch their method or come up with his own method of removing the columns. So, it was like two heads are better than one type of thing. So, this engineer told them he didn't believe you could ever tighten this cable enough to lift the deck of the 50 year old stadium enough by the slightest amount to take the weight off of those old columns. And, that he believed that the design would work once you got the column out. But, in order to get the column out, you're going to have to support it from underneath, or jack it up a fraction of an inch to get the load off that column because of so much settlement in the stadium.

The stadium had settled tremendously over the years. It would - to exaggerate - it looked like a roller coaster. If you could draw a straight line on a piece of paper from one end of the stadium to the other, the home plate area had settled as much as 12 inches. Now, spread over from end to end, the stadium is more than 1/4 of a mile long. So, spread over a great distance, it wasn't really noticeable to the naked eye. In fact, if you did a survey, it went up and down like a roller coaster.

Anytime, when it came time on the first day to jack out the columns - the engineer who represented Praeger Kavanagh Waterbury on site - had a PhD in Structures.

And he was Asian. And he was from a different culture, so he was wary of New York contractors. I think he felt that most New York contractors were just looking to take shortcuts and do things as quickly as possible, and not follow procedures. So, he wouldn't go along with the suggestion. He wanted them to try the first column his way. They put all these gauges on this column and tightened the cable. The gauges were showing the weight, or load, on the column. I can't explain exactly how they worked, because it was a little bit above my head, to be honest with you. But, the point being that they tensioned the cable and they tensioned the cable. The gauge never moved. It never showed any relief or reduction of the load on the column. They stopped and said, "What do we do now?"

And, Koch's Engineers said that this was what we were trying to explain to you. "Why don't you let us weld a little seat on the side of the old column and put a little hydraulic jack there, like when you jack up your car, and we'll jack up the deck just enough to get daylight on the top of the column? Just enough to know that the weight is off that column." This was after they unbolted the connections. It would be held with jacks. "Meanwhile, we tension the cables to the amount of tension that you designed, because we agree with you that that amount of tension on these cables is going to hold the deck up with no problem. But, we've got to get the weight off of the old columns, and we'll never get it off by trying to pull from behind, like on a seesaw. We've got to relieve it some other way."

He didn't want to go for it, but he said he'd think about it. I had become friendly with this engineer. And, like I said, he had all these degrees. After work, we would play tennis in the park across the street. That night, after we played tennis, he comes to me and says, "Steve, what do you think about their idea about lifting up the weight?" We hadn't taken out the first column yet. His name was Ken Diao. I said, "Ken, I don't think they're trying to trick you or anything. It seems to make good, logical sense to me. And there doesn't seem to be any danger or any harm. They're going to get clearance on the column. They're going to jack it up just a shade. You're going to get cable tension the way you want. And then very gently, they're going to lower the jack. And if the upper deck doesn't move, and you've still got clearance, you're home free." He said, "You know, I think maybe you're right." So, the next day he gave them the okay to do it that way, and it worked like a charm.

But, what always amazed me, and I know this is self serving - but I thought to myself, "Oh, my God! I'm a dumb bricklayer." I started as a bricklayer in the business. My father was a bricklayer. I said, "I'm a dumb bricklayer. This guy's got a PhD in Structures, and he's relying on my recommendation. That's scary!" (we laugh)

M.W.: But you know what, a lot of folks without degrees have a lot of common sense.

S.K.: That's what it really came down to. What it came down to was that he trusted me. We had become friends. He knew I wasn't trying to take any shortcuts. I wasn't a contractor for profit on this job. Like you say, it was logical. But, he had this fear that the contractors for profit that low bid this job were just looking to cut corners to save a buck, and that kind of scared him. Anyway, we removed the first column that way, and it worked perfectly. He was satisfied, and all the rest of the columns were removed by jacking the weight off them just a slight bit, tensioning the cables, and then cutting out the column. As a matter of fact, I have a little black and white photo on my desk here of the first one we took out. I believe it was of February or March of 1975. I also have a photo of the last one. The date on the back of the photo says the last column was removed on March 10, 1975.

M.W.: That's wonderful information!

S.K.: I wrote on the back here. What happened is that I had these pictures taped in a little scrapbook, and over the years with the heat of storing them in the attic, and when I tried to separate them, I lost some of the backing. This looks like it was Column 33 in Section 5. Oh, wait, I see it. It's in right field. That would be Column 33. Okay. I don't know why I put that on there.

M.W.: I'm glad you did for historical purposes.

S.K.: Yeah.

M.W.: Steve, I've heard different things. Was Yankee Stadium actually falling apart? And, did it need the renovation?

S.K.: I've never read anything about it, but I can tell you that when Karl Koch stripped concrete off some of the steel columns that were encased in concrete, and he was supposed to cut them at a certain point, and actually add on a new section of column to an old column, it was frightening. Because, there were places where the steel was so corroded inside the concrete from water getting in, that it was razor thin and falling apart and crumbling. And many, many of the connections (where you added on a new piece of steel to an old piece, whether it be splice plates, welding, etc.) had to be changed because there wasn't enough old steel to make a solid connection. Reinforcing was a joke. When we chopped out concrete, the reinforcing bars in concrete were as thin as spaghetti in places. They had just corroded away over the years.

M.W.: So, are you saying that the grandstand could have fallen with spectators in it?

S.K.: I'm not saying that because I'm not qualified to say that. I don't know. All I know is that it looked pretty scary in places. That's for sure. I wondered what held it up.

M.W.: It's sounds like the White House when Harry Truman was there. They said it stood out of habit.

S.K.: I would say that was true of Yankee Stadium. And these expansion joints that we replaced were prime examples. There were three expansion joints, as I recall. I think the first one was at Column 9 that was in right field. All we were supposed to do - I want to say - was chop two or three feet of the old concrete on each side of the expansion joint and put in this new expansion joint assembly, then replace the concrete that we had chopped out, putting in new reinforcing bars and tying them in with the old reinforcing bars. And that's when it became obvious that there was virtually no reinforcing left in these things.

M.W.: So, it needed the renovation.

S.K.: Oh, it needed the renovation. In my mind, and a lot of the contractors' minds, was that it needed to be taken down and rebuilt.

M.W.: You mean level the whole stadium?

S.K.: Yep.

M.W.: Oh My God!

S.K.: Not so much because of the danger of failure. More from a practical standpoint. A lot of the construction guys, not most, were of the opinion that it would probably had been cheaper to demolish the whole thing in one swoop, just implode it, and build a new one in less time and for less money.

M.W.: I show in the book that Matt Troy and others on the city council were constantly against the money getting poured into the Stadium. The expenses just kept getting higher and higher.

S.K.: At that time, this was 40 years ago, who knows? A new one could have been built with less effort and you would have had a nicer stadium. It wouldn't have had the nostalgia behind it...you talked about problems. The column thing turned out to not be a serious problem. We just had to find a new approach to cut the columns out.

But, one of the most serious problems which did created a lot of problems...I mentioned to you already how the stadium had settled over the years...there was a foundation study that had been done. Unless you read the foundation study carefully, you probably wouldn't have been familiar with how bad the settlement was. And I hate to be critical of the designers. But, as we got into the mechanical work in the building, specifically down in the basement, duct work...we had trouble fitting duct work, because there was not enough ceiling height. And the mechanical engineers were always arguing with us..."What do you mean there's not enough height?" There's supposed to be whatever the dimension was, a 10 foot ceiling, for instance, and you only had a 12 inch duct...you can still have a 9-foot ceiling, etc. Things like that. Then we would say, "Yeah, but you're not taking into consideration the settlement." They'd say, "What settlement?" Not to public knowledge at the time, but they finally admitted they had not read the Foundation Study. They didn't think it would affect them or apply to them, so they never read it.

Again, if you can visualize this…if you can visualize horizontal lines representing the different floor levels…let's just take the first floor…I'll call it the ground floor. In theory, it's supposed to be a horizontal line. But, as I explained, it was more like a roller coaster. Behind home plate was the worst. Now, if you picture the worst area that is now 12 inches down from its theoretical position, here's the problem where they screwed up. When it settled, the whole building settled. So, the floor, lets call it the basement floor, and the ground floor, being the ceiling of the basement…they all settled together. So, if there was 9 or 10 feet of height between the basement floor and the ceiling originally, there was still 9 or 10 feet of height because it all settled together. Well, the architect designed the remodeled stadium to rip out the entire basement floor and put in a new floor dead level. But, they didn't straighten out the next floor up. So, if the ceiling came down 12 inches, and the floor is ripped out and a new one is put in dead level, unless you went down an extra 12 inches, which they didn't do, you're going to lose that 12 inches. It was expensive to correct this situation.

If you can visualize a cross-section of the field level stands, naturally they are sloped liked theater seating. If you're up in the back row, you're higher up, and if you're down at field level, you're lower down. In a cross section, that creates a triangle of wasted space because the area under those seats is level. Let's say the ceiling of the ground floor is basically level. Meanwhile, the seats at the field are sloping upwards to the next level. So, there's a triangle of space under the seats that's really wasted space, sort of like attic space. So, what the designers and engineers had to do when there wasn't room to get duct work under low beams, whereas normally we would just pass under the beam, we chopped holes in the ceiling and turned the duct work vertical. We then went up in this attic space, back across over the top of the beam, chopped another hole, and went back down, then came out the other side. I know it's all difficult to visualize, but the ceiling height issue in the basement became a real problem for getting air conditioning duct work and heating duct work from one section over to the next section because of lack of head room.

M.W.: It sounds very time consuming.

S.K.: It was time consuming. It gave the mechanical contractor an excuse for time delays and he got paid extra costs to reroute duct work. And someone else got paid extra costs to chop holes in concrete that wasn't supposed to get chopped. It was a pain in the neck. But, the embarrassing part from the designer's standpoint was…looking back, I don't know whose responsibility it was in the first place, but the mechanical engineer's position was that "I never have to read a foundation report. That usually goes to the soils people, and has to do with what kind of foundation it is due to soil conditions." But, buried in there was this whole world of information about the settlement, and no one seemed to grasp the fact that this settlement was going to affect the alterations to the degree that it did. But, like everything else, it got worked out and corrected. But, there were many areas in the basement where the ceiling heights were lowered beyond what people wanted it to be.

M.W.: Was Yankee Stadium well built or not well built?

S.K.: Oh, I think it was well built. But, I mean it's how they did things 50 years ago. Are you talking about the new or old Stadium?

M.W.: The one you were at…the renovated Stadium.

S.K.: Oh, it was well built.

M.W.: I took some photos of what looks like logs, or telephone poles. I guess they were piers to keep the Stadium level. For instance, go to page 166.

S.K.: Page 166. Those are wood pilings. We drove piles for the foundations for the escalator towers. You're looking at the extreme left field where the escalator tower was going to go. In fact, if you go to the picture just to the right of it on the other page, where the guard is walking past, that's the formwork coming up for the escalator tower that's sitting on top of the piles that you refer to as the wood pilings. In other words, they drove wood pilings, then put in the foundations, then came up with the escalator tower.

M.W.: So, I guess that's the same with pages 179 and 180.

S.K.: Oh, yeah. Absolutely. That's the other escalator tower in right field. There were three escalator towers.

M.W.: Right. I thought those were foundations like you see in old houses.

S.K.: That's what they were. That's correct. These were then cut off and concrete was poured around them for a footing. Then you come up with the structure above it.

M.W.: But, these were not in the old Stadium. You guys put them in, is that correct?

S.K.: That's right, that's right. These were brand new for the new escalator towers.

M.W.: I thought they were from the old Stadium.

S.K.: No, no, no, no, no. These are brand new for the new escalator towers.

M.W.: Do you know where the cement was being dumped during demolition phase of the renovation?

S.K.: I have no idea. It's something, that frankly, we didn't even give a second thought to at the time.

M.W.: A number of people thought it may have been dumped in New York City area to different construction sites.

S.K.: It could be. There was nothing sacred about it. It was just rubble. The fact that it came from Yankee Stadium - I don't think anybody at the time got too excited over it.

M.W.: Jay Schwall said there was a man named Kahn, in upstate New York that melted down most of the copper frieze.

S.K: That could be. I don't know. I think I read someplace in your book where there was some disagreement as to whether there was copper in it or there wasn't copper in it.

M.W.: Well, Jay Schwall said it was 100 percent pure copper. I really asked Jay about that because I knew how important it was to people. He said it was 100 percent copper. I came across so many different answers.

S.K.: Copper would be valuable, of course. And, it probably made sense because it didn't rust out.

M.W.: Do you have any more funny stories?

S.K.: Yes, but I won't keep you much longer, because it's been a long day. I have some funny personal stories, if you're interested.

M.W.: Sure, sure.

S.K.: Let me give you one that's not a funny story, but...in the visitor's locker room, I personally salvaged...they had the old style Coca Cola cooler chest on wheels. You can lift up the top and pull out a bottle of Coke. That's the only piece of memorabilia that I really hung onto. It was old and the inside was galvanized. The inside was beginning to rust. But, it worked. It was modern enough that it plugged into the wall. It was refrigerated. I guess the real old ones used chunks of ice instead. Anyway, I managed to get that into the back of a Jeep I was driving - obviously with some help, and took it to the first home I was living in Bayside, Queens, New York. And we kept that in the garage until we got transferred to Chicago. We used it for barbeques and backyard picnics, and whatever, and it was the talk of the neighborhood, because everybody knew it was the Coca Cola cooler from Yankee Stadium! (laughs) That was just a fun thing for me.

You mentioned American Seating in your book. I was sent by the city to Grand Rapids, Michigan, to count seats, if you can believe this. I really didn't physically count every seat. But, the city had a provision in their contract that if something was manufactured and stored off-site, the contractor was entitled to be paid for it, provided it was confirmed that it was properly stored and had an insurance policy to protect it in case of fire, theft, etc. Being how we were falling behind schedule from the original schedule, theoretically, although we made it in the end, American Seating wanted to get paid for their seats. So the city sent me out to Grand Rapids and I went to this warehouse...what they really did was count boxes of seats because they were all in parts or pieces. So, that was an interesting trip for me.

Visits from some of the famous people - Joe DiMaggio. On one of Joe DiMaggio's visits, because I think he came to the Stadium twice...on one of his visits, and I've got his autograph from that day, as a matter of fact...I think it was July of 1975, the word went out that workers were hanging around the trailer, waiting to see Joe. We had a procedure to where the visitors, no matter who they were, and the Press, would have to come into the trailer where I was, and get a pass to tour the Stadium. They also had to get a hard hat. I was the guy who most of the days would give out the passes. So, Joe was supposed to come, but he was delayed. In the meantime, I had work to do. I got called out to the field, which means that you leave the construction trailer and go into the site. I got my hard hat, and a couple of Walsh co-workers asked where I was going. I said, "I have to go out to the job." They said, "Now? Joe DiMaggio's coming!" I said, "I have things to do. I have to go."

So, I go out to the Stadium, and I'm out there for several hours. Low and behold, I'm walking around, and they were demolishing the Bleachers. In the distance I see someone walking around near one of the columns. I look, and I see its Joe DiMaggio. He was with a photographer and reporter. I got Joe's autograph. When I came back to the trailer, the guys said, "You missed Joe." I said, "No, I didn't miss him. I got to see him." They asked, "Where did you get to see him?" I said, "Out in the Bleachers." I had a little pocket diary, and he happened to sign it on the date that I saw him. He signed his name across my little pocket diary.

M.W.: So you kept a diary of the renovation? Wow!

S.K.: No, no. I didn't keep a diary. It's one of those little calendar memos that you get as advertisement from people. I kept it as a notebook in my pocket. I didn't keep copious notes in it. It just happened to be what I had in my pocket, so I had it with me.

The other thing that I did that was a personal thing was embarrassing. I was inside the trailer and hear some people come in. Somebody says, "Where's Steve Koch?" I said, "I'm over here." He says, "I'm supposed to see him for a pass." I was in the midst of doing something, it was hectic, and I didn't even look at the guy. He comes over, and I had a pad of passes. You just write one, tear it off, and give it to the person. I didn't even look up at him. I said, "What's your name?" He said, "It's Gifford." I said, "What's your first name?" With frustration in his voice, he said, "Frank." I looked up and said, "Oh! Frank Gifford! Hello, Mr. Gifford!" I never felt so stupid! (we both laughed) I wasn't really paying attention. Those are the kinds of things that made the job fun at times.

M.W.: I understand that there were about 500 workers at the site. Is that right?

S.K.: You know, I don't remember, but I think that was at the very peak. And, it might have been a little bit of a stretch. It varied. I couldn't swear that we ever got that high. But, it was close.

M.W.: Are there any closing thoughts that you have on anything, Steve?

S.K.: No, not at the moment. Is there anything for me that you'd be interesting in having, such as any photographs? I have five Opening Day tickets unused, if you'd like to use it as a photo.

M.W.: I wanted to use that in the book, but the Yankees organization never gave me permission to use that or anything else.

S.K.: From my calendar - I don't know how I ended up with two of these, but I've got a June 1974 page ripped out of my pocket calendar with Joe DiMaggio's signature. I've got a July 1974 page from my pocket calendar, also with Joe DiMaggio's name.

M.W.: If you want to send them, I can put them in the book, if they're yours.

S.K.: I'd be happy to send a copy to you.

M.W.: That would be neat.

S.K.: I'm going to read more of the book, and if I come up with any new thoughts to talk to you about, I'd be happy to do it. I'm looking here at my notes…cracks in the concrete façade. You're not interested in that.

M.W.: What was that?

S.K.: The painting contractor for NAB-Tern had the job of painting all the exterior walls, which were concrete. There were a lot of cracks. And they wanted to patch the cracks. This is where the one time I got misquoted as being the Chief Engineer for Walsh. I was walking around with a couple of the Department of Public Works (DPW) guys, and they were arguing about these cracks. The painter said he would fill them in and do the best he can, but it won't repair them. They would crack again. One of the city guys wanted to make a big deal over the cracks, like, would the walls fall down, would they be structurally safe, and all this nonsense. That's when I just piped up and said, "The wall is only a façade. The building structure, as far as safety, is steel. Yeah, the concrete might crumble and a piece of it may fall out, but the building will never fall down. It has nothing to do with supporting the building. It's not structural concrete." It's just like what they would do today with plaster board, except that this was concrete. "Oh!" That's when the light dawned for the DPW employees. That's when there was some quote in the paper that said, "Walsh Construction's Chief Engineer, Steve Koch said that cracks in the concrete are okay." I nearly got fired.

M.W.: Amsterdam Color Works in the Bronx supplied the paint for the Stadium. Victor Strauss of Ben Strauss Industries was the painter.

S.K. That's who I thought it might have been. I think it was Victor Strauss. In fact, I thought I had a picture of Victor Strauss here. I have a big, fancy picture here, but it's not Victor Strauss. In August 1974, somebody took an 8 1/2"x11" color photo of me standing in front of a bulldozer with the excavation contractor, I guess, Ted Cohen, and one of Ted Cohen's men. God, was I really that young? My little pocket protector with all the pens and pencils that my daughter makes fun of. She said, "Dad, you wore a pocket protector? Oh! How tacky!" I see I also had a little Skil in my pocket, like I was somebody important. Oh well, you bring back memories, Michael.

M.W.: I'm happy to do it. I'm glad Suzanne contacted me.

S.K.: It's funny how it all happened.

M.W.: I know there's a lot of people out there that I've never contacted. A number of people have died and other people…where are they? I don't know.

S.K.: Right, right.

M.W.: You probably know there was a laborer on the job whose name was Joe DiMaggio.

S.K.: Yes, yes, I did know that. I think I read that in the book. It did not surprise me. It's a common Italian name. It's not that unique. It's just like I met Steve Koch and he thought I was being a smart ass. (laughs)

M.W.: Right. Is there anything you want people to know that is not known about the renovation or Yankee Stadium itself that should be known?

S.K.: There isn't anything, frankly, that jumps out in my head that would mean anything to anybody or be of real significance. Off the top of my head, I can't think of anything.

M.W.: I just didn't know that the columns were in such bad shape. We didn't deal with it because we were fans just going to the games, so we had no idea about that.

S.K.: The columns that were obstructing your view, those were solid. Those were okay. The columns in the back of the stadium that were buried in concrete…what happens is that concrete gets cracks…and then water infiltrates inside the concrete and lays there, and rots away the steel. The columns that were exposed are in the best condition.

M.W.: So, those were fine.

S.K.: Yes, those were fine because those are repainted on a regular basis. And the ones that were holding up the Stadium were just like the Whitestone Bridge. They get sandblasted and painted regularly, and those are fine. You see, those you can see the deterioration. The problem was the deterioration that you couldn't see because that was buried inside of the concrete. That's where the problem was.

Whether it was reinforced steel or a structural column encased in concrete - either way, when you chop away the concrete you see what's left inside, you say, "Oh My God! How did this thing stand up?" I'm sure there were others where we didn't chop away the concrete that were still there. Well, not anymore, since they took the building down.

Oh, well. I think I've about had it.

M.W.: Steve, thank you so much.

S.K.: You're welcome, Michael. [16]

S.K: You said that when the tape cut off last time we talked, that you lost some of the information. I'm not sure how much we need to talk about, but I think you lost the part about my mother-in-law, Angela, or "Angie," as we called her.

M.W.: Yes, that was lost.

S.K.: I was just commenting at the time that she was a big baseball fan. Her father-in-law was actually an umpire, so with her, especially with her very modest background, she was so thrilled to be at the Opening Day game, and that her son-in-law was involved with the construction.

That one photo of my family that I sent you that was taken on Opening Day in 1976, with Suzanne, Kim, myself, and Jean...the reason Jean is not in it is that she was the one taking the picture. I think I mentioned to you in the past, after the game, we were able to go back to George Steinbrenner's office, where he had a little reception for guests. They served cocktails and hors d'oeuvres. My mother-in-law ended up sitting on the couch in Steinbrenner's office between Governor Brendan Byrne of New Jersey, and Governor Hugh Carey of New York. It was a big thrill for her. She was raised in a Catholic orphanage in Staten Island, had very little exposure to the outside world, and she just couldn't believe that she was sitting there at the new Stadium with people at that level. That was a big thrill for her.

M.W.: It sounds like she may have been a peace keeper between those two governors.

S.K.: (Laughs). She may have been. It was certainly one of those days where politics wasn't the topic of conversation. The other thing I mentioned to you is that she was always a big fan of Joe Garagiola, Sr. As you know, his son, Joe, Jr., worked for the Yankees. I got pretty friendly with his son, and ended up mentioning to him that the sun rose and set with his father. So, he was kind enough to one day bring me an 8 1/2"x11" black and white photo of his dad, who was kind enough to have written on it, "Best Wishes to Angie, Joe Garagiola." As I tell you this, I have no idea what happened to the photo. My mother-in-law passed away about

10 years ago, and I was the one emptying out her house. She was alone by then, and I don't ever recall finding the photo, but I know she enjoyed getting it.

M.W. My grandmother (Rose) was a big fan of Lawrence Welk. One day I wrote to him and he was nice enough to inscribe a color photo to her. She was very happy to have it because she always watched his show on TV. She proudly displayed it in a frame in her kitchen in Brooklyn.

S.K.: The one photo I sent you...when I took her with me on one of the days when we toured the Stadium...she had a big thrill when she did that.

M.W.: Not many people get to do that.

S.K.: Yes, not very many.

M.W.: Let me ask you about Mark Ravitz, the gentleman who had the questions about the louvers pertaining to the section around Michael Burke's office. He would like to know what was put in that area of the Stadium.

S.K.: I can't remember exactly where that louver was located or what was behind it. In general, they were nothing more than just ventilation louvers, either in the concourses where you walked in the back of the Stadium, or in some cases, mechanical equipment rooms for ventilation. But, it would not have been inside a private office. It might have been on the level where his office was, but I don't recall a louver in anybody's office. That wouldn't make sense.

M.W.: I spoke to him earlier today. He received a copy of my book Monday. He loves the book! Mark told me on page 170 I captured a perfect picture of the exact area he's talking about.

S.K.: Oh, okay. Those real tall louvers were against the ramps in the concourses where people walked up and down. I can't tell you after about 40 years which louver was in which location or which office. But, like I said, in general they were never in anybody's office. My recollection is that most of the offices were towards the interior, not the exterior of the building.

M.W.: Here's another question brought up by Mark, regarding page 170. You have square windows, then louvers on both sides of the windows. Why would there be square windows instead of louvers all the way across?

S.K.: I really don't remember, to be quite honest with you.

S.K.: One of the guys I remember at the Stadium, and he certainly didn't leave me with a great impression, was Howard Cosell.

M.W.: I didn't like him.

S.K.: Talk about a guy who was stuck on himself! Oh my God! He was a piece of work. I had the occasion...he came to the Stadium...it must have been shortly before or after it opened. Steinbrenner was working in his office on a daily basis. For some reason the elevator wasn't working, because I remember walking up these ramps to bring Cosell up to Steinbrenner's office to show him where it was. People would not have been able to find it unless somebody directed them to the office. So, I was escorting him up to Steinbrenner's office. He began telling me how well he knew Steinbrenner and what he'd done for him. He did this sort of boasting, and he had no reason to impress me. I was just a construction worker to him. I thought that this guy was just so full of himself. But, anyway, I took him up to Steinbrenner's office (laughs).

And, George Steinbrenner himself was not the most friendly guy - or at least to strangers, or people that he didn't employ or were not on his team, or friends. Because I happened to ride with him a couple of times a week on the elevator as he was coming into the Stadium to go to his office, and I was going to the Stadium to do my job. We got into the elevator, and I can't remember him ever saying, "Good morning."

M.W.: Did he give a lot of input into the work you were doing, or did he not mention it?

S.K.: No, no, he did none of that. It was through the city. He didn't get involved in any of that. This person that you wrote about - Perry Green - I don't know what his connection was, but nobody had a lot of respect for Perry Green. I hate to say that. Perry Green was, I'm sure by education, was an architect. And, whether he was hired by the Steinbrenner family or another reason, what he did at the Stadium, I can't tell you. He had an office or trailer. I can't remember anybody ever consulting him for anything, or his getting involved in any decision making. The design was already completed by the time he got there. And, if it was a construction problem, he didn't get involved in solving the construction problems. So, it was sort of strange as to what his role was. He didn't have much to do with the Stadium.

M.W.: Did you ever meet Michael Burke?

S.K.: Not formally. I was across the table from him, but I didn't deal with him or meet him in a way as to where I could tell you any good stories.

M.W.: I love Michael Burke. He was a great gentleman!

S.K.: Kim got to know a lot of the staff of the Yankees. They were all nice guys. They were fun to be with. They were not like George Steinbrenner. I remember Mike Rendine. I think he was the ticket manager. Of course, everybody was always trying to be nice to him so they could get good seats to the games. Some of the grounds crew…there was an old timer. I wish I could remember his name.

M.W.: Was it Jimmy Esposito?

S.K.: Jimmy Esposito was the head of the ground crew. The one I'm thinking of only had one arm. He was a heck of a nice guy and one of the hardest workers. When you saw how he was able to cradle a rake and rake the infield, and do his job with just one arm, it was very admirable. He was also a very nice guy. Jimmy Esposito was well liked.

M.W.: Is there anything you would like to add that is of great importance?

S.K.: I don't think so, Michael. It was a great experience. It's amazing when you get older and you think back that not only were you there many years ago, but the building is gone. It was a great time.

M.W.: When I was talking to Mark, he was shocked that I was able to walk onto the baseball field during the renovation. There wasn't much security, and I was just a regular guy able to walk about freely. Nowadays you'd probably get arrested or shot.

S.K.: That's true, that's true.

M.W.: Back then, the memorabilia industry was in its infancy, so the memorabilia we see today wasn't important.

S.K.: It was definitely different then.

I may have told you this. We brought the kids, Suzanne and Kim, in one night. My wife and I were tennis players, and I heard that Billie Jean King was going to be there. The Stadium was almost completed, and hadn't opened yet. She was going to be there filming a commercial for a soda company with her brother, Randy Moffitt, who pitched for the Giants. That was a funny experience, to watch them film the commercial. It was after hours, so nobody was at the Stadium. The four of us were in the first or second row behind home plate, just watching them.

It was one of those typical scenes for producers, where they go through a million takes until they get it correct, because there's always interference, or someone messes up a word, or something goes wrong. It was sort of a play on words between Billie Jean and her brother. I wish I could remember the lines, as it was cute. But, what we remember about it is that they thought they finally had it down pat. Just when they were shooting the end of the commercial, the elevated subway line behind the bleachers came roaring by, and that sound ruined the take.

Billie Jean was so frustrated that she said, "Oh, shit!" She then turned around and saw our two young daughters there, and came over and apologized for her foul language. The kids remember that to this day (laughs).

Anyway, Michael, it was a pleasure talking with you.

M.W.: Same here, Steve, as always.

S.K.: If you have anything that comes up or have any other questions, I'll be happy to tell you what I can.

M.W.: Thank you, Steve. And, if I can do anything for you, please let me know. [17]

Top photo shows Steve Koch and his daughters, Suzanne (left), and Kim (right). Steve's Mother-in-Law, Angela Miles, shows a nice batting style in the bottom left photo. Lucky Steve lives the dream of standing on the Yankee Stadium pitcher's mound in the bottom right photo. Photos courtesy of Steven Koch.

Views of grandstand during Yankee Stadium renovation. Photos courtesy of Steven Koch.

Crew dismantling a column during 1970s renovation. Photo courtesy of Steven Koch.

Concrete stringer being hoisted at Gate 6. Photo courtesy of Steven Koch.

Steve Koch (left) and Ken Diao inspecting reinforcing steel placement in preparation for concrete placement on the new upper deck, June 1974. Photo courtesy photo of Steven Koch. Below are two autographs of Yankee legend Joe DiMaggio obtained by Steve Koch.

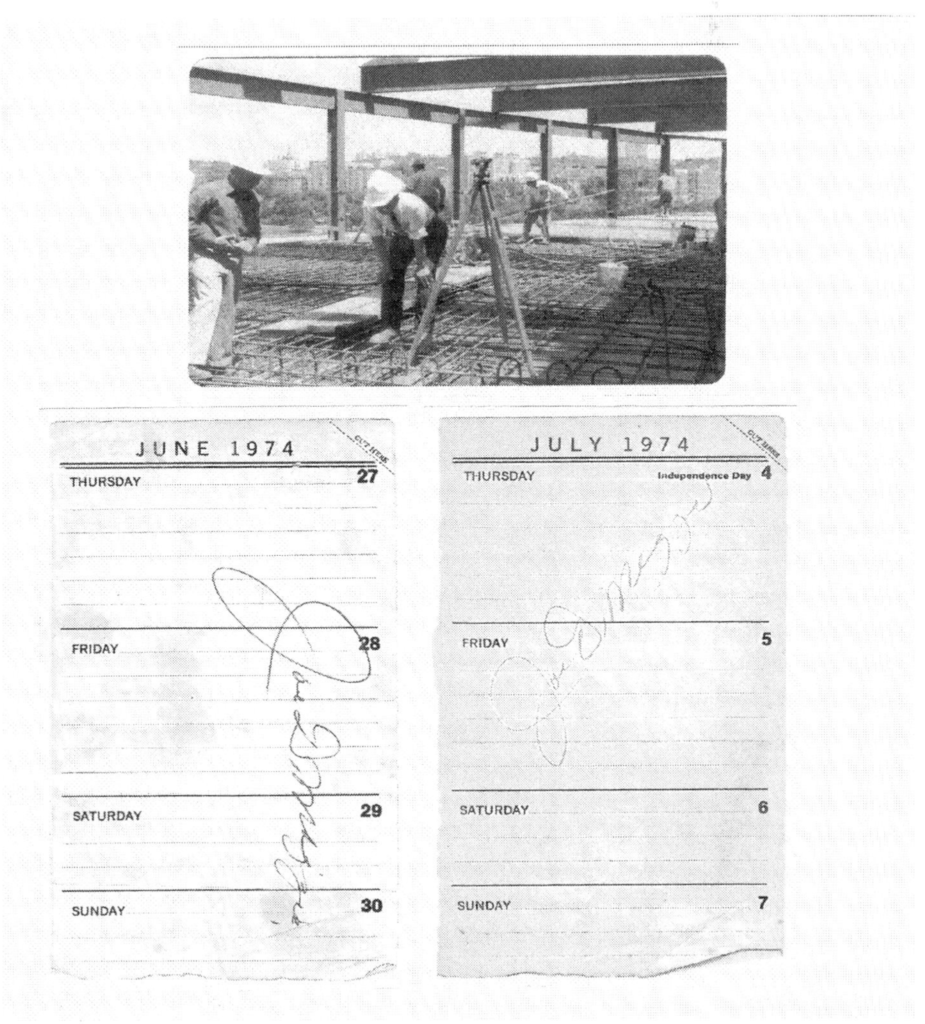

Ted Cohen (2nd from left) and Steve Koch (far right) at Yankee Stadium worksite. Photo courtesy of Steven Koch.

UNISTRESS

Unistress Corporation (www.unistresscorp.com), located on 72 acres in Pittsfield, Massachusetts, manufactured the precast concrete stadia pieces for the iconic Yankee Stadium frieze in the 1970s Yankee Stadium modernization. These panels, each weighing 8,000 to 9,000 pounds, had been bolted above the bleachers, and made Yankee fans feel right at home.

Unistress also produced the stringers used to hold 10 rows of seating in the Upper Deck of the renovated stadium. In addition, the company supplied precast concrete for the parking garage and escalator pods.

The Unistress/Yankee tradition continues today, as Unistress built three parking garages for the new Yankee Stadium, which opened in 2009.

Unistress is the seventh largest precut manufacturer in the country. Unistress is a subsidiary of Petricca Industries, a third generation family owned and operated business founded in 1969. They've completed more than 500 precast structures in the northeast, such as multi-level parking garages for 1,000 or more vehicles, bridges, commercial and industrial buildings, stadiums, and railway stations. They've won numerous Precast/Prestressed Concrete Institute (PCI) and other awards for their superior quality of work.

Unistress provided concrete segments for the massive "Big Dig," which was the Boston Central Artery/Tunnel. This project lasted from 1991 until its completion in 2006.

Unistress recently landed a $70 million contract to provide concrete deck panels for the new Tappan Zee Bridge in New York. This is the largest contract in the company's history. [18]

My deepest thanks to Rick Petricca, Vice President of Unistress, for his kindness in responding to my inquiry about Unistress and his company's role in the remodeling of Yankee Stadium.

Chapter Eight

MORE PHOTOS AND MEMORIES OF YANKEE STADIUM

ROGER MARIS TRIBUTE

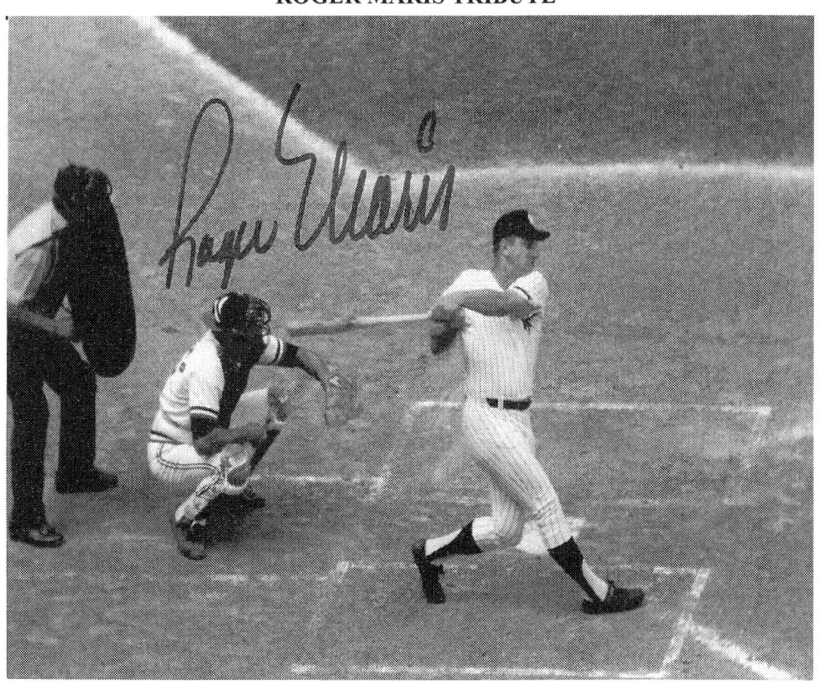

While I have a deep love and respect for the New York Yankees and their proud history, there are always some people that touch our hearts more than others. Of course the usual heroes come to mind, such as Babe Ruth, Lou Gehrig, Joe DiMaggio, Mickey Mantle…the list can go on forever.

Growing up in the 1960s in West Hempstead, Long Island, New York, I was also an autograph collector. The first autograph request I sent was to Joe DiMaggio at the 1967 Yankee Old Timers' Day game. I was hooked. I later sent to Joe and other Yankees at other Old Timers' Day games, as well as to the Stadium. Later, I came across home addresses of ballplayers.

Roger Maris was one of them. Like many of the baseball players of Roger's era, Roger was kind enough to autograph anything I would send him. Mickey Mantle did, too. I was surprised that Mickey did so as well because he was such a superstar, that I didn't think he'd take the time to comply with such a mundane request. Sometimes it's nice to be wrong.

The reason that Roger remained so close to my heart, was because of his kindness towards me. We'd met briefly in 1964, when my dad took us to a game. I guess it must have been inside Gate 4 or 6. I was only nine years old. A Yankee in a uniform nearly ran into us. He said, "excuse me." We didn't know who it was. When he turned to go into a door, the number "9" told us who it was. I exclaimed to my dad, "That's Roger Maris!" That was the only time we'd met in person, although he'd never remember it, I'm sure. Yet, seeing a Yankee in uniform like that still gives me a great thrill when I remember it.

I have a very hard time with unfairness. It doesn't have to be against me. I like the good guy to win and people to do what's right. It makes life so much nicer. One of my earliest battles was defending Roger Maris. I wrote a "Letter To The Editor," and *Newsday* did publish it on May 14, 1972. It read:

In Defense of...

I'm writing to all news media through Newsday to disprove a mistake that the press made 12 years ago. It concerns ex-Yankee Roger Maris. He was chasing after Babe Ruth's 60 home runs. The media made Roger out to be a bad person because there were times he wouldn't want to be interviewed, or so I've read in baseball magazines. It was because Roger had a hard and nervous time thinking about breaking Babe's record. He couldn't take all the questions thrown at him day after day and wanted to have peace and privacy. When I'm nervous I try to keep to myself, too. It had to be the worst time in Roger's life!!!

Now it's 12 years later, and peace for Roger Maris. I sent for his autograph quite a few times, and he always signs what I send him. I also sent Roger baseball cards and some other things to keep to show my gratitude. He even sometimes sends them back to me autographed. Ted Williams, who the press also mocked, is quite a nice person too. He's also kind to me the way Roger is. There are others who I send to. Most of these very famous people give me the same courtesy Roger and Ted do.

I feel that all the media owes Roger Maris and Ted Williams a very deep apology for the rough treatment of the past. I've given my story. That's my opinion. What's yours?

Mike Wagner
West Hempstead

Yes, the copy is smudged, but I still feel pride when I look at it. Even little achievements feel noteworthy.

While in the Air Force at Langley Air Force Base in Virginia, from 1982 thru 1990, I went to Spring Training for about seven years. One year I decided to go to the Boston Red Sox camp in Winter Haven, Florida, to see if baseball God, Ted Williams was there. I asked a man who worked there if Ted was around. He pointed to a distant ball field.

Even though I'm a Yankee fan, I felt a surge of excitement. I was surprised at how tall Ted was. He was also so nice to the fans and signed anything for us. When someone asked him a baseball question when a bunch of us were sitting near the field, we all stopped talking to hear Ted's answer. Like Roger, Ted was a gem.

My favorite Yankee games were the Old Timers' Day games. Seeing our heroes, taking photos, and sometimes meeting some was pure heaven! The photo I took of Roger was at the June 21, 1980 Old Timers' Day game. I love his level swing! I had a number of reprints made. Roger was kind enough to sign them for me through the mail. I sent him some to keep. He was ALWAYS wonderful to me.

When he died in 1985 from cancer, I cried for three days straight. The day after he died I was scheduled to play Santa Claus at a local hospital. Although not in the mood to do so, I rationalized that "Roger would want me to do it." It's not easy when your beloved hero dies. It took me years to get over it. Even now while writing this - 27 years later, it still hurts. Love is great when your loved one is alive and well. When they're not, then it's a different story. My mom died at age 41 in 1975 of cancer. Both of these wonderful people left us far too early.

Baseball binds people together in so many ways. Some things in life do that. Years ago I wanted to give a tribute to Roger Maris - one of my biggest heroes. I suppose I haven't had the forum until now. That's the beauty of self-publishing. You can get personal if you wish. Maybe you're not supposed to. I don't know. But, I felt that if I were to ever write a book, it would have warmth and humanity in it.

I learned that from my parents, Michael Burke, my Aunts Elsie and Elaine, Dale Carnegie, Leo Buscaglia, Ellen Kreidman, and many others. I have quite a few heroes, as do so many other people. For whatever reason, certain people touch us more than others.

Mickey Mantle affected us through his great talent although he played with terrible pain. Lou Gehrig does so as well because of his tragic end.

People such as Bill "Moose" Skowron, Bobby Richardson, Abraham Lincoln, Superman, and so many more of my heroes have affected me in a positive way. Roger Maris touched me the most, although we'd met only briefly. Michael Burke, president of the Yankees in the 1960s and 1970s was the same way, although I did have the joy and honor of meeting him and getting his autograph at Yankee games. Also, Roger persevered in hitting 61 home runs in 1961 to eclipse Babe Ruth's record of 60, although it was under the most trying circumstances. Roger still did his best. We build up our heroes and connect with them for whatever reason. Having such role models is what helps us get through life. We think of them and they give us the strength to go on. You don't have to be famous to be a hero.

One such person was Yvette Maldonado, who lived near Hicksville, New York. I was working at a check printing company in that town during the 1980s. Yvette was possibly the first person who let me see it was okay to be in touch with my feelings. She physically touched everyone. Just thinking about it now, I can still feel her warmth and love for others. Yvette is one such person who has made me a better and more caring and loving person. I pass on her gift daily, as human touch and encouragement is so important to our mental, spiritual, and physical well being. Other heroes are waitresses, the mailman, the trashman, nurses…anyone who performs their job on a daily basis. Or, anyone who makes us a better person, and spreads light in the world.

We are all living encyclopedias. We bring our experiences in life with us wherever we travel. Part of this experience is that my being ambidextrous was fun when playing stickball while growing up. I could bat as Mickey, Roger, Yogi…every Yankee batter. Then I could pitch as Whitey, Al Downing, or Jim Bouton...every Yankee pitcher. Life isn't too dull when you're an oddball.

In closing, Roger, this is my tribute to you. You'll forever have my deepest love and respect because of the fine gentleman you were. Thank You, Roger. In fact, this applies to all of my heroes for making me a more loving and nicer person.

Opera star Robert Merrill singing the National Anthem prior to the Yankees Old Timers' Day game of June 21, 1980. Yankee announcer and Master of Ceremonies, Frank Messer, is in the foreground. Merrill wore uniform number 1 1/2.

Mel Allen (L) and Frank Messer (R), during the Yankee Old Timers' Day game of Saturday, June 21, 1980.

Yankee Stadium from 158th Street and Walton Avenue, October 3, 2006. Below, Yankee Stadium with the Macombs Dam Bridge Approach in the foreground, October 7, 2007. Photographs © Gary Dunaier

Yankee Stadium with the pedestrian walkway over the Metro-North railroad tracks, October 3, 2006. Below, Yankee Stadium as seen from the Major Deegan Expressway. Photographs © Gary Dunaier

Right field bleachers and Grandstand, April 21, 2008. Courtesy of Matthew King.

Frieze photo showing thickness of the icon in renovated Yankee Stadium, April 21, 2008. Photo is taken from bleachers. Courtesy of Matthew King.

Loading dock & Upper Deck, April 21, 2008. Courtesy of Matthew King.

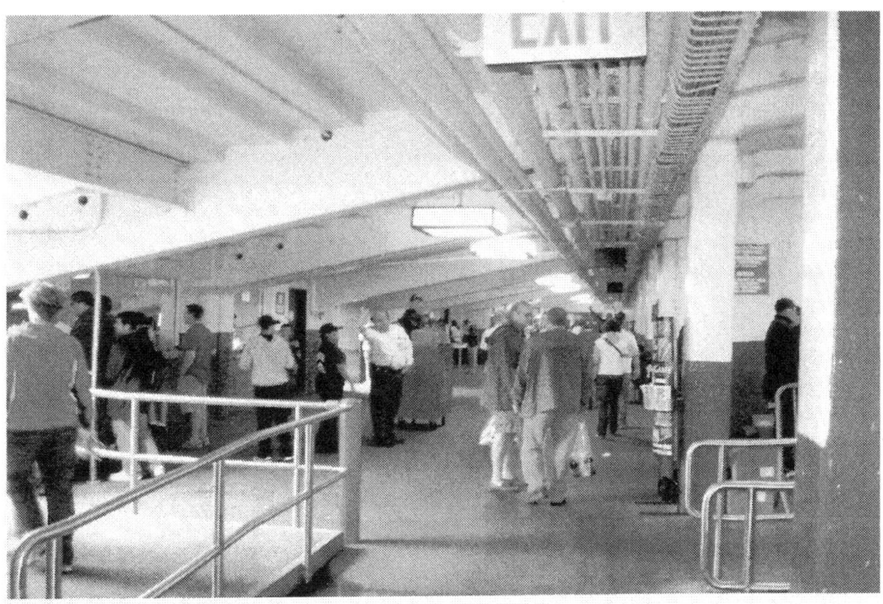

Interior Bleacher Concourse, April 21, 2008. Courtesy of Matthew King.

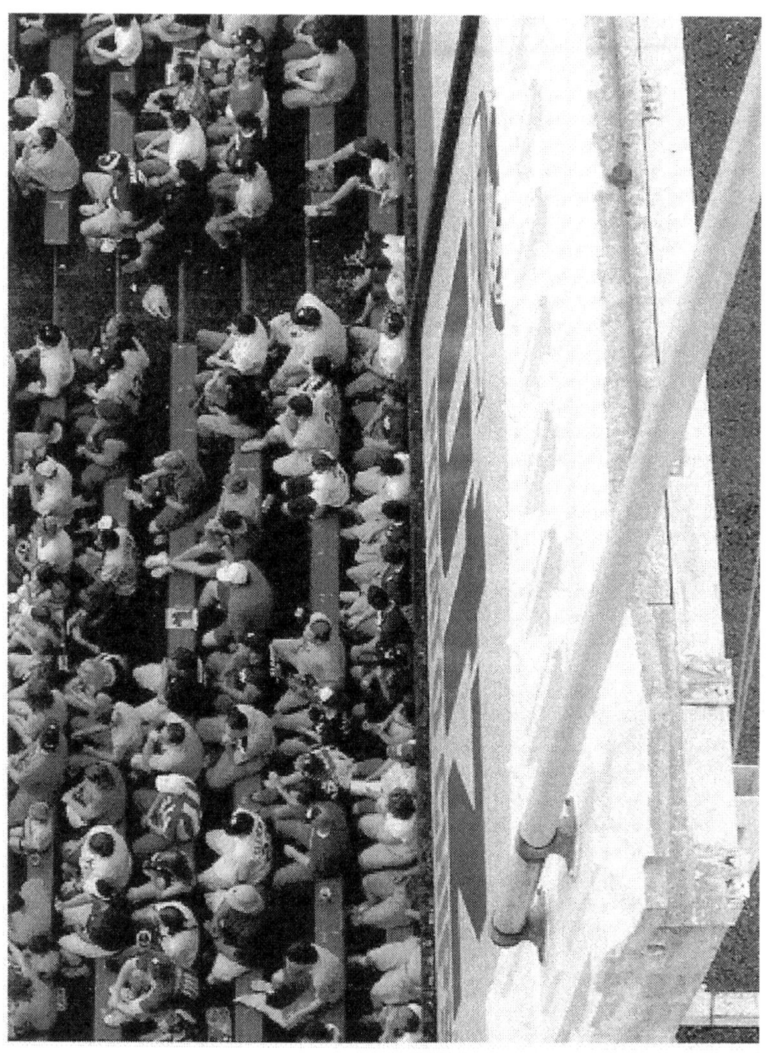

Unusual view of top of right field frieze from Tier Reserved 35, Row X, Seat 12, July 1, 2008. Photo © Gary Dunaier.

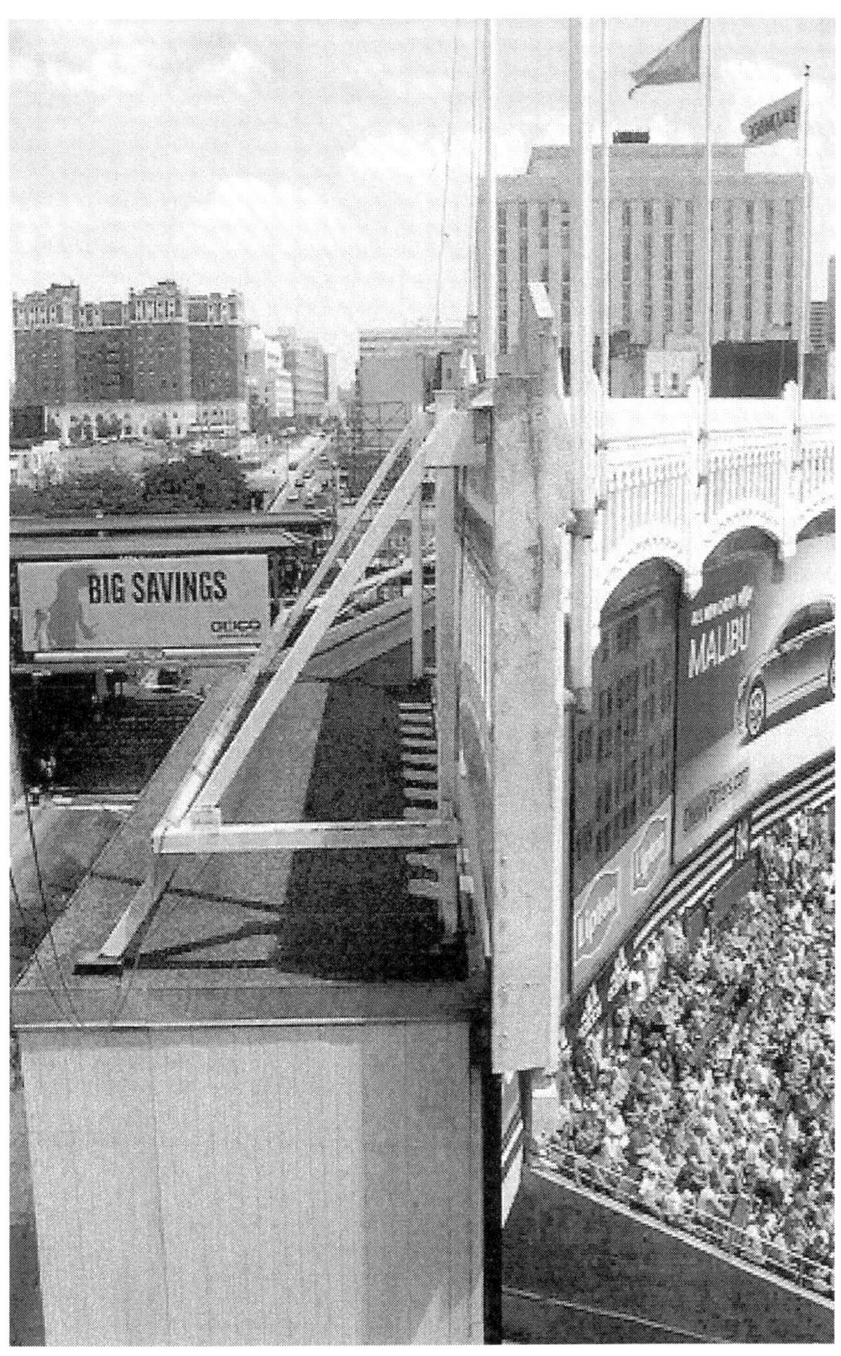

View of frieze from left field side, July 19, 2008. The Bronx County Courthouse is in the rear of the frieze. Photograph © Gary Dunaier

View of Yankee Stadium from inside el train, September 20, 2008. Courtesy of Matt Visco.

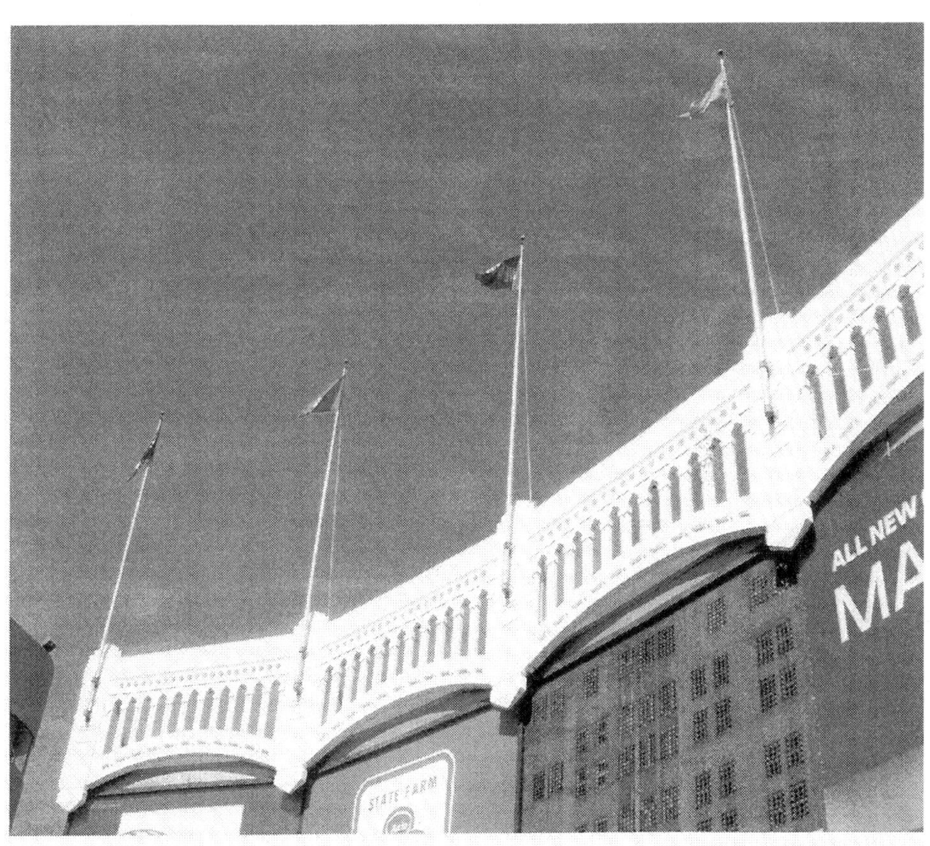

View of frieze from left field bleachers, September 20, 2008. Courtesy of Matt Visco.

Center Field Speaker System, September 20, 2008. Courtesy of Matt Visco.

Last game at Yankee Stadium, September 21, 2008. Above, representatives of the 1923 Yankees and other Yankees greats take the field. Below, the game is on. Andy Pettitte pitched the Yankees to a 7-3 win over Chris Waters of the Baltimore Orioles. The game lasted 3 hours and 5 minutes before 54,610 fans. This historic event began at 8:15 p.m. Photos are courtesy of Steve Alevas.

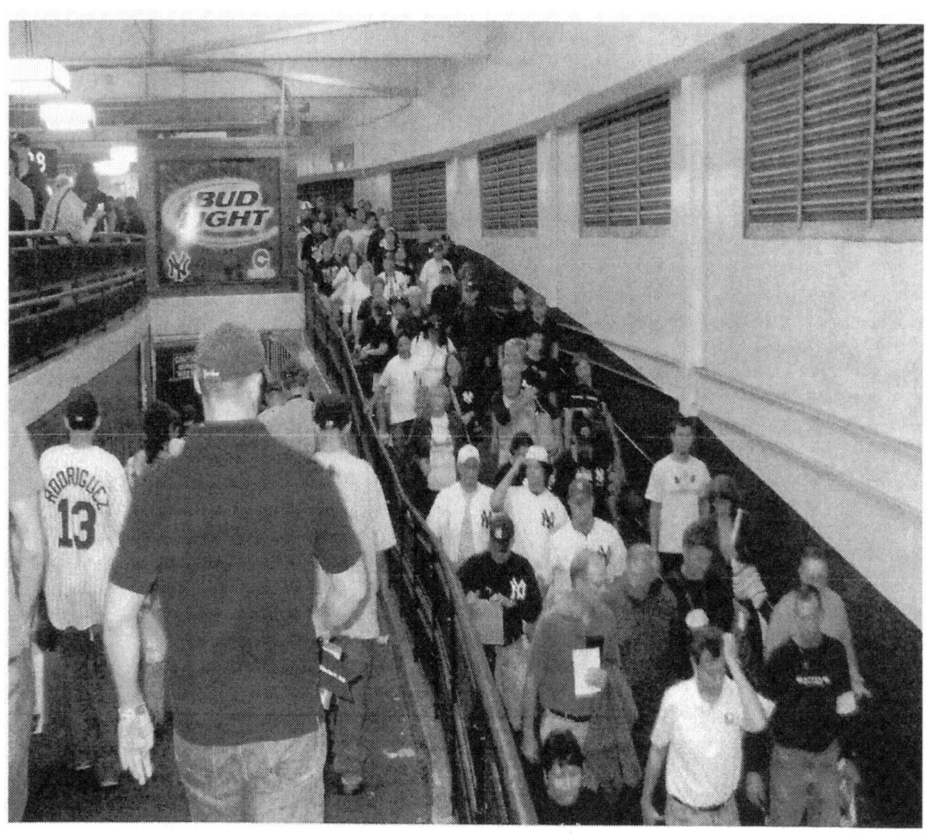

Fans exiting scissor ramp. Last game at Yankee Stadium, September 21, 2008. Photo courtesy of Matt Visco.

JOHN MEEKS' YANKEE STADIUM MODEL

John Meeks has built a 1/120 scale model of Yankee Stadium as it appeared in June of 1973. Made of mostly styrene plastic, this magnificent model will make you feel as though you are in Yankee Stadium.. Go to www.baseball-fever.com. Then go to the thread that says, "Ballparks, Stadiums & Green Diamonds." John's thread in that section is "Yankee Stadium Model Circa 1973," by stadiumbuilder.

RICK KAPLAN'S YANKEE STADIUM 3D AUTO CAD MODEL

Rick Kaplan has created an extraordinary 3D AutoCAD model of Yankee Stadium from the late 1960s or early 1970s. This interactive gem is finished in 3D Studio Max. His breathtaking work can be found on his website at http://www.digitalcentrality.com/Yankee_Stadium/.

DAVE KRAMER'S 1923 YANKEE STADIUM 3D MODEL

Dave Kramer has been working on a sensational digital model of Opening Day in 1923. Dave is including the neighborhood, as well. His superb project may be seen on www.baseball-fever.com. Then type in the thread that says, "Ballparks, Stadiums & Green Diamonds." Dave's thread may be found by typing "1923 Yankee Stadium 3D Renderings." The works of John Meeks and Rick Kaplan will also be found in the "Ballparks, Stadiums & Green Diamonds" thread.

The Atlantic Coast Line Trestle, in Richmond, Virginia, was completed in 1911. This cement arch bridge is one of many similar structures that dot the east coast of the United States. Note the great similarity to the Yankee Stadium frieze. It's conceivable that one of these bridges may have served as the inspiration for the Stadium's famous trademark. Photo courtesy of Chris Jones.

Chapter Nine

THE HEROES SPEAK II

YANKEE STADIUM DEMOLITION RESPONSES

The new Yankee Stadium rises in the background above the site of the demolished Yankee Stadium in the foreground, June 1, 2010. Photo courtesy of Eric Okurowski of www.stadiumpage.com This is the photo I enclosed with my query letter.

On the next page is a general version of the letter I used to ask former baseball players, managers, and umpires about their feelings about the demolition of Yankee Stadium. The vast majority of the responses were letters. Some responses came by telephone and e-mail.

I felt it was important to list those that responded by only signing the demolition photo of Yankee Stadium or baseball cards so readers could see who actually responded. I sent out about 750 letters. I may or may not write a book about this sad event. In case this does not come to pass, I felt it would be important to publish these answers for the sake of history.

Date

Dear Mr. _________,

I'm a New York Yankees fan who is 55 years old. I grew up in West Hempstead, Long Island, New York, from 1956 thru 1977, and had the pleasure and honor of going to many New York Yankees games.

I'm collecting information about the demolition of Yankee Stadium, as I'm writing about the efforts of myself and others to save Gate 2 or an exterior wall of Yankee Stadium. We hoped to have a portion of this sacred Stadium preserved as a permanent monument. Sadly, however, our efforts failed, and nothing is left. Gate 2 was demolished on March 31, 2010, and the end for Yankee Stadium came in May of 2010. A photo is enclosed of the current site.

I would like to know your thoughts about the demolition of Yankee Stadium for inclusion in my book. Since you've had the pleasure and honor of playing at the Stadium as a New York Yankee or opposing player, I would think that you would have a very interesting point of view that spectators such as myself would like to hear. And/or if you have a story about Yankee Stadium you'd like to share, please feel free to do so, as it would be an important part of the history of The House That Ruth Built.

If you would like to see the history of the demolition, go to Baseball Fever (www.baseball-fever.com). Then go to the subject that says "Ballparks, Stadiums, & Green Diamonds." Then go to the thread that says "Yankee Stadium Demolition."

Thank you for your time and kindness, Mr. _________. I look forward to hearing from you. God Bless you. If you would like to write a letter, e-mail, or phone call, please do whatever you wish. Whatever is easier for you.

Respectfully,

Michael Wagner [1]

PERSON AND RESPONSE DATE	RESPONSE
Ruben Amaro, Sr. September 26, 2010	Hi Michael: Our Minor League season & scouting season are coming to the end. Just as our beloved Old Yankee Stadium. Every time I hear the names like Yogi Berra, Whitey Ford, Jeter, Cano, Rodriguez, Torre, & many more privileged names, that not only participated in the old ball park, but also wrote history because they lost and won - I've only lost. I didn't write any history while in the most demanding, big, beautiful, impressing, & frightful stage and uniform. I wish I did - just a small, minute chapter. I can only tell you that the memories of seeing Mickey, Roger, Elston, Mel, Clete, Big Pete & Little Pete (our club house guys), & Soares and Seager (our trainers), & the rest of our group that included Richardson, Tresh, Murcer, Rizzuto (our radio announcer), Crosetti (our 3rd base coach), just walking in our club house & then seeing the sun to start our life has signifcantly made my life more special. Ruben Sr. [2]
Brad Arnsberg January 7, 2011	My funniest memory of Yankee Stadium was that is where I had my first M.L. start against the Orioles in the 1987 season. I loved the fans & the Stadium, as they either loved you or hated you. There was no in-between. It was a very fair "pitchers" park & the new stadium is a joke, & quite the contrary. I wish you and your family a very happy & healthy 2011, & GO STRO'S! Brad Arnsberg [3]
Julio Becquer July 7, 2010	Great stadium to play where the greatest ballplayers of our generations played. It was my greatest moment in my life, the first time I set foot in Yankee Stadium. Being from Cuba - this was it. Julio Becquer [4]
Bill "Lefty" Bell Negro Leagues November 15, 2010	Bill sent me an autographed baseball card and bio. [5]

Vern Benson
July 6, 2010

Signed a Yankee Stadium demolition photo. [6]

Dennis "Bose" Biddle
Negro Leagues
August 17, 2010

Signed a photo of the demolition and a signed baseball card. [7]

Milt Bolling
July 1, 2010

Dear Michael - I dislike seeing Yankee Stadium demolished; however everything seems to have an ending, whether we approve or not. Playing in Yankee Stadium was an awe inspiring event. Milt Bolling [8]

Bobby Bonilla
July 10, 2010

Bobby sent me a signed baseball card. [9]

Dick Bosman
September 21, 2010

I will always remember walking up the steps and seeing the façade over the 3rd deck in right field, the monuments on the field in center field, and my first start there in 1966-pitching to Mickey Mantle, all the memories of the old stadium. It's hard to put into words how many memories I have over the years that are associated with the stadium.

Didn't pitch too bad in there for the most part, always liked to come there for a series. Pretty special for a kid out of Kenosha, Wisc! Dick Bosman (Dick also signed a photo of the demolition.) [10]

Lou Brissie
September 21, 2010

Lou sent me two signed baseball cards. [11]

Bobby Brown
Baseball Player &
A.L. President 1984-1994
June 8, 2011

Dear Mr. Wagner, I believe all the players who played in the old Yankee Stadium were saddened to see it demolished. On the other hand I feel most of us realize that there comes a time when large structures like the Yankee Stadium, Briggs Stadium, Comiskey Park, etc. reach an age when they cannot be renovated and have to be destroyed.

I was even more saddened when the Stadium was renovated in 1974 (?) and the outfield and fence measurements were drastically reduced. That in my opinion took away a lot of the drama and mystique of the old Yankee Stadium.

Sincerely, Bobby Brown (Robert W. Brown M.D.) [12]

Gates Brown
September 1, 2010

Signed a Yankee Stadium demolition photo. [13]

Bert Campaneris
July 14, 2010

Signed a Yankee Stadium demolition photo. [14]

Sonny Carroll
Negro Leagues
September 29, 2010

I do not think they should get rid of them. "Sonny" Carroll God Bless You. [15]

Paul Casanova
December 22, 2010

Signed a Yankee Stadium demolition photo. [16]

Wayne Causey
August 21, 2013

A great place to play. Too bad it is gone! WC [17]

Phil Cavaretta
August 17, 2010

Signed a Yankee Stadium demolition photo.
Phil Cavaretta MVP 1945 "CUBS" [18]

Ed Charles
August 12, 2010

Signed a Yankee Stadium demolition photo. [19]

Gino Cimoli
August 23, 2010

Signed a Yankee Stadium demolition photo. [20]

Allie Clark
Umpire
December 25, 2010

Just recently I received a letter postmarked August 26, 2010. The delay in my response to you has everything to do with the fact I did not receive your letter until now.

With pleasure I share my thoughts with you about Yankee Stadium, the old one, or more accurately, the refurbished Yankee Stadium. As I'm sure you know the Yanks actually played at Shea Stadium during the summers of 1974 and 1975 while the old original ball park was being "modernized."

I, like yourself, have fond memories of the old Yankee Stadium. I grew up in Trenton, New Jersey and was a Yankee fan also. I remember fondly my dad taking me to the stadium when I was about eight or nine years old. I remember the excitement I felt that day and days leading up to "the EVENT". Wow, was that day ever so special.

As time went on and I grew to manhood, my chosen profession was that of being a professional baseball umpire. I was fortunate enough to spend 26 seasons as an American League Umpire and MLB Umpire.

I remember vividly the first time I walked on the field as an umpire in Yankee Stadium. Of course I was remembering that day years earlier that I was there with my dad. We sat in the upper deck along the first base side. That day at the stadium I worked at second base and more than a time or two I looked up to where we sat…and just remembered. Pretty good stuff.

During the course of my career I was fortunate enough to "open" three new ball parks. Camden Yards in Baltimore - Jacobs Field "The Jake" in Cleveland - The Ball Park in Arlington, of course the Texas Rangers new field. I also closed Memorial Stadium in Cleveland. Four great experiences and memories. Each and every new ball park that opened was more magnificent than the last. And so it continues. We (of the sentimental sort) might hate to see a ballpark like Yankee Stadium torn down, however I guess it's progress. The new ball park in the Bronx, from all reviews, is super magnificent. And the kids today will remember, as they reach their golden years the likes of Jeter, and Mo, and Andy and Jorgy. Where you and I remember The Mick and Yogi and Gil McDougald, and Al Downing and Bob Turley, et. al. the kids of today deserve their own…and new memories that are unimpeded by the likes of our memories.

Sure I'm sorry to see Yankee Stadium go…but ya know what…it was time…and besides, that's what the Hall of Fame is for. To make everyone know and remember the players, plays, stadium et. al. of yesterdayear. And I don't mind that.

Michael, I'll share with you a memory that was even special for an old umpire like myself near the end of my career. Our crew was scheduled to go from Chicago and Wrigley Field with an off day to Baltimore. It so happened we were reassigned because of a make-up rain day to go to Boston on the day off. So, on consecutive days, a Wednesday, Thursday and Friday, I worked in Wrigley Field, Fenway Park and Camden Yards. Thinking back on that week, it became special even for an old, weathered ump like me. Pretty neat, huh!~

Once again, Michael, I apologize for the delay in answering your letter. Fans are the life line and blood of our sport and I, for one, answer each and every note I receive. Thanks for taking the time to write. I wish you well with your book endeavor. I'd love to own a copy when published.

To you and your family, I wish you a very Merry Christmas and Happy and Safe Holiday Season.
Very Sincerely, Al Clark (e-mail) [21]

Allie Clark
July 22, 2010

Allie sent me a signed baseball card. [22]

Horace Clarke
July 8, 2010

My sympathy is with you for not leaving some part of the stadium, but the good part is that the new one is next door and in the Bronx rather than taking it to another neighborhood.

When I first joined the Yankees I stayed at the old Concourse Plaza Hotel only a couple blocks from the stadium. I vividly remember the first day I entered the park as a player. The first thing I did was walked out to the monuments in center field.

As a boy I remember when I would listen to the radio and hear players like DiMaggio, Ford, Berra, Rizzuto and the likes playing the Dodgers in World Series. At that time I never had the wildest dream that I would one day play for the team that I was a fan of.

Rizzuto was my favorite since I too was a shortstop. It was an honor to play for the best organization in baseball in the world and also to most of my ten years as a big leaguer at Yankee Stadium.

Horace Clarke, 1965-1974 2nd Base, #20
(Horace also signed a Yankee Stadium demolition photo.) [23]

David Clyde
August 10, 2010

Dear Mr. Wagner, I had the pleasure of seeing games at the Original Yankee Stadium, before remodeling, as I lived in New Jersey when I was 12 and 13. I also had the honor of being in uniform on the playing surface of the Original Yankee Stadium in 1973, my rookie season, but not pitching in the only series I was with the team that year.

The Original Stadium had an aura about it with the monuments being in the field and not behind a fence as they were in the remodeled version because when we returned to the Remodeled Stadium the aura was gone. I guess we call the New Yankee Stadium progress along with the demolished remodeled old stadium. Sometimes I wonder. David Clyde [24]

Drew Coble
Umpire
August 31, 2010

Michael, I remember thinking about all the history every time I walked into Yankee Stadium. There was a feeling that was different from all the other ballparks. I feel very thankful that I had the chance to umpire there.

Drew Coble, AL Umpire #37, Retired [25]

Jerry Coleman
August 20, 2010

Mr. Wagner - 1923-2009 - In Life Things Change - as did Yankee Stadium. I accept that -

Jerry Coleman [26]

Casey Cox
July 14, 2010

I did not know about saving Gate 2, but I believe some part of Yankee Stadium should be saved. [27]

Bud Daley
July 6, 2010

The first time I went to Yankee Stadium I was with the Cleveland ball club. I walk in and what a thrill. Too bad people won't have the thrill I had. [28]

Cot Deal
July 6, 2010

Signed a Yankee Stadium demolition photo. [29]

Billy DeMars
July 9, 2010

Mike, It's pretty hard to look back 62 yrs to the time I played at Yankee Stadium. I also was born & raised in the Bay Ridge section of Brooklyn, so as a kid it was Dodgers & Yankees, not so much Giants.

When I stepped on the field in 1948 it was thrilling just knowing that this is where all the great Yankees played. In fact that day in '48 they still had DiMaggio, Rizzuto, Keller, Henrich, Stirnweiss, Dickey, Reynolds, Raschi, Lopat, etc. Pretty famous players.

That was no worse when the Dodgers packed up and moved to Cal. It was devastating. Time goes on & things change. We see it every day. Take care.

Billy DeMars

(Billy also sent me a signed baseball card.)[30]

Don Demeter
September 9, 2010

I can remember, while hitting in the Stadium - I'm standing where Ruth stood - I too, am sad nothing was preserved for the fans in N.Y.

DD [31]

Bobby Doerr
July 1, 2010

Dear Michael, On Memorial Day 1938 we played to 83,500 fans. They say it was 85,000 because of some free passes.

That day our pitcher threw at Jake Powell and they got into a fight. Cronin was thrown out of the game and when he went through the Yankee dugout they started fighting again. Think that is where the rivalry started to take place.

Thought the Yankee Stadium was a hard place to hit. Tall stands and shadows between home & the pitcher and white shirts in centerfield was hard to pick up the pitches. Left center and center field was a lot of field. DiMaggio played it so good. Hope your book goes good.

Best Wishes, Bobby Doerr [32]

Al Downing
July 3, 2010

Dear Michael, I'm writing a book myself of my career and I'd answer some of the questions you've asked! [33]

Carl Erskine
July 5, 2010

Hello Michael. Thanks for writing. Yes I've pitched several innings at Yankee Stadium. In 1952, 5th game, on the 5th Oct and it was my 5th wedding anniversary - leading 4-0 until - yes the 5th I gave up 5 runs. The game went 11 innings and we, the Dodgers, won 6-5. I got the complete game victory. Also I pitched 9 no hit innings. The Yankees got hits in only 2 innings.

Vince Scully & Red Barber were the Dodger broadcasters. Vince Scully said he was watching for any other 5's. He swears that when I struck Berra out to end the game in the bottom of the 11th inning he looked at the stadium clock - it was 5 past 5 o'clock.

Carl Erskine (Carl also sent me his e-mail address.) [34]

Jim Evans
Umpire
September 6, 2010

Hi Michael, I enjoyed working in the classic stadiums of the American League - Yankee Stadium, Fenway, Tiger Stadium, etc. Any time you worked there you felt like you were stepping back into history.

My first time to YS was in Sept. of 1971 and Bob Sheppard came by and introduced himself.

My memories there include my first World Series (1977) and my last World Series (1996). I worked two others in between but those are certainly my most memorable.

In addition to all the arguments and battles with Billy Martin, I was on the field for Reggie's 3 home runs in the 1977 WS, Jim Abbott's no-hitter and David Cone's perfect game.

One of the most inspiring experiences was standing for the National Anthem at home plate where Babe Ruth, Joe DiMaggio, Lou Gehrig, Yogi Berra, Mickey Mantle and many other greats stood, and listening to Robert Merrill sing the Star Spangled Banner.

I will always treasure my experiences at the Stadium and consider these some of my fondest memories. I am sorry to hear that no permanent monument is being provided at the site.

Yours truly, Jim Evans

(Jim also sent me a couple of business cards.) [35]

Don Ferrarese
July 10, 2010

There was no stadium like Yankee Stadium. I was always in awe just being there.

My 3 double game tied Babe Ruth, while he was pitching for the Red Sox. It probably will never be broken unless they eliminate the D.H.

I met Babe in 1947 at a high school All-Star game when we practiced in the stadium. I'll send you some stuff and I appreciate your interest.

Regards, Don Ferrarese

Call me if you want for more info.

(Don also enclosed a signed photo of the Yankee Stadium demolition and a few signed and unsigned photos and articles of himself, as well as a business card.) [36]

Boo Ferriss
July 8, 2010

Michael: This is in reply to your letter about Yankee Stadium that I received recently. No doubt you're one of thousands of Yankee fans who have sad thoughts about the demolition of the stadium.

I was an opposing player (Red Sox) of the Yankees, but I am saddened to see it destroyed, great history and tradition like Fenway Park - "the House that Ruth built."

I loved pitching in the Stadium, great atmosphere and environment, might call it hallowed ground. Pitching there in the late 1940s was one of the highlights of my career.

After winning 8 straight games to start my career in 1945, I lost my first game there on June 10 - a 3-2 loss played in a light rain. The game had been a sellout of 65,000 or so, but the rain cut it to about 45,000. A tough loss, but a great thrill to pitch there.

In 1946 we battled the Yankees for the pennant, and you could count on Fenway and the Stadium being packed anytime we played. Fans loved the Ted Williams - Joe DiMaggio hitting duels, both teams with great players. No fire laws back then so fans could sit in the aisles.

Two big thrilling moments for me came the latter part of the season. In a night game on August 9, I won a 4-3 game before over 68,000, pitching all 9 innings. In a Labor Day Sept. 2 doubleheader I won a complete game (5-2 first game) before a crowd of over 73,000 - what a great sight seeing the Stadium overflowing with excited fans. Of course, I have sad thoughts about the Yankees beating us the last two games of the 1949 season to win the pennant by one game.

I saw first hand some of the greatest Yankee teams in the late 1950s when I was the Red Sox pitching coach (1955-59). I saw some of Mickey Mantle's greatest feats. Well, I could go on and on.

Baseball has been a blessing to my life, and I am indeed grateful. The wonderful associations and endured friendships are priceless.

I wish you great success with your book, and my thanks for contacting me.

Best regards, Dave "Boo" Ferriss

(Dave also sent me a signed copy of his bio as a 2002 Boston Red Sox Hall of Fame Inductee.) [37]

Paul Foytack
July 12, 2010

Paul left a message on my telephone. We talked quite a while about baseball. He had some great stories. Paul's comment about the demolition of Yankee Stadium:

	It's too bad because it was a great place to play. I guess it had to be done. I haven't thought about it much after that. I did dream of playing there when I was a kid. The only game I went to before I played was in 1949. I remember seeing Joe DiMaggio. [38]
Jim Fregosi January 7, 2011	Signed a Yankee Stadium demolition photo. [39]
Ned Garver July 8, 2010	Sent two signed baseball cards. [40]
Joe Ginsberg July 6, 2010	Everything gets old and new things takes its place. Joe signed a Yankee Stadium demolition photo. [41]
Stanley "Doc" Glenn Negro Leagues August 25, 2010	Signed an index card for me. [42]
Mike Hegan August 28, 2010	Mike, Sorry to see all of the stadium gone! It would have been nice to keep some kind of physical memorial. My greatest memory will be the fact that I had the final at bat at the stadium. Mike Hegan [43]
Jack Heidemann August 18, 2010	Mike, I remember going into Yankee Stadium as a rookie 1970. Wow. It was also "Old Timers' Game." Mantle, Maris, Ford, Stengel, I can name them all. They were my team growing up. Never thought of getting an autograph. Bad decision!!! To me, centerfield should have been preserved with statues. Just to tear it down…I don't know. But, just like players…once too old… just replace. Like Mom/Dad with kids…now kids Mom/Dad with more kids. Thanks for writing, Jack Heidemann. (Jack also sent two signed photos and a business card.) [44]

Solly Hemus August 23, 2010	Dear Michael - I never had the opportunity to play in Yankee Stadium but I did coach while being with Cleveland. The first time I was in the Stadium I could recall all the great players that played in The Stadium - Ruth, Gehrig, Mantle - just a few. The new stadium is beautiful. Best wishes - Solly Hemus (Solly also signed a Yankee Stadium demolition photo.) [45]
Ray Herbert August 16, 2010	Ray wrote on a Yankee Stadium demolition photo. "Won my 20 Game in 1962. Was 20-9. [46]
Mike Hershberger August 18, 2010	It was a thrill to play there. But also a bigger thrill to play against Mantle, etc - Since I came up with the White Sox my biggest thrill was playing in Comiskey Park. I have 5 shirts from the park. Mike Hershberger [47]
Chuck Hinton August 25, 2010	Sorry about the demolition. I do know that the Yankees had a good team. It was fun reading about your team. Keep the faith and God Bless you. Chuck [48]
Jay Hook August 26, 2010	Thank you for your interest in baseball. Jay Hook [49]
Ralph Houk July 3, 2010	Ralph sent me two signed baseball cards. [50]
Rex Hudler August 19, 2010	Mr. Wagner, What a blessing to be a 1st born Yankee! Got my first big league hit there over Bill Buckner's head at 1st Base. When they put that on the scoreboard the crowd roared and cheered. It was cool. Yogi was my first manager. Billy Martin was next 84-85. Fond memories. All my best. [51]

John James August 28, 2010	It was certainly an honor to have played there. John James [52]
Alex Johnson May 29, 2012	Like you, a fan. My short time in Yankee uniform only relights memory of the giants - Babe, Gehrig, etc. Alex also signed a Yankee Stadium demolition photo. [53]
Cliff Johnson September 9, 2010	Cliff sent a signed baseball card [54]
Ben Jones Negro Leagues July 7, 2010	Ben sent two photos of himself, one of which is signed. [55]
Dalton Jones August 17, 2010	Telephone Interview.

DJ: I played two and a half years of minor league baseball, and in 1964 was brought up to the Boston Red Sox. I began my nine complete seasons in the major leagues. My first game ever to dress out for a major league ball game was at Yankee Stadium.

Here was a southern boy that was brought up there, and I had never been to New York, much less Yankee Stadium. And, my first experience, of course, was to go into the clubhouse. I was all excited to be there to begin with, walking…oh, gosh…you had to take a couple of turns, if I remember right, under the stands to go to batting practice.

I walked into the third base dugout, which back then really was a dugout. It was really deep. I walked up on that precious field, and it was just unbelievable. I could not believe it! I'd been sort of taken away by the city itself.

Walking onto the field and taking batting practice…I'll never forget it. I wasn't going to play. Whitey Ford was pitching. I'm a left handed hitter, so they weren't going to start me. I'll never forget taking batting practice and having the thought that Babe Ruth, Lou Gehrig, and all those guys stood at the same spot. It was really some kind of thrill!

Bob Turley was our pitching coach. Bob had pitched for the Yankees, of course. If I remember right, it was Bob who walked me out to right field and pointed up to the façade where Mantle had hit the façade with a home run, just missing hitting the ball out of the stadium by a foot. I told him, "I don't even know if I could pop a ball that high standing right here." It was just amazing. And going out to the monuments, which were then in center field…it was just a big thrill for me.

That's about it, Michael. I can't really remember anything else. I do remember a kid named Billy Rohr pitching a one-hitter. I do believe it was in that series.

MW: I remember that. I think Elston Howard broke that up.

DJ: Elston Howard broke that up in the 9th inning.

MW: Your first time at the Stadium, when you were taking batting practice, did you hit any into the seats?

DJ: I don't remember. I tell everybody that during my rookie year, I didn't know if I should play ball or get autographs. So, I don't remember exactly what happened. I guess I did pretty good. I hung around for nine years. Anyway, Yankee Stadium was my first experience ever dressing out as a major league baseball player. And it was quite a thrill.

MW: I understand Ted Williams got you to sign with the Red Sox because he was one of your heroes.

DJ: Actually, he came down in 1961. A guy named Rusty Staub played with Jesuit out of New Orleans, and I played with Istrouma High School in Baton Rouge. We ended up playing in the state playoffs. Ted came down to see us both. They couldn't talk to us until after graduation.

Ted came to my house with George Digby. George Digby is the scout that actually signed me. Ted had been one of my heroes, and I actually I had fallen in love with the Boston Red Sox quite early in my life. Why, I don't know, other than him. Ted might have had a little to do with it. I think my mind was pretty much made up that I wanted to play with them.

MW: It's nice to play with a team you want to play with. What an honor!

DJ: There were only 20 teams in existence at the time – 10 in each league. Eighteen scouts came parading through. Atley Donald of the Yankees was one of them. It was really a decision that I had to make in more ways than one because I didn't know if I wanted to play college ball or what. I had an offer from some of them, too. But I felt...I don't know...I was so young that it's hard to remember back then what my reasoning was. I kind of felt like, "Hey, that's the Yankees saying they have a lot of good ballplayers in front of you before you make it with that ball club."

MW: That's true. It would have probably limited your playing time.

DJ: Maybe so. Maybe so. But, Boston, of course, was hurting at the time. I ended up playing about two and a half years in the minors, then coming up at the age of 20. It turned out right. (laughs).

MW: That it did. I was in the Air Force from 1982-1992. For seven or eight years I went to Spring Training. One year I decided, "I wonder if Ted Williams is down here." So I went to the Red Sox camp at Winter Haven. I went to one of the fields asked somebody if Ted was here. He pointed to a field in the distance. Sure enough, Ted was there. He was so tall! A bunch of us were sitting near the field. Ted joined us. Somebody asked him a question about a batter that was at the plate and his swing. We all shut up because that was a Baseball God talking. (DJ laughs)

Ted was absolutely wonderful! I followed him to his truck. It was an old cream colored Ford or Chevy. I was the only person with him. I asked, "Mr. Williams, would you please sign my book?" He said, "Sure!" I could still hear him dotting those two "i's" in "Williams." He hit them hard. He was wonderful, great to the fans. And, me being a Yankee fan, I even bought a Winter Haven Red Sox T-shirt because of Ted. I know it's sacrilegious, but...(DJ laughs)

DJ: That rivalry has been around for a long time. We had a fan who was so in love with the Red Sox that he came every Spring Training. He had multiple sclerosis. Somebody offered him a Mickey Mantle bat and he reluctantly took it. He said,

"I'll stick it in the back someplace." That rivalry was something.

MW: I know. One time the Yankees beat the Red Sox in a doubleheader. We were going back to our cars in the parking lot, and people were chanting, "Red Sox suck, Red Sox suck." This must have been about 1972. I'm sure the Red Sox fans at Fenway said the same thing about the Yankees.

DJ: Yeah. I remember in those days that we weren't that good a ball club in '64, '65, and the start of '66. After '66 is when the "Impossible Dream" caught on for '67. Leading up to that, we were really pushovers.

We'd go into Yankee Stadium, and I remember this distinctly – it was almost like the fans were pulling for the underdog, and the fans would almost tolerate you for four or five innings. I don't know if they were playing with us. Then if we'd get a lead, they'd turn on us like…(laughs). That's when they'd become Yankee fans again. It was unusual.

MW: When the Red Sox came to the Stadium, did they fear coming to the Bronx, or did the team look forward to it?

DJ: No, there wasn't any real fear. I guess in those days we really didn't have a real good ball club. We were always the underdog. My gosh, the Minnesota Twins and Chicago White Sox owned us. I think we played each team 18 times a year and the Twins and White Sox each beat us 16 times. So, it wasn't just the Yankees. We probably did better against the Yankees than these other two clubs.

MW: Me being a fan and you being an actual baseball player, you have a perspective that the fans don't have.

DJ: You'd have to put yourself in a position of a ball club that was not expected to win. So you feel like you're going out there as an underdog. The last thing you'd do is tighten up because nobody thought you were going to win anyway.

MW: I understand that. I don't know if you want to talk for yourself, the Red Sox, or ballplayers in general. Did Yankee Stadium intimidate ballplayers because of its size, Death Valley, or just the huge size of the field?

DJ: I can only speak for myself, not anyone else. It was intimidating in a good way. It was so huge! There was nothing else like it around, and to go in there, and get to play every now and then, was a thrill to me. It was the ultimate experience. I can't take away from the Fenway Park experience because it has a lot of history, too, with Williams, Doerr, and those guys. Yankee Stadium was special in its own way in that regard. Ruth played there, Gehrig played there, and all that. Back then we used to know a little about history. I don't know if today's ballplayers know about history.

MW: Probably not.

DJ: That's about it, Michael. I appreciate what you are doing.

MW: Thank you, Mr. Jones. It's been an honor to talk to you. If I can do anything baseball wise or not, please let me know.

DJ: Thank you, Michael. [56]

Fred Kipp
August 27, 2010

Fred signed a Yankee Stadium demolition photo. [57]

Lou Klimchock
August 31, 2010

Lou signed a Yankee Stadium demolition photo. [58]

Steve Kline
January 20. 2011

Michael - Thank you for your interest. Old Yankee Stadium was quaint. Close to the field for spectators, but pillars that block the view throughout. Sadly it had grown too small for "New York." Athletic and other new, bright, dazzling stadiums were built and N.Y. was not to fall behind on the glitz wagon.

However, when you go to Wrigley or Fenway you know the ghosts and the stadiums call of hallowed ground, baseball lore and history. I can only hope the "New Yankee Stadium" can embody that spirit. The "old ghosts" will need that to move into the new digs. [59]

Bobby Knoop Telephone Interview
February 13, 2011

The demolition was long overdue. It was not a real comfortable place. They had 4 showers for us, and only one of them worked. They rebuilt it, repaired it, and made it comfortable, and it was a comfortable place. It was a fun place to play. I knew the first time that I went to play in Yankee Stadium that I wanted to see where Mickey Mantle hit the right field façade.

It was not an easy field to play on. The left field foul line was difficult to play because it was so deep. There was not much room at the foul lines. But, it was a fun field to play on. We had no fear of playing at Yankee Stadium because the Yankee clubs that played against us were not that competitive.

I was there for an Old Timers' Day game, and saw players like Mantle and DiMaggio and a capacity crowd.

I remember hitting my only grand slam at Yankee Stadium on a "Game of the Week."

The "old" Stadium with all of its history and glory, and the type of attendance the Yankees have…it was time to do something. Renovation would cost too much, and it would be obsolete in 5 years.

**Fenway Park is always being renovated. Fenway is a terrible place…you couldn't even stand in the dugout.

I love to go to New York, but can only do so for four or five days. I'm from the Midwest, so that's about all I can take. I remember my first real Italian meal was in Brooklyn. A lady in the Gino Cimoli fan club made a wonderful, Italian meal. I've loved Italian food ever since.

The Stadium has wonderful memories for me.

**My remarks concerning Fenway only meant that the accommodations - locker room and dugouts were difficult. The tradition of playing Boston in Fenway, like old Yankee Stadium, was priceless. [60]

Andy Kosco
August 28, 2010

Signed a Yankee Stadium demolition photo. [61]

Ted Kubiak

Ted sent me an e-mail on September 4, 2010, and another one on September 20, 2010. We spoke on the phone a few days before Ted sent me his second e-mail. Both e-mails follow:

September 4, 2010 e-mail:

Hi: I can appreciate your feelings about losing what I consider the cathedral of baseball. I am including some of my own thoughts about growing up around it and playing there in a book I'm writing myself so I'm a little hesitant to share what I've already written because I do go into what it was like to be inside the locker room and on the field.

Maybe if you have a specific question I can answer you. I hope you understand my position. Who knows if my book will ever see a publisher but it's about my forty years in the game with a little different twist than the normal "baseball life story." Let me know. I would love to read yours when it's finished. Ted Kubiak [62]

September 20, 2010 e-mail:

Hi, Mike, Good to talk to you the other day. Regarding the demolition of the Stadium, it is the end of just about all my memories of the way baseball used to be. Fenway is still alive but the loss of Yankee Stadium is more personal and was somewhat the symbol of baseball for me as I grew up. I lived only an hour away and only got there a few times but the team was always in the news much like it is today so I felt as though I knew the players. The Stadium and its façade, front ticket gazebos and turnstiles are etched in my mind.

As I said I knew the interior which I am writing a little about but being interested as I am in the early history of the game, I at least have a couple of seats and the memories. Losing it may have been an inevitability because of age and the times. I would imagine Old-timers Days will lose a little but the tradition of the Yankees and everything connected with them will live.

I haven't seen the new one, not sure I will or really care to. It would certainly be interesting to compare the luxury it no doubt has to the simplicity of the old one. I could liken the interior I saw to what maybe an old castle might have been like. I hope someday to see your writings. Not sure how much this helped. Ted [63]

Jim Landis
August 21, 2010

Being a C.F. there was sure a lot of room to cover.

J.L. [64]

Ted Lepcio
August 16, 2010

Dear Michael - Thank you for remembering that players such as T. Lepcio could possibly contribute to your project.

First of all, I personally after my playing days were over have often thought of all the parks I played in. Every one of those that were demolished had great history in a small way. Parks such as Griffith Stadium, Crosley Field, Tiger Stadium, Comiskey, Baltimore, Cleveland - and of course Yankee Stadium!

Ted Williams (who liked me as a person) used to point to where some of the great hitters hit balls (i.e.) J. Foxx - Greenberg, etc.

Getting to Yankee Stadium for a moment and me being born in Utica, N.Y. It was magical for me to play at the stadium. It was, as you know, intimidating to say the least. I also believe once they tear down Fenway many will have the same sentiments as you. I believe some parts of the real great ones should be made over to have everyone see how it was.

I can go on with this script but enough is enough. I wish you luck with the book.

Regards, Ted Lepcio [65]

Phil Linz
August 19, 2010

Signed a Yankee Stadium demolition photo. Phil also sent me a business card and a baseball card showing a playful photo of him playing a harmonica, while Yogi Berra has his fingers in his ears. Both are in New York Mets uniforms. [66]

Jim Lonborg
September 13, 2010

Dear Michael - It is too bad that some of the great old stadiums are replaced. Some day it will happen to Fenway Park. So much of it is economics and profitability, but that goes with the equation.

Some of the new parks they are building are fantastic for the fan. The history of games played will always be there.

I loved walking into Yankee Stadium in 1965 for the first time and walking out to the monuments in center field. I loved warming up for a game in front of the dugouts too, looking at Whitey Ford and Mel Stottlemyre.

Little did I know at the time - Sept. 20, 1968, that I would give up Mickey Mantle's last home run #536 in Yankee Stadium. Not a thrill at the time, but historically a significant moment to share with one of my childhood heroes.

Have a great summer.

Sincerely, Jim Lonborg [67]

Stan Lopata
September 9, 2010

Dear Mike, To me Yankee Stadium was another big league ball park. I only was there 4 times when the Phillies played the Yankees in the World Series in 1950.

I don't believe it was the ball park but the players that played in it: Ruth, Dickey, Gomez, Rizzuto, Coleman, Bauer and the other great Yankee players.

Stan Lopata [68]

Lee MacPhail
Yankee Executive
July 7, 2010

I regret seeing changes in historic Yankee Stadium.

Lee MacPhail [69]

Charlie Maxwell
August 17, 2010

Signed a Yankee Stadium demolition photo. [70]

Mike McCormick
October 7, 2010

Nostalgic park as a visitor or Yankee player. Disappointed nothing remains except typical of today's parks.

Mike McCormick [71]

Larry McCoy
Umpire
August 30, 2010

Sent signed photo of himself. [72]

Lindy McDaniel
August 17, 2010

Dear Michael, Yes history does matter, and I have many great memories in the stadium "Ruth Built."

In these economic times it is hard to understand why a new stadium was built. Now people pay $95.00+ for a ticket. I have a bullpen bench that came from the old stadium.

One of my favorite photos is of myself and my two boys taken by the monuments in center field. Check out my website and blog where I write short articles about baseball and religion.
Lindy McDaniel (www.lindymcdaniel.com)
(Lindy also sent a nice signed color photo as a Yankee.) [73]

Scott McGregor
September 21, 2010

Signed a Yankee Stadium demolition photo. [74]

Jack McKeon
March 5, 2011

Sorry to see old Yankee Stadium go down. I saw many games at the Stadium growing up.

My best memories are catching a foul ball from bat of the "Scooter" at age 10.

Also knowing I was the last Mgr. to win a World Series game at Yankee Stadium in 2003. [75]

Sam Mele
August 19, 2010

Signed a Yankee Stadium demolition photo. [76]

Rudy Meoli
August 23, 2010

Dear Michael, Sorry to hear about the failed effort!

I remember standing in dead centerfield looking toward home plate thinking "that is a long way." Of course I was standing between the monuments.

Also playing a day game on "Bat Day." 65K people you couldn't talk without yelling in the person's ear.

Whatever happened to Bat Day!

Best Regards, Rudy [77]

John "Mule" Miles
Negro Leagues
August 19, 2010

Hello Michael! Thank you for writing. I enjoy hearing from baseball fans.

Yes I have played baseball in New York. Have great memories of the Polo Grounds and Yankee Stadium. Yes it was "sad" when I heard about the demolition of Yankee Stadium.

Not only ball parks changing, but the players. Major League players are not role models. They are focused on individual goals, huge contracts, dreadlocks, baggy uniforms and steroids. They set bad example for young kids.

I played for the love of the game. No huge salary, but with the "God" given talent I had to play the game and become a professional baseball player. I have no regrets. I am not complaining, just explaining.

John "Mule" Miles

(Mr. Miles signed a Yankee Stadium demolition photo.) [78]

George Mitterwald
September 12, 2010

All good things come to an end. Just like all of our lives will come to an end. The first original stadium was awe inspiring the first time you walk into it. That's the one that should have been saved. I hear the new stadium is just beautiful and modern. [79]

Don Mueller
August 26, 2010

Don sent a signed photo of himself as a New York Giant. [80]

Russ Nixon
August 26, 2010

My fondest memory of Yankee Stadium was Oct 1st 1961 catching for the Red Sox when my roomie Roger Maris hit his 61 home run.

Russ Nixon

Gate #2 was our escape route. What memories. [81]

Jim Northrup
September 13, 2010

Signed a Yankee Stadium demolition photo. [82]

Billy O'Dell November 12, 2010	Signed a Yankee Stadium demolition photo. Billy also sent a signed photo as a Baltimore Oriole. [83]
Bob Oldis August 17, 2010	Playing in Yankee Stadium in the World Series with Pittsburgh in 1960 in 2 games that we won has to be a great memory. Thanks, Bob Oldis [84]
Nate Oliver September 17, 2010	I felt the sadness like most people. But life goes on!! [85]
Dave Pagan August 26, 2010	Dear Michael, I loved it very much in Yankee Stadium. I wished it was not torn down. I played in the Stadium that Ruth built in '73 and as for a few pillars & center field being a mile away with the monuments in playable territory, I was sad to see it go. After they renovated to the New Yankee Stadium it was still beautiful, and it never changed a whole lot. There was a lot of things that reminded me of the first stadium. Why did they build a new ball park when Fenway Park is still the same today as it was when I played? The Green Monster in left and a very short right field down the line. I'm disappointed. Dave Pagan [86]
Steve Palermo Umpire September 10, 2010	Michael, Sad to see the 'House' torn down. I worked many games at the Stadium. One in particular was Dave Righetti's no-hitter on July 4, 1983. It was a typical Boston vs. New York game. The crowd was raucous & on their feet, especially in the late innings. Dave and I had a special relationship since that day. I get to see him in Spring Training and sometimes during the season. He's a good guy.

I hope your memories will last. The Stadium was a special place for all of us who took the field. The great players and umpires who preceded us left their spirit for us to enjoy.

All The Best, Steve [87]

Lance Parrish
November 18, 2010

Mike - Just like in the closing and eventual leveling of Tiger Stadium where there was so much history & so many memories I am saddened to see the great Yankee Stadium suffer the same fate.

Every time (as a player) you competed on the surface of Yankee Stadium you knew that you were competing on the same field as so many great players throughout history had competed on. That made the games very special & the experience itself very "personally" satisfying.

I'm sure every living Yankee fan or even a visiting fan can remember when they walked through the tunnel & sat in their seat for the first time. So many memories and experiences shared with family and friends.

I really came to love Yankee Stadium & always looked forward to playing there. The passion of the Yankees fans always made it an experience to remember.

Oh well - time marches on.

Take care, Lance Parrish [88]

Dan Pasqua
March 4, 2013

I'll never forget the thrill of Yankee Stadium!

Dan Pasqua [89]

Maurice Peatros
Negro Leagues
December 23, 2010

The Stadium was third major league park I played in (Crosley Field & Forbes Field were the first). Got a bloop single off Satchel Paige (K.C. Monarchs) there. I was ducking a high hard one! He cursed me (SMILE). MP [90]

Gary Peters
August 19, 2010

It was an honor and a great thrill every time I played in the old Stadium.

Gary Peters [91]

Fritz Peterson July 3, 2010	I started the last game in the original House that Ruth built & ended up with the lowest E.R.A. there of all time. F.P. (Fritz signed a Yankee Stadium demolition photo on which he wrote, "Mike, I miss this place! Fritz Peterson." Fritz also sent me a signed 1973 baseball card. [92]
Billy Pierce August 19, 2010	To Michael, I thought old Yankee Stadium was one of the greatest parks ever built and I was very disappointed to see it torn down. Bill Pierce [93]
Joe Pignatano August 13, 2010	Mike, Yankee Stadium was a landmark. They shouldn't have to demolish it. Today it's dollars and cents. There was no reason to destroy it. J.P. [94]
Juan Pizarro August 30, 2010	Signed a Yankee Stadium demolition photo. [95]
Herb Plews August 26, 2010	Dear Michael - You are truly one of the many loyal baseball fans. I couldn't believe the old stadium site had already been so cleaned. The new stadium is unbelievable. Appearance from the outside sure resembles the old one. I always felt lucky and very privileged to have played there. Growing up in their farm system I always had high hopes of being a Yankee, but never quite that good. Michael, I can't quite recall the exact year, '58 or '59, we (Washington Senators) opened the season in N.Y. I remember it well. We formed in the area where the monuments were located. Robert Merrill sang that day and then we all marched towards the infield at which time we faced home plate while our national anthem was played. Talk about being excited. My emotions were at their highest. It was always special playing in Yankee Stadium. I'm sorry efforts failed so a small token from the old stadium couldn't have been preserved. But you gave a gallant effort. Hope you have enjoyed a great summer. We're all looking towards the playoffs. Our Rockies have sure hit the skids.

I hate to see a great player like Roger Clemens in trouble. All those players had so much natural ability. I don't know why they even gave drugs a thought. A real shame! Stay well Michael.

My best regards always - Herb Plews [96]

Mack Pride, Jr. Telephone Interview
Negro Leagues
September 16, 2010

M.W.: What are your feelings about the demolition of Yankee Stadium?

M.P.: BAD! There are so many ways you could think of that. How old was the Stadium?

M.W.: It was built in 1923.

M.P.: That's old. They're having problems right here in Colorado. There's buildings right here in Colorado that inspectors go into that's busted with cracks. I can understand people because this is a sentimental thing. But, if you can, it's good to keep a certain portion of a thing, if you can. But I don't get into that. There's too much politics in that.

What I'm saying is that I hate that it happened because you do have so many spectators that are sentimental. But, then too, things have changed so much. Things have gotten older, just like they do in Colorado. You have all these old buildings, these old highways, sewers that are over 100 years old, man. They need replacing. When one of those main lines bust, cars fall into a big hole.

Good Writing! Mack A. Pride, Jr.

(Mack signed a Yankee Stadium demolition photo that I sent him.) [97]

Frank Quilici
August 16, 2010

Hi Michael, I'll try to answer your letter. It's too bad the Yankees didn't get a chance to see the Twins new baseball stadium - "Target Field." They took an 8 1/2 acre piece of ground and turned it into a modern museum for fans to reminisce on all our previous minor & major league stadiums that not only the Minnesota Twins occupied but included the former AAA parks in Minneapolis & St. Paul. (Minneapolis Millers & St. Paul Saints). They also acknowledged their former players, Hall of Famers and championship teams. It truly is an outstanding, state of the art stadium.

Billy Martin, who was our 3rd base coach in 1965, took me as a rookie when we played the Yankees in my first appearance against them into the bowels of Yankee Stadium. We walked down the corridor and came upon a door that was old and kind of out of the way. We went in and up some stairs and came into a room that looked like a storage bin. There was a pot belly stove at the back and some benches there. Billy said "Sit down there," and asked me if I knew where we were. I said, "I have no idea." Billy said, "You are sitting in the same room that Babe Ruth, Lou Gehrig, Tony Lazzeri, and those great 1920, 30, 40 teams used for their locker room." It was a thrill for me to reminisce.

I love Billy. He was a true blooded Yankee and a guy that loved history, read all about the great leaders & generals and had a lot of their attributes. I was with him in October of the year he died. He told me he was the happiest he had ever been.

We were coming home from the Mantle Golf Tourney in Loma Linda, MO. He told me he had a contract with Chiquita Banana and wanted me to think about coming to the East Coast to start a baseball camp for tough kids. He told me Steinbrenner was still paying him and life was good.

We said goodbye and hugged each other like brothers and said goodbye. It's the last time I saw or heard from Billy.

That Christmas season he died & we lost one of the most unique talented wild guys that ever put on a Yankee uniform.

Frank Quilici [98]

Merv Rettenmund
August 19, 2010

Michael, Enjoyed your letter. What a thrill to play in old Yankee Stadium. I understand where you are coming from, but when they did the first renovation they ruined the park. No façade, no park distance to the fences changed in every direction, monuments from the field to the bullpen.

Again demolition took place long before they tore it down. The façade made the park special, the façade gave the park all the shadows you see in old World Series games.

Thanks, Merv Rettenmund [99]

Bobby Richardson
July 23, 2010

Michael, I guess no matter what the "House that Ruth built" is across the street - the old is no more. Great to play there & after they played at Shea for 2 years I was asked by "Geo" - (He just passed away) to have the prayer of dedication as they moved back in. I was coaching then at Univ. of S.C. That seems so long ago.

Sincerely, Bobby [100]

Mickey Rivers
December 9, 2010

Signed a Yankee Stadium demolition photo. [101]

James Robinson
Negro Leagues
August 21, 2010

Dear Mr. Wagner, I received your letter and share the sad feelings re: the saving of Gate 2.

Recently I attended a Yankee game and found it difficult to look across at the vast emptiness where the old stadium once stood.

My memories of the old Yankee Stadium are vivid, including regular season games, World Series games, Negro League doubleheaders and N.Y. Giant football.

I am proud to say that my first game as a Negro League player was at Yankee Stadium in August 1952. At the time, I was a member of the Philadelphia Stars. In 1958, my final year in the league, I returned to the stadium as a member of the Kansas City Monarchs.

At eighty years old, I am still an avid baseball fan. I enjoy the new Yankee Stadium but sincerely miss the old ball park and the memories of the great events that took place there.

Yours truly, Jim Robinson

(Jim included his e-mail address & a signed baseball card). [102]

Ed Roebuck October 14, 2010	Ed sent a signed index card and signed 1958 baseball card. [103]
Rich Rollins July 8, 2010	Dear Mr. Wagner:- Yes I have some great memories of playing in Yankee Stadium 1961-1970. These will never go away playing against the Yankee greats of that era! Money talks doesn't it. This one is beyond me! Good luck to you and your efforts. God Bless, Rich [104]
Phil Roof July 7, 2010	I have many good memories of Yankee Stadium, from 1965 thru 1988. I hate to see old Stadiums torn down. New stadiums all over are fan friendly. That's progress. Catching Catfish Hunter when we were with the K.C. & Oakland A's. That was a thrill. I hit a home run there. I played against many great players who wore the pin stripes, Mantle, Maris, Pepitone, Richardson, Clete Boyer, Stottlemyre, W. Ford, Elston Howard and many more. That was a thrill trying to compete against the Yankees and we didn't compete very well. A lot of good memories that I can cherish for a long time. Phil Roof [105]
Al Rosen July 1, 2010	Al sent a signed baseball card. [106]
Bob Savage July 23, 2010	Leaning against the dugout, Babe Ruth passed him and patted him on the "ASS." I believe this was the day they honored him. It was his day. Babe was retiring. Bob is 88 years old. His memory is gone, but he has told me this story many times. He has no opinion about the demolition of Yankee Stadium. He felt it was an honor just to be there, even though they didn't win many games. He pitched maybe an inning or two. He says you have to realize he was on a last place club. Also Yogi Berra hit his 1st home run on Bob's pitch.

Thank you for the mail and interest. He still gets requests for autographs.

(Besides the note I received, Bob's family member also sent a signed baseball card of Bob). [107]

Bob Saverine
July 22, 2010

I think the old Yankee Stadium kept Joe DiMaggio and Mickey Mantle from having the all-time record baseball statistics. I played centerfield there and it was a long run to the fences. DiMaggio and Mantle were hurt regularly when they hit long balls from left center to right center.

I saw Mantle in Baltimore and Washington D.C. and he hit home run after home run in regular parks. There was no pitching to him there.

Bob Saverine [108]

Chuck Schilling
July 10, 2010

Even though I was not a Yankee fan growing up on Long Island (New Hyde Park), I always had great respect for the House that Ruth Built.

I happened to be playing 2nd base for the Red Sox when Maris hit #61, so I consider myself part of the glorious history of Yankee Stadium.

Chuck Schilling [109]

Johnny Schmitz
July 6, 2010

Signed a Yankee Stadium demolition photo. [110]

Art Schult
July 12, 2010

Dear Michael, In answer to your letter of 7/2 I will attempt to give you an idea of how I felt about Yankee Stadium.

The house that Ruth built was the epitome of class as stadiums go. From the roof & stands all the way to the locker rooms it was class. No other stadium gave me that kind of feeling, but each ball park had its "own" aura.

I had mixed feelings about Yankee Stadium, because it was the last one of the 3 ball parks I played in there. I always looked forward to coming home to my home and family. When the Dodgers and Giants went west and I went to the N.L., the only time we came east was to Philly, which meant a 90 mile drive to home. (No Fun).

Hope this note will aid you in your endeavor.
Regards, Art Schult [111]

Dick Schofield
July 20, 2010

Mike - Sorry nothing left of ball park.

In Pitt. They saved left field where Maz H.R. beat Yankees. Home plate is in a building.

So I'm sorry they didn't save some part of stadium.
Sincerely, Dick [112]

Don Schwall
July 12, 2010

Michael, I remember the first game I pitched at Yankee Stadium in 1961. I was pitching the second game of a doubleheader. The manager, Pinky Higgins, told me to stay at the hotel and take the subway from Grand Central Station.

I will never forget when the train went above ground and I saw all of Yankee Stadium from right field with 58,000 people in their seats. It was a great thrill to know I was going to pitch at the greatest shrine in baseball.

To add to my joy I pitched 9 innings and beat what I consider the best baseball team of the modern era - the 1961 New York Yankees.
Regards, Don Schwall, 1961 A.L. ROY

(Don signed a Yankee Stadium demolition photo.) [113]

Bobby Shantz
July 1, 2010

Dear Sir: Nice to hear from you. I always loved to pitch in the old Yankee Stadium. The Yankees always had a great ball club in those days. When I was pitching for the Phila. A's in 1952, I pitched my best ball game against the Yankees. I pitched a <u>14</u>

inning complete game against them and beat them 2-1. I'll never forget it!!

Sincerely, Bobby Shantz

(Bobby signed a Yankee Stadium demolition photo.) [114]

Roland Sheldon
July 3, 2010

My only point of view. I still cannot believe there is a new "Yankee Stadium." All our history whether baseball, culture, etc. is contrived and belittled. This country is going down the tubes, people are too greedy and lazy in my opinion. We must restore morality and values so missed in our society.

Rollie Sheldon [115]

Norm Sherry
January 7, 2011

Hi Mike, To answer your question - I was in Yankee Stadium as a coach & mgr - never as a player.

I visited N.Y. in 1951 after finishing my Minor League season in Newport News, VA. I did go to the Stadium - it was very impressive as it was the 1st Major League park I had ever seen.

Entering the field from the dugout and stepping on to the field gave me quite a thrill - just thinking that Ruth & Gehrig had played there - my boyhood idols-

Sincerely, Norm [116]

Roy Sievers
August 18, 2010

Mr. Wagner, You know it's a shame to tear down the old ball parks. It happens in every baseball city - the parks are shorter, giving the hitters the advantage of hitting home runs, which the public wants to see.

Yankee Stadium was a tough park to play in - especially left field - where I played. The sun would go down, putting shadows in the centerfield area.

Just think of all the great players who played there, DiMaggio - Ruth - Gehrig - Berra- Gomez - Reynolds - Rizzuto - Ford...I could go on and on.

The fans always treated me good in the Stadium. My favorite managers were Casey Stengel and Ralph Houk.

Hope this works out for you, Mike.

Roy Sievers [117]

Charlie Silvera
August 18, 2010

Michael, Sorry for the delay bit I answer my fan mail about every three months -

I was at an old timers game in July & everything was just about flattened.

The new park is great but to me old Yankee Stadium was something special. On my first visit to the old stadium I went to see the field first, not the club house (1947).

I'm glad you have the same feeling as I for the old Stadium. Too bad it couldn't be considered a National Monument & not torn down.

Thanks for your interest, Charlie Silvera [118]

Curt Simmons
January 8, 2011

Curt sent a signed baseball card. [119]

Eric Soderholm
January 8, 2011

Signed a Yankee Stadium demolition photo. [120]

Daryl Spencer
January 5, 2011

Michael, Sorry Michael, I have no feelings about Yankee Stadium. I played for the N.Y. Giants at the end of the 1952 season and all of the 1953 and 1956-1957 seasons. I have never even been in Yankee Stadium, so I have no regrets to see it torn down.

The only ball parks still standing that I played in are Dodger Stadium, Wrigley Field and Fenway Park (played one Spring Training game there).

The sad thing about all the new parks is that they were all built it seems like for the big corporations. The poor guy with 2 or 3 kids can't even afford to go to 1 or 2 games a year because of the prices they charge.

Good luck with your book.

Daryl Spencer [121]

Marty Springstead
Umpire
September 11, 2010

Michael - Received your letter regarding Yankee Stadium.

As far as saving Gate 2 or an exterior wall is no doubt out of the question, as plans are already made to use that piece of property. They could however have a monument to tell people where the old stadium once stood. In Minn. for example, they have a home plate in the floor where the original H.P. was. This is in the "Mall of America."

The sad thing about the old stadium was the memories that were lost, all the ole' Yankee teams and players, the champion prize fights, the Beatles, the Pope, the N.Y. football Giants & the greatest game with Balt., the N.D. - Army great games, etc.

I enjoyed working in the stadium and being on the field with some of the greats, Mantle, Maris, etc., not to mention all the great visiting team players. Growing up in the Bronx, it was extra special to me, because in school we'd play a lot of games across the street.

Good luck in your venture & thanks for writing.

Kindest Regards, Marty Springstead [122]

Herman Starrette
January 9, 2011

Mike, There should be a memorial of some type. Someone would have to protect it & keep it up, or maintenance.

I loved Yankee Stadium & have memories of the stadium. So much history, but time goes on. It's just like building a house. You have one & someone has to build one better. Keep up with the Joneses. Hope this is a little help for you.

God Bless, Herman Starrette (Orioles) [123]

Dick Stigman January 7, 2011	Michael, I'll never forget my 1st appearance in Yankee Stadium. I came in in relief of Mudcat Grant (7th) (1960 w/ Cleveland). With men on base and faced Gil McDougald, Maris, Mantle, & Skowron. Got out of the inning and ended up winning the game. My walk from the bullpen in left field was also memorable as I prayed & sang to keep myself calm. It seemed that I got to pitch every time we played the Yankees, not always winning, but usually pitching well. Casey Stengel said "that Stigman always gives us trouble." I guess we have to accept change in our lives, but memories live on. God Bless you. Sincerely, Dick Stigman (Dick also sent a signed brochure & signed baseball card). [124]
Hal Stowe January 24, 2011	Signed a Yankee Stadium demolition photo. [125]
Frank Tepedino August 26, 2010	They should have had every living Yankee come to the old park and each one of us carry some of the sacred dirt from the old infield and sprinkle it over the new one. Let Mr. Steinbrenner cut the ribbon with all of us behind him. Best Always, Frank Tepedino (Frank signed a Yankee Stadium demolition photo and baseball card). [126]
Luis Tiant September 7, 2010	Signed a Yankee Stadium demolition photo. [127]
Virgil Trucks August 25, 2010	Dear Mr. Wagner, I will do the best I can in answer to your questions about Yankee Stadium. First, I think it was a terrible decision to destroy such a historic stadium, place, or what ever you want to call it. Because the history of baseball was invented in The United States of America. I know other stadiums in the U.S.A. have been torn down. But no comparison to the House that Babe Ruth Built,

with names like Lou Gehrig, Bill Dickey, Charlie Keller, Tommy Henrich and many more young ones. Joe DiMaggio, Mickey Mantle, Lefty Gomez, Whitey Ford, and you can add to this I'm sure.

The big thrill for me as my first trip to play in Yankee Stadium in 1942 was to think, I'm on the same field as so many great baseball men have played on. There was and still is nothing greater to me, and finishing my career with the Yankees in 1959.

Dressing in both club houses is a dream come true. Also, as a climax to all of this, that I had the honor and pleasure of meeting Babe Ruth, Ty Cobb, and most of the legendary players before me.

Well Mike, this is about all I have to say, and hope it will keep you in your endeavor. May God Bless you and your memories of Yankee Stadium, also the new one.

Sincerely, Virgil Trucks

P.S. - I wrote a book, so I use these pages for stationery, and a card for Major League Stats.

2X All Star/1949-1954/WS Champs 1945 vs. Cubs

Virgil Trucks

(Virgil also sent a signed baseball card). [128]

Sandy Valdespino
March 15, 2010

Signed a Yankee Stadium demolition photo. [129]

Bill Virdon
July 2, 2010

My only memories are my playing in three games during the 1960 World Series. It was great winning 2 of three games especially because the Yankees were the greatest and Yankee Stadium was their home.

Bill Virdon [130]

Jose Vizcaino
August 11, 2010

Dear Mr. Wagner: Thank you for your recent correspondence requesting my thoughts for consideration of your book.

The following answers are in response to your inquiry:

It is sad that the stadium is gone because it's the most historical field in history. The sensation of walking in for the first time to the Yankee locker room, and walking out onto the field where before you stood the likes of Mr. Joe DiMaggio and Mr. Babe Ruth is indescribable; a feeling that to this day overwhelms me.

The image of the original stadium will forever be ingrained in my mind. The surge of energy from that infield is so powerful. It gives off a feeling you will only get there.

Again, thank you for contacting me. I wish you the best of luck in your writing endeavors.

Kind Regards, Jose Vizcaino [131]

Vic Voltaggio
Umpire
September 6, 2010

Dear Michael, I received your letter on September 1st and was delighted to hear that someone besides myself is still interested in preserving our "Baseball History."

I was fortunate to have worked many games at the "Stadium" and I have many memories looking back over my twenty year career in the American League. The very first major league game that I worked was at Yankee Stadium on April 4, 1977. My crew chief was one great guy, Marty Springstead. The other guys on the crew were household names in umpiring. Larry Barnett and Jim Evans. It was a very cold day, around 34 degrees as I remember and the Milwaukee Brewers were in town.

I also remember that in 1979 while working a series between the Yankees and the Red Sox on Monday Night Game of the Week, I went out on a fly ball to left center and stepped in a sprinkler hole and tore the meniscus in right knee. I was told by a groundskeeper that it was the same hole that Mickey Mantle had stepped in years before. I had surgery the very next day and missed the rest of the season.

I loved Yankee Stadium and I was never intimidated by the city or the fans. I am originally from South Jersey and had been to the stadium as a child with an uncle who was a diehard Yankee fan.

I am enclosing for you one of my challenge coins to better explain what I am doing these days since I retired from the American League in 1996. I am a former Marine and I and my wife have been extremely active with the Marine Corps League since my retirement. I have worked my way through the chairs at the Detachment, Department, Division and National levels and I was just recently elected as the National Commandant. I get to travel the country as a voice for Veterans Affairs and I get to entertain members of Congress with some Baseball Stories.

I watch very little baseball on television these days because the commentators have taken the fun out of the game. The Ernie Harwells and the Phil Rizzutos are gone and now all we have are a bunch of diehard "Homers" who make up things as they go along. In St. Pete, we have the Rays and we also have Dwayne Staats and Kevin Kennedy, two of the worst I have ever heard. I can't stand to listen to them.

I miss the real announcers and with all of the former ball players in the booth giving their opinions, it has become a joke. They don't know the rules and all they do is talk about themselves. It is not the game that I was part of for 24 years and I miss it.

I wish you luck and godspeed.

Regards, Vic [132]

Bill Wakefield
August 16, 2010

Signed a Yankee Stadium demolition photo. [133]

Fred Whitfield
September 8, 2010

Michael: Thanks for asking me the questions you had about the Stadium. It broke my heart when I heard they were tearing it down. I sure had some fond memories there, played against some of the best players in the history of the game there. I also had the pleasure of meeting Mrs. Ruth there. It was a beautiful place.

I was a country boy for a small town in Alabama, Vandiver - population: 250 or less "ha, ha." I was blessed by God just being able to play in the majors, and Yankee Stadium sure was a

Blessing & Joy: I hit a lot of homers there, and they all jumped on my head then in the fight we had with them "ha, ha."

Thanks Michael for asking, so take care and good luck on the book. Send me one if possible.

Fred [134]

Dave Whitney
Negro Leagues
August 26, 2010

Dear Sir: Some parts of history should never be destroyed. I appreciate your efforts in that respect.

It was a tremendous thrill for me to play in the stadium since I was only twenty-two at the time. I remember getting three hits the first time I played in the stadium.

Thanks for your interest.

Dave Whitney KC. Monarchs [135]

Bob Wiesler
August 20, 2010

Signed a Yankee Stadium demolition photo. [136]

Stan Williams
July 5, 2010

Michael - I'm busy putting reports into my P.C. (Wash. Nat'ls), so this note will be terse.

Yes - I pitched 2 yrs. For the Yankees & came into the 'Old-Park' with several clubs. I even pitched in the 1960 All-Star game there. As a Yankee I was probably at the bottom of my productive years - (Bad Arm), but I always got a thrill just going to the park - because of all the tradition & legends that played there. I only wish I could have been more productive, as a N.Y.Y., though. I also was pitching coach there - several times - & "George" fired me every time he got angry at the Mgr. -

One cute story - a "Yogism." One day in 1980, (Yogi & I - both coaches for Howser), it rained so hard that the dugout filled up 'til it was even with the field. During the delay we all went into the Mgr's office. Someone turned on the T.V., showing the movie: "The Great Escape." Yogi - looked, saw Steve McQueen & said "Hey, he musta made that one before he died." That's not a knock on 'Yogi' - he's a fine man & I love him dearly. He just makes fun quotes at times and all enjoy them.

Regards - Good Luck with your book-
Stan Williams, ex-Yankee

P.S. - I pitched in the Polo Grounds and it's gone, too. Must be getting old - SW [137]

Walt "No Neck" Williams July 27, 2010	Signed a Yankee Stadium demolition photo. [138]
Gordon Windhorn July 8, 2010	Dear Michael - Thank you for your nice letter...always enjoy hearing from good baseball fans. Fans, like you, is what made the game what is today...players don't appreciate the fans today and this is a mistake. I really don't know much about what was done with the parts of old Yankee Stadium. I thought, for sure, that a lot would be saved. My time there was short but it was very special! Sincerely, Gordy Windhorn [139]
Bob Wolff Sportscaster August 12, 2010	Dear Michael, The old Yankee Stadium houses many wonderful memories for me. I broadcast the Don Larsen perfect World Series game there. I called the Colts-Giants overtime NFL Championship there, called "the greatest football game ever played," called Mickey Mantle's towering home run which hit the façade about a foot from becoming the first home run to go out of the ball park, many World Series games and classic events. But Yankee Stadium is not alone in stadium demolitions. I would believe that every professional stadium I broadcast or telecast in during the years has suffered a similar fate. Many college stadia remain intact, but professional sports is a big business influenced by many new developments. Along with

television came rights money for clubs and networks televising their games. Gate receipts were just part of the income.

Salaries of the players rose from thousands to millions of dollars as players wanted part of the new jackpot.

To take care of the increased expenditures, baseball and indoor arenas started to build luxury suites for their wealthy patrons and corporations, and most early parks weren't built for that. New buildings also included restaurants, and other amenities which brought in further income, redid the press section and, playing more to adults who could afford this than kids, baseball became more of a spectator sport. Fewer youngsters play baseball today than in the early years - but the baseball attendance is far greater than ever, so economically it's paying off for the team owners.

This happens all over. For over fifty years I've been broadcasting Madison Square Garden events. This is the fourth Madison Square Garden.

Memories do fade and that's the process of sports, too.

But they are treasured by those who experienced them and I can fully understand your passion for the past and wish you well with your work. A book is a great way to remember.

I have wonderful Yankee Stadium memories. They're an important part of my career. I must admit, that although I have filed-away clippings of my playing career, I have watched with renewed enjoyment watching my children and grandchildren make headlines of their own. That's exciting to me today.

I love the old sentiment, but am working in the present on the longest-running broadcaster in history - and I'm extremely grateful to have worked and enjoyed these many decades.

Best wishes for all your endeavors.

Bob Wolff, HOF '95 [140]

Al Worthington
July 4, 2010

Dear Michael, You really made a big jump from New York to Texas.

The first time I saw Yankee Stadium I believe it was 1957…a fight, I think I saw two fights there. As a player I went to Yankee Stadium in 1964, 65, 66, 67, 68, 69-71, & 72.

The first time I went into Yankee Stadium as a player I was "awed." The history behind Yankee Stadium made me feel very small and maybe I should not be here, as I thought of all the great Yankee players and all the World Series they had won.

As I look back I am honored to have played in Yankee Stadium.

It does seem unreal that the stadium should be torn down.

Where you thought of New York, you think of the Empire State Building, the Statue of Liberty, and Yankee Stadium. It seems a piece of America is missing. What a loss for New York.

Even though I live in Alabama losing something like Yankee Stadium is like losing a best friend.

Sincerely Yours, Al Worthington

(Al also sent a signed newspaper clipping of himself and a signed religious brochure). [141]

Ed Yost
January 8, 2011

Signed a Yankee Stadium demolition photo and two signed photos of himself. [142]

Gus Zernial
July 14, 2010

Signed a Yankee Stadium demolition photo. [143]

Chapter Ten

YANKEE STADIUM ADVERTISERS IN PROGRAMS AND YEARBOOKS

The following are from advertisements in the New York Yankees programs sold in the years listed. It seemed interesting to see what products were advertised in years past. Capitalized, bold, underlined type, etc are how the words appeared in the score cards. The type faces varied, with a good number of them showing photos of cigarettes, beer, whiskey bottles, ice cream, etc.

<u>1923</u>

Yankee Stadium Opening Day Program vs. Boston Red Sox – April 18, 1923 15 cents
Adams Black Jack Chewing Gum
Between The Acts Mild Havana Blend Little Cigars – 15 cents
Camel Cigarettes
Socony Gasoline and Motor Oil, 26 Broadway, NY
Lucky Strike Cigarettes – "It's Toasted"
Murad Turkish Cigarettes
Apper Brothers Clothes
Childs Foods – Food For Mankind
Hotel Savoy, 58th to 59th Street, New York City
Chesterfield Cigarettes – Sold On The Grounds
Osborn Engineering Co., Cleveland, Ohio, Architects and Engineers of Yankee Stadium, Also for the Polo Grounds, and other baseball parks
GEM Safety Razors, $3.00 Deluxe Models – Now $1.00
Huyler's, America's Foremost Fine Candy – Chocolate Bars and Taffy, sold exclusively on these grounds
White Rock "The World's Best Table Water"
Muriel Cigars – "A hit whenever lit."
Rosoff Sand and Gravel Corp., supplied all the gravel used in constructing the Stadium
Hudson River Night Lines – Daily Sailings to Albany, Troy, and the North
The Corn Exchange Bank, New York, Beaver and William Streets
Flor De Melba – The Cigar Supreme – on sale at all stands on the grounds
Spalding – "The Ball that made Base Ball"
Melachrino Cigarettes – "The One Cigarette Sold the World Over" – On Sale Here
J.W. Fiske Iron Works – Supplied the Turnstile used to enter Yankee Stadium
Taylor-Fichter Steel Construction Co. of New York – They Furnished and Erected All Structural Steel for the Stadium
Otto Stahl's "Ready to Eat Meats," Frankfurters – served at Yankee Stadium
Daly Bros. Company, Contractors and Excavators, New York
Edwards & Booth, General Insurance Brokers, New York – Insurance & Surety Bonds

Sinclair Oils, Sinclair Refining Company, Chicago
Genuine "Bull" Durham Tobacco – 50 Good Cigarettes 10 cents
Wadsworth, Howland, & Co., Inc. – Furnished all the Paint, Enamels, and Concrete Coatings used in Yankee Stadium
Harry M. Stevens, Publisher

1937

Score card - 5 cents
Regal Shoes - Compare
Between The Acts Little Cigars 10 for 15 cents
Muriel Cigars – "For a real hit…ASK THE BOY FOR…MURIEL 10 cents
Harry M. Stevens, Inc., Publisher, Offices: 320 Fifth Ave., NY
Camel Cigarettes – "I Get A Lift With a CAMEL"
JACOB RUPPERT'S Light BEER Dark – SOLD HERE AND EVERYWHERE
WARD'S ROLLS – The delicious Frankfurter Rolls – served at Yankee Stadium
Wear Shirts with TruBenized Collars. They'll keep you cool! Won't wilt, wrinkle, pucker, curl or kink! Empire State Building, New York City
Chesterfield Cigarettes – A sure hit – THEY SATISFY
Try a Delicious Stahl-Meyer FRANKFURTER – served at Yankee Stadium
THE SHOREHAM HOTEL, Washington, D.C., Single Room and Bath $4.00 and $5.00 Double Room and Bath $6.00 and $8.00 – Washington Home of the Yankees
THE COPLEY-PLAZA, Boston, Massachusetts
THE BENJAMIN FRANKLIN – 1200 MODERN ROOMS EACH WITH A PRIVATE BATH - The Yankees' Home in Philadelphia
HOTEL CLEVELAND – Headquarters in Cleveland for the Yankees and all ball clubs and fans. Rooms from $2.50 for one, $4. for two
HOTEL CHASE, Saint Louis – The Yankees stay at this Nationally Known Hotel – Every Convenience – Reasonable Rates
DEL PRADO HOTEL, Lake Michigan and 53rd Street, CHICAGO – 400 ROOMS – 400 BATHS EUROPEAN: $3.00 and up
Truly Warner Hats and Shoes – Genuine Panama $2.95, Feather Weight Straws $1.85 White Reverse Calf Shoes $3.98
OLD GOLD, America's Double-Mellow CIGARETTE
Chesterfield Cigarettes – for the good things smoking can give you. They Satisfy
GEM Micromatic BLADES For Perfect Shaves – Use a Gem in a Gem
G.G.G. Clothes
BARNEY'S – Many Nationally Advertised CLOTHES At Cut Prices – THE ONLY STORE OF ITS KIND IN NEW YORK
LUCKY STRIKE CIGARETTES – "Luckies are gentle on my throat"- Jimmie Dunn
A.G. Spalding & Bros. – 14 out of 16 Major League teams play in Spalding uniforms
Corn Exchange Bank Trust Company – William and Beaver Streets, New York
Beech-Nut Gum – Six hits! "Gee, they're hits, all right!"
White Rock – mineral water
SCHRAFFT'S CHOCOLATE COVERED BARS - A sure hit! 5 cents
GULDEN'S MUSTARD
HORTON'S Manhattan Special Ice Cream – SERVED HERE EXCLUSIVELY
Book-Cadillac Hotel – preferred by the Yankees when in Detroit – 1200 Rooms From $3.00

New York and the New Yorker Hotel New York Headquarters for the New York Yankees
CANADA DRY – "IT'S GINGERVATING" The Champagne of Ginger Ales
Certified Cremo Cigars - was 5 cents. NOW 3 for ten cents
SINCLAIR – SINCLAIR-BABE RUTH BASEBALL CONTEST – free EVERY WEEK!
2 NASH 8's! 20 RCA Victor AUTO RADIOS. Also 500 AUTOGRAPHED LEAGUE BASEBALLS
Tune in Babe Ruth – Wednesday and Friday Nights – 10:30-10:45 WABC

1942

Score Card - 10 cents
Harry M. Stevens, Inc., Publisher, OFFICES: 320 FIFTH AVE., N.Y.
CAMEL Cigarettes – 28% LESS NICOTINE
THREE FEATHERS RESERVE BLENDED WHISKEY, 86.8 Proof
FOR VICTORY BUY UNITED STATES DEFENSE BONDS AND STAMPS
Between The Acts LITTLE CIGARS 10 for 15 cents
MURIEL CIGARS - For a real hit...ASK THE BOY FOR MURIEL 10 cents
RENAULT AMERICAN CHAMPAGNE – A toast to VICTORY – BUY DEFENSE BONDS AND STAMPS
WARD'S TIP-TOP BREAD – Enriched WITH VITAMIN AND FOOD IRON
RUPPERT BEER – "BOY! MAKE MINE RUPPERT
Douglas Shoes – You, too, will make a HIT in Douglas Shoes
GALLAGHER'S STEAK HOUSE, 228 WEST 52nd STREET (West of Broadway)
Chesterfield Cigarettes – EVERYWHERE YOU GO – It's Chesterfield – They Satisfy
THE COPLEY-PLAZA, BOSTON, MASSACHUSETTS, One of the World's Finest Hotels
White Rock SPARKLING MINERAL WATER, IT IS THE DUTY OF EVERY AMERICAN TO **KEEP FIT!**
Corn Exchange Bank Trust Company – Head Office – William and Beaver Streets, NEW YORK
HOTEL CLEVELAND, Cleveland – Headquarters in Cleveland for the Yankees, and all ball clubs and fans. Rooms from $3.00 for one, $4.50 for two
ASTOR HOTEL, TIMES SQUARE, "MEET ME AT THE ASTOR" – New COLUMBIA ROOM, Luncheon from $1., Dinner from $2 – The BAR-CAFÉ, Luncheon from 95 cents, Dinner a la Carte
OLD GOLD CIGARETTES
G.G.G. Clothes
ADAM HATS – SCORE AGAIN!
GEM SINGLEDGE BLADES – GEM REPEATS ITS GREATEST SALE! 12 for 39 cents. Reg .55 pack
LUCKY STRIKE CIGARETTES – With men who know tobacco best – IT'S LUCKIES 2 TO 1
SPALDING – EXCLUSIVE in BOTH Major Leagues!
HORTON'S ICE CREAM – Packed in individual box with spoon.
SCHRAFFT'S CHOCOLATE COVERED BARS – During the Game – It's SCHRAFFT'S
Gulden's Mustard – SERVED HERE EXCLUSIVELY
BRUCKNER BEVERAGES – Thirsty??? Call the Boy For BRUCKNER BEVERAGES. Since 1871
DRAKE'S CAKE – THE ROOTER'S SNACK – AS GOOD AS THE BEST YOU EVER ATE!
DEL PRADO HOTEL – Lake Michigan at 53rd Street, CHICAGO – Chicago Headquarters for American League Clubs – 400 ROOMS-400 BATHS – EUROPEAN: $3.00 and up
The YANKEES prefer the Book-Cadillac Hotel while in Detroit – 1200 Rooms – From $3.30
Beech-Nut Gum – CHAMPION year after year
THE SHOREHAM HOTEL, Washington, D.C. – Washington Home of the Yankees
THE BENJAMIN FRANKLIN – A GREAT NAME, A GREAT HOTEL – The Yankees' Home in Philadelphia – 1200 MODERN ROOMS EACH WITH A BATH
HOTEL CHASE – BASEBALL HEADQUARTERS IN ST. LOUIS
Stevens Metal Products Company – Niles, Ohio – Steel Containers – From 10 to 110 Gallon Capacity

THE COMMODORE – Right at Grand Central – 42nd Street and Lexington Avenue – Rooms: $3.50 to $7.15 – Twin-bedded rooms - $6.60, $7.15, $7.70, and $8.80
CANADA DRY – "The Champagne of Ginger Ales"
Garcia y Vega Cigars – No finer cigar made 10 cents and up
SINCLAIR – "SAVE WEAR WITH SINCLAIR" – HELP WIN THE WAR – BUY DEFENSE BONDS AND STAMPS

1951

Score Card – 10 cents
Publisher: HARRY M. STEVENS, Inc., 320 FIFTH AVENUE, NEW YORK
Camel Cigarettes – CAMELS – Cool and Mild!
MELROSE RARE Blended Whiskey – The Perfect Rose to Remember – Symbol of Gracious Living
BRIGGS PIPE MIXTURE & MURIEL CIGARS – A couple of "SMOKING HITS"
GOTTFRIED'S - BREAD-ROLLS-CAKES-PASTRIES – GOLDEN CRUST PRODUCTS – Enjoy 'Em at home, here at the ball park, and at the finest restaurants and cafes all over town
DU MONT TELEVISION – NEXT TO SEEING IT IN PERSON! You'll see it best over DU MONT TELEVISION
BEECH-NUT GUM – That's what makes a hit with me – It's Always Refreshing
Emerson LIFE-TESTED Television and Radio – Every 5 Seconds Someone buys an EMERSON-AMERICA'S BEST BUY
PARK & TILFORD RESERVE WHISKEY – An American Favorite – The PREMIUM Whiskey at a POPULAR Price!
SCHENLEY RESERVE Blended Whiskey – leads the league in good taste! Try it today!
DeSoto – For extra value today…and tomorrow! SEE YOUR DESOTO-PLYMOUTH DEALER
Seagram's 7 Crown 'Blended Whiskey – Sure as a Home Run – Say Seagram's and be Sure
Corn Exchange Bank Trust Company – ESTABLISHED 1853 – HEAD OFFICE – William and Beaver Streets - NEW YORK
London Character Shoes – woven with a difference! $13.95
Chesterfield Cigarettes – MILDER! PLUS NO UNPLEASANT AFTER-TASTE Always Buy CHESTERFIELD
THE BRASS RAIL – Four Great American Restaurants
OLD GOLD Cigarettes – If you want a TREAT instead of a TREATMENT…smoke OLD GOLDS
GEM – Feather Weight RAZOR
G.G.G. CLOTHES – So comfortable you can slide safely in-to home in your G.G.G.
LONGINES – THE WORLD'S MOST HONORED WATCH – USED BY ALL MAJOR LEAGUE UMPIRES FOR TIMING ALL BASEBALL GAMES –INCLUDING THE WORLD SERIES
LUCKY STRIKE Cigarettes – Be Happy- Go Lucky! LUCKIES TASTE BETTER THAN ANY OTHER CIGARETTE!
CORBY'S BLENDED WHISKEY – For whiskey with striking quality, look for CORBY'S PARROT
SCHRAFFT'S – Always ask for SCHRAFFT'S Delicious CHOCOLATE COVERED CANDY BARS AND PEPPERMINT PATTIES
GULDEN'S MUSTARD – Your Frankfurter Tastes Better because it's SPREAD with GULDEN'S MUSTARD – SERVED HERE EXCLUSIVELY
Seagram's Gin – As Modern as Tomorrow! BASEBALL HAS COME OF AGE – Now Gin has come of Age
DRAKE'S CAKE – THE ROOTERS SNACK- AS GOOD AS THE BEST YOU EVER ATE!
TROMMER'S BEER – Any inning-STRETCH for TROMMER'S BEER…better because it's all-Malt and Hops!
COLGATE LEADS THE LEAGUE IN smooth shaving! "Choice of Champions in Every Sport"
White Rock Ginger Ale and Sparkling Water – Perfect Mixers at Any Party!

HYGRADE'S ALL BEEF FRANKFURTERS – Enjoy them at home, too. In cellophane packages and cans.
BALLANTINE! – Make the world-wide friendship sign-ASK THE MAN FOR BALLANTINE!
Majors CABIN GRILL RESTAURANT – a sure winner....for the finest steaks! 33 WEST 33 ST., N.Y.
LANOLIZE YOUR SHOES WITH ESQUIRE BOOT POLISH
EHLERS GRADE "A" Coffee – HOME RUN? With Ehlers waiting for you after the game you'll RUN HOME! THE BEST COFFEE AT ANY PRICE!
MRS. WAGNER'S PIES – Always A Winner!
Stahl-Meyer FRANKFURT – THE FINEST-**NOW** AS ALWAYS! AT HOME.....or AT MAJOR SPORTING EVENTS
HORTON'S ICE CREAM – FOR A REAL ICE CREAM TREAT! Get a Horton's – 1851 – 1951
CANADA DRY – ASK THE BOY for CANADA DRY – "The best of them all"
Garcia y Vega – A famous name for over 65 years –1882- THE BONDED HAVANA CIGAR – Made in Tampa
SINCLAIR – World's First ANTI-RUST GASOLINE – CONTAINS RD-119 – Super Power, too

1961

Score Card - 15 cents Yearbook: 50 cents
CAMEL Cigarettes – Have a real cigarette...have a CAMEL – Jackie Jensen, Warren Spahn, Roger Maris, Whitey Ford, and Pete Runnels are pictured smoking Camels.
Elsie Brand Ice Cream (Borden's) – ELSIE SAYS: TRY MY ICE CREAM – FROSTICK and ICE CREAM CONE
TOP BRASS – TAKE CARE OF YOUR HAIR...YOU'VE ONLY GOT IT ONCE!
AMF – BOWL WHERE YOU SEE THE "MAGIC TRIANGLE"
Schenley – After the game enjoy Schenley the only whisky with whipped-in smoothness
Parliament Cigarettes – WHY is Parliament's ¼ in recess so important to you? BECAUSE tobacco tastes better when the filter's recessed
Four Roses Blended Whiskey – The Good Life includes Four Roses
Northeast Airlines – MOST JETS TO FLORIDA
Chevron Gas Stations
Coca Cola – BE REALLY REFRESHED...PAUSE FOR COKE!
Beech-Nut Gum – Big Leaguers chew Beech-Nut Gum! It's FLAVOR-IFIC
J.W. Dant 10 Year Old Charcoal Perfected Whiskey
ESQUIRE 'NO ODOR' BOOT POLISH – Leading the League in Shoe Shines
SWEET-ORR Casual Wear – An All-Star Selection for 90 years
Mutual of New York (MONY) Insurance – **MONY** TODAY MEANS **MONEY** TOMORROW!
Ehlers Golden Blend Coffee – LEADS THE COFFEE LEAGUE IN FLAVOR SATISFACTION
G.G.G. Clothes – Sold only in America's finest stores
Old Spice – MEN WHO 'LIVE" OUTDOORS...choose cool, skin-soothing Old Spice AFTER SHAVE LOTION
GEM Blades – ATTENTION MEN WITH TOUGH BEARDS! Get Extra Tough GEM Blades and GEM PUSH-BUTTON RAZOR in handsome Presentation Case with Gem blades in dispenser $1.00
KENT Cigarettes – You'll feel better about smoking with the taste of KENT
PALMOLIVE Rapid-Shave – **Super-Soaks** AND **Super Softens** EVEN THE TOUGHEST BEARD – For The FASTEST, SMOOTHEST SHAVES POSSIBLE – REGULAR AND MENTHOL
BEEFEATER – The imported English Gin that doubles your martini pleasure
CHEMICAL BANK NEW YORK TRUST COMPANY –
Great Western New York State Champagne – "ON THE BALL" for 100 years!
PARK & TILFORD – The Finest Tasting Whiskey of its Type
Seagram's Blended Whiskey – SAY Seagram's AND BE Sure

Garcia y Vega Cigars – Connoisseur's Choice SINCE 1882 – THE BONDED HAVANA CIGAR
Marlboro Cigarettes – The filter cigarette with the unfiltered taste – Make yourself comfortable-have a Marlboro
GOTTFRIED FRANKFURTER ROLLS – **NEW YORKS** FINEST! – SERVED HERE!
QUALITY – PALL MALL HERBERT TAREYTON LUCKY STRIKE TAREYTON Cigarettes
Gulden's Mustard – Tops at 'home plate'! Great on franks!
Stahl-Meyer – THESE FRANKFURTS ARE HICKORY SMOKED!
Ruppert Knickerbocker – SATISFY YOUR BEER THIRST BETTER
SEAGRAM'S EXTRA DRY GIN – TOP OF THE LEAGUE IN DRYNESS
Newport Cigarettes – refreshes while you smoke
OLD GOLD Cigarettes – Old Gold Spin Filters
LONGCHAMPS RESTAURANTS – AFTER THE GAME…for great food and great drinks mixed with Lighter, Livelier White Rock
Canada Dry – Spectating is more sparkling…with Canada Dry Ginger Ale…
SCHRAFFT'S – Our Proudest and Finest for you to Give
Ballantine Beer – the 'crisp' refresher…bubbling with pride at sponsoring the New York Yankees on radio and television for 15 straight great years.
Sinclair DINO GASOLINE At Regular Price – At *Sinclair* We Care…About You…About your Car

1973

Score Card: 30 cents Yearbook: $1.50 (50th Anniversary of Yankee Stadium)
Camel, Salem, Winston Cigarettes – LEADS THE LEAGUE IN TASTE!
Seagram's 7 Crown. It's America's whiskey.
Marlboro Cigarettes
MANUFACTURERS HANOVER – It's Any Car Loan season.
Schaefer Beer – when you're having more than one – available at all concession stands.
SUN DEW – Tasty Fruit Drinks – WARM WEATHER WINNER!
BEEFEATER DRY GIN – First name for the martini
CUTTY SARK BLENDED SCOTS WHISKY – If our Yanks are a bunch of runs behind in the ninth…"Don't give up the ship!"
KENT MENTHOL, KENT, Newport, TRUE Cigarettes – The All-Star Line-up.
AMERICAN EXPRESS The Money Card – For men who hunger after victory.
ILGWU – Baseball. The Great American Game. STOP IMPORTING UNEMPLOYMENT
Budweiser Beer – When you say Budweiser you've said it all!
PLANTERS Peanuts – Hey sport! Go with the winner! PLANTERS
Seagram's 100 PIPERS Scotch Whisky – It's made proudly. Drink it that way.
PALL MALL, Tareyton 100's, LUCKY TEN, Silva THINS, Iceberg 10 Cigarettes – TOP LINE-UP FOR TASTE
Old Grand-Dad Fifth, Pint, Quart KENTUCKY STRAIGHT BOURBON WHISKEY – TRIPLE PLAY
DATSUN – THE OFFICIAL YANKEE CAR – PRIDE OF THE YANKEES – 610 2-Door Hardtop
Getty Gasoline – More miles for your money.

1976

Score Card: 50 cents Yearbook: $1.50
Ambassador. Representing Scotch at its lightest.
JOIN THE NAVY. Be someone special. GET AN EXTRA BASE HIT
Miller Beer – Miller time – America's quality beer since 1855.
WALSH CONSTRUCTION COMPANY – GOOD LUCK YANKEES – 1976 – From The

CONSTRUCTION MANAGER of Your New Stadium

Old Grand-Dad KENTUCKY STRAIGHT BOURBON WHISKEY – When you ask a lot more from life. If you ask a lot more from your team, shouldn't you expect as much from your Bourbon?

Winston Cigarettes – I know my taste.

THE 1976 TOYOTA CELICAS. WE GOT IT. IT'S THE IMPORT CAR OF THE YEAR.

Jack in the Box – NEW SEASON, NEW BALL GAME! THERE YOU HAVE IT, FANS…

NEW YORK LIFE Insurance – Where the name of the game is life, call New York Life.

MANUFACTURERS HANOVER – It's banking the way you want it to be. Manufacturers Hanover makes 2,000 loans a week to people just like you.

The New Dodge Street Van. It's the first van that comes factory-customized.

BEEFSTEAK CHARLIE'S – CHARLIE'S GOOD DEALS ARE A HIT IN NEW YORK. CHARLIE'S STEAK $4.99, CHARLIE'S ROAST PRIME RIB $4.99, CHARLIE LOVES KIDS 99 CENTS

POLLY-O There's more to Polly-O than just New York's best Ricotta and Mozzarella.

Key APPLIANCE **CO-OP STORES – WE GIVE YOU MORE FOR A LOT LESS!**

Schenley Canadian O.F.C. CANADIAN WHISKY – In a league by itself.

French's PURE PREPARED MUSTARD – You've put us on top – we make your life delicious.

J&B RARE SCOTCH – You can always count on J&B for consistent quality. That's why we're confident that once you try it, you'll become an ardent fan too.

Yankees Away From Home – the Ponchartrain – Detroit's Preferred Hotel; The Pfister Hotel & Tower, Milwaukee, Wis; Hollenden House, Cleveland, Ohio; The Lord Baltimore Hotel, Baltimore, Maryland; Leamington Hotel & Motor Inn, Minneapolis, Minn; Royal Inn of Anaheim, Anaheim, Calif.; Executive House, Chicago, Illinois.

KENT, Newport, TRUE, OLD GOLD FILTERS Cigarettes – "TAKE US OUT AT THE BALL GAME"

Jackson's – Fordham Road's First Restaurant – Steak & Lobster is our middle name

PEPSI – Call your own time-out. Pepsi-Cola salutes the Yankees and their new Stadium.

AMC Pacer – The first wide small car. EVERY NEW PACER IS BACKED BY THE AMC BUYER PROTECTION PLAN

Boulevard AMC-Jeep- Bayside Queens – THERE IS SOMETHING ALWAYS HAPPENING AT THE HOME OF THE GOOD SPORTS

GAF – Photo Equipment – THE GAF NOSTALGIA MACHINES

TOWN AND COUNTRY TRAVEL OF MANHATTAN LTD./HOLIDAYLAND, INC. – PLAY BALL WITH THE WORLD CHAMPIONS OF TRAVEL

Colonial – NEW YORK YANKEES label BEEF FRANKS and COLD CUTS – The greatest double play combination of the year.

UNIVERSITY CHEVROLET, Jerome Ave. at 167th St., Bx. – Always Tries to **save you more**

WILKINSON SWORD- The name on the world's finest blades.

Dunhill PERSONNEL AGENCY, 342 Madison Ave., N.Y., N.Y. 10017

SPORTS PRODUCTS CORP., Cleveland, Ohio 44122 – The World's Largest Manufacturer of Plastic Helmets - $25.00 each

Johnnie Walker Red – In a league by itself.

Borkum Riff Pipe Tobaccos - Introducing Borkum Riff Champagne. Another one of life's simple pleasures.

Getty Unleaded Regular gasoline – Our price and performance are a whole new ballgame. High Octane. Low price.

Datsun Saves – THE WINNING LINE-UP FROM DATSUN.

Beck Beer – Drink Beck's only if the Yanks win this game. Germany's best premium beer is too good to be wasted on a lost cause.

AMC – THE BUYER PROTECTION PLAN Company. We stand behind our cars.

BEEFEATER – The Gin of England.
TERMINAL PRINTING & LITHOGRAPHING CO. – 41 FIRST STREET, HOBOKEN, N.J.
Gabriel – New shocks can save wear on your tires.
Professional SPORTS Publications – The ad you're reading right now is worth a lot more than it cost.
The Marines – The tough team to join has no second string.
Marlboro Cigarettes – Come to where the flavor is. Come to Marlboro Country.

Publisher: Professional SPORTS Publications, 310 Madison Avenue, New York, NY 10017

Chapter Eleven

End Notes

A TEAM AND HOME ARE BORN End Notes

1. "American League Here: Another Baseball Team Proposed for New York Next Season," *The New York Times*, September 7, 1902.

2. "Grounds For Baseball: President Johnson Says American League Is Sure of a Site," *The New York Times*, February 8, 1903.

3. "Troubles In Baseball: Laborers on American League Grounds Want More Wages," *The New York Times*, March 31, 1903.

4. "Big Day For Baseball: New York American League Team Will Open New Grounds To-day," *The New York Times*, April 30, 1903.

5. "Griffith's Men Win First Game At Home," *The New York Times*, April 11, 1905; "Clark Griffith The Pitcher-Manager," *Sandusky Evening Star,* Sandusky, Ohio, April 26, 1904; "Baseball Results: American League," *The Post-Standard,* Syracuse, New York, May 17, 1904; "Patsy Dougherty Statistics," http://www.baseball-reference.com/d/doughpa01.shtml; "1904: Boston Herald tells of Red Sox trade "Dougherty as a Yankee," 1st known reference to the New York club as Yankees," http://www.brainyhistory.com/ days/june_ 21.html.

6. "What's In The Name Yankees?," *The Galveston Daily News*, Galveston, Texas, May 24, 1939; "15,000 See Yankees Take First Game," *The New York Times*, April 15, 1906.

7. "15,000 See Yankees Take First Game," *The New York Times*, April 15, 1906.

8. "Yankees" Beaten In Opening Game," *The New York Times*, April 17, 1907.

9. "Chance Signs to Manage Yankees," *The New York Times*, January 9, 1913.

10. "New Tags For Chance's Men Now In Order," *The Anaconda Standard,* Anaconda, Montana, February 2, 1913.

11. Ibid.

12. "Girth of a Nation: The New York Yankees adopted pinstripe uniforms in an effort to disguise Babe Ruth's girth," http://ww.snopes.com/sports/baseball/pinstripes.asp.

13. "Yankees Pick Site For New Ball Park," *The New York Times*, January 30, 1921.

14. "Statements Clash Regarding Stadium," *The New York Times*, January 31, 1921.

15. "Not Just Jerry: There's a Quirky Story To the Way Jerome Avenue Got Its Name," The Bronx Journal Online, http://lehman.cuny.edu/deanhum/langlit/tbj/sep00/local.htm.

16. "Yankees To Build Stadium In Bronx," *The New York Times*, February 6, 1921.

17. "Yankee Stadium To Seat 80,000 Fans," *The New York Times*, December 18, 1921.

18. Swanson, Harry. *Ruthless Baseball: Yankees Purified by Fire Stadium Construction*," Bloomington, Indiana: Author HOUSE, 2005, xxi. (hereafter cited at "Swanson"). Numerous details about which companies were given contracts to perform particular jobs in the construction of Yankee Stadium, as presented in this chapter of "*Babe's Place*," used information from Harry Swanson's book. Specific page numbers are cited in subsequent notes. I am truly indebted to Mr. Swanson for the generous use of his wonderful reference book.

19. "Work Begins Today On Yankee Stadium," *The New York Times*, May 6, 1922.

20. Swanson, xxi, 92.

21. Swanson, 115, 89; "Standard Fire Insurance Policy of the State of New York (Policy #407857), September 16, 1922," ebay, December 29, 2002; "Standard Fire Insurance Policy of the State of New York (Policy #14661), January 18, 1923,"; http://www.baseball-fever.com/showthread.php?97584-1923-Yankee-S..., August 22, 2011.

22. Swanson, 90, 100-101, 104-107, 115; "Souvenir Programme: Yankee Stadium-Opening Day, April 18, 1923," Harry M. Stevens, Publisher; Jane Primerano, "Edison Cement Plant: N.J. Plant Cemented in History," *The Express-Times*, http://www.rootsweb.ancestry.com/~njwarren/edison.html; "Yankee Stadium's Big Engineering Task," *The New York Times*, April 1, 1923.

23. Blueprint, "Elevations: Yankee Stadium Letters and Frieze," The Osborn Engineering Co, Cleveland, Ohio, drawn July 25, 1927; Swanson, 103 (façade); "Vintage Original Yankee Stadium Sign "S,'" ebay, December 31, 2009; "Lot 441: 1923 Letter "U" From Yankee Stadium," Lelands Auctions, November 2010, November 19, 2010; "New York NY Yankee Stadium Baseball Sign "M,"" ebay, February 26, 2007; "New Air View of

Yankee Stadium; Giant Copper Bat for Weather Vane," *The Mansfield News*, Mansfield, Ohio, October 9, 1923.

24. Swanson, 93-99.

25. Swanson, 117-118.

26. Swanson, 122.

27. Swanson, 129-130.

28. "Yankee Field Is Given Final Touch," *The New York Times*, November 28, 1922.

29. Swanson, 164-165.

30. Swanson, 143.

31. "Yankees' New Park Almost Completed," *The New York Times*, March 11, 1923; Swanson, 142, 147-148.

32. Swanson, 162-163.

33. "Comparison Shows Yanks' Park Larger," *The New York Times*, February 4, 1923; Baseball Historian, "Fred Lieb quickly dubbed it "The House that Ruth built," http://www.baseballhistorian.com/html/American_heroes.cfm?page=6.

34. e-mail, Richard Lillard to Michael Wagner, Blueprint of Yankee Stadium Field Dimensions, ca.1922, January 14, 2010.

35. "Giants and Yanks Start Active War," *The New York Times*, January 6, 1923.

36. "ASG reminds of Stadium's rich history: Cathedral in the Bronx part of America's heritage," July 14, 2008, http://www.sny.tv/news/article.jsp?ymd=20080714&content_id=1467.

37. "Yanks' New Stadium To Be Opened Today," *The New York Times*, April 18, 1923.

38. "Ticket Speculators Arrested At Stadium," *The New York Times*, April 19, 1923.

39. "74,200 See Yankees Open New Stadium; Ruth Hits Home Run," *The New York Times*, April 19, 1923.

40. Harvey Frommer, "*Yankee Stadium Firsts (A Very Partial List)," http://baseballguru.com/hfrommer/analysishfrommer65.html.

41. "Harding Sees Ruth Drive Out Home Run," *The New York Times*, April 25, 1923.

42. "Ruppert Completes Deal for Yankees: Formally Announces Purchase of Houston's Interest in New York Club," *The New York Times*, May 22, 1923.

43. "60,000 Will See Giants Play Yanks," *The New York Times*, October 10, 1923.

44. "Ruppert Plans To Increase Yank Field to 85,000," *The New York Times, The Bridgeport Telegram*, Bridgeport, Connecticut, October 31, 1923.

45. "Yankees Announce Changes At Stadium," *The New York Times*, February 3, 1924.

46. "Honor Babe Ruth At Stadium Today," *The New York Times*, May 14, 1924.

47. "Work On Stadium Will Start Today," *The New York Times*, February 1, 1928; "1928 Signed Osborn Engineering Yankee Stadium Construction Specification for the "House That Ruth Built," Geppi's Memorabilia Roadshow," http://www.gmrs.com/item/.asp?Auction=1&ItemNo=35904; "Lot 441;1928 Yankee Stadium Contract Signed Ruppert," ebay, April 25, 2005.

48. "Yankees Plan New Stand: Stadium Left and Centre Field Bleachers to Be of Concrete," *The New York Times*, March 4, 1933; "Yankees Will Enlarge Stadium To Seat 84,000 at Ball Games," *The New York Times*, February 5, 1936.

49. James P. Dawson, "Decision Revealed At Contest's End," *The New York Times*, October 7, 1947; Jack Hand, "Yankees Sold To Trio Headed By MacPhail;" *Daily Kennebec Journal,* Augusta, Maine, January 27, 1945.

50. John Drebinger, "Yankees Contract For Stadium Lights, *The New York Times*, November 16, 1945.

51. John Drebinger, "Yankee Stadium Lights to Eclipse Those at All Other Sports Plants," *The New York Times*, January 16, 1946.

52. "1947 World Series," http://en.wikipedia.org/wiki/1947World_Series; "Television History – the First 75 Years," http://www.tvhistory.tv/1947 QF.htm; Maribeth Keane, "An Interview With Vintage Television Set Collector Steve McVoy," *Collectors Weekly*, ttp://www.collectorsweekly.com/articles/an-interview-withvintage-te..., August 19, 2008.

53. "Automatic Canteen Gets Stadium Pact," *The New York Times*, October 17, 1963; "Automatic Canteen Makes Pitch to Hawk Hot Dogs for Yankees," *The New York Times*, September 13, 1963; James J. Nagle, "Executive Moves And Attains Goals," *The New York Times*, November 8, 1964.

54. William N. Wallace, "C.B.S. Buys 80% of Stock In Yankee Baseball Team," *The New York Times*, August 14, 1964; Leonard Koppett, "Webb Sells 10 Per cent Interest in Yanks to C.B.S. for $1.4 Million," *The New York Times*, March 2, 1965; "Dan Topping Leaves Yankees," *Daily Tribune*, Great Bend, Kansas, September 20, 1966.

55. Joseph Durso, "Yanks' Sale to C.B.S. Stirs Senate Moves for Inquiry," *The New York Times*, August 15, 1964.

56. William N. Wallace, "C.B.S. Buys 80% of Stock In Yankee Baseball Team," *The New York Times*, August 14, 1964.

57. Joseph Durso, "Yanks' Sale to C.B.S. Stirs Senate Moves for Inquiry," *The New York Times*, August 15, 1964.

58. Ibid.

59. Ibid.

60. Ibid.

61. Leonard Koppett, "Yanks: Healthy, Wealthy but Unwise," *The New York Times*, October 18, 1964.

62. Ibid.

63. Joseph Durso, "C.B.S. Tells of Plans for Yankees," *The New York Times*, December 26, 1965.

64. Leonard Koppett, "C.B.S. Will renew Houk's Option," *The New York Times*, September 21, 1966.

65. Leonard Koppett, "Burke Setting Tempo for Yankees' New Image," *The New York Times*, May 21, 1967.

66. Ross Newman, "Yankee Aim: Remold Old Image," *Independent Press Telegram*, Long Beach, California, April 26, 1967.

67. Michael Burke. *Outrageous Good Fortune*. Boston-Toronto. Little Brown and Company, 1984, 266, 267, 307; "Yankee Stadium Frieze. (1967 Facelift)," http: //www.baseball-fever.com/showthread.php?74744-Yankee-Stadium..., March 2, 2009.

68. "New York Yankees Golden Era Is Still Glowing," *Constitution-Tribune*, Chillicothe, Missouri, August 24, 1967; http://www.baseball-fever.com/showthread.php?58009-Yankee Stadium (THIS IS THE YANKEE "HALL OF FAME"), May 24, 2012; http://www.baseball-fever.com/showthread.php?t= 58009-Yankee Stadium (kiosks in

the stadium), May 24, 2012; http://www. baseball-fever.com/showthread.php?58009-Yankee Stadium (partial listing of Yankee Telephonic Hall of Fame Displays), May 25, 2012.

69. "Comprehensive Study and Report for Modernization of Yankee Stadium, Borough of the Bronx, City of New York," 69 pages, June 30, 1972.

70. New York Yankees year-by-year results," http://newyork.yankees.mlb.com/ nyy/history/year_by_year_results.jsp.

TO STAY OR NOT TO STAY END NOTES

1. "Yanks Ponder Need to Leave Stadium," *The Post-Standard*, Syracuse, New York, January 28, 1971.
2. "N.Y. Giants Consider Move to New Jersey," *Greeley Tribune*, Greeley, Colorado, March 25, 1971.
3. Ibid.
4. Carl Zeitz, "Giants to move to Hackensack, N.J," *The Oneonta Star*, Oneonta, New York, August 27, 1971.
5. Robert Lipsyte, "Yankees, Why?" *New York Times*, May 6, 1971.
6. "Worst Foot Forward," *New York Daily News*, June 15, 1971.
7. Thomas P. Ronan, "Governor Signs Bill Allowing Purchase Of Stadium by City," *The New York Times*, July 7, 1971.
8. Dick Young, "Young Ideas," *New York Daily News*, July 9, 1971.
9. Joseph Durso, "Yankees and Mets Oppose Sharing of Shea Stadium," *The New York Times*, August 28, 1971; "Mets Threaten to Move If Forced to Share Shea," *The Stars And Stripes*, September 2, 1971.
10. Martin Tolchin, "Leviss Now Backs Plan For Stadium," *The New York Times*, September 3, 1971.
11. Maurice Carroll, "With Votes on Yankee Stadium Plan Lined Up, Mayor Is Ready to Start Pushing Project," September 20, 1971.

12. Maurice Carroll, "City Officials Report Substantial Progress in Plans to Save Yankee Stadium," *The New York Times*, October 8, 1971.

13. Maurice Carroll, "Planners Favor City Stadium Plan," *The New York Times*, November 4, 1971.

14. Joseph Durso. "Yanks Say Mayor Will Seek Funds," *The New York Times*, November 23, 1971.

15. "Renovation Study Set: Yankee Stadium First Plan Passes," *The Lincoln Star*, Lincoln, Nebraska, December 8, 1971.

16. Red Smith, "Lindsay and the Quarterback Sneak," *The New York Times*, January 7, 1972.

17. "Letter to the Editor," *New York Daily News*, December 16, 1971.

18. "Shea Stadium For Yankees," *The Odessa American*, Odessa, Texas, February 1, 1972.

19. Maurice Carroll, "1.8-Billion Capital Budget Is Proposed by the Mayor," *The New York Times*, February 1, 1972.

20. Arthur Mulligan, "Taxpayers Sue to Bar $ for Yankee Stadium," *New York Daily News*, February 10, 1972.

21. Ibid.

22. "Ralph Blumenthal, "Yankees To Stay 30 Years In Pact Approved By City," *The New York Times*, March 24, 1972.

23. Ibid.

24. Edward Ranzal, "Yanks, City Sign 30-Year Stadium Lease," *The New York Times*, August 17, 1972; Letter, Michael Burke to Mark Ravitz, February 3, 1971.

25. Joseph P. Fried, "Plan for Renovation Of Yankee Stadium Includes Elevators," *The New York Times*, August 15 1972.

26. Edward Ranzal, "Yanks, City Sign 30-Year Stadium Lease," *The New York Times*, August 17, 1972.

27. Letter, Robert C.Y. Young to the Author, "Yankee Stadium Renovation," November 15, 2003.

28. "Aide to Lindsay is 'Landlord' of Yankee Stadium," *The New York Times,* October 8, 1972.

1973 AND THE BEGINNING OF THE END End Notes

1. Joseph Durso, "C.B.S. Sells the Yankees for $10-Million," *The New York Times*, January 4, 1973.

2. Ibid.; "Obituaries: Michael Burke, once president, part-owner of baseball's Yankees," *Syracuse Herald-Journal*, Syracuse, New York, February 6, 1987.

3. Joseph Durso, "C.B.S. Sells the Yankees for $10-Million," *The New York Times*, January 4, 1973.

4. Ibid.

5. Ibid.

6. Ibid.

7. Murray Chass, "New Owner Held Yanks in Awe as Boy," *The New York Times*, January 4, 1974.

8. Ibid.

9. 1973 New York Yankees Yearbook.

10. Edward Ranzal, "Cost of Renovation At Yankee Stadium Climbs $7-Million," *The New York Times*, April 6, 1973.

11. Alfred Miele, "Tab for Work on Stadium Jumps 6.9 Million," *New York Daily News*, April 6, 1973.

12. Steve Cady, "Memories Are Full but Many Seats Empty on Yankee Anniversary," *The New York Times*, April 10, 1973.

13. Joseph Durso, "50 Years of Stadium Memories," *The New York Times*, April 15, 1973.

14. Murray Chass, "Burke's Eclipse With Yankees Explained," *The New York Times*, May 14, 1973.

15. Ibid.

16. Ibid.

17. George Dugan, "Leaders Address 70,000 Witnesses," *The New York Times*, July 9, 1973.

18. Steve Jacobson, "Mays Retires: End of a Love Affair," *Newsday*, September 21, 1973.

19. Yankee Stadium Blowout! Everything Must Go!," http://www.baseball-fever.com/showthread.php?71363-Yankee-Stadium-Pre-Renovation, August 5, 2010; Letter, Ken Smith, Director, Baseball Hall of Fame to L.L. Schwall, "Thank you for donations to the Hall of Fame," October 3, 1974; Vic Ziegel, "The Stadium's Final Night," *New York Post*, September 29, 1973.

20. e-mail, Larry Wiederecht to Michael Wagner, "YS Reconstruction," February 27, 2008.

21. Author interview With Harvey Levene (Telephone), April 8, 2008.

22. Sam Goldpaper, "Houk Out As Yanks' Manager," *The New York Times*, October 1, 1973; Alfred Miele and Bruce Drake, "Yank Fans Steal 1st, 2d & Home," *New York Daily News*, October 1, 1973; Ed Comerford, "The Old Gray Stadium Ain't What It Used to Be," *Newsday*, October 1, 1973.

23. e-mail, Roy Slezak to Michael Wagner, "I Attended The Last Game Also," January 31, 2009.

24. Sam Goldpaper, "Houk Out As Yanks' Manager," *The New York Times*, October 1, 1973.

25. Ibid.

26. Will Grimsley, "Before the Wreckers, A Nostalgic Goodbye," *Newsday*, October 2, 1973.

27. e-mail, Roy Slezak to Michael Wagner, "Memories of a True Baseball Fan Meeting the Widows of the Legends," February 4, 2009.

28. Letter, The City of New York, Department of Public Works, Herbert J. Simins, Commissioner, to Invirex Demolition Inc. And Cuyahoga Wrecking Corp., "Yankee Stadium…Notice of Award," August 24, 1973; Telephone interview notes, Jay Schwall, June 30, 2011; Interview corrections, Jay Schwall, July 7, 2011.

29. Glenn Fowler, "Bids Raise Cost Of Stadium Work," *The New York Times*, December 5, 1973.

30. Telephone interview notes, Jay Schwall, June 30, 2011; Interview corrections, Jay Schwall, July 7, 2011; Ad, Yankee Stadium Demolition Items For Sale, *The New York Times*, October 28, 1973; Joe Trimble, "Wreckers Dig Up Yank Memorabilia," *New York Daily News*, November, 1973; Edward Kirkman, "No Game Today: Memories for Sale," *New York Daily News*, November, 1973.

31. Interview corrections, Jay Schwall, July 7, 2011; Joe Trimble, "Wreckers Dig Up Yank Memorabilia," *New York Daily News*, November, 1973.

32. Telephone interview notes, Jay Schwall, June 30, 2011; Interview corrections, Jay Schwall, July 7, 2011; "Part of Ruth's House Can Be Part of Your Home," *New York Daily News*, ca. November, 1973.

33. Maury Allen, "Memories of Old Yankee Stadium Linger On…," *Baseball Digest*, August 1976, pp. 55-56.

34. Anthony McCarron, "First goodbye: Old Yankee Stadium said farewell in 1973," *New York Daily News*, September 21, 2008.

35. Larry Merchant, "Nostalgic Kick (Yankee Stadium Demolition Items For Sale)," *New York Post*, ca. September 1973.

36. "Yankee Stadium Blowout! Everything Must Go!," http:// www.baseball-fever.com/ showthread.php?71363-Yankee-Stadium-Pre-Renovation, August 5, 2010.

37. Joe Gergen, "Fans Rummage at Yankee Stadium," *Newsday*, ca. November, 1973.

38. Ad, Winston Cigarettes/E.J. Korvettes, "Get your Yankee Stadium Seat," ca. May 1974.

39. Anthony McCarron, "First goodbye: Old Yankee Stadium said farewell in 1973," *New York Daily News*, September 21, 2008.

40. Interview corrections, Jay Schwall, July 7, 2011; "Inventory of Memorabilia From Yankee Stadium, 5/18/98," *J. Peterman Catalog*, Christmas '98.

41. Interview corrections, Jay Schwall, July 7, 2011; "Reconstruction Scores At The "House That Ruth Built,"" *Constructioneer*, February 18, 1974.

42. Interview corrections, Jay Schwall, July 7, 2011.

43. Blueprint, "Elevation Of Frieze, Part "D,"" The Osborn Engineering Co., Cleveland, Ohio, October 20, 1921; "New Yankee Baseball Stadium Topped By Copper Cornice Weighing 15 Tons," *The Olean Evening Herald*, Olean, New York, January 16, 1923; "New Air View of Yankee Stadium; Giant Copper Bat for Weather Vane," *The Mansfield News*, Mansfield, Ohio, October 9, 1923.

44. Ad, "Tons of Toncan went into this stadium," United Alloy Steel Corporation, 1923, ebay, March 10, 2008.

45. Charles Phelps Cushing, "86,000 pounds of Copper and 86,000 Fans at World Series," *Bulletin of the Copper & Brass Research Association*, October 1937.

46. Telephone interview notes, Jay Schwall, June 30, 2011.

47. Interview corrections, Jay Schwall, July 7, 2011; "Reconstruction Scores At The "House That Ruth Built,"" *Constructioneer*, February 18, 1974; List from Jay Schwall of Yankee Stadium Demolition figures, ca. 2004.

48. Interview corrections, Jay Schwall, July 7, 2011; "Yankees to Get Biggest Scoreboard for $300,000," *The New York Times*, February 12, 1959.

49. Murray Chass, "Tigers Get Houk As Pilot," *The New York Times*, October 12, 1973.

50. Joseph Durso, "Yankees Hire Replacement For MacPhail," *The New York Times,* November 2, 1973.

51. "Broadcast," http://www.brainyhistory.com/topics/b/broadcast.html; Stephen Borelli, "'Voice of God' presides over Yankees," http://www.usatoday. Com/sports/baseball/ comment/ sbcoll15.htm; Marley Seaman, "'Good evening ladies and gentlemen' Talking to the longtime voice of New York sports," *Herald Community Newspapers*, http://www. liherald.com/site/news.cfm?newsid= 15137971&BRD=1601&PAG= 461&depti..., February 5, 2006.

52. Stephen Borelli, "'Voice of God' presides over Yankees," http://www.usatoday.Com/sports/baseball/comment/sbcoll15.htm.

53. "Yank Equipment Man Recalls Stadium Opening," *The Lima News*, Lima, Ohio, April 15, 1973.

54. George Vecsey, "A gracious Yankee's career ends," *Syracuse Herald Journal*, Syracuse, New York, August 15, 1985.

55. Edward Ranzal, "Troy Threatens to Delay Funds For Work at Yankee Stadium," *The New York Times*, November 16, 1973.

56. Ibid.

57. Ibid.

58. Edward Ranzal, "$15.9-Million More Is Voted for the Stadium Project, *The New York Times*, November 17, 1973.

59. Edward Ranzal, "Council's Finance Group Delays Stadium Decision," *The New York Times,* November 21, 1973.

60. Edward Ranzal, "City Seeks To Aid Yankees At Shea," *The New York Times*, November 10, 1973.

61. Edward Ranzal, "Council Votes $15.9-Million for Stadium And $50-Million for Convention Center," *The New York Times*, November 28, 1973.

62. John Darnton, "Yanks Get Lease For Shea Stadium," *The New York Times*, December 29, 1973.

TWO YEARS ON THE ROAD End Notes

1. John Darnton, "Lindsay at a Farewell Party," *The New York Times*, January 1, 1974.

2. Michael Stern, "Coalition of Bronx Leaders Drafts Job-Creation Program to Revivify Borough," *The New York Times*, March 11, 1974; John Patterson, Jr., "Can the South Bronx Save New York?," *The New York Times*, October 4, 1975.

3. Wayne Minshew, "The Hammer hits the big one," http://www.sportingnews.com/archives/aaron/152207.html.

4. Murray Chass, "Yanks Open Here Today; Mets Visit Phils," *The New York Times*, April 6, 1974.

5. "Burke Named Head of NBA Club," *The Lima News* (Ohio), May 23, 1974.

6. "Riddled Yankee Stadium Draws DiMag," *Delta Democrat-Times*, Greenville, Mississippi, July 8, 1974.

7. Ibid.

8. Allan M. Siegal, "Stadium Repairs Touch All Bases," *The New York Times*, August 29, 1974.

9. Telephone interview with Ralph Drewes, September 19, 2007; e-mail message, Peter Kasten, United State Bronze to Michael Wagner, "Plaques," June 12, 2008.

10. Allan M. Siegal, "Stadium Repairs Touch All Bases," *The New York Times*, August 29, 1974.

11. Ibid.

12. Telephone Interview with Dick Muller, June 15, 2008; e-mail from Steve Koch, October 12, 2013.

13. Allan M. Siegal, "Stadium Repairs Touch All Bases," *The New York Times*, August 29, 1974.

14. Joe Donnelly, "Martin Hustles for a Winner," *Newsday*, March, 1976.

15. "Phil Rizzuto Can't Help Feeling Sad Over Changes," *Florence Morning News*, Florence, South Carolina, December 18, 1974.

16. Bob Snyder, "Crouse-Hinds lights Chiefs as well as Yanks," *Syracuse Herald Journal,* Syracuse, New York, February 16, 1975.

17. "The Tight Grip Of Inflation," newspaper article, unknown newspaper, August 9, 1975.

18. Peter Kihss, "Stadium Project Put At $57-Million," *The New York Times*, July 17, 1975.

19. Letter, Robert C.Y. Young to Michael Wagner, November 15, 2003; "Stadium's New Big 'Bat' Proves A Hit in First Appearance Here," *The New York Times*, July 27, 1975; Telephone Interview, Joe Garagiola, Jr., September 20, 2008; e-mail, Mariano Molina/MD Consulting Engineers, New York City, to Michael Wagner, August 20, 2008.

20. "Stadium's New Big 'Bat' Proves A Hit in First Appearance Here," *The New York Times*, July 27, 1975.

21. Larry Fox, "Grass at Yankee Stadium: Taxpayer the Big Loser," *New York Daily News,* July 29, 1975.

22. Joseph Durso, "Martin Starts Job With Yanks; Players Are Divided on Virdon," *The New York Times*, August 3, 1975.

23. Edward Ranzal, "Cost For Stadium Put At 66-Million," *The New York Times*, October 11, 1975.

24. Ibid.

25. George F. Will, "Absurd, But Ah, New York Will Have Its Stainless Steel 'Bat,'" *The Daily Courier*, Connellsville, Pennsylvania, October 23, 1975.

26. "Was the Stadium Worth It?," *New York Magazine*, April 19, 1976; e-mail, David Andres/DeLea Sod Farms, East Northport, New York, to Michael Wagner, October 5, 2008.

27. "Yankee Stadium Spiral," *The Sporting News*, November 8, 1975.

28. Dick Young, "They Could Play Now at New Yankee Stadium," *New York Daily*

News, November 13, 1975.

29. Letter, Robert C.Y. Young to Michael Wagner, June 29, 2011.

30. "'House Ruth Built' Won't Be The Same," *The Times Recorder*, Zanesville, Ohio, November 21, 1975; Telephone Interview with Steve Koch, June 30, 2013.

31. Martin Waldron, "Yanks Get Windfall As City Shifts Plans," *The New York Times*, December 1, 1975.

32. Ibid.

33. Ibid.

34. Ibid.

35. Ibid.

36. Leonard Koppett, "Paul Defends Yanks' Role In Stadium Building Costs," *The New York Times*, December 6, 1975.

37. "Yankees to Open Rebuilt Stadium April 15," *The New York Times*, December 7, 1975.

38. Robert Carroll, "Stadium Cost, Like Topsy…Keeps Growin'," *New York Daily News*, December 7, 1975.

39. "Pontiac Dome Revives Fever," *The Coshocton Tribune*, Coshocton, Ohio, December 14, 1975.

1976 ROUND TWO END NOTES

1. Report, "Yankee Stadium Project Final Environmental Impact Statement," New York City Department of Parks and Recreation, February 10, 2006; e-mail, Ed H. Brunjes to Michael Wagner, "Just a few suggestions for accuracy in your book," November 14, 2008; "Was the Stadium Worth It?," *New York Magazine*, April 19, 1976.

2. Report, "Yankee Stadium Project Final Environmental Impact Statement," New York City Department of Parks and Recreation, February 10, 2006; "About Abraham Beame – Richmond Hill Historical Society," http://www.richmondhill history.org/abeame.html.

3. "Construction Management and Prime Contractors for The Modernization of Yankee Stadium," Warren Weil Public Relations, April 13, 1976.

4. Shirley Povich, "Faithful Remake of Venerable Baseball Colossus," *News Journal*, Mansfield, Ohio, March 10, 1976; "Refurbished Yankees' Home Boasts Brand New Interior," *Bridgeport Sunday Post*, Bridgeport, Connecticut, February 29, 1976.

5. "Construction Management and Prime Contractors for The Modernization of Yankee Stadium," Warren Weil Public Relations, April 13, 1976; Telephone Interview, Ralph Terowsky, April 13, 2009; Telephone Interview, Harry Swanson, March 4, 2007; Letter, Ralph Drewes to Michael Wagner, August 10, 2011. Telephone Interview, Ralph Drewes, September 19, 2007.

6. Telephone Interview, Doug Walker, May 24, 2007; "Yankee Stadium Pedestrian Bridge," http://www.ehbrungesassociates.com/profile.html; "America's Favorite Architecture," http://en.wikipedia.org/wiki/America's_Favorite_Architecture.

7. "Old Yankee Stadium," http:/www.baseball-fever.com/showthread.php?t=43850& page =2, September 29, 2007, pp. 1, 11-12.

8. Murray Chass, "Yankee Stadium: Modern Comforts and Hairdryers," *The New York Times*, March 7, 1976; George Vecsey, "Stadium Suites Keep Rich in Style, *The New York Times*, October 20, 1976.

9. e-mail, SCI to Michael Wagner, "Yankee Stadium Modernization," August 21, 2008; Interview Corrections from Anthony Adonetti, Structural Contours, Inc. (SCI), Greenwich, Connecticut, August 1, 2011; e-mail, Anthony Adonetti to Michael Wagner, "Yankee Stadium Rehabilitation," May 29, 2010.

10. "'76 Opening Day Tomorrow: New Yankee Stadium," *New York Post*, April 14, 1976.

11. Dave Anderson, "Bring Money, Yankee Fans," *The New York Times*, May 9, 1976.

12. Ibid.

13. Ibid.

14. Ibid.

15. "Yankee Fans Flock to 'Opening Day,'" *The New York Times*, March 2, 1976.

16. "'76 Opening Day Tomorrow: New Yankee Stadium," *New York Post*, April 14, 1976; "Construction Management and Prime Contractors for The Modernization of Yankee Stadium," Warren Weil Public Relations, April 13, 1976.

17. "Construction Management and Prime Contractors for The Modernization of Yankee Stadium," Warren Weil Public Relations, April 13, 1976.

18. Telephone Interview, Victor Strauss, September 18, 2007.

19. Ibid.; "Yankee Stadium Renovation: Medallions," http://www.baseball-fever.com/showthread.php?t=58009-Yankee-Stadium…, September 13, 2008.

20. Telephone Interview, Stephen Offerman, September 20, 2007; Blueprint, Slocum and Fuller, "Paint Specifications," October 1, 1973.

21. "Construction Management and Prime Contractors for The Modernization of Yankee Stadium," Warren Weil Public Relations, April 13, 1976.

22. Information written on Yankee Stadium renovation photos I sent to Ralph Drewes, November 5, 2007; "Fans to Have Clear View," *New York Post*, April 14, 1976.

23. Telephone Interview, Joe Garagiola, Jr., September 20, 2008.

24. Michael Burke, *Outrageous Good Fortune*: *A Memoir By Michael Burke*, Boston: Little Brown & Company, 1984, 307; Television Documentary, National Geographic Channel, "*Break It Down: Yankee Stadium*," airing April 28, 2011, http://www.cinamablend.com/

Television/Break-It-Down-Yankee-Stadium."

25. Richard Sandomir, "A Distinctive Façade Is Recreated at New Yankee Stadium," *The New York Times*, April 14, 2009.

26. "Fans to Have Clear View," *New York Post*, April 14, 1976; Joseph Valerio, "Yankee Stadium Reclaims Role As a World Showcase," *New York Post*, April 14, 1976.

27. George deLucenay Leon, "Sound on the Mound," *Sound & Communications*, June 1976.

28. Information Specifications Sheet, American Seating, Grand Rapids, Michigan, "Stadium chair model 406," n.d.; New York Yankees Dedication Program, April 13, 1976.

29. Yankee Stadium Renovation, "Row K of the Upper Reserved," http://www.baseball-fever.com/showthread.php?t=58009&page=18, July 9, 2008; Yankee Stadium Renovation, "Counting Rows At Yankee Stadium," http://www.baseball-fever.com/ showthread.php?t=58009&page==37, January 11, 2009; Yankee Stadium Renovation, "Row U and Row K," http://www.baseball-fever.com/ showthread. php?t=58009 &page =22, August 10, 2008.

30. Blueprint, "Modernization Of Yankee Stadium: Cross Sections," Sheet S-A, 38 of 173, October 1, 1973; Blueprint, "Modernization Of Yankee Stadium: Exterior Elevations & Cross Sections," 40 of 173, October 1, 1973; Blueprint, "Yankee Stadium-Part D-Addition, Elevations," The Osborn Engineering Co, Cleveland, Ohio, drawn July 25, 1927.

31. Handout, "Yankee Stadium," New York Yankees, Parks Administration Building, Flushing, New York 11368, 1974 or 1975.

32. Press Release #141-76, The City of New York, Mayor Abraham D. Beame today officially rededicated the completely renovated Yankee Stadium, April 13, 1976; Murray Schumach, "Beame Is at the Top of Batting Order For Dedication of Renovated Stadium," *The New York Times*, April 14, 1976; e-mail, Steve Koch to Michael Wagner, December 7, 2013.

33. Maury Allen, "Mike Burke Made It Happen," *New York Post,* April 15, 1976.

34. Murray Schumach, “Beame Is at the Top of Batting Order For Dedication of Renovated Stadium,” *The New York Times*, April 14, 1976; Maury Allen, “Mike Burke Made It Happen,” *New York Post,* April 15, 1976.

35. Murray Schumach, “Beame Is at the Top of Batting Order For Dedication of Renovated Stadium,” *The New York Times*, April 14, 1976.

36. Dave Anderson, “No Carpet in Billy Martin’s Office,” *The New York Times*, April 15, 1976; Phil Pepe, “Infield a Bit Wavy but New Stadium Stunning,” *New York Daily News*, April 15, 1976.

37. Phil Pepe, “Infield a Bit Wavy but New Stadium Stunning,” *New York Daily News*, April 15, 1976.

38. Yankee Stadium Renovation, “It’s still old but it’s more modern,” http://www.baseball-fever.com/showthread.php?t=58009&page=37, January 11, 2009.

39. Phil Pepe, “Infield a Bit Wavy but New Stadium Stunning,” *New York Daily News*, April 15, 1976.

40. Murray Chass, "Yanks Go Home Again Today, to Bronx," *The New York Times,* April 15, 1975.

41. *The New York Post*, photos with captions, April 20, 1976.

42. “A Yankee Quipper Now,” *Newsday,* April 16, 1976.

43. Joseph Durso. “Yankees Win First Game In Rebuilt Stadium,” *The New York Times*, April 16, 1976.

44. Joe Donnelly, “The Housewarming’s a Winner,” *Newsday*, April 16, 1976.

45. Ibid.

46. Sheila Moran, “Stadium: Mixed Emotions,” *New York Post*, April 16, 1976.

47. Ibid.

48. Dave Hirshey, "Shoeshine Boy Back on Feet; Pizza Pies Get Slice of Action," *New York Daily News*, April 16, 1976.

49. Malcolm Moran, "For Some, 'Rejuvenation' Falls Shy," *Newsday*, April 16, 1976.

50. Ibid.

51. e-mail, Dr. Cary Goodman to Michael Wagner, "Re: Your story in my book, 'Babe's Place,' (corrections from telephone interview of June 30, 2011)" August 4, 2011.

52. Joseph Durso. "Yankees Win First Game In Rebuilt Stadium," *The New York Times*, April 16, 1976.

53. Ibid.

54. Will Grimsley, "Yankee Stadium Welcomes 54,028 for Home Opener," *Florence Morning News*, Florence, South Carolina, April 16, 1976.

55. Dave Hirshey, "Shoeshine Boy Back on Feet; Pizza Pies Get Slice of Action," *New York Daily News*, April 16, 1976.

56. "A Smashing Intro For 'House That Ruth Built,'" *The Daily Times*, Salisbury, Maryland, April 16, 1976.

57. Joseph Durso. "Yankees Win First Game In Rebuilt Stadium," *The New York Times*, April 16, 1976.

58. Murray Chass, "Yanks Go Home Again Today, to Bronx," *The New York Times*, April 15, 1976.

59. John L. Hess, "Stadium's Costs Now Seen As Loss," *The New York Times*, April 15, 1976.

60. Ibid.

61. "Yankee Pinstripe Still Shows Through Houk's Uniform," *The Daily Oklahoman*, Oklahoma City, Oklahoma, May 14, 1976.

62. Eleanor Blau, "Moon Rally Draws 25,000, Half of Stadium Capacity," *The New York Times*, June 2, 1976.

63. Murray Chass, "Yanks Getting Big Crowds, Big Headaches at Stadium," *The New York Times*, June 8, 1976.

64. Thomas Rogers, "Court Order Stops Yanks From Ending Free-ticket Arrangement for Children," *The New York Times*, June 22, 1976.

65. Dick Young, "Yanks shut off free ticket program," *The New Mexican*, Santa Fe, New Mexico, June 27, 1976.

66. Joseph Durso, "Old-Time Yanks Return to Site of Past, Present Glory," *The New York Times*, August 8, 1976.

67. Michael Katz, "A Rebuilt Stadium Little Aid in Bronx," *The New York Times*, August 10, 1976.

68. Pranay Gupte, "Residents Near Yankee Stadium Say City Reneged on Renovation Promise," *The New York Times*, August 21, 1976.

69. Ibid.

70. Clinton Cox, "The angry neighbors of Yankee Stadium," *Sunday News Magazine*, February 27, 1977.

71. Ibid.

72. Ibid.

73. "Demonstrators, Youths and Fans Make Up Mob Scene at Stadium," *The New York*

Times, September 29, 1976.

74. Obituary, "Jimmy Esposito Dies at 69; Supervised Stadium Upkeep," *The New York Times*, October 10, 1986.

75. Murray Chass, "Jackson Signs Yankee Contract For Five Years and $2.9 Million," *The New York Times*, November 30, 1976.

76. "Reggie 'succumbs' to Steinbrenner's 'charm,' money," *The Post-Crescent*, Appleton, Wisconsin, November 30, 1976.

Anthony Adonetti, president of Structural Contours, Inc., Greenwich, Connecticut, was kind enough to write the portion of "*Babe's Place*" with regard to "Formwork" and "Falsework," located in this chapter. Mr. Adonetti also generously supplied photos of the work being done.

THE HEROES SPEAK I End Notes

(The 1970s Renovation of Yankee Stadium)

1. Letter sent by Michael Wagner to various respondents, various dates.

2. Allen, Bernie. 7 March 2005, letter.

3. Anderson, Sparky. 10 February 2005. Sparky signed a renovation photo.

4. Appel, Marty. 7 January 2004, telephone interview.

5. Bando, Sal. 20 February 2005, letter.

6. Barber, Red. 10 November 1981, letter.

7. Barber, Red. 18 March 1986, letter.

8. Barnett, Larry. 15 January 2005, letter.

9. Bartholomay, William. 4 June 2008, letter.

10. Bavasi, Buzzie. 15 January 2008, letter.

11. Berra, Yogi. 21 March 2005, letter.

12. Blackwell, Ewell. 27 March 1975, letter.

13. Blanchard, John. 15 November 2006, New York Yankees Fantasy Camp, Tampa, Florida, oral taped interview.

14. Bolling, Milt. 20 November 2007, letter.

15. Borom, Red. 5 November, 2007, letter.

16. Bosman, Dick. 17 December 2007, e-mail.

17. Bouton, Jim. 11 January 2004, oral taped interview/e-mail.

18. Bragan, Bobby. 10 January 2008, letter.

19. Bressoud, Ed. 6 November 2007, letter.

20. Brissie, Lou. 20 January 2008, letter.

21. Brown, Bobby (1940s Yankees). 22 February 2005, letter.

22. Byrne, Tommy. 25 October 2004, letter.

23. Carrieri, Joe. 20 March 2008, letter.

24. Casanova, Paul. 29 January 2008. Paul signed two renovation photos.

25. Chapman, Ben. 25 March 1985, letter.

26. Clarke, Horace. 8 February 2005. Horace signed two renovation photos.

27. Coan, Gil. 14 November 2007, letter.

28. Coleman, Jerry. 2 December 2004, letter.

29. Combs, Earle. 18 August 1975, letter.

30. Conlan, Jocko. 18 August 1975, letter.

31. Costas, Bob. 5 February 2008, letter.

32. Cottier, Chuck. 6 November 2007, letter.

33. Coveleski, Stanley. 20 September 1975, letter.

34. Crandall, Del. 22 March 2008, letter.

35. Creamer, Robert. 18 April 2008, letter.

36. Crosetti, Frank. 4 October 1976, letter.

37. Culp, Ray. 25 March 2008, letter.

38. Daley, Bud. 22 February 2005, letter.

39. Denkinger, Don. 26 January 2008, letter.

40. Doerr, Bobby. 17 October 2004, letter.

41. Downing, Al. 15 November 2006, New York Yankees Fantasy Camp, Tampa, Florida, oral taped interview.

42. Dugan, Joe. 22 May 1975, letter.

43. Dugan, Joe. 18 August 1975, letter.

44. Engel, Bob. 25 January 2008, letter.

45. Ermer, Cal. 1 May 2008, letter.

46. Erskine, Carl. 29 March 2005, letter.

47. Feller, Bob. 25 October 2004, telephone call.

48. Franks, Herman. 14 January 2008, letter.

49. Gamble, Oscar. 15 November 2006, New York Yankees Fantasy Camp, Tampa, Florida, oral taped interview.

50. Garagiola, Joe, Sr. 21 February 2005, letter.

51. Garagiola, Joe, Jr. 7 January 2004, telephone interview.

52. Gardner, Billy. 8 January 2008. Billy sent two signed renovation photos.

53. Garver, Ned. 14 January 2008, letter.

54. Gehringer, Charles. 24 November 1974, letter.

55. Gehringer, Charles. 18 August 1975, letter.

56. Gehringer, Charles. 4 October 1976, letter.

57. Gernert, Dick. 14 January 2008, letter.

58. Gibbs, Jake. 18 January 2008, letter.

59. Giuliani, Rudolph. 22 December 2004, letter.

60. Goetz, Russ. 26 January 2008, letter.

61. Grimes, Burleigh. 18 August 1975, letter.

62. Groat, Dick. 22 October 2004, letter.

63. Grossbardt, Michael. 18 February 2009, e-mail.

64. Gutteridge, Don. 11 January 2008, letter.

65. Haller, Bill. 19 February 2005, letter.

66. Harshman, Jack. 21 March 2008, telephone interview.

67. Hartung, Clint. 8 January 2008. Clint sent two signed renovation photos.

68. Harwell, Ernie. 20 March 2008, letter.

69. Hatton, Grady. 22 March 2008, letter.

70. Hemus, Solly. 8 January 2008, letter.

71. Henrich, Tommy. 16 September 1981, letter.

72. Herzog, Whitey. 19 February 2005, letter.

73. Hickman, Jim. 22 February 2005, letter.

74. Honig, Donald. 2 April 2008, letter.

75. Houk, Ralph. 3 August 2003, Live Oak, Texas, interview.

76. Howard, Elston. 18 August 1975, letter.

77. Howard, Frank. 8 January 2008. Frank sent a signed baseball card.

78. Hoyt, Waite. 17 September 1974, letter.

79. Hunter, Billy. 27 March 1975, letter.

80. Jansen, Larry. 8 January 2008. Larry sent a signed card.

81. John, Tommy. 15 November 2006, New York Yankees Fantasy Camp, Tampa, Florida, oral taped interview.

82. Joost, Eddie. 19 February 2008, letter.

83. Jorgens, Arndt. 8 September 1975, letter.

84. Kasko, Eddie. 21 March 2008, letter.

85. Kemmerer, Russ. 10 January 2008, letter.

86. Kibler, John. 19 February 2005, letter.

87. Kiner, Ralph. 18 March 2005, letter.

88. Koch, Ed. 19 July 2007, letter.

89. Koenig, Mark. 3 August 1974, letter.

90. Koenig, Mark. 20 October 1975, letter.

91. Koenig, Mark. 24 September 1981, letter.

92. Koosman, Jerry. 24 February 2005, letter.

93. Kuzava, Bob. 8 January 2008, letter.

94. Law, Vern. 26 October 2004, letter.

95. Leonard, Buck. 7 December 1975, letter.

96. Lindstrom, Fred. 3 September 1976, letter.

97. Linz, Phil. 12 January 2008, letter.

98. Lopat, Ed. 3 August 1974, letter.

99. Lopez, Hector. 19 February 2005, letter.

100. Lopez, Hector. 15 November 2006, New York Yankees Fantasy Camp, Tampa, Florida, oral taped interview.

101. MacPhail, Lee. 8 February 2005, letter.

102. Mantle, Max, Sr. 22 March 2008, telephone interview.

103. Marion, Marty. 10 March 2005, letter.

104. Maris, Roger. 14 November 1978, letter.

105. Martin, Morrie. 18 January, 2008. Morrie sent a signed renovation photo.

106. Maxwell, Charlie. 8 January, 2008. Charlie sent a signed card.

107. McCarthy, Joe. 23 January 1974, letter.

108. McCarthy, Joe. 18 January 1975, letter.

109. McCarthy, Joe. 18 August 1975, letter.

110. McCarthy, Joe. 9 August 1976, letter.

111. McDaniel, Lindy. 18 August 1975, letter.

112. McDaniel, Lindy. 17 March 2005, letter.

113. McDevitt, Danny. 17 March 2008. Danny sent a signed photo.

114. McDougald, Gil. 30 June 1974, letter.

115. McDougald, Gil. 25 October 2004, letter.

116. Mead, Charlie. 12 January 2008, letter.

117. Medich, George (Doc). 28 March 2005, e-mail.

118. Mele, Sam. 24 March, 2008. Sam sent a signed renovation photo.

119. Metro, Charles. 7 April 2008, letter.

120. Mize, John. 2 September 1975, letter.

121. Morabito, Mickey. 26 May 2005, letter.

122. Moses, Gerry. 15 April 2005, letter.

123. Mossi, Don. 1 February 2008, letter.

124. Nicholson, Bill. 3 March 1975, letter.

125. Noren, Irv. 27 March 1975, letter.

126. O'Dell, Billy. 7 August 2008. Billy sent a signed renovation photo.

127. Oldis, Bob. 28 January 2008, letter.

128. O'Malley, Peter. 24 January 2008, letter.

129. Pagliaroni, Jim. 30 January 2008, letter.

130. Pasqual, Camilo. 2 April 2008, letter.

131. Pattin, Marty. 1 February 2008, letter.

132. Peckinpaugh, Roger. 18 August 1975, letter.

133. Perry, Jim. 6 March 2008, letter.

134. Pesky, Johnny. 19 February 2005, letter.

135. Peterson, Fritz. 31 January 2005, letter.

136. Phillips, Dave. 3 March 2005, letter.

137. Picone, Mario. 5 March 2008. Mario signed two renovation photos.

138. Pignatano, Joe. 19 January 2008, letter.

139. Pillette, Duane. 11 January 2008, letter.

140. Pipgras, George. 27 May 1975, letter.

141. Plews, Herb. 17 March 2008, letter.

142. Quilici, Frank. 13 February 2008, letter.

143. Reese, Rich. 17 March 2008, letter.

144. Reichardt, Rick. 26 January 2008, letter.

145. Rettenmund, Merv. 25 January 2008, letter.

146. Reynolds, Allie. 3 August 1974, letter.

147. Reynolds, Allie. 18 August 1975, letter.

148. Rhodes, Dusty. 14 January 2008, letter.

149. Rhodes, Dusty. 18 January 2008, telephone interview.

150. Rice, John. 1 March 2005, letter.

151. Richardson, Bobby. 23 November 2004, letter.

152. Roberts, Robin. 25 October 2004. Robin sent signed card.

153. Roebuck, Ed. 9 January 2008, letter.

154. Roof, Phil. 22 February 2008, letter.

155. Rosen, Al. 16 January 2008, telephone interview.

156. Ruth, Mrs. Babe. 9 March 1974, letter.

157. Salerno, Al. 22 March 2005, letter.

158. Savage, Bob. 5 February 2008, letter.

159. Scheib, Carl. 26 January 2008, letter.

160. Schilling, Chuck. 27 March 2008, letter.

161. Sewell, Joe. 18 January 1975, letter.

162. Sewell, Joe. 18 August 1975, letter.

163. Shantz, Bobby. 27 March 1975, letter.

164. Shantz, Bobby. 23 October 2004, letter.

165. Shawkey, Bob. 18 August 1975, letter.

166. Shea, Frank (Spec). 3 August 1974, letter.

167. Sheldon, Roland. 24 February 2005, letter.

168. Sheppard, Bob. 5 February 2005, letter.

169. Shore, Ernie. 18 August 1975, letter.

170. Sievers, Roy. 22 February 2005, letter.

171. Simmons, Curt. 11 January 2008. Curt sent me a signed card.

172. Simpson, Harry. 27 March 1975, letter.

173. Skowron, Bill. 3 August 2003, Live Oak, Texas, interview.

174. Skowron, Bill. 27 October 2004, letter.

175. Snider, Duke. 27 June 2007. Duke signed a renovation photo.

176. Snyder, Jerry. 19 March 2008, letter.

177. Snyder, Russ. 22 January 2008, letter.

178. Springstead, Marty. 19 February 2005, letter.

179. Staley, Jerry. 8 September 1975, letter.

180. Starr, Dick. 31 January 2008, letter.

181. Stephens, Gene. 12 February 2008, letter.

182. Stock, Wes. 12 February 2008, letter.

183. Strickland, George. 10 January 2008, letter.

184. Talese, Gay. 21 March 2008. Gay signed two renovation photos.

185. Terry, Ralph. 27 March 1975, letter.

186. Terwilliger, Wayne. 16 April 2008, letter.

187. Tiant, Luis. 4 February 2008. Luis signed two renovation photos.

188. Tresh, Tom. 15 March 2008, letter.

189. Triandos, Gus. 15 January 2008. Gus signed two renovation photos.

190. Trucks, Virgil. 12 January 2008, letter.

191. Valentine, Bill. 18 February 2005, letter.

192. Valentinetti, Vito. 20 February 2008, letter.

193. Vargo, Ed. 8 March 2005, letter.

194. Vecsey, George. 20 April 2008, letter.

195. Vernon, Mickey. 27 February 2008. Mickey sent me a signed card.

196. Waslewski, Gary. 26 January 2008, letter.

197. Watson, Bob. 8 April 2008, letter.

198. Watt, Ed. 14 January 2008, letter.

199. Whitaker, Steve. 14 May 2008. Steve signed two renovation photos.

200. White, Roy. 15 November 2006, New York Yankees Fantasy Camp, Tampa, Florida, oral taped interview.

201. Wickersham, Dave. 14 January 2008.

202. Williams, Dick. 22 February 2005, letter.

203. Williams, Stan. 19 February 2005, letter.

204. Williams, Walt (No Neck). 7 February 2008, letter.

205. Witt, Whitey. 3 August 1974, letter.

206. Witt, Whitey. 18 August 1975, letter.

207. Witt, Whitey. 20 October 1975, letter.

208. Wolff, Bob. 16 January 2008, letter.

209. Worthington, Al. 23 January 2008, letter.

210. Yost, Ed. 15 January 2008. Ed signed two renovation photos.

211. Yvars, Sal. 14 January 2008, letter.

212. Zernial, Gus. 25 June 1975, letter.

THEY WERE THERE End Notes

1. Letter, Robert C.Y. Young to Michael Wagner, November 15, 2003.

2. Ed H. Brunjes to Michael Wagner, "Just a few suggestions for accuracy in your book," November 14, 2008.

3. e-mail, Tim Crowley/The Crowley Group to Michael Wagner, Jerry Crowley, January 12, 2009.

4. Telephone Interview with Harvey Levene, April 8, 2008.

5. Telephone Interview with Victor Strauss, September 18, 2007; e-mail, Victor Strauss to Michael Wagner, "Final Draft of Yankee Stadium Renovation Book," September 11, 2008; e-mail, Victor Strauss to Michael Wagner, "We are now located in Manhattan," September 12, 2008.

6. Telephone Interview with Stephen Offerman, September 20, 2007.

7. Telephone Interview with Ralph Drewes, September 19, 2007; Notes written by Ralph Drewes on Yankee Stadium renovation photos I sent him, November 5, 2007; Letter, Ralph Drewes to Michael Wagner, August 10, 2011.

8. Telephone Interview, Ralph Terowsky, April 13, 2009.

9. e-mail, Michael Wagner to Mariano Molina, "Yankee Stadium Renovation," August 20,

2008; e-mail, Mariano Molina to Michael Wagner, "Attached is some information regarding the Yankee Stadium project," August 20, 2008.

10. Telephone Interview #1 with Dick Muller, September 26, 2007.

11. Telephone Interview #2 with Dick Muller, June 15, 2008.

12. Telephone Interview with Doug Walker, May 24, 2007.

13. Telephone Interview with Jerry Marshall, August 22, 2008.

14. Telephone Interview with Larry King, August 30, 2008.

15. e-mail, Suzanne Koch Fabrizio to Michael Wagner, "Memories from Yankee Stadium, by Suzanne Koch Fabrizio," June 8, 2013.

16. Telehone Interview #1 with Steven Koch, June 30, 2013.

17. Telephone Interview #2 with Steven Koch, September 15, 2013.

18. Telephone Interview with Rick Petricca of Unistress, September 14, 2014.

Chapter Twelve

BIBLIOGRAPHY

Books

Burke, Michael. *Outrageous Good Fortune*. Boston-Toronto: Little Brown and Company, 1984.

Durso, Joseph. *Yankee Stadium: Fifty Years of Drama*. Boston, Massachusetts: Houghton Mifflin Company, 1972.

Leventhal, Josh. *The World Series: an illustrated encyclopedia of the fall classic.* New York: Black Dog & Leventhal Publishers, 2001.

Sullivan, Neil J. "*The Diamond In The Bronx*," New York: Oxford University Press, 2001, 2008.

Swanson, Harry. *Ruthless Baseball: Yankees Purified by Fire Stadium Construction.* Bloomington, Indiana: Author HOUSE, 2005.

e-mails/interviews/letters

Adonetti, Anthony. e-mail, August 21, 2008; telephone interview, August 22, 2008; letter, September 8, 2008; e-mail, May 29, 2010; interview corrections, August 1, 2011.

Andres, David. e-mail, October 5, 2008.

Brown, Abraham. Notes, Texas artist, "Yankee Stadium Architecture," February 2, 2008.

Brunjes, Ed H. e-mails, November 14 and 18, 2008.

Burns, Gordon. Press Releases, Warren Weil Public Relations, 405 Park Avenue, New York, N.Y. 10022, numerous press releases regarding various aspects of the renovation of Yankee Stadium, "The Modernization of Yankee Stadium," April 13, 1976.

Concepcion, David. e-mail, September 7, 2008.

Costello, Mark. e-mail, January 13, 2009.

Crowley, Tim. e-mail, January 13, 2009.

Drewes, Ralph. Telephone interview, September 19, 2007; notes written on Yankee Stadium renovation photos, November 5, 2007; letter, August 10, 2011.

Dunaier, Gary. e-mails, September 7, 2008; September 24, 2008; November 6, 2008; September 13, 2009; September 14, 2009.

Fabrizio, Suzanne. e-mail, "Memories from Yankee Stadium by Suzanne Koch Fabrizio," June 8, 2013.

Gagliano, Rich. e-mail, "Yankee Stadium Renovation Photos," October 22, 2006.

Garagiola, Joe Jr. Telephone interview, September 20, 2008.

Gates, James L. Jr. (Library Director, Baseball Hall of Fame). e-mails, September 13 and 17, 2010.

Goodman, Dr. Cary. Telephone Interview, June 30, 2011.

Jones, Chris. e-mails, February 8, 17 and 25, 2009.

Kasten, Peter. e-mail, June 12, 2008.

Kelleher, Brian (aka "Mack Maloney). e-mail, November 7, 2008.

Kelly, Patricia D (Photo Archivist, Baseball Hall of Fame). Letter, December 16, 2008; e-mails, January 26, 2009; October 21, 2010.

King, Larry. e-mails, September 18, 2008; July 19, 2010.

King, Matthew. e-mail, October 13, 2008.

Koch, Steven. Telephone Interview #1, June 30, 2013; Telephone Interview #2, September 15, 2013.

Leavitt, David. Letter, November 13, 2008.

Lenaz, John. e-mail, December 31, 2008.

Levene, Harvey. Telephone interview, April 8, 2008.

Lillard, Judith. e-mails, September 26, 2008; October 30, 2008; November 3, 2008.

Lillard, Richard. e-mail, January 14, 2010.

Lindau, Herman A. e-mail, August 24, 2008.

Long, Jim. e-mail, September 18, 2008.

Marshall, Jerry. Telephone interview, August 22, 2008; e-mails, September 3 and 9, 2008.

McNally, Peter. e-mail, September 22, 2008.

Meeks, John. e-mails, April 27, 2009; October 3, 2011.

Molina, Mariano. Letter with DVD, August 25, 2008; e-mails, August 20 and 27, 2008; September 9, 2008; August 12, 2009.

Muller, Dick. Telephone interview #1, September 26, 2007; interview #2, June 15, 2008; e-mails, July 10, 2008; September 9, 2008.

Offerman, Stephen. Telephone interview, September 20, 2007.

Reid, Tim. e-mails, May 2, 2009; July 1, 2010.

Rim, Kurt K. Letter, Chairman, The Osborn Engineering Company, March 31, 2005.

Ruppert, K. Jacob. e-mail, March 30, 2008.

Schechter, Gabriel. e-mails, June 30, 2011; July 1, 2011.

Schwall, Jay (L.L.). e-mail, November 8, 2008; telephone interviews, June 24 and 30, 2011; telephone interview corrections, July 7, 2011; August 4, 2011.

Simins, Herbert J. Letter, The City of New York, Department of Public Works, Commissioner, to Invirex Demolition Inc. And Cuyahoga Wrecking Corp., "Yankee Stadium…Notice of Award," August 24, 1973.

Slezak, Roy. e-mail, February 4, 2009.

Smith, Ken. [Director, Baseball Hall of Fame] Letter to L.L. Schwall, "Thank you for donations to the Hall of Fame," October 3, 1974.

Strauss, Victor. Telephone interview, September 18, 2007; e-mail, September 11, 2008.

Sugar, Bert Randolph. Letter to L.L. Schwall, "Re: Signed Yankee Stadium Home Plate," July 9, 1999.

Swanson, Harry. e-mails, October 30, 2006; September 19, 2007; December 8, 2008; telephone interview, March 4, 2007.

Terowsky, Ralph. Telephone interview, April 13, 2009.

Thompson, Jackie. e-mail, August 21, 2008.

Turnow, Brad. e-mail, October 24, 2009.

Visco, Matt. e-mails, April 9, 2007; July 12, 2008; October 19, 2008; December 8, 2011.

Walker, Doug. Telephone interview, May 24, 2007; letter, March 7, 2008.

Wiederecht, Larry. e-mail, February 27, 2008.

Young , Robert C.Y. Letter, "Yankee Stadium Renovation," November 15, 2003; letter, June 29, 2011.

Various Media

Auction, "Lot 347. Blue Prints for Old Yankee Stadium," Lelands, August 2005.

Blueprint, "Paint Specifications," Slocum and Fuller, October 1, 1973.

Blueprint, "Yankee Stadium Blueprint – Original Working Print 1922! (American Bridge Company)," 1922, ebay, February 5, 2005.

Handout, "Yankee Stadium," New York Yankees, Parks Administration Building, Flushing, New York 11368, 1 page, 1974 or 1975.

Information Specifications Sheet, American Seating Company, Grand Rapids, Michigan, "Stadium chair model 406," n.d.

Program, "30th Annual New York Yankees Old Timers' Day," August 7, 1976.

Television Documentary, National Geographic Channel, "*Break It Down: Yankee Stadium*," airing April 28, 2011, http://btbfansite.proboards.com/index.cgi?board=general &action= print…, April 12, 2011.

Newspapers

The following newspapers were utilized:

Advocate, Newark, Ohio
Anaconda Standard, Anaconda, Montana
Bennington Banner, Bennington, Vermont
Boston Herald
Bridgeport Sunday Post, Bridgeport, Connecticut

Bridgeport Telegram, Bridgeport, Connecticut
Bucks County Courier Times, Levittown, Pennsylvania
Charleston Gazette, Charleston, West Virginia
Chicago Tribune
Chronicle Telegram, Elyria, Ohio
Constitution-Tribune, Chillicothe, Missouri
Coshocton Tribune, Coshocton, Ohio
Daily Courier, Connellsville, Pennsylvania
Daily Freeman, Kingston, New York
Daily Kennebec Journal, Augusta, Maine
Daily Messenger, Canandaigua, New York
Daily Times, Salisbury, Maryland
Daily Tribune, Great Bend, Kansas
Davenport Democrat And Leader, Davenport, Iowa
Delta Democrat-Times, Greenville, Mississippi
Express-Times, Lehigh Valley, New Jersey
Florence Morning News, Florence, South Carolina
Fort Wayne Daily News, Fort Wayne, Indiana
Frederick Post, Frederick, Maryland
Fresno Bee, Fresno, California
Galveston Daily News, Galveston, Texas
Greeley Tribune, Greeley, Colorado
Indianapolis Star, Indianapolis, Indiana
Independent, Long Beach, California
Independent Press Telegram, Long Beach, California
Lethbridge Herald, Alberta, Canada
Lima News, Lima, Ohio
Lincoln Star, Lincoln, Nebraska
Lowell Sun, Lowell, Massachusetts
Mansfield News, Mansfield, Ohio
Modesto News Herald, Modesto, California
Nevada State Journal, Reno, Nevada
Newport Daily News, Newport, Rhode Island
Newsday, Long Island, New York
News Journal, Mansfield, Ohio
New York Daily News

New York Post
New York Times
Odessa American, Odessa, Texas
Olean Evening Herald, Olean, New York
Oneonta Star, Oneonta, New York
Pacific Stars & Stripes
Post-Crescent, Appleton, Wisconsin
Post-Standard, Syracuse, New York
Public Ledger-Philadelphia, Philadelphia, Pennsylvania
Sandusky Evening Star, Sandusky, Ohio
San Antonio Express News, San Antonio, Texas
Star-Ledger, Newark, New Jersey
Stars And Stripes
St. Petersburg Times, St. Petersburg, Florida
Syracuse Herald, Syracuse, New York
Syracuse Herald-Journal, Syracuse, New York
The New Mexican, Santa Fe, New Mexico
The News, Frederick, Maryland
Times Recorder, Zanesville, Ohio
Valley Morning Star, Harlingen, Texas

Periodical and Internet Articles

100th anniversary," http://www.mlb.com/NASApp/mlb/mlb/news/mlb_20010331_originaleight_news.jsp.

"161st Street/River Avenue (Yankee Stadium) (IRT Woodlawn Line)," http://www.nycsubway.org/perl/stations?198:3161.

"1904: Boston Herald tells of Red Sox trade "Dougherty as a Yankee," 1st known reference to the New York club as Yankees," http://www.brainyhistory.com/days/june_ 21.html.

"1928 Signed Osborn Engineering Yankee Stadium Construction Specification for the "House That Ruth Built," Geppi's Memorabilia Roadshow," http://www.gmrs.com/item/.asp?Auction=1&ItemNo=35904.

"1974-75 Renovation/"Yankee Stadium II," http://en.wikipedia.org/wiki/Yankee_ Stadium.

"1999 Ford C. Frick Award Winner Arch McDonald," http://www.baseballhallof fame.org/hoofers_and_honorees/frick_bios/mcdonald_arch.htm.

"American Bridge—Manufacturing History," http://www.americanbridge.net/company/ mfg/abmhistory.php, February 5, 2005.

"America's Favorite Architecture," http://en.wikipedia.org/wiki/America's_Favorite _Architecture.

"Astor, William Waldorf Astor, 1st Viscount," http://education.yahoo.com/reference -encyclopedia/entry?id=3155.

"Ballparks of Baseball: The Fields of Major League Baseball: Hilltop Park," http://www. ballparksofbaseball.com/past/HilltopPark.htm.

"Billingham has no issues with giving up Aaron's 714th HR," http://www.sportsline. Com/mlb/story/10266340, July 23, 2007.

"Biography: Red Barber," http://www.chatteringmagpie.com/essays/red_barber. html.

Borelli, Stephen, "'Voice of God' presides over Yankees," http://www.usatoday.com/ sports/baseball/comment/sbcoll15.htm.

"Brad's Ultimate New York Yankees Website:" http://www.ultimateyankees.com/history. htm.

"Broadcast," http://www.brainyhistory.com/topics/b/broadcast.html.

"Bronx – New York – History," http://www.americatravelling.net/usa/new_york/Bronx _history.htm.

"Chronology of outfield dimensions," http://www.bokrags.com/Yankee_Stadium.

"Eddie Layton," http://ultimateyankees.com.eddielayton.htm.

"Giants Stadium: History of Giants' Stadium," http://www.giants.com/gameday/GiantsStadium.asp.

Frommer, Harvey."*Yankee Stadium Firsts (A Very Partial List)," http://baseball guru.com/hfrommer/analysishfrommer65.html.

"Girth of a Nation: The New York Yankees adopted pinstripe uniforms in an effort to disguise Babe Ruth's girth," http://ww.snopes.com/sports/baseball/pinstripes.asp.

"Heavy Duty Falsework Systems," http://www.sciglobal.com/falsework/25kw.html, November 16, 2007.

Horsley, Carter B. "The Upper East Side Book: Ruppert & Yorkville Towers," http:/www.thecityreview.com/ues/thirdave/ruppert.html.

"Improvements underway for Yankee Stadium area," *Real Estate Weekly*, July 23, 1993, http://www.highbeam.com/doc/1G1-14170335.html.

"Jerome Avenue in history:," *Bronx Blotter, 50th Precinct, Jerome Avenue, 2002*, http://kraybill.home.mindspring.com/50/02jerome.html.

"Jerome Avenue," http://jerome-avenue.co.tv/.

"Klepper Marshall King Associates Ltd., http://goliath.ecnext.com/comsite5/bin/pdlanding=1&referid=1868&accession_number=00…

Lasseter, Diana. "scrap-heap rollup hits New Jersey," *Business News New Jersey*, http://findarticles.com/p/articles/mi_qa6206/is_199806/ai_n24334984/, June 1, 1998.

Markusen, Bruce. "Frank Messer: The Passing of a Yankee Broadcaster," http://www.baseballlibrary.com/baseballlibrary/submit/Markusen_Bruce1.stm.

"Mel Allen (Melvin Allen Israel)," http://www.jewishvirtuallibrary.org/jsource/biography/Allen.html.

Moore, Donald, "Oakland A's History: Finley Fires Andrews," http://athletics.scout.com/2/683126.html.

"New York Yankees: Ballpark: Yankee Stadium History," http://newyork.yankees.mlb.com/NASApp/mlb/nyy/ballpark/stadium_history.jsp.

"New York Yankees: History: Yankees All-Time Broadcasters," http://newyork.Yankees.mlb.com/NASApp/mlb/nyy/history.broadcasters.jsp.

"New York Yankees: History: Yankees Timeline: 1937 Stands Expansion," http://newyork.yankees.mlb.com/NASApp/mlb/nyy/history/timeline2.jsp.

"New York Yankees: Nickname/Franchise/Highlights," http://www.angelfire.com/sd/slopitch/yankee.html.

"No. 1 Pick: Hunt Auctions," http://sportsantiques101.com, July 11, 2008.

"Not Just Jerry: There's a Quirky Story to the Way Jerome Avenue Got its Name," *The Bronx Journal Online*, http://lehman.cuny.edu/deanhum/langlit/tbj/sep00/local.htm.

"Oakland Athletics," http://en.wikipedia.org/wiki/1973_World_Series.

"Old Yankee Stadium," http:/www.baseball-fever.com/showthread.php?t=43850&page=2, September 29, 2007.

"Origin of the Name "New York Yankees," http://www.baseball-fever.com/showthread.php?t=64650, July 23, 2007.

"Original Yankee Stadium Brick with Receipt," Geppi's Memorabilia Roadshow, http://www.gmrs.com/item/asp?Auction=1&ItemNo35903, July 24, 2006.

"Osborn Architects and Engineers - About Us," http://www.osborn-eng.com/about_background.html.

"Patsy Dougherty Statistics," http://www.baseball-reference.com/d/doughpa01.shtml.

Pietrusza, David. "Ban Takes Manhattan," http:/www.davidpietrusza.com/Ban-Takes-Manhattan.html.

Primerano, Jane. "Edison Cement Plant: N.J. Plant Cemented in History," *The Express-Times*, http://www.rootsweb.ancestry.com/~njwarren/edison.html., n.d.

"Renovated Yankee Stadium: Color coded tickets," http://www.baseball-fever.com/showthread.php?t=45054, September 29, 2007.

"Riverside Drive Viaduct," http://www.morningside-heights.net/rivbrid.htm.

"Ross Lewis Yankee Stadium 1973-1976 Farewell Photographs," http://www.ys-stadium photos.com/source1/htm.

"Service Begun on the Jerome Avenue Line (June 1917)," http://www.nycsubway.Org/dual/psr_jerome.html.

Silverman, Dan. "Saluting the AL's Original Eight: The junior circuit celebrates its 100th anniversary," http://www.mlb.com/NASApp/mlb/mlb/news/mlb_20010331_originaleight_news.jsp.

Stamford Demolition Services, "Stamford Wrecking Company," http://Stamford wrecking.com/about.html.

"Standard Fire Insurance Policy of the State of New York (Policy #14661)," http://www.baseball-fever.com/showthread.php?97584-1923-Yankee-S..., August 22, 2011.

"The Edison Papers: "Cement," "Edison's Companies," Rutgers, The State University of New Jersey, Piscataway, New Jersey, http://edison.rutgers.edu/contact.htm.

"The Lackawanna Cutoff-Then & Now: Paulins Kill Viaduct," Photo courtesy of The Lackawanna Railroad in Northwest New Jersey by Larry Lowenthal and William T. Greenberg Jr., Tri State Railway Historical Society, http://history.gsmrrclub.org/history 5i.html, 1987.

“The Town of Enfield, Connecticut – 1997 Inductees: Michael Burke,” http://enfield-ct.gov/content/91/151/1569/3015.aspx, n.d.

“Unistress,” http://www.unistresscorp.com/Precast_structures.html.

Wilkins, Michael. “Today in New York history: Babe suffers the ‘bellyache heard ‘round the world,’” *NY History Examiner*, April 5, 2010, http://www.examiner.com/history-in-new-york/today-new-york-history…

“Yankee Stadium,” http://www.nabconstruction.com.gencon.html.

“Yankee Stadium, “htpp://www.projectballpark.org/major/yankee.html.

“Yankee Stadium 1920s thru 1950s. (Telephonic Hall of Fame,)” http://www.baseball-fever.com/showthread.php?t=22080&page=14, December 31, 2006.

“Yankee Stadium Demolition, “Re: Catwalks,” http://www.baseball-fever.com/showthread.php?78640-Yankee-Stadium…, page 4, May 27, 2010, page 15, May 25, 2010, page 16, May 27, 2010.

"Yankee Stadium Facts,” http://reg18.k12.ct.us/lolhs/stark/facts.htm.

“Yankee Stadium Frieze:1967 Facelift,” http://www.baseball-fever.com/showthread.php?74744-Yankee-Stadium..., March 2, 2009.

“Yankee Stadium Frieze: Gauge Thickness of Frieze,” http://baseball-fever.com/showthread.php?t=74744&page=2, March 19, 2008.

“Yankee Stadium Pedestrian Bridge,” http://www.ehbrunjesassociates.com/profile.html.

“Yankee Stadium Pre-Renovation: Scoreboards,” http://www.baseball-fever.com/showthread.php?t=71363&page=43, March 25, 2008.

"Yankee Stadium Pre-Renovation: Yankee Stadium Blowout! Everything Must Go!,” http://www.baseball-fever.com/showthread.php?71363-Yankee-Stadium-Pre-Renovation, August 5, 2010.

"Yankee Stadium Renovation 1973-1975, http://www.baseball-fever.com/showthread.php?t=58009&page 2, March 4, 2007, pages 6 thru 9, February 21, 2008 thru April 21, 2008; page 8, April 8, 2008; pages 18, 19, July 9, 2008; page 22, August 10, 2008; page 29, September 13, 2008; page 37, January 11, 2009.

Magazine Articles

"1923 New York Yankees Team Roster," *Sports Illustrated*, http://sportsillustrated.cnn.com/baseball/mlb/all_time_stats/rosters/american_league/nya/1923.1...

1973 New York Yankees Yearbook.

1976 New York Yankees Yearbook.

1976 New York Yankees Scorebook & Official Magazine.

Ad, "Jenkins Valves," *The Architectural Record Magazine*, October 1924.

Ad, "Johns-Manville Asbestos Roofing," *The Saturday Evening Post*, ca. 1923.

Ad, "Tons of Toncan went into this stadium," United Alloy Steel Corporation, 1923, ebay, March 10, 2008.

Ad, Yankee Stadium Demolition Items For Sale, *Wrecking & Salvage Journal*, October, 1973.

"Baseball: AL East," *Sports Illustrated*, August 26, 1976.

Cerrone, Rick. "A Look Back: Yankee Stadium Came Down Piece By Piece," *Yankees Magazine*, May, 2004.

Coffey, Wayne, "Part Four: Birth of The Bronx Zoo," http://www.nydailynews.com/features/thestadium/the_magazine/partfour_01.html, August 17, 2008.

"Comprehensive Study and Report for Modernization of Yankee Stadium, Borough of the Bronx, City of New York," *Praeger Kavanagh Waterbury Engineers, Architects*, 69 pages, June 30, 1972.

Cox, Clinton. "The angry neighbors of Yankee Stadium," *Sunday News Magazine*, February 27, 1977.

Cushing, Charles Phelps."86,000 pounds of Copper and 86,000 Fans at World Series," *Bulletin of the Copper & Brass Research Association*, October 1937.

"Cuyahoga and Invirex in joint venture; win Yankee Stadium," W*recking & Salvage Journal*, September, 1973.

Fimrite, Ron. "Bowie Stops Charlie's Checks," *Sports Illustrated*, June 28, 1976.

"Inventory of Memorabilia From Yankee Stadium, 5/18/98," *J. Peterman Catalog*, Christmas '98.

Invirex Demolition, Inc., Company Magazine, n.d.

Johnson, Kyle and Clark, Carol. "The Ballpark and the City: Yankee Stadium Renovation," *New York Affairs Magazine*, n.d.

Keane, Maribeth. "An Interview With Vintage Television Set Collector Steve McVoy," *Collectors Weekly*, http://www.collectorsweekly.com/articles/an-interview-withvintage-te..., August 19, 2008.

Leon, George deLucenay, "Sound on the Mound," *Sound & Communications*, June 1976.

Levy, Eric. "When the Yankees Were on the Top (of the Hill): Playing Ball in the Medical Center Garden," *Columbia University P&S Journal*, Spring/Summer 2003.

Lipsyte, Robert. "A Diamond In The Ashes," *Sports Illustrated*, April 26, 1976.

Minshew, Wayne. "The Hammer hits the big one," http://www.sportingnews.com/

archives/aaron/152207.html.

Murdock E. "The Tragedy of Ban Johnson," *The Sporting News*, July 14, 1927.

"New York Highlanders 1903 All-Time Roster," http://sportsillustrated.cnn.com/baseball/mlb/stats/alltime/rosters/highlanders/1903.html.

New York Yankees Dedication Program, April 13, 1976.

Pileggi, Nicholas (text) and Lewis, Ross (photos), "Was the Stadium Worth It?," *New York Magazine*, April 19, 1976.

Randolph, John Brooks, "Yankee Stadium: Going, Going, Gone," *Argosy*, ca October 1973.

"Reconstruction Scores At The "House That Ruth Built,"" *Constructioneer*, February 18, 1974.

Report, "Yankee Stadium Project Final Environmental Impact Statement," *New York City Department of Parks and Recreation*, February 10, 2006.

Riess, Steven A. "The Baseball Magnate and Urban Politics in the Progressive Era, 1895-1920," University of Chicago, 1999.

Selter, Ron. "Hilltop Park," The Society For American Baseball Research, August 2002.

"Souvenir Programme: Yankee Stadium-Opening Day, April 18, 1923," Harry M. Stevens, Publisher.

"Stadia-Part II: The Yankee Stadium, New York," *The American Architect and the Architectural Review*," November 7, 1923.

"The Stadium, 1920s: Grand Opening," *New York Yankees Magazine*, 2008.

Twersky, Mordechai I. "Remembering the Manager That Got Away," http://bats.Blogs.nytimes.com/2011/07/23/remembering-the-mamager-tha…

Walters, John. "Yankee Stadium for Sale: Home plate and old seats at J. Peterman's ain't cheap," *Sports Illustrated*, November 2, 1998.

Wilson, Walt. "Yankees, Giants, and Dodgers Met in 1931: Mayor Jimmy Walker's Charity Match," *The Society For American Baseball Research*, December 2004.

"Yankees Baseball: 100 Years: The 1900s," 2003 New York Yankees Yearbook.

"Yankees return to "Home of Champions" in legendary "House that Ruth Built," *Pinstripes*, April, 1976.

"Yankees vs. Giants 1923, Worlds Championship Series Program, 1923, Harry M. Stevens, Publisher, 1923, (*The Great World Series Program Collection: Volume 29*), Robert D. Opie/Publisher, 2829 Toyon Drive, Santa Clara, CA 95051, 1982.

"Yankee Stadium Spiral," *The Sporting News*, November 8, 1975.

THE HEROES SPEAK II End Notes

(The Demolition of Yankee Stadium, 2010)

1. Letter sent by Michael Wagner to various respondents, various dates.

2. Amaro, Sr., Ruben. 26 September 2010, letter.

3. Arnsberg, Brad. 7 January 2011, letter.

4. Becquer, Julio. 7 July 2010, letter.

5. Bell, Bill "Lefty". 15 November 2010, signed biography and baseball card.

6. Benson, Vern. 6 July 2010, signed Yankee Stadium demolition photo.

7. Biddle, Dennis "Bose". 17 August 2010, signed Yankee Stadium demolition photo and signed baseball card.

8. Bolling, Milt. 1 July 2010, letter.

9. Bonilla, Bobby. 10 July 2010, signed baseball card.

10. Bosman, Dick. 28 September 2010, e-mail, signed Yankee Stadium demolition photo.

11. Brissie, Lou. 21 September 2010, signed baseball cards.

12. Brown, Bobby. 8 June 2011, letter.

13. Brown, Gates. 1 September 2010, signed Yankee Stadium demolition photo.

14. Campaneris, Bert. 14 July 2010, signed Yankee Stadium demolition photo.

15. Carroll, Sonny. 29 September 2010, letter.

16. Casanova, Paul. 22 December 2010, signed Yankee Stadium demolition photo.

17. Causey, Wayne. 21 August 2010, letter.

18. Cavaretta, Phil. 17 August 2010, signed Yankee Stadium demolition photo.

19. Charles, Ed. 12 August 2010, signed Yankee Stadium demolition photo.

20. Cimoli, Gino. 23 August 2010, signed Yankee Stadium demolition photo.

21. Clark, Al. 25 December 2010, e-mail.

22. Clark, Allie. 22 July 2010, signed baseball card.

23. Clarke, Horace. 8 July 2010, letter, signed Yankee Stadium demolition photo.

24. Clyde, David. 10 August 2010, e-mail.

25. Coble, Drew. 31 August 2010, letter.

26. Coleman, Jerry. 20 August 2010, letter.

27. Cox, Casey. 14 July 2010, letter.

28. Daley, Bud. 6 July 2010, letter.

29. Deal, Cot. 6 July, 2010, signed Yankee Stadium demolition photo.

30. Demars, Billy. 9 July 2010, letter, signed baseball card.

31. Demeter, Don. 9 September 2010, letter.

32. Doerr, Bobby. 1 July 2010, letter.

33. Downing, Al. 3 July 2010, letter.

34. Erskine, Carl. 5 July 2010, letter, signed Yankee Stadium demolition photo.

35. Evans, Jim. 6 September 2010, letter.

36. Ferrarese, Don. 10 July 2010, letter, signed Yankee Stadium demolition photo, other photos.

37. Ferriss, Dave, "Boo". 8 July 2010, signed biography.

38. Foytack, Paul. 12 July 2010, telephone interview.

39. Fregosi, Jim. 7 January 2011, signed Yankee Stadium demolition photo.

40. Garver, Ned. 8 July 2010, two signed baseball cards.

41. Ginsberg, Joe. 6 July 2010, letter, signed Yankee Stadium demolition photo.

42. Glenn, Stanley "Doc". 25 August 2010, signed index card.

43. Hegan, Mike. 28 August 2010, letter.

44. Heidemann, Jack. 18 August 2010, letter, signed photos.

45. Hemus, Solly. 23 August 2010, letter, signed Yankee Stadium demolition photo.

46. Herbert, Ray. 16 August 2010, signed Yankee Stadium demolition photo.

47. Hershberger, Mike. 18 August 2010, letter.

48. Hinton, Chuck. 25 August 2010 letter.

49. Hook, Jay. 26 August 2010, letter.

50. Houk, Ralph. 3 July 2010, signed two baseball cards.

51. Hudler, Rex. 19 August 2010, letter, signed baseball card.

52. James, John. 28 August 2010, letter.

53. Johnson, Alex. 29 May 2012, letter, signed Yankee Stadium demolition photo.

54. Johnson, Cliff. 9 September 2010, signed baseball card.

55. Jones, Ben. 7 September 2010, signed photo.

56. Jones, Dalton. 17 August 2010, telephone interview.

57. Kipp, Fred. 27 August 2010, signed Yankee Stadium demolition photo.

58. Klimchock, Lou. 31 August 2010, signed Yankee Stadium demolition photo.

59. Kline, Steve. 20 January 2011, letter.

60. Knoop, Bobby. 13 February 2011, telephone interview.

61. Kosco, Andy. 28 August 2010, signed Yankee Stadium demolition photo.

62. Kubiak, Ted. 4 September 2010, e-mail.

63. Kubiak, Ted. 28 September 2010, e-mail.

64. Landis, Jim. 21 August 2010, letter.

65. Lepcio, Ted. 16 August 2010, letter.

66. Linz, Phil. 19 August 2010, signed Yankee Stadium demolition photo, unsigned photo.

67. Lonborg, Jim. 13 September 2010, letter.

68. Lopata, Stan. 9 September 2010, letter.

69. MacPhail, Lee. 7 July 2010, letter.

70. Maxwell, Charlie. 17 August 2010, signed Yankee Stadium demolition photo.

71. McCormick, Mike. 7 October 2010, letter.

72. McCoy, Larry. 30 August 2010, signed photo.

73. McDaniel, Lindy. 17 August 2010, letter, signed photo.

74. McGregor, Scott. 21 September 2010, signed Yankee Stadium demolition photo.

75. McKeon, Jack. 5 March 2011, letter.

76. Mele, Sam. 19 August 2010, signed Yankee Stadium demolition photo.

77. Meoli, Rudy. 23 August 2010, letter.

78. Miles, John "Mule". 19 August 2010, letter, signed Yankee Stadium demolition photo.

79. Mitterwald, George. 12 September 2010, letter.

80. Mueller, Don. 26 August 2010, signed photo.

81. Nixon, Russ. 26 August 2010, letter.

82. Northrup, Jim. 13 September 2010, signed Yankee Stadium demolition photo.

83. O'Dell, Billy. 12 November 2010, signed Yankee Stadium demolition photo, signed photo.

84. Oldis, Bob. 17 August, 2010, letter, signed Yankee Stadium demolition photo.

85. Oliver, Nate. 17 September 2010, letter.

86. Pagan, Dave. 26 August 2010, letter.

87. Palermo, Steve. 10 September 2010, letter.

88. Parrish, Lance. 18 November 2010, letter.

89. Pasqua, Dan. 4 March 2013, signed photo.

90. Peatros, Maurice. 23 December 2010, letter, signed baseball card.

91. Peters, Gary. 19 August 2010, letter.

92. Peterson, Fritz. 3 July 2010, letter, signed Yankee Stadium demolition photo, signed baseball card.

93. Pierce, Billy. 19 August 2010, letter.

94. Pignatano, Joe. 13 August 2010, letter.

95. Pizarro, Juan. 30 August 2010, signed Yankee Stadium demolition photo.

96. Plews, Herb. 26 August 2010, letter.

97. Pride, Mack A., Jr. 16 September 2010, telephone interview, signed Yankee Stadium demolition photo.

98. Quilici, Frank. 16 August 2010, letter.

99. Rettenmund, Merv. 19 August 2010, letter.

100. Richardson, Bobby. 23 July 2010, letter.

101. Rivers, Mickey. 9 December 2010, signed Yankee Stadium demolition photo.

102. Robinson, James. 21 August 2010, letter signed baseball card.

103. Roebuck, Ed. 14 October 2010, signed baseball card and signed index card.

104. Rollins, Rich. 8 July 2010, letter.

105. Roof, Phil. 7 July 2010, letter.

106. Rosen, Al. 1 July 2010. Signed baseball card.

107. Savage, Bob. 23 July 2010, letter, signed baseball card.

108. Saverine, Bob. 22 July 2010, letter.

109. Schilling, Chuck. 10 July 2010, letter.

110. Schmitz, Johnny. 6 July 2010, signed Yankee Stadium demolition photo.

111. Schult, Art. 12 July 2010, letter.

112. Schofield, Dick. 20 July 2010, letter.

113. Schwall, Don. 12 July 2010, letter, signed Yankee Stadium demolition photo.

114. Shantz, Bobby. 1 July 2010, letter, signed Yankee Stadium demolition photo.

115. Sheldon, Rollie. 3 July 2010, letter.

116. Sherry, Norm. 7 January 2011, letter.

117. Sievers, Roy. 10 August 2010, letter.

118. Silvera, Charlie. 18 August 2010, letter, signed Yankee Stadium demolition photo.

119. Simmons, Curt. 8 January 2011, signed baseball card.

120. Soderholm, Eric. 8 January 2011, signed Yankee Stadium demolition photo.

121. Spencer, Daryl. 5 January 2011, letter.

122. Springstead, Marty. 11 September 2010, letter.

123. Starrette, Herman. 9 January 2011, letter.

124. Stigman, Dick. 7 January 2011, letter, signed photo.

125. Stowe, Hal. 24 January 2011, signed Yankee Stadium demolition photo.

126. Tepedino, Frank. 26 August 2010, letter, signed Yankee Stadium demolition photo, signed baseball card.

127. Tiant, Luis, 7 September 2010, signed Yankee Stadium demolition photo.

128. Trucks, Virgil. 25 August 2010, letter, signed baseball card.

129. Valdespino, Sandy. 15 March 2010, signed Yankee Stadium demolition photo.

130. Virdon, Bill. 2 July 2010, letter, signed photo.

131. Vizcaino, Jose. 31 August 2010, letter.

132. Voltaggio, Vic. 6 September 2010, letter.

133. Wakefield, Bill. 16 August 2010, signed Yankee Stadium demolition photo.

134. Whitfield, Fred. 8 September 2010, letter.

135. Whitney, Dave. 26 August 2010, letter.

136. Wiesler, Bob. 20 August 2010, signed Yankee Stadium demolition photo.

137. Williams, Stan. 5 July 2010, letter.

138. Williams, Walt "No Neck". 27 July 2010, signed Yankee Stadium demolition photo.

139. Windhorn, Gordon. 8 July 2010, letter.

140. Wolff, Bob. 12 August 2010, letter.

141. Worthington, Al. 4 July 2010, letter, signed brochure.

142. Yost, Ed. 8 January 2011, signed Yankee Stadium demolition photo, two signed photos.

143. Zernial, Gus. 14 July 2010, signed Yankee Stadium demolition photo.

INDEX

A

B

C

D

E

F

<u>G</u>

H

I

J

K

L

M

N

O

P

Q

R

S

<u>T</u>

U

V

W

X

Y

Z

Although Mark Costello did not participate in renovating Yankee Stadium, he has brought up some excellent points regarding this project. Therefore, his e-mail, on the following three pages is included in this chapter of the book.

1/13/2009
Mike,

It was nice speaking with you today. Here is a slightly updated version of my 1/11/2009 post in your Baseball Fever thread. Please feel free to use the portions of it that you like in your book and go ahead and mention my name in connection with it.

Best of luck in having the book published and I am looking forward to buying a copy. I think that it's great that you've tackled this heretofore relatively unexplored topic. With the new stadium opening this year, there is naturally a heightened interest in the old building and the major renovation in the 1970s so your timing should be good.

If I can be of further assistance, don't hesitate to contact me.

Regards,
Mark Costello
Amityville, NY

Hello Mike & Spiderico,

I've just recently found this website and have really enjoyed reading through the thread. Mike, if it's not too late to tweak your book, I'd like to weigh in on a couple of points.

My first visit to Yankee Stadium was in 1962. Over the years, I've always had an interest in knowing the differences in detail between the pre and post renovated stadium versions. Until I saw this great thread, I thought that I was about the only one who was! Anyway, my two items here are as follows:

1. Number of New Rows Added to the Upper Deck - All the while reading this thread, I've seen various numbers quoted with 10 being the most prevalent. Each time, I said to myself, "No - it was 11", but figured that I better read the whole thread until I respond. I'm glad I did because with Spiderico's good explanation here, I think that I have an idea of what actually happened during the renovation.

I've counted the new rows a number of times while at the Stadium and always came up with the number 11. It was easy to identify the new rows as they were constructed of pre-cast concrete panels set on top of the upper deck extension supports. So you can see the lines where the individual horizontal and vertical (riser) sections meet. The old section was concrete poured in place without the seams. Also, earlier in this thread, several people mentioned that the last old row is now row K. The first new row is above the high step referred to. Therefore, the new rows are L, M, N, P, R, S, T, U, V, W, X or 11 in all, there being no rows O and Q (or I).
On the other hand, Spiderico correctly, I believe, counts 34 rows (33 seating and 1 aisle) in the renovated stadium and his picture clearly shows 24 rows (23 seating and 1 aisle) in the old stadium, a difference of 10 rows.

So here's my theory and see what you guys think. If you look at Spiderico's pre-1937 photo, you can see that the 24th row is connected to the exterior wall, which appears to be a bearing wall of fairly substantial construction. Now having done quite of bit of home renovation work myself, I know that it is often difficult to cleanly remove one section of wall, ceiling, etc. without damaging the adjoining sections. So when the roof and the exterior upper wall were removed during the renovation (and I agree with all of you guys that these were major losses, by the way. Always has bugged me since.), I think that the horizontal section of row 24 was also cut away leaving 23 rows. Then the new row L was set on top on the riser of old row 23 creating the high step that all those people tripped on.

Therefore, I believe that during the stadium renovation, one upper deck row was removed and 11 new rows were added for a total difference of 10 additional rows. Sorry about the long winded explanation here but I wanted to get this out there.

2. The Colors of the Frieze - Whole lot of good discussion here. I think that we all now agree that the original frieze was made of copper and was painted white in 1967. What happened between 1923 and 1967 is still somewhat murky, though, as there doesn't seem to be many good close-up color pictures of the frieze available from those years.

Referring the picture of the one remaining scrap below (taken from post 821 of this thread and rotated 90 degrees to its correct orientation), you can see the white, green, and bare copper-brown sections. The point I want to make pertains to the green sections. A previous post stated that the green part was oxidation of the original copper. It's possible that some of the green is, but the green stripe on the left side of the picture midway down looks very much like a layer of green paint that preceded the eventual white coating.

Considering this, it appears that the frieze was painted green at some point. Posts in the Pre-Renovation thread (which I'm now part way through) have pointed out that the original 1923 frieze section appeared to be a different shade than the 1928 LF and 1937 RF sections. There's a picture taken during the 1943 World Series that shows the LF extension to be darker than the original part. So maybe the frieze was painted green after that.

I haven't seen any reference to Yankee Stadium being repainted prior to 1967, or any discussion on the Stadium's original 1923 seat colors, for that matter. I suspect that it was repainted in the 40s, though, as I doubt the original 1923 paint job could have lasted 44 years. Perhaps it was repainted right after WWII when Topping/Webb/MacPhail bought the team. I know that changes in the field level box seats were made before the 1946 season and the auxiliary scoreboards were installed in 1949. Maybe the seats and frieze were painted light green as part of one of these upgrades.

Well, that's my thinking. Thanks guys for all the great ideas and photos throughout.

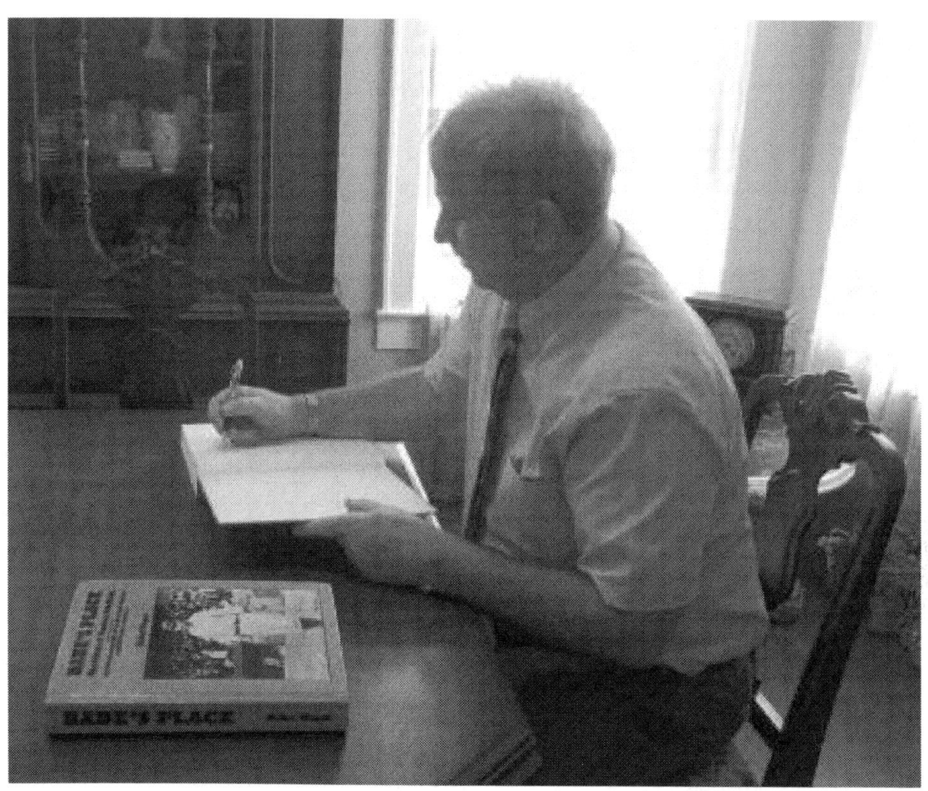

Michael Wagner was an Air Force historian for 21 years. He's been a New York Yankees fan since he was a child. Michael grew up in West Hempstead, New York, and currently lives in Temple, Texas, with his wife, Carolyn. This is his first book. Michael can be contacted at his e-mail: *babesplace03@yahoo.com*, or website: *www.babes-place.com*

Book cover designed by Brad Turnow (his website is: *www.historyoftheyankees.com*)

SOME DREAMS NEVER DIE!

Made in the USA
Middletown, DE
15 February 2022

61123814R00353